This is a study of the politics of a rural English county between the first and third Reform Acts. It examines the political behaviour of the landed and farming classes in the context of the local society and economy. But it also deals with the relationship of county to national politics. Party politicians were never able to ignore the personal ties and local loyalties that, even in an age of railways and cheap newspapers, counted for much in a rural constituency. And there were times when members of Parliament found it hard to influence an electorate of farmers determined to protect their means of livelihood.

OXFORD HISTORICAL MONOGRAPHS

Lincolnshire Politics 1832-1885

BY

R. J. OLNEY

OXFORD UNIVERSITY PRESS
1973

Oxford University Press, Ely House, London W. 1
GLASGOW NEW YORK TORONTO MELBOURNE WELLINGTON
CAPE TOWN IBADAN NAIROBI DAR ES SALAAM LUSAKA ADDIS ABABA
DELHI BOMBAY CALCUTTA MADRAS KARACHI LAHORE DACCA
KUALA LUMPUR SINGAPORE HONG KONG TOKYO

ISBN 0 19 821848 6

Printed in Great Britain

To my parents

and in memory of K.B. McFarlane

Fur they knaws what I beän to Squoire sin fust a coomed to the 'All;
I done moy duty by Squoire an' I done moy duty boy hall . . . .

Thaw a knaws I hallus voäted wi' Squoire an' choorch an' staäte,
An' i' the woost o' toimes I wur niver agin the raäte . . . .

Alfred Tennyson, 'Northern Farmer, Old Style', 1864

PREFACE

This book is, I hope, no more and no less than its title claims: it describes the politics of a rural English county between the first and third Reform Acts. But it is not intended to be simply a contribution to the history of Lincolnshire, for its purpose is at least partly to explore the relationship between local and national politics in nineteenth-century England. In that connection it can claim no more than to make a very small contribution to an exceedingly complicated subject.

It is all too easy to bridge the gap between Westminster and the constituencies in a superficial manner, either by making passing reference to national affairs in a locally-centred study ('No doubt the fall of the government was eagerly discussed in the smoking-rooms of Bourne and the drawing rooms of Grimsthorpe'); or by supporting general statements about English politics with local examples divorced from their local context. It sometimes turns out that a feature of the local political scene is very much *sui generis*, and that local politics went their own way almost oblivious of national opinion and wider issues. But in other cases it seems that what happened in Lincolnshire does have interest and relevance for the historian of English national politics. It is useful, for instance, to test generalizations about the nature of landed interests and the voting habits of tenant farmers by reference to specific examples. Generalizations about electoral behaviour at specific general elections can also be examined. More directly, the interaction of local and national politics can be studied through the careers of individual Members of parliament, revealing their sometimes conflicting attitudes towards constituency supporters on the one hand and party leaders on the other. A description of local agricultural movements, moreover, must contribute to a history of the agricultural interest in English politics, even if it turns out that local farmers were ordinary delegates to, rather than leaders of, the national organizations that championed the farmers' cause.

Lincolnshire has been chosen for this study because it was, in the nineteenth century, a predominantly rural county, and an important agricultural one. It was not, therefore, typical of the majority of English counties; nor was it, perhaps, typical even of the rural counties. But its largely agricultural electorate, and its comparative isolation from the major metropolitan and provincial centres of English political life, make it an unusually pure specimen of rural political organization and agricultural opinion.

In the first part of the book, the 'Survey', attention is paid to the local background and framework of county politics—the differing regional characteristics, estate patterns, and agricultural economies that were all reflected in the county poll books. The political complexion of the farming class is examined, both as regards its relations with the landlords and also as regards its characteristic political activities, the ploughing meeting and the market ordinary.

The 'Narrative' attempts a coherent description of the development of county politics during the period. Although election movements are discussed and voting analysed, the intention is to show that what happened between elections was also important. Whilst urban and religious movements are not wholly neglected, the principal attention is paid to the issues which agitated the farmers—the malt tax, local taxation, and, above all, Protection. The Lincolnshire boroughs do not make much of an appearance in the picture; but, in a sense, that was their choice rather than mine.

The Narrative also discusses techniques of electioneering and problems of party management, selecting for detailed treatment the Liberal party in North Lincolnshire from 1850 to 1857. Later developments in local party management are related to the extension of national party organization, the spread of urban methods into rural politics, and the decline of the independent country gentleman.

Recent historical writing on English rural politics is discussed in the Bibliography. My greatest single debt to a published work is undoubtedly to *Politics in the Age of Peel*, by Norman Gash. And I have been greatly stimulated by D.C. Moore's unpublished thesis 'The Politics of Deference', the only work to date to discuss the whole period of English rural politics from 1830 to 1885.

The debt I should like to acknowledge most deeply and fully, however, is to my supervisor, Mr. A.F. Thompson, who guided my footsteps as a green researcher with unfailing kindness, and but for whose encouragement my thesis would never have been completed. Dr. A.D. Macintyre has most kindly read and most invaluably commented on the manuscript at more than one stage of its development. Mrs. Joan Varley, former county archivist of Lincolnshire, initiated me into Lincolnshire studies with the utmost patience and helpfulness. My examiners, Miss Betty Kemp and Mr. Michael Brock, made many criticisms and suggestions which have helped me in revising the thesis for publication. Sir Francis Hill not only gave me the benefit of his great local knowledge, but also allowed me to see part of the manuscript of his forthcoming volume on *Victorian Lincoln*. Others to whose kindness and learning I am indebted are Mr. Michael Lloyd, county archivist of Lincolnshire, my colleague Miss Judith Cripps, Dr. James Obelkevich, Mr. Travis L. Crosby, Miss Joan Gibbons, and the late G.S. Dixon.

Many people have generously made their private archives available to me, and I recall with particular pleasure two visits to Casewick, where the Hon. Mrs. N. Trollope-Bellew hospitably allowed me to see the Trollope muniments. For permission to make published use of manuscript material I am grateful to the Most Hon. the Marquis of Salisbury, the Rt. Hon. the Lord Monson, the Rt. Hon. the Lord St. Oswald, J.N. Heneage, Esq., the National Trust (Hughenden Manor, High Wycombe, Bucks.), and the National Union of Conservative and Unionist Associations.

Miss B. Coysh most professionally typed my thesis, and I have been fortunate in having Mrs. Margaret Matheson to prepare a typescript for the press. In the work of adapting the thesis for publication I have been sustained above all by the wise advice and patient encouragement of Ruth, my wife.

November 1971

CONTENTS

LIST OF MAPS

ABBREVIATIONS

Amer.Hist.Rev.	*American Historical Review*
ANC	Lincolnshire Archives Office, Ancaster MSS.
BNL	Lincolnshire Archives Office, Brownlow MSS.
Bodl.	Bodleian Library, Oxford
Brit.Mus.	British Museum
D.N.B.	*Dictionary of National Biography*
Econ.Hist.Rev.	*Economic History Review*
Eng.Hist.Rev.	*English Historical Review*
Harl.Soc.	*Harleian Society*
Hist.Journ.	*Historical Journal*
Journ.Brit.Stud.	*Journal of British Studies*
Kelly	*The Post Office Directory of Lincolnshire,* ed. E.R. Kelly
Journ.Roy.Ag.Soc.	*Journal of the Royal Agricultural Society of England*
Journ.Stat.Soc.	*Journal of the Statistical Society of London,* later the *Royal Statistical Society*
L.A.O.	Lincolnshire Archives Office
Lincs.Chron.	*Lincolnshire Chronicle*
Lincs.Hist.	*Lincolnshire Historian*
MON	L.A.O., Monson MSS.
Parl.Deb.	Hansard's *Parliamentary Debates*
Parl.Papers	*Parliamentary Papers*
Pol.Stud.	*Political Studies*
P.R.O.	Public Record Office
R.C.	Royal Commission
S.C.	Select Committee
Stamf.Merc.	*Lincoln, Rutland, and Stamford Mercury*
STUBBS	L.A.O., Stubbs Deposit
TGH	L.A.O., Taylor, Glover, and Hill Deposit
TD'E	L.A.O., Tennyson d'Eyncourt MSS.
Trans.Roy.Hist.Soc.	*Transactions of the Royal Historical Society*
V.C.H.	*Victoria County History*
Vict.Stud.	*Victorian Studies*
White	William White, *History and Gazetteer of Lincolnshire*
YARB	L.A.O., Yarborough MSS.

PART ONE

SURVEY

1

THE COUNTY

A POLITICAL observer, casting his eye over the English provinces in, say, the 1830s, would have found little to arrest his attention in the county of Lincoln. He would have observed that no prominent national politician had a Lincolnshire interest of any consequence, and that the county lacked the vigorous political tradition of Yorkshire or the popular movements of Birmingham or Manchester.

Yet, for the historian, there are many arguments in favour of turning from the orators and men of national influence, the mass meetings and the torchlight processions, and exploring instead the grass roots of rural politics, and even the soils that nourished those roots, in an agricultural shire. It can be discovered that the dullest county Member could exhibit interesting political behaviour, and that even farmers, those supposedly least politically-minded of electors, could exert a strong influence on the forms and issues of county politics in the period 1832-85.

Nor was excitement always lacking in Lincolnshire. The protectionist movement of 1850-2, for example, was a very determined and a very spirited affair. But it is true that Lincolnshire, remote from the chief population centres of England, was not easily influenced by reports of agitations in London and the provincial capitals. It was isolated from its immediate neighbours by the Humber to the north, the Trent to the west,[1] and the Fens (more particularly before the great drainage operations of the early nineteenth century) to the south. Even in the railway age, although its communications with the Midlands and the West Riding were improved, Lincolnshire could boast of only one town, Grantham, directly connected with London and the north.

Not only was the shire divided from its neighbours: it was

[1] In 1830 Gainsborough was still the only bridging-point across the Trent below Newark. Below Gainsborough the Trent separates the Isle of Axholme from the rest of Lindsey.

also divided within itself. It had one lord lieutenant and one high sheriff, but contained four administrative counties, the City of Lincoln and the several Parts of Lindsey, Kesteven, and Holland, each with its own court or courts of quarter sessions. Together they made up a shire that was second only to Yorkshire in size among the English counties, and it is not surprising that Lincolnshire contained—and still contains—marked regional differences. The whole shire was classified by the 1851 census as a north midland county, along with Leicestershire, Nottinghamshire, Rutland, and Derbyshire. But, whilst Lindsey shared many characteristics with Nottinghamshire and the southern parts of Yorkshire, Kesteven might have been grouped with Northamptonshire, or Holland with Cambridgeshire.

All these factors would have counted for little had Lincolnshire possessed one or more major centres of population, where large-scale political movements could be generated. But in 1831 Lincolnshire's total population of 320,000 was scattered sparsely over an area of 2,700 square miles. There were 78 places with over 1,000 inhabitants, but they contained only 43 per cent of the county's population.[2] Only one town had a population of over 10,000, and that was Boston, with 11,240. Lincoln, the county town, took second place with 9,831, and the four next largest towns had under 7,000 inhabitants—Louth with 6,927, Gainsborough with 6,658, Spalding with 6,395, and Stamford with 5,837. None of these six places was an industrial town in the modern sense. They relied for their prosperity mainly upon agriculture, and owed their importance to their sea, canal, or river trades.

Before 1832 the importance of Lincoln in the politics of the undivided county was less than that of Leicester, for instance, in Leicestershire, or Norwich in Norfolk.[3] Lincoln was the place, of course, from which the two knights of the shire were returned; and its importance as a social centre was enhanced by the fact that it was also an assize town and the seat of a bishopric. But, though lying more or less in the centre

[2] 'Places' means townships or municipal boroughs where separate totals are given in the census of 1831 (*Parl. Papers*, 1833, xxxvi), otherwise parishes.

[3] See J.H. Plumb, 'Political History, 1530-1885', *V.C.H.* Leics., ii. 102ff.; B.D. Hayes, 'Politics in Norfolk, 1750-1832', Cambridge Ph.D. thesis, 1957, p.266 *et passim.*

of Lincolnshire, it was many miles from the more remote corners of the shire; and towns such as Louth, twenty-six miles to the north-east, and Stamford, forty-six miles to the south, tended to go their own ways both socially and politically. In the early nineteenth century no major political interest in the county, with the possible exception of that of the Chaplin family,[4] was located close enough to Lincoln to exert a direct influence on the city. And no Member for Lincoln succeeded in transferring himself to a county seat, although one, Richard Ellison,[5] attempted to do so.

In 1832 Lincoln became the returning town for the division of North Lincolnshire, which corresponded with the Parts of Lindsey. But it lay on the edge of the new constituency. It was separated from Great Grimsby and Louth by the chalk uplands of the Wolds; and both Gainsborough, in the north-west, and Boston, in the south-east, exercised an independent influence in their respective parts of the division.

The City of Lincoln returned two Members to parliament between 1832 and 1885.[6] The principal local influence was that of the Sibthorps of Canwick. Colonel Charles de Laet Waldo Sibthorp (1783-1855) held one of the seats from 1826 to 1832, and again from 1835 until his death. A tory of an old-fashioned and eccentric kind, he was a strong supporter of the agricultural interest in the House of Commons. But in Lincoln he relied upon the support of the clergy and upon generous treating. In 1852 the sixth baron Monson, whose Lincolnshire seat was at Burton-by-Lincoln, and whose family had once possessed a strong whig interest in the city, wrote to his son W.J. Monson: 'I think it is quite disgraceful the way Sibthorp is always received and the horrid stuff he talks that they cheer. In fact there are few places so far behind in real intelligence as Lincoln, either hot tories and bigoted chapter clergy, or else democrats, the sensible men are few.'[7]

4 For whom see below, p.18.

5 For whom see below, p.92.

6 For the representatives of the Lincolnshire boroughs, 1832-85, see below, Appendix A, p.252.

7 Lincolnshire Archives Office, Monson MSS., MON 25/10/1/3/2/52, 8 July 1852. The 6th baron, a whig, s. his cousin, a tory, in 1842, and d. 1861. His son, the 7th baron (1829-98), sat for Reigate (Lib.), 1858-62, was a Lords whip from 1882, and was cr. Viscount Oxenbridge in 1886. He m., 1869, the widow of the 2nd earl of Yarborough.

The 'democrats' owed their growing strength, from the 1840s onwards, to the development of Lincoln as a manufacturing town. Of the six largest towns in the county in 1831, only Lincoln steadily increased its population in the following sixty years. Messrs. Clayton and Shuttleworth started their iron foundry in 1842, and in 1846 the Midland Railway reached Lincoln from Nottingham. The leading radical of the city for many years was Charles Seely, the owner of a large Lincoln flour mill which supplied the Nottingham bakers, and a business associate of Clayton and Shuttleworth.[8] He and his supporters became skilled in interrupting county meetings called to advocate Protection, but they found it difficult to make headway against the tories in city politics. As late as 1859 Nathaniel Clayton reminded a meeting of reformers that 'Lincoln . . . was a city not easily to be moved on political matters, as it was a place which almost stood by itself—isolated, as it were, in the midst of an agricultural district.'[9] The triumph of the Lincoln Liberals came finally in 1868, when, at the first general election after the Reform Act of 1867, they returned both the Members for the city without a contest.[10]

The other parliamentary borough in Lindsey was Great Grimsby. A small port in the early nineteenth century, its representation was reduced in 1832 from two seats to one. But between the 1840s and the end of the century it grew rapidly, owing principally to its railway connection with Sheffield and Manchester, and to the associated improvement of the docks and harbour. By 1885 it had overtaken Lincoln as the largest town in the county.[11]

Between 1832 and 1885 the principal landed influence in the borough was that of the Pelhams of Brocklesby. Charles Anderson Pelham (1781-1846), first earl of Yarborough, was both the leading whig and the largest landowner in Lindsey, and his seat at Brocklesby was only a few miles from Grimsby.[12]

[8] Charles Seely, b. 1803, was M.P. (Lib.) for Lincoln, 1847-8 and 1861-85. He became a moderate Liberal in the 1860s.

[9] *Stamford Mercury*, 14 Jan. 1859.

[10] See also the forthcoming volume on *Victorian Lincoln* by Sir Francis Hill.

[11] See also Edward Gillett, *A History of Grimsby*, 1970, esp. pp.212ff.

[12] M.P. (whig) for Lincs., 1807-23; cr. earl of Yarborough and baron Worsley, 1837. See also below, p.13.

His interest in the borough was supplemented by that of the Heneage family, which also owned substantial property there. Edward Heneage (1802-80)[13] represented Grimsby from 1835 to 1852.

During the period 1852-80, however, the Yarborough and Heneage interests languished. Although the second earl of Yarborough (1809-62)[14] was for some years chairman of the railway company which brought prosperity to the town, the railway interest liked to play its own hand in Grimsby politics. And a further independent interest was built up during the middle years of the century by George Tomline (1812-89), of Riby Grove, who was returned for the borough in 1868. An erratic politician, he had been a Conservative in the 1840s, but by 1868 counted as an independent Liberal.[15]

However important these influences, no single interest could hope to control the electors of Grimsby in the period 1832-85. Their politics had a salt flavour and distinctly fishy smell: corruption was extensive. 'These fishermen are very independent', wrote a Grimsby solicitor to the third earl of Yarborough in 1873, 'and generally vote with a popular man or one likely to serve their own personal interests, rather than from any strong political feeling'.[16] In order to counteract the venality of the freemen the borough boundaries were extended in 1832 to include several rural parishes. This did not have a profound effect on the politics of the borough, but it may well have reduced Grimsby's influence in North Lincolnshire between 1832 and 1867, by introducing a kind of insulating layer between the borough and the county.

The principal urban influence in Lindsey politics, at least until the 1850s, was that of Louth. A municipal borough, its population rose to about 10,000 by the middle of the century, making it the largest town in the division of North Lincolnshire without separate representation in parliament. Its prosperity

13 Brother of G.F. Heneage, for whom see below, p.15.

14 Son of the 2nd baron and 1st earl, by Henrietta, niece and heiress of Sir Richard Worsley, of Appuldurcombe, I.O.W. He was M.P. (whig) for Newtown, I.O.W., 1830-1; Lincs., 1831-2; and N. Lincs., 1832-46. Lord lieut. of Lincs., 1857-62.

15 He sat for Sudbury, 1840-1 (Lib.); for Shrewsbury, 1841-7 (Cons.) and 1852-68 (Lib.); and for Grimsby, 1868-74 (Lib.); stood for E. Suffolk, 1874, and N. Lincs., 1881.

16 L.A.O. Daubney MSS., IV/4/37.

grew with the development of high farming on the Wolds, for a large region of which it was the principal market town. Its corn and wool were carried by a short canal to the sea, and thence to London and Yorkshire.

There was no dominant political interest in the borough, and feeling often ran high. In the early nineteenth century the balance of power lay with the tories, led by local landowners such as the Chaplins of Tathwell, and supported by a large number of resident clergy. But an independent and nonconformist group (chiefly Liberal in general politics) began to make headway after 1832, assisted by the reform of the corporation and later by the spread of the Wesleyan Reform movement. The Liberals were never able for long, however, to control either the corporation or the vestry, and often it seems to have been a middle party of moderate churchmen, of mixed politics, who held the balance. But for most of the period 1832-85 there was a far from certain correspondence between municipal and county politics. Supporters of the Liberals in North Lincolnshire might be found supporting the Church party in Louth itself, and, more surprisingly, it was not unknown for borough Liberals to give Conservative votes for the county.[17]

Gainsborough, the other large unrepresented town in North Lincolnshire, lacked the political vitality of Louth, at least before 1870. The explanation is partly connected with local government. Gainsborough had no municipality to foster political feeling in the intervals between parliamentary elections, although it acquired a local board in the 1850s. But economic factors were also important. Gainsborough's prosperity had been founded on its river trade, and it had built up a large carrying trade from Hull and Grimsby. But, though made a port in 1840, Gainsborough was seriously affected by the coming of the railway, and its decline was not arrested until the later 1860s. Unlike the shipping port of Boston, however, the depression of trade at Gainsborough did not feed a strong protectionist movement in the town. Perhaps urban influences from Newark, the next large town up the Trent, and East Retford, the nearest parliamentary borough, were significant in this connection.

[17] *Stamf. Merc.*, 28 Mar. 1879.

If local interests were sometimes hard to reconcile in Lindsey, the case was far worse in the South Lincolnshire constituency that was created in 1832. The Parts of Kesteven and Holland, of which it was composed, insisted upon their separate identities, and in one important matter, that of drainage, their interests were at times antagonistic. Kesteven's rainfall became Holland's floods, and Holland therefore expected Kesteven to contribute to the cost of fenland drainage. It is true that Kesteven included, on its eastern border, low-lying lands similar to those of Holland. But the western side of Kesteven lay beyond the upland region of the limestone Heath. Whilst Bourne and Sleaford looked towards Holland, Grantham looked towards Leicestershire and the valley of the Trent.[18]

Grantham returned two Members to parliament between 1832 and 1885. Before 1868 its electorate was small, and mostly under the influence of the large landowners whose estates surrounded it. In the period before 1852 these influences were almost entirely tory. The first earl Brownlow (1779-1853)[19] had a strong interest in the borough, and so had the eighth earl of Dysart (1794-1878).[20] The Brownlow interest was generally given to the Welby family,[21] three generations of which sat for Grantham between 1802 and 1868. The Hon. F. Tollemache (1804-88), younger brother of the eighth earl of Dysart, occupied the second seat at various dates between 1837 and 1874, beginning his career as a Conservative, but sitting as a Liberal from 1859.

In 1868, on a greatly enlarged register, the Liberals secured both seats. Their triumph reflected the growth of Grantham from an agricultural market town into an industrial and railway centre. In 1852 it was linked, by the 'towns' line of the Great Northern Railway, with London and Doncaster, and more immediately with Peterborough, Newark, and East Retford.[22] And the agricultural implement factory of

[18] See David Grigg, *The Agricultural Revolution in South Lincolnshire,* Cambridge, 1966, p. 46.

[19] M.P. (tory) for Clitheroe, 1802-7; lord lieut. of Lincs., 1809-52. He m., 1810, a dau. and coheir of Sir Abraham Hume, 2nd bart., and a grand-dau. of the last earl of Bridgwater. See also below, p. 17.

[20] M.P. (tory) for Ilchester, 1827-30. He s. his father, Sir William Manners (later Talmash) in 1833, and his grandmother, the countess of Dysart, in 1840.

[21] For whom see below, p. 18.

[22] Charles H. Grinling, *The History of the Great Northern Railway*, 1903, pp. 117, 121.

Messrs. Hornsby expanded rapidly in the middle years of the century. Grantham never came to have much influence, however, in South Lincolnshire politics. Its railway communication with other parts of Kesteven was slow to develop, and the building of the towns line only served to emphasize its position on the periphery of the county. The borough Liberals took little interest in South Lincolnshire contests, and the Hornsby family, mindful of its rural customers, played a cautious part in county politics.

Stamford returned two Members between 1832 and 1868, and one Member between 1868 and 1885. The second marquis of Exeter (1795-1867)[23] controlled both seats before 1868, and they were usually reserved for tory politicians of national standing rather than for Lincolnshire gentry. There was an undercurrent of Liberal opposition in the town, but it was not until the 1870s that the Exeter interest was successfully challenged. Lying in the extreme south of the county, Stamford was connected, commercially and politically, more with Rutland and Northamptonshire than with Lincolnshire.

Sleaford, the returning town for South Lincolnshire until 1867, owed its rising commercial importance in the early nineteenth century to the drainage of the Kesteven fens. Situated on the road from Lincoln to Boston, it was open to political influences from both those places, and it had important connections with the grazing interest.[24] Like Louth (although a town of smaller size and less consequence), it lay between an upland and a lowland region; but unlike Louth, it lacked local tory influences of any great significance. Much of the town was owned by the Hervey family, earls and later marquisses of Bristol; but the first marquis (1769-1859) was non-resident, his politics were of an uncertain tone, and he did not exact regular voting from his tenants. From the 1860s the political importance of Sleaford, again like that of Louth, declined. Railways were slow to reach the town, and its growth was hindered by a lack of building land.

Lincoln exercised little influence on Kesteven politics, partly because its liberty extended into Kesteven on the southern side of the city. Bracebridge, Branston, Canwick,

23 Lord lieut. of Rutland (1826-67) and Northants. (1842-67); recorder of Stamford; P.C., 1841.

24 See below, p. 29.

and Waddington did not vote for South Lincolnshire, and thus had an effect similar to that of the rural extension of the Grimsby boundary, in providing an obstacle to borough influence. More important for north Kesteven, economically and politically, was the Nottinghamshire borough of Newark.

Holland comprises three principal natural regions: a strip of marshland along the Wash; the townlands, a narrow and slightly elevated crescent of land running from Boston and Spalding through Holbeach to Long Sutton; and the interior fens. The population in 1800 was concentrated in the townlands, and the fens were regions of swamp and rough pasture, subject to periodic inundation, and inhabited by a few poor commoners whose wildness was noticed by Arthur Young.[25] By 1850 the immense tracts of Deeping Fen and the South Holland Fens had been much improved by drainage, and rendered capable of supporting a more intensive agriculture. But they remained sparsely populated; and those new freeholders, whose creation stemmed from the great fenland enclosures, and who greatly swelled the number of electors in Holland between 1800 and 1832, were never thoroughly canvassed. Even after 1832 Holland remained politically apathetic and slow to respond to popular movements. The issues which occasionally excited it were generally local in character: rates, tithes, charities, and so on. Typical is the following report of an agricultural meeting near Spalding in January 1850: 'Protection was indeed named, but only as a forlorn hope. One of the landed proprietors shrewdly remarked . . . that in a thinly populated district like theirs, they would be doing more good by attacking local abuses, than in political or national movements.'[26]

Despite the building of railways and the improvement of roads, the rivers of Holland were still, in the mid-nineteenth century, its main arteries of communication. Boston derived some of its character from Lincoln, which it served as the out-port of the Witham. The Nene conveyed some of the radicalism of Peterborough and Wisbech to its outfall near Long Sutton and Holbeach. And the backward and benighted

[25] Arthur Young, *A General View of the Agriculture of the County of Lincoln*, 1799, pp. 223 f.

[26] *Stamf. Merc.*, 14 Jan. 1850.

town of Spalding was linked, politically and physically, with Crowland and Stamford by the sluggish waters of the Welland.

Boston, a two-Member borough, had the largest electorate of the five Lincolnshire boroughs in the early 1840s, though by the 1860s it had been overtaken by both Lincoln and Grimsby. At the time of the first Reform Act it also had the strongest radical tradition of the Lincolnshire constituencies. John Wilks, founder of the Protestant Society for the Protection of Religious Liberty, sat for Boston from 1830 to 1837.[27] But from the middle of the century the movement declined, and personal and financial considerations began to dictate the choice of candidates. The Conservative candidates had always been selected partly for their ability and willingness to spend money in the town, and the constituency came to have a reputation for corruption. Seaports had a strong tendency to corrupt practices in the nineteenth century, and Boston, like Hull and Grimsby, was no exception. The decline of the port of Boston in the railway age encouraged the port's employees to look for easy money from parliamentary candidates, whilst its employers were encouraged to look favourably on the protectionist movement.[28]

There was a whig, or orange, interest in the borough in the early nineteenth century, fostered by the banker William Garfit (1774-1856), and represented from time to time by members of the Willoughby, Heathcote, and Pelham families. The twenty-second baron Willoughby de Eresby (1782-1865)[29] represented Boston from 1812 to 1820,[30] when he was succeeded by his son-in-law G.J. Heathcote (1795-1867).[31] But this interest too was founded more on financial than on landed influence.[32] It does not seem to have carried much weight after 1832.

[27] See Raymond G. Cowherd, *The Politics of English Dissent, 1815-48*, 1959, p.17.

[28] See below, p. 123.

[29] He s. his father as baron Gwydir in 1820, and his mother as baron Willoughby de Eresby in 1828. See also below, p. 19.

[30] He sat as P.R. Drummond Burrell.

[31] M.P. (whig) for Boston, 1820-30 and 1831-2; S. Lincs., 1832-41; and Rutland, 1841-56. He s. his father as 5th bart. in 1851, and was created baron Aveland in 1856, by Palmerston. See also below, p. 19.

[32] Garfit wrote to Heathcote in 1832: 'The misfortune is that the large fortunes of both your families are so magnified here that the people consider the expense to you as a mere trifle, and I fear there is no means of making them think otherwise' (L.A.O., Ancaster MSS., 3 ANC 9/13/63).

Spalding, the largest unrepresented town in South Lincolnshire, was freer than Louth or Gainsborough from landed influence, and was potentially a much more formidable stronghold of dissent than those two Lindsey towns. The drainage of the neighbouring fens, moreover, vastly increased the possibilities of Spalding as an agricultural market town, and it was eventually connected by railway directly with Peterborough and London. But it was the Welland trade which had been the principal business of the town; and whilst the railway increased the trade of Peterborough, that of Spalding suffered from the poor condition of the Welland navigation. It was a principal source of grievance against Boston in the 1830s that the corporation of that borough made Stamford and Spalding contribute to Boston in the form of harbour dues, whilst Boston did nothing for Stamford and Spalding by way of assisting the improvement of the Welland outfall.[33] The Liberals of Spalding became more vocal in the 1850s and '60s than they had been in the 1830s, and were later still considerably encouraged from Peterborough. But throughout the period 1832-85 there was very little co-operation between the Spalding Liberals and those of Boston.

33 *Stamf. Merc.*, 10 Oct. 1833.

2

THE LANDED INTEREST

IF POLITICAL movements were sometimes originated in the towns of Lincolnshire, their issue was generally determined in the countryside. It might almost be laid down as a rule, that the more intense and noisy urban politics became, the less notice was taken of them by the country people. Even the great magnates did not necessarily benefit in the rural districts from their influence in the boroughs. Lord Yarborough was a power in Lindsey, and Lord Brownlow a power in Kesteven, not because of their respective interests in Grimsby and Grantham, but because of their broad acres and social position in the county. Lord Dysart, who (it was said) once threatened to take the roofs off his houses in Grantham if his tenants voted contrarily, cut no ice in Kesteven at all, despite the fact that he owned more land in it than Brownlow himself. Dysart had the broad acres, but he did not care to cultivate a political interest in the county. Nor would he have found it an easy matter had he tried, for, as will be shown, Kesteven was already mapped out politically in a way that would not have allowed him much elbow-room.

This mapping-out of the countryside into spheres of political influence was an important feature of Lincolnshire politics between 1832 and 1885, but it applied only to certain regions in the county. Lincolnshire as a whole was not an overwhelmingly aristocratic part of England. In 1873 only 28 per cent of its area was taken up with estates of over 10,000 acres.[1] The figure was not much more than the English average (24 per cent), and much less than the figure for the neighbouring county of Nottingham (38 per cent), where lay the ducal realms of Clumber, Welbeck, and Thoresby. Lincolnshire was, in fact, a county of small proprietors: in 1873 45 per cent of its total number of landowners had estates of under one acre, 44 per cent had estates of between one and fifty acres, and only 11 per cent had estates of over

[1] F.M.L. Thompson, *English Landed Society in the Nineteenth Century*, 1963, p.32.

fifty acres.[2] But the small proprietors were not evenly distributed through the county. They were concentrated in Holland and in certain areas of Lindsey, leaving part of Lindsey and most of Kesteven in the hands of the yeomanry, gentry, and nobility. Important as the yeomanry were in rural politics as voters, they could not count for much, in a large constituency like North or South Lincolnshire, as wielders of landed influence. It is to the influential noblemen and gentry of the county that the rest of this chapter will be devoted.

Lindsey was dominated by one very large estate, that of the Anderson Pelham family, barons (and later earls of) Yarborough. Its 55,272 acres in 1873 greatly exceeded even the 35,209 acres of the Cavendish Bentincks (dukes of Portland) in Nottinghamshire;[3] and, unlike Portland's estate, Yarborough's was rivalled by no other of comparable size in its division. The Lumleys (Lords Scarbrough) and the Willoughbys (Lords Willoughby de Eresby) were the only other noble families to own over 10,000 acres in Lindsey, and they were both the non-resident proprietors of somewhat scattered estates.

The major part of the Yarborough property was a compact group of estates, centred on the principal family seat of Brocklesby, and extending from near Barton-on-Humber in the north towards Market Rasen in the south-west and Louth in the south-east. Most of the estate was on the Wolds, the major upland region of Lindsey, and the importance of this wold property was enhanced by the fact that, apart from the Tathwell estate of the Chaplin family, there was no other major estate in that part of the county.

The solidity of the Brocklesby estate, and the wealth of its principal tenants, made it the ideal centre for a powerful landed interest. And in fact, for much of the period 1832-85, the Brocklesby interest was consolidated by the adherence of a number of adjacent estates. This is best shown by reference to the North Lincolnshire contest of 1841, when the pattern of voting in the poll book reveals the extent of the first earl of Yarborough's influence. It was possible at that time to walk a distance of twenty-five miles, from East Barkwith,

2 Summary of Return of Owners of Land, *Parl. Papers*, 1876, lxxx.
3 Return of Owners of Land, *Parl. Papers*, 1874, lxxii.

Map I. Diagram of certain Lindsey parishes, showing pattern of landed influence, 1841
(Sources: *Poll Book*, 1841; *White*, 1842; O.S. 1", 2nd edn., 1890-

near Wragby, to East Halton, on the Humber, without once setting foot on tory soil.[4]

Adjoining the south-westernmost parishes of the Brocklesby estate, in the neighbourhood of Market Rasen, lay the properties of the Angerstein and Tennyson d'Eyncourt families, and south of these were the Heneage and Boucherett estates. West of this central group of estates, on the left bank of the Ancholme, lay the Norton Place estate of the Cholmeley family, whilst in the south-east the Heneage estate met that of the Vyner family. In 1841 John Angerstein (d. 1858),[5] Charles Tennyson d'Eyncourt (1784-1861),[6] Ayscough Boucherett (1791-1857),[7] George Fieschi Heneage (1800-64),[8] Sir Montague John Cholmeley (1802-74),[9] and Robert Vyner (1789-1872)[10] all gave their interests to Yarborough's son, the whig candidate.

The tory interests in Lindsey were far from negligible, but, with the whigs holding the centre of the division, the tories had perforce to content themselves with influencing its perimeter. In the north-west the strongest interest, throughout the period 1832-85, was that of the Sheffield family of Normanby.[11] The Gainsborough and Wragby districts were mainly tory, but with no predominating interests. In the east of the division, however, the marshlands that stretched from the Humber to the Wash, the case was somewhat different. In the Louth neighbourhood the Chaplin influence was supplemented by that of the Fytche, Allenby, Smyth, and

[4] See Map I.

[5] About 11,500 acres in Lindsey, 1841, but no seat; M.P. (whig) for Greenwich, 1835-7. (Sizes of estates have been roughly computed from directories (esp. *White*, 1842) in conjunction with the Return for 1873.)

[6] About 3,500 acres in Lindsey, 1841; seat Bayons Manor. M.P. for Grimsby, 1818-26; Bletchingley, 1826-30; Stamford, 1831-2; and Lambeth, 1832-52. A Liberal with some radical leanings in the 1830s.

[7] 5,800 acres in Lindsey; seat at N. Willingham. Later a Conservative.

[8] 10,760 acres in Lindsey, including property in the borough of Grimsby; seat Hainton. M.P. (whig) for Grimsby, 1826-30; Lincoln, 1831-5, 1852-62. Connected by marriage with the Anderson Pelhams.

[9] 6,000 acres in Lindsey and 4,500 (*c.* 1841) in Kesteven. Principal seat Easton, near Grantham. M.P. (whig) for Grantham, 1826-31; N. Lincs., 1847-52 and 1857-74.

[10] 14,500 acres in Lindsey; seat Gautby. Son of a whig Member for the county (1796-1802), but not himself an active politician.

[11] Sir Robert Sheffield (1786-1862) owned 9,370 acres in Lindsey. Stood for N. Lincs., 1832. For many years chairman of quarter sessions at Kirton in Lindsey.

other families. Robert Adam Christopher (1804-77),[12] Member for North Lincolnshire from 1837 to 1857, had a seat near Alford, in which neighbourhood he exercised the principal influence. And in the Spilsby area Lord Willoughby de Eresby had a large estate,[13] including most of the town of Spilsby itself.

It was estates like Willoughby's, occupied mainly by small farmers, which ensured that, in contests such as that of 1841, the tories could send more tenants to the poll in Lindsey than their opponents. But voting in these tory parts of the division did not produce a clear pattern in the poll book. There was no large block of tory influence to rival the Brocklesby complex, and the presence of many smaller proprietors in the Marshes meant that even within individual parishes tory landlords commanded more often the majority, rather than the total, of the votes.

Kesteven differed markedly from Lindsey in the complexion of its landed interest. There was no single estate in Kesteven large enough to outweigh the rest, as the Yarborough estate did in Lindsey. Rather, Kesteven was characterized by the large number of proprietors who owned estates of between 7,000 and 20,000 acres—a large number, that is, in comparison with the figure for the total area of the administrative county, which was only half the size of Lindsey. Most of these substantial landowners, moreover, were resident on their Kesteven estates, whereas Lindsey had many non-resident proprietors. The aristocracy of Kesteven was led by such noblemen as Brownlow and Willoughby de Eresby, but it was composed largely of what might be called the greater gentry—the families of Heathcote, Chaplin, Thorold, Welby, Whichcote, and the like. Some of these families were of ancient Lincolnshire ancestry, and they were all of sufficient standing to provide county Members from amongst their ranks. They mostly lacked the wider influence of the titled magnates, but within the county the magnates could not do without them in their political schemes.

[12] About 7,000 acres in Lindsey. Returned for Ipswich, 1835, but unseated on petition. Born R.A. Dundas, he took the name of Christopher in 1835 and that of Nisbet Hamilton in 1855.

[13] 11,000 acres.

Nor was there a lack of lesser gentry, families such as the Reeves of Leadenham or their neighbours the Fanes of Fulbeck. These gentry, whose estates of up to five or six thousand acres would have ranked much higher in less aristocratic counties, did not carry a great deal of political weight in Kesteven. Nevertheless, their contributions to local Conservative funds (they were nearly all Conservative) were appreciated, and they might be asked to second, if less frequently to propose, the nomination of candidates at county elections.

Grantham was the centre of the most compact group of large estates in Kesteven, and the Grantham neighbourhood was the most strongly Conservative region in Lincolnshire. The social, if not the political, leaders of this important interest were the dukes of Rutland, whose seat of Belvoir, though just within the Leicestershire border, was only a few miles from Grantham. Although the Belvoir interest in the borough was withdrawn in the early nineteenth century, the fifth duke of Rutland (1778-1857) was recorder of Grantham, and a name to conjure with for many miles about. The Waltham Agricultural Society, under his patronage, drew on a large area of Kesteven for its subscribers and competitors. And the Belvoir Hunt listed among its supporters most of the gentry of the Grantham and Sleaford neighbourhoods.[14] Such considerations might excuse, if they could not justify, the appointment of the duke's eldest son, the marquis of Granby, to the lord-lieutenancy of Lincolnshire in 1853.

The Rutland interest in county politics, however, was concentrated in Leicestershire, and the duke owned only 3,000 acres in Lincolnshire. Of more weight in the latter county was Granby's predecessor in the lord-lieutenancy, the first earl Brownlow. He has already been mentioned in connection with his Grantham interest, but his main concern was the county, and his chief ambition to return one of the Lincolnshire Members. This he never achieved, but in Kesteven his property of over 17,000 acres could not but give him a prominent voice in its political affairs.

Between Belvoir and Belton (the Brownlow seat) lay the

[14] T.F. Dale, *The History of the Belvoir Hunt,* 1899; King's *Hunting Map of the Country round Belvoir Castle.*

seat of the Welby family at Denton.[15] And south of Grantham were the estates of the Turnor family, whose seat was Stoke Rochford.[16] Both these families contributed to the tory ascendancy in the Grantham neighbourhood. But there was no solid phalanx of tory parishes, as the 1841 poll book for South Lincolnshire reveals. No significant influence was exercised on the Dysart estate, which also lay in this region. And Sir Montague Cholmeley, of Easton, a close neighbour of Christopher Turnor and a marriage connection of Sir. W.E. Welby, was a whig.

Between Grantham and Lincoln, partly on the upland Heath and partly along its fenland border, lay a group of tory estates which, in the first half of the nineteenth century, rivalled that of the Grantham region in importance. At its centre lay Blankney, the seat of Charles Chaplin (1786-1859).[17] Chaplin was a tory, but his toryism was very different from Brownlow's. Brownlow was an earl with his eye on a marquisate. Chaplin was an independent country gentleman, rich enough to be independent, and independent enough to remain a gentleman, though he might easily have secured and supported the dignity of a peerage. Brownlow wished to build up a powerful county interest: Chaplin already had one. He had sat for Lincolnshire from 1818 to 1831, and his father had occupied the same seat before him. What Brownlow might hope to do by dipping into his purse, Chaplin could do through his popularity as a landlord, magistrate, and sportsman. None the less, when it came to counting votes, Chaplin's interest had essentially the same foundation as Brownlow's. The Blankney estate had pretty well as numerous a tenantry as the Belton, and Chaplin, like Brownlow, could count on the political support of most of his neighbours. In 1841 most of the Kesteven Heath voted tory, and even parishes without direct influence were carried with the predominating local interest.

In southern Kesteven the chief cluster of estates represented

15 Sir William Earle Welby (1768-1852) sat (tory) for Grantham, 1807-20. About 9,500 acres in S. Lincs., 1841, increased by purchase to nearly 12,000 by 1873.

16 Christopher Turnor (1810-86) sat for S. Lincs., 1841-7. About 10,000 acres in Lindsey in 1841, and 5,500 in S. Lincs. (increased to about 9,000 by 1873).

17 About 15,500 acres in S. Lincs., and about 7,500 acres (the Tathwell estate, occupied by his cousin Frederick Chaplin (1803-63)) in Lindsey.

the decline of a great whig interest, that of the former dukes of Ancaster. Their seat at Grimsthorpe, near Bourne, was the grandest house in Lincolnshire, the fitting residence of a line which held the lord-lieutenancy of the county from 1701 to 1809. The dukedom of Ancaster, however, became extinct in the latter year, and Grimsthorpe descended, with the barony of Willoughby de Eresby, in the female line. The twenty-second baron Willoughby was a whig at the time of the first Reform Act, but in 1841 he gave both his Kesteven and his Lindsey interest to the tories.[18]

In 1827 his daughter (and eventual heir) married Gilbert John Heathcote, son of Sir Gilbert Heathcote, fourth baronet. Sir Gilbert had extensive property in Kesteven, lying just to the north of the Grimsthorpe estate, and was also one of the leading proprietors in Rutland, where he had his principal seat.[19] He was Member for Lincolnshire in the whig interest from 1796 to 1807, and for Rutland from 1812 to 1841. His influence in southern Lincolnshire in the early years of the nineteenth century had been extensive, supported as it was by a numerous tenantry and a very ample fortune. But after 1807 he allowed it to languish, and his son, who succeeded him in 1851, was similarly lukewarm in politics. The South Lincolnshire Liberals found it hard to do anything with him, but equally hard to act without him. And the marriage connections of the Heathcotes with the Willoughby and Tollemache[20] families, which could have given them an access of influence, served rather to encourage their apathy.

Between Grantham and Newark, in the wapentake (or hundred) of Loveden, lay a small group of estates which nevertheless played an important part in county politics in the early years of the century. Sir John Thorold (d. 1831),[21] tenth baronet, contested the county as an independent whig in 1823. His estate stretched from his seat at Syston, on the edge of the Heath, into the lowlands of north-west Kesteven, where it met that of Sir Robert Heron (1765-1854),[22] of Stubton. Heron shared Thorold's politics, and together they

[18] About 13,500 acres in Kesteven. [19] 17,500 acres in Kesteven.
[20] Sir Gilbert Heathcote, 4th bart., m., 1793, Katherine Sophia, eldest dau. of Louisa, countess of Dysart.
[21] 11,000 acres in Kesteven and 1,500 in Lindsey.
[22] 2,500 acres. M.P. (whig) for Grimsby, 1812-18; Peterborough, 1819-47.

influenced most of Loveden, which had more freeholders than any other wapentake in Kesteven.[23] Heron was a trustee of the Syston estate during the minority of Thorold's son; but after he attained his majority in 1837 the eleventh baronet veered towards the Conservative party. Another landowner in this neighbourhood was George Hussey Packe (1796-1874),[24] whom Heron persuaded to stand for Newark in 1847, and who later sat as a Liberal for South Lincolnshire between 1859 and 1868.

Holland scarcely merits inclusion in this chapter. Owing to the great size of its parishes, and the fragmentary nature of its pattern of landownership, it is difficult for the historian, as it was for the contemporary politician, to estimate the total size of properties and assess the influence they carried. Several of the leading Kesteven proprietors had estates in Holland,[25] but none resided on them, lacking as they did the necessary visual, social, and sporting attractions. There were a few large corporate landowners in the Fens, but they possessed no influence, even if their agents sometimes did. Most of Holland was in the hands of small proprietors, who were neither very susceptible to influence themselves, nor capable of influencing others.

An exception must be made, however, in the case of some resident families who exercised influence in the region between Spalding and Boston—Everard of Fulney and Gosberton, Moore of Spalding, Tunnard of Frampton,[26] Beridge of Algarkirk, Gleed of Donington, and Calthorp of Swineshead. They were a social group between yeomanry and squirearchy, but their wealth often equalled that of much larger proprietors in less fertile areas of the county. In the absence of a resident aristocracy it was they who sat on the magistrates' bench, and managed drainage and other local affairs; and at election times, though they by no means pulled

[23] See 'A List of the Freeholders of the County of Lincoln. . .', a MS. survey compiled for Lord Yarborough in 1825 (Lincoln City Library, D Coll./SMI). I am indebted to Sir Francis Hill for this reference.

[24] 4,000 acres in Kesteven; seat Caythorpe. Connected by marriage with the Heathcote family. His brother, whom he s. 1867, was M.P. (tory) for S. Leics., 1836-67.

[25] Principally the Custs (lords Brownlow).

[26] See below, p. 30 and n.

together, they could muster very respectable bodies of adherents.

In large divisions, as North and South Lincolnshire were between 1832 and 1867, landownership by itself could not decide a contest, in the way that it could in Rutland. In that little county the balance of power might be affected if even a small estate changed hands, and at one period the manufacture of faggot votes by the creation of small freeholds was practised on both sides.[27] In Lincolnshire it is hard to give specific examples of the purchase of estates for political reasons, although such reasons may have played a part in Christopher's purchase of the Well Vale estate in 1837,[28] or Exeter's purchase of the Postland estate, near Crowland, earlier in the century. Nor can a positive instance be given of an estate's being sold when its political value had been lost, although Lord Fortescue's sale in 1855 of the Billingborough estate, which lay next to Heathcote territory, may be a case in point.

The political allegiance of smaller proprietors, moreover, was never entirely determined by the fact that they lived close to the borders of a great landed interest. But there is no denying the pull of an interest such as the Brocklesby, particularly at times when party-political feeling was decreasing or dormant. It may probably be seen in operation in the case of two squires in the Horncastle neighbourhood, Sir Henry Dymoke and Joseph Livesey, who voted tory in 1841, but later came over to the Brocklesby interest. In the meantime, however, that interest had suffered a serious defection: Ayscough Boucherett went over to the tories after the death of the first earl of Yarborough. Even powerful interests, therefore, lacked stability, and were subject even in their heyday to changes of allegiance.

In conclusion, it is worth passing briefly from the fields of Lincolnshire to the streets of London, from the political topography of Belton to that of Belgravia. In the 1840s most of the Lincolnshire landowners with estates totalling more than 7,000 acres could and did maintain a town as well as a country house. There were a few exceptions. Sir Thomas

27 See, for instance, *Stamf. Merc.* 29 Oct. 1841.

28 Scottish Record Office, Biel Muniments, GD/6/976.

Whichcote was too attached to rural sports, and the sixth Lord Monson too financially embarrassed, to join the London season. On the other hand men like Sir John Trollope[29] and Sir Henry Dymoke, men of rank though not of vast substance, had houses in the capital, though in its slightly less fashionable parts. The possession of a town house was, of course, a great asset to an aspiring county candidate, without being a *sine qua non.* It was possible to stay, like Sir Robert Heron, at Brooks's Club. And country gentlemen of larger means, but lacking a permanent London establishment, could always rent a house for a season if necessary.

In the 1840s the great magnates still filled Grosvenor Square and the Piccadilly neighbourhood. Yarborough occupied 17 Arlington St., Willoughby 142 Piccadilly, Rutland 7 Bolton St., and so on. But Belgravia was the height of fashion, and there in the 1840s we find Lord Brownlow established in 12 Belgrave Square, Chaplin in 6 Eaton Square, and three Lincolnshire neighbours, Welby, Cholmeley, and Turnor, occupying neighbouring houses in Upper Belgrave Street.[30]

[29] Sir John Trollope (1800-74) owned under 3,000 acres in S. Lincs. in 1841, increased to over 4,000 (worth over £7,750) by 1873. He was M.P. (Cons.) for S. Lincs., 1841-68; was President of the Poor Law Board, 1852; and was cr. baron Kesteven, 1868. He m., 1847, a dau. of Sir Robert Sheffield, 4th bart.

[30] Welby took No.8, Cholmeley 10, and Turnor 12 (*Royal Blue Book*, 1841, 1842; *Webster's Royal Red Book for April 1847*).

3

THE AGRICULTURAL INTEREST

THE LARGE estates discussed in the previous chapter were not only mainly rural, but also predominantly agricultural. The two do not, of course, necessarily go together. Northamptonshire was one of England's most rural counties in the middle of the nineteenth century, but the existence of rural industries meant that the proportion of its male population engaged in agriculture was relatively low. Lincolnshire, on the other hand, had very little rural industry. In 1861 the proportion of its adult male population engaged in agriculture was higher than for any other English county except Rutland and Huntingdon.[1]

Rutland and Huntingdon, moreover, were pygmy counties compared with Lincolnshire. The latter grew 294,014 acres of wheat in 1866, a total exceeding even the figure for Yorkshire (290,793 acres), and far outstripping those for Norfolk (189,398 acres), Essex (181,062 acres), and Suffolk (178,021 acres). At the same date Lincolnshire (with 141,001 acres) gave pride of place as a barley grower to Norfolk (with 186,925 acres), but it grew more barley than Suffolk (138,496 acres) or Essex (109,636 acres). Lincolnshire's total flock of sheep numbered 1,088,204, compared with 769,126 for Devon and 731,243 for Kent, its nearest rivals.[2]

With its vast acreage of wheat and barley, it is not a surprise to find that as much as 42·8 per cent of its cultivated area was devoted to corn crops in 1866. This figure was considerably higher than the English average of 33·2 per cent, and was exceeded only by the great arable counties of

[1] In 1861 Northants. had only 35 per cent of its population living in places with over 2,000 inhabitants, compared with 37 per cent for Lincolnshire. But at the same date only 36 per cent of its adult male population was directly engaged in agriculture, compared with 48 per cent for Rutland and Hunts., and 45 per cent for Lincolnshire. (See the census of 1861. 'Directly engaged in agriculture' includes the census categories of farmer, grazier, farmers' relatives over 15 years of age and living on the holding, agricultural labourer, shepherd, farm servant, and 'others engaged in agriculture'.)

[2] *Parl. Papers,* 1866, lx, 6-9.

Cambridge (56·7 per cent), Suffolk (52·3 per cent), Essex (51·4 per cent), Huntingdon (49·1 per cent), Bedford (46·7 per cent), Hertford (45·4 per cent), and Norfolk (44·5 per cent).

Of Lincolnshire's total corn acreage, 49·6 per cent was given over to wheat, a figure surpassed only by Cambridgeshire (49·8 per cent) among the major arable counties of England. But only 24 per cent of Lincolnshire's arable lands were devoted to barley, compared with 42 per cent in Norfolk, 38 per cent in Rutland, 34 per cent in Suffolk, and 27 per cent in Essex. Lincolnshire had 78·4 sheep per hundred acres, compared with the four principal sheep counties of Dorset, Westmorland, Kent, and Rutland, all of which had over 100 sheep per acre.[3]

Lincolnshire emerges from these figures as one of the most important corn-growing counties in England, and, within that group, the leading wheat specialist. It was this emphasis on wheat that chiefly distinguished it from the great East Anglian barley-growing counties, but it was also distinguished from other arable counties by the number of sheep it supported. Lincolnshire as a whole cannot be classified, like Rutland, as a sheep-and-barley county. Nor did it have a sizeable acreage, in the 1860s, of permanent pasture.[4] To call it a sheep-and-wheat county, therefore, might be the most accurate general description.

Unfortunately, detailed agricultural returns do not exist for the early nineteenth century. Nor does the return of 1866 distinguish between the Parts of Lindsey, Kesteven, and Holland. There were in fact important regional differences within the shire, and important agricultural changes between 1800 and the 1860s, changes which had a considerable influence on county politics.

In the mid-nineteenth century the pride of Lincolnshire farming was the intensive cultivation of its upland regions, the Wolds, Cliff, and Heath.[5] A hundred years previously they had been almost barren, supporting at most a number

[3] Ibid.

[4] Only 28 per cent of its acreage was laid down in permanent pasture in 1866, a figure below the English average but similar to those for Herts., Hunts., Beds., and Berks. (*Parl. Papers,* 1866, lx, 6).

[5] See Map II.

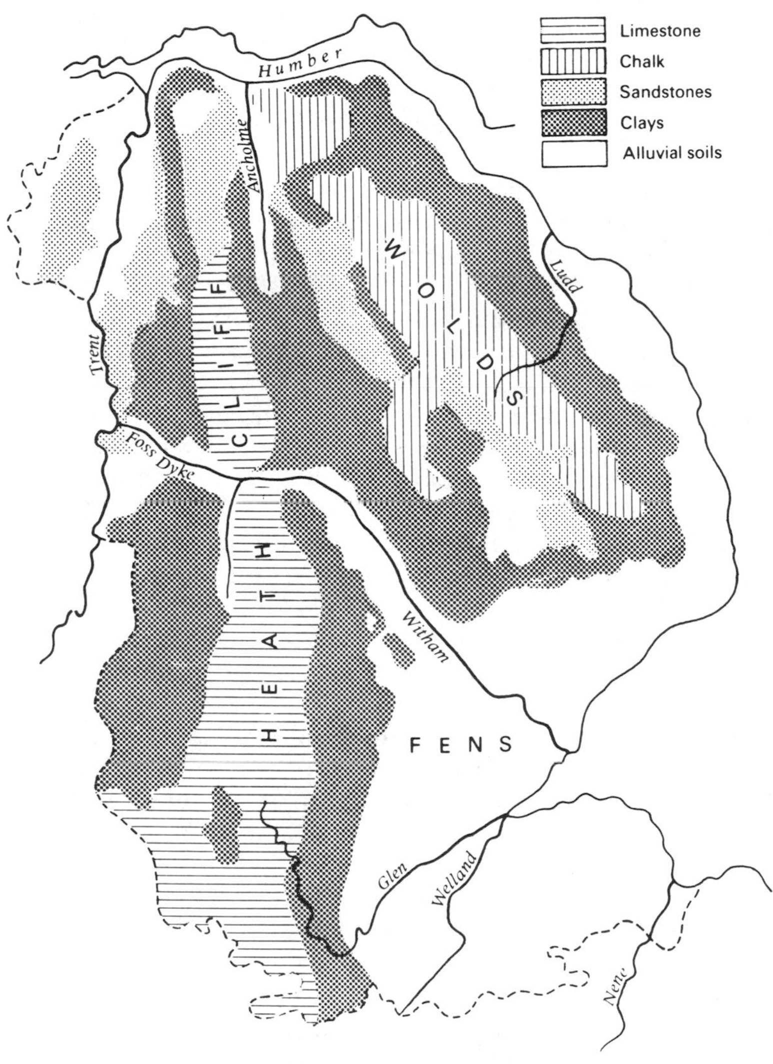

Map II. Surface geology of Lincolnshire
(Based on J.A. Clarke's Geological Map of Lincolnshire, 1850, *Journ. Roy. Ag. Soc.* xii [1851], p. 258)

of rabbit warrens and a few flocks of sheep. The Heath was enclosed and turned over to arable by the end of the eighteenth century, but at that date a large area of the Wolds was still unimproved. When Arthur Young made his agricultural tour of Lincolnshire, he noticed large tracts of gorse near Brocklesby: 'It is a beautiful plant to the foxhunter. Lord Yarborough keeps a pack of hounds; if he has a fall I hope it will be into a furze bush; he is too good to be hurt much: but a decent pricking might be beneficial to the country.'[6] Parishes on the Brocklesby estate were among the last to be enclosed, towards the end of the Napoleonic Wars. But when Cobbett rode over the area in 1830, he found it 'not downs, as in Wiltshire; but cultivated all over'.[7] Most of the sheep walks and rabbit warrens had disappeared. In their place were wide arable fields, yielding good crops of barley and wheat, and supporting large herds of cattle and flocks of sheep. Cultivation was on the Norfolk pattern, the sheep being folded on the turnip fields for winter feeding. It was the sheep which provided the big profits for the large wold farmer. But their maintenance was possible only as an integral part of arable farming. By 1850 wheat had superseded barley on the Wolds, but the latter was still the principal crop on the lighter soils of the Kesteven Heath.

High farming on these uplands required tenants of large capital. The initial expenses—enclosure, and the erection of buildings—were the landlord's responsibility. But it was then the task of the tenant so to manage his thin soil that it could eventually support regular cropping. His investment in fertilizers was heavy, and his labour bill enormous—or rather, it would have been enormous had he paid his labourers a living wage. But his greatest capital investment was in his stock. Altogether it was reckoned that the improvement of a wold farm from rough pasture cost eight pounds an acre. And wold farms were large. Holdings of a thousand acres were not uncommon. In 1832-3, 26,384 wold acres on the Brocklesby estate were farmed by 46 tenants in holdings of over 300 acres. Of this area 15,244 acres were held by only

[6] Arthur Young, *A General View of the Agriculture of the County of Lincoln*, 1799, p. 224.

[7] William Cobbett, *Rural Rides*, new edn., 1853, p. 587.

20 tenants, in farms of 600 acres and upwards.[8] In addition, many of the wold farmers occupied 100 or more acres of lowland pasture for summer grazing. Tenancies were usual on the Wolds, but the lowland farms were often owner-occupied.

In 1800 the outstanding feature of Lincolnshire agriculture had been its rich grazing lands, stretching through the coastal Marshes from the Humber to the Wash. In 1850 this region was still three-quarters in permanent pasture, supporting large flocks of sheep. But in breeding the lowland farmers had lost ground to the upland in the intervening period. And on the lowlands the arable acreage had been steadily increasing. Poor pasture was being broken up for crops of wheat and beans, and the more progressive farmers, such as William Loft of Trusthorpe,[9] had begun to introduce turnip cultivation.

In the low-lying clay lands of Lindsey, particularly in the region from around Wragby to north of Brigg, between the Cliff and the Wolds, holdings were generally small, and farming methods backward. In some areas as much as half the land was in permanent pasture, but, as towards the coast, there was a steady process of conversion to arable. The old rotation of fallow, wheat, and beans survived in many places as late as 1850, lack of drainage being the chief obstacle to more intensive cultivation. Some of the small farmers maintained a few sheep and cattle, but many were dependent on the wheat crop. Little barley was grown in the lowlands, and it was generally below malting quality.[10]

Small farms were particularly numerous in the Isle of Axholme and in some of the parishes north of Boston. The fertility of these regions supported a spade husbandry that relied almost entirely upon wheat and potatoes, though in Axholme vegetables for the Doncaster market were also grown. Only one-seventh of the Isle was in grass, around 1850, and there were very few sheep.

[8] L.A.O., Yarborough MSS., YARB. 5 (Surveys).

[9] William Loft (d. 1854) farmed 500 acres of wold land, as a tenant, and 500 acres of marsh, his own property, in 1847. Founder of the Alford Agricultural Society. A strong Conservative and protectionist (*Parl. Papers*, 1847-8, vii, 439-43; *Stamf. Merc.*, 19 May 1854; William Loft, 'On different varieties of wheat. . .', in *Journ. Roy. Ag. Soc.* ix (1848-9), pp. 281-3).

[10] See J.A. Clarke, *On the Farming of Lincolnshire,* 1852 (reprinted from the *Journ. Roy. Ag. Soc.*).

The farmers of the Isle deserve some attention, since many of them were freeholders and had votes for the county. Holdings of under twenty acres were numerous, and many were comprised of scattered strips in the open fields of Haxey and Epworth. The smallholder often rented small plots in addition to his own property. But his great desire was to achieve an independent livelihood from his own land. In order to raise the purchase money he often took a mortgage that proved too great a burden in hard times; and in that way he came under the influence of the mortgagees, often attornies, who were frequently willing to exert that influence for political purposes. On the whole, however, the simple and independent-minded farming communities of the Isle were an unpredictable element in county politics.[11]

Although a similar conversion from pasture to arable, and spread of mixed farming, took place in South Lincolnshire between 1800 and 1850, it was still at the latter date a more pastoral region than Lindsey. This was true more particularly of Kesteven, where sheep farming was carried on extensively in parts of the upland as well as the lowland region.[12]

Southern Kesteven, between Grantham and Stamford, was an area of limestone upland, overlaid in places with heavier clay soils. In 1800 it had been largely given over to grazing. By 1850 there was more arable, but it was generally badly drained and occupied in small farms. Barley was the usual crop on the lighter lands. There were one or two large farmers, outstanding among them being Richard Healy of Laughton, who maintained a large flock on several hundred acres of rented land, part pasture and part grass.[13] But on the Willoughby and Heathcote estates small farms were usual, and the region was remarkable more for its woods, parks, and game preserves than for the excellence of its farming. The Grimsthorpe tenantry were a very different body of men from the Brocklesby tenantry at the other end of the shire.[14]

Like Lindsey, however, Kesteven had its rich lowland grazing grounds. The two principal areas were to the east of

[11] Report of S.B.L. Druce, assistant commissioner, R.C. Agricultural Distress, *Parl. Papers*, 1889, xii, 118 ff.; see also Chaplin's comments, below, p. 189.

[12] See Grigg, *Agricultural Revolution, passim.*

[13] S.C. British Wool Trade, *Parl. Papers*, 1828, viii, 445 ff. He also farmed 125 acres of his own.

[14] Grigg, op. cit., p. 91. See also below, pp. 36 ff.

the limestone region, in the fenside parishes of the Stamford, Bourne, and Sleaford neighbourhoods, and in parts of western Kesteven, north and north-west of Grantham. Trollope's property near Stamford included a good deal of pasture. And one of the grazing families of the Bourne district, Lawrance of Dunsby, was later to provide one of the Members for the county. In western Kesteven the Thorold and Heron estates were partly in grazing country. And a close neighbour of Thorold was J.C.L. Calcraft (1770-1851),[15] of Ancaster, a substantial grazier and owner-occupier, and one of Heathcote's leading supporters in South Lincolnshire politics in the 1830s. It may be noticed that W.E. Welby, Trollope's successor as Conservative Member for South Lincolnshire, also had territorial connections with the grazing interest. Apart from the property near the family seat of Denton, there were estates near Folkingham, in south-east Kesteven, and also north-west of Grantham, near those of Heron and Thorold.[16]

The management of the Heath was similar to that of the Wolds, except that its generally lighter soils required less drainage but more artificial manures. Wheat was the principal crop by 1850, but barley was also important, especially on the lighter lands of the Chaplin estate. Chaplin's income from his heath lands increased ninefold following their enclosure and improvement, and his property on the level of the Witham fens had derived similar benefit from the drainage undertakings of the late eighteenth century.[17] He was thus familiar with the two most important features of Lincolnshire agriculture in the early nineteenth century, and his position in county politics owed something to this familiarity, as well as to the large income which went with it. In South Lincolnshire politics, however, the heath farmers were not sufficiently numerous to occupy the position that the wold farmers held in Lindsey.

15 For whom see *Parl. Papers*, 1828, viii, 445 ff. Later a Conservative.

16 See below, p. 171, for Welby and the grazing interest in 1868.

17 Philip Pusey, 'On the Agricultural Improvements of Lincolnshire', in *Journ. Roy. Ag. Soc.* iv (1843-4), p. 304; J.S. Padley, *The Fens and Floods of South Lincolnshire*, 1882, p. 53; Clarke, op. cit., p. 84.

In 1800 Holland had been chiefly pastoral, the principal graziers, such as the Tunnards of Frampton,[18] occupying the fertile belt of the townlands. The drainage of the fens, however, was followed by a rapid increase in the wheat production of the region, and by 1850 the characteristic Holland farmer was a small occupier of twenty to fifty acres, depending on wheat for at least part of his livelihood. Oats, the chief fenland crop in 1800, decreased in importance as underdraining and manuring increased the productivity of the soil. Management was not always good, however, particularly on the estates of the larger absentee and corporate landowners. The growing of potatoes was becoming more common in the middle of the century, especially by those small owner-occupiers of which Holland as well as the Isle of Axholme had its complement. The richness of much of the soil, and the absence of restrictive covenants in many cases, meant that in a period of low wheat prices fenland farmers could diversify their crops. Around 1850, for instance, mustard and chicory were tried instead of wheat.[19]

Returning to a general view of the county, it can now more clearly be seen what Lindsey, Kesteven, and Holland had in common, and how they differed in their agricultural practices. The agricultural economy of Lindsey was the one to depend most heavily on the wheat crop. Even its well-stocked upland farms could not function efficiently without it, and the small lowland farmers relied throughout the period 1832-85 on good wheat prices for their prosperity. The importance of the Brocklesby interest was naturally enhanced by the fact that its leading tenants were also (at least in the early nineteenth century) among the most prosperous and progressive farmers in Lindsey. But of more weight in the electorate were the smallholders of the Marshes and the Isle. The fact that these farmers were mainly wheat producers, and the fact that they were mostly outside the usual channels of political influence, had together a most profound effect upon North Lincolnshire politics. Protection was the great cry of the wheat growers throughout the period,

[18] C.K. Tunnard (d. 1837), of Frampton House, was invited to stand for Boston in the orange interest in 1832, but declined (3 ANC 9/14/172).

[19] *Stamf. Merc.*, 7 Feb. 1851.

and nowhere was there to be found, once aroused, a stronger spirit of protectionism than among the marshmen and islonians.[20]

If Lindsey, with its high arable farming tradition but numerous small farms, somewhat resembled Nottinghamshire in its agriculture,[21] in Kesteven we are nearer to sheep-and-barley farming of the Rutland type. And this particular pattern of farming influenced Kesteven politics, more especially before 1850, just as the wheat production of Lindsey influenced the politics of that particular county. Barley growers agitated for the modification or repeal of the excise duty on malt for the same reason that the wheat growers agitated for the maintenance and later the reimposition, of protective duties on imported foreign grain. Their principal concern was in both cases the maintenance of high prices and steady markets for their product. But where the barley growers were also graziers a further element seems to have been present in their behaviour. It was not a mere coincidence that the leading grazing areas of South Lincolnshire, the wapentake of Loveden, the Sleaford neighbourhood, and the hinterland of Boston, were also the centres of the independent tradition in county politics.[22]

Holland, whose grazing interest had been so important in 1800, came by 1850 to resemble more the wheat-growing districts of Lindsey than the stock-farming of Kesteven. But even its resemblance to Lindsey was not very strong, for, as already described, the farmers of Holland could diversify their crops more easily than the occupiers of less fertile soils. This may help to explain why, in the period of depression from 1848 to 1852, the agriculturists of Holland were less militantly protectionist than their Lindsey neighbours.[23]

[20] See also p. 106 below for a discussion of Protection in the politics of the 1830s.

[21] For comparative sizes of farms among English counties see *Parl. Papers*, 1886, lxx, 114; and for sizes of farms within Lincolnshire see Joan Thirsk, *English Peasant Farming*, 1957, at p. 298.

[22] See below, pp. 52 ff.

[23] See below, pp. 154 ff.

4

LANDLORD-TENANT RELATIONS

THE DISCUSSION of the landed interest in Chapter 2 assumed that at county elections Lincolnshire landlords could command, or at least strongly influence, the votes of their agricultural tenants. It must now be enquired how far this was in fact the case, and what social and economic as well as political factors lay behind the electoral behaviour of the rural voter between 1832 and 1885.

Tenants farming under leases were rare in nineteenth-century Lincolnshire, and very few of the farmers who were enfranchised in 1832 came on to the register as fifty pound leaseholders.[1] The overwhelming majority qualified as tenants-at-will under the fifty-pound occupational franchise. It was these voters whose subservience, according to the radicals' fears, would bolster the power of the great landlords in rural constituencies; and those fears were given at least a colour of justification by the behaviour of the new electorate. In South Lincolnshire there were 44 parishes, at the time of the 1841 election, owned, exclusive of glebe, by a single proprietor.[2] Of these parishes, 32 voted at that election with absolute regularity.[3] That is to say, in each of those 32 parishes *all* the voters (both freeholders and tenants, but almost all tenants), cast their votes in the same way—all plumping for Handley, for instance, or splitting between Trollope and Turnor. In 1868 there were 38 parishes, in the new South Lincolnshire constituency, owned by a single proprietor, and of these 23 voted with absolute regularity, a proportion of 61 per cent.[4] There were eleven close parishes[5] in South Lincolnshire where the voting was regular in 1841,

[1] See below, Appendix B, Table III. [2] *White*, 1842.

[3] *The Poll Book for the . . . Southern Division of the County of Lincoln*, Sleaford, 1841.

[4] *Kelly*, 1868; *White*, 1872; *The Poll Book . . . for the Southern Division of the County of Lincoln, Nov. 1868*, Sleaford, n.d.

[5] That is, parishes where all the soil (exclusive of glebe) was in the hands of one proprietor.

again in 1857, and again in 1868 (the only three contests between 1832 and 1872). Of these, seven were the 'demesne' parishes of influential landlords—Belton (Brownlow), North Stoke (Turnor), Aswarby (Whichcote), Culverthorpe (Houblon), Holywell (Reynardson), Ashby-de-la-Launde (King), and Syston (Thorold). Two other parishes out of the eleven were owned by the Welby family. The spectacular case, however, is the Cust property at South Kyme, where the voters were consistently Conservative, 29 of them in 1841, 25 in 1857, and 37 (including 12 twelve-pound occupiers) in 1868.

These were estates with established political traditions, but even a landlord who changed his course might expect to carry the greater part of his tenantry with him. In the early 1830s Willoughby de Eresby had not exercised any direct influence on the politics of his Grimsthorpe tenants, but in 1839 they were asked to rally to the whig Member (Heathcote), and in 1841 to vote for Trollope and Turnor, the two tory candidates. At the 1841 election a few tenants plumped for Trollope, but most split between Trollope and Turnor. There were no Handley (Liberal) voters on the estate.

This was, admittedly, in a rather benighted corner of Kesteven. But Lindsey, too, can furnish examples of tenant loyalty. At the North Lincolnshire election of 1852 Yarborough's tenants voted for Cholmeley, the Brocklesby candidate, with great regularity. An estate rental of 1853-4 gives 129 tenants whose holdings could enfranchise them as fifty-pound occupiers. Of those 129, 109 can be traced in the North Lincolnshire poll book of 1852. And of those 109, 107 gave plumpers for Cholmeley.[6]

This uniformity is the more remarkable, since the second earl of Yarborough, in his political attitude towards his tenants, was careful not to incur the accusation of heavy-handedness. Tory squires such as Sir John Beckett, of Somerby, near Gainsborough, might refuse to let their tenants be canvassed by the opposition. But in 1850 Yarborough made a public declaration, in a letter to the *Stamford Mercury*, of his rejection of such methods: 'I am satisfied no person can say that I have attempted at any time to control the free

[6] YARB 5 (estate rentals); *Poll Book of the North Lincolnshire Election taken in July, 1852 . . .*, Boston, 1852.

expression of opinion on Politics by my Tenantry'.[7] At the first election for North Lincolnshire in 1832 Yarborough, then (as Charles Pelham) himself a candidate, had expressed himself proud that his father allowed his tenantry to vote as they pleased, and had voiced the wish that every landlord in the country would do the same.[8] The poll book for this election suggests that all the tenants on the Brocklesby estate gave one vote to their landlord's son, but that they did what they liked with their second vote. The same pattern emerges from the contest of 1835. In the late 1830s both the first earl of Yarborough and his son, now Lord Worsley, were converted to the ballot; and the latter, speaking in a Commons debate in 1838, went so far as to repent of his vote for the enfranchisement of the tenants-at-will in 1832, since it had not been accompanied by a measure of protection against undue influence.[9]

The evidence for Lincolnshire suggests that in general whig landlords wielded their influence with more tact and caution than their opponents. Sir Montague Cholmeley wrote to G.J. Heathcote in connection with the South Lincolnshire election of 1832: 'I shall be very happy to give you one of my votes, and I have this day written to my tenantry to say I should be glad if they could conscientiously do the same, tho' I should not *demand* it of them against their consciences. I have however not the least doubt you will get them all if you can find time to canvass them.'[10] Similarly Lord Ebrington informed Heathcote in 1839 that he and his father, Earl Fortescue, would support him: 'Though we have never been in the habit of *pressing* any of our tenants for their votes I will take care that they shall be informed of the interest I feel in your behalf.'[11]

The agent might not share the scruples of his employer or client. William Cragg of Threekingham informed Heathcote later the same month that he had conveyed Fortescue's wishes to the Kesteven tenants. 'I also wrote to Messrs. Smith and Wilkinson to say if any particular tenant required a further

[7] *Stamf. Merc.*, 18 Jan. 1850.
[8] *Stamf. Merc.*, 21 Dec. 1832.
[9] *Parl. Deb.* 3rd Ser. xliii, 682, 12 June 1838. The question debated was the earl of Cawdor's interference in a Carmarthenshire election.
[10] 3 ANC 9/13/61. [11] 3 ANC 9/13/383.

hint to let me know.'[12] At the time of the 1841 election, however, Cragg's hints were of a tory character, and Ebrington had to come down to South Lincolnshire in person, after his return for Plymouth, in order to reclaim his father's erring tenants.[13] There is no doubt that, especially where the landlord was an absentee, the influence of the agent on the spot was considerable. Land agents such as John Burcham of Coningsby were men of power in their own right.[14] And even the Brocklesby agent may not have been guided entirely by the noble principles of his master.[15]

Whatever the means of communication chosen by the landlords, they commonly assumed that their tenants would naturally wish to oblige them. The coercion of tenants was widely regarded as an abuse of the landlord's power, but it was often stated that he had a legitimate influence over his tenants, an influence which reflected the harmony of a well-run estate. A remarkably full statement of this doctrine came from Sir Charles Monck, of Belsay Castle, Northumberland, in a letter to his North Lincolnshire tenants in 1852.

> Nothing is more agreeable to the Constitution, and to all ancient usages of the Kingdom, or more advantageous to true liberty [Monck was a Whig], than that landlords should endeavour by all fair means to lead their tenants. The Queen leads the Nation, and landlords in a similar manner lead their tenants. But there is a common interest between the Queen and the nation: so also between landlords and their tenants . . . I expect of my tenants that they shall not engage their votes before they have communicated with me and come to know my wishes . . . . If it shall after that appear that my wishes and yours are in contrarity there then ought to be the fullest explanation and consideration between us . . . . I promise you that to the opinion of the majority I will submit. But . . . if I am bound to set an example of submission to the majority, the minority must be bound to follow that example, that the estate might not be divided, but act with its full weight for the benefit of all.

Monck went on to emphasize his good relations with his tenants, despite their holding their farms at will, and concluded by explaining his reasons for supporting Cholmeley at the forthcoming poll. The tenants consulted with each

12 3 ANC 9/13/389. 13 *Stamf. Merc.*, 9 July 1841.

14 For the extent of his influence in 1824 see 'A List of the Freeholders of the County of Lincoln . . .'.

15 See an admittedly unsatisfactory reference in Donald Southgate, *The Passing of the Whigs*, 1962, p. 93.

other as Monck proposed, and were happy to inform him that, although they were less sanguine than he about the effects of Free Trade, they were all ready to concur in his wishes and plump for Cholmeley.[16]

Despite the second earl of Yarborough's renunciation of direct political influence on his tenantry, it may none the less be assumed that he fully expected a measure of conformity on his estates. In other than political matters he certainly left his tenants in no doubt as to his feelings, and the few of his letters to his tenants which survive, though polite in form, sometimes broach subjects which the twentieth century might think none of his business. Thus he was annoyed, in October 1846, to learn that one of his tenants had held a shooting party on the day of his father's funeral. 'I wish', he wrote to his agent, 'you would see George Dodds and endeavour to get all particulars for my return when I will consider what steps to take to shew my displeasure.' What those steps were is unrecorded. But in the case of one tenant who had evicted a labourer from a cottage, Yarborough evicted the tenant himself from his farm, although he offered the holding to the offender's brother to show his regard for one of the estate's oldest families. In another case, in offering a farm to the son of a former tenant, Yarborough expressed the hope that he would when in occupation abandon the low amusement of steeple-chasing.[17]

On the Grimsthorpe estate the tenants were selected for their docility, and kept under the eye of a watchful agent. In 1857 he wrote to Lord Willoughby's principal agent in London about finding a tenant for a farm near a newly constructed line of railway: '[As it] will now become a *prominent* farm, it is desirable to be particular to get a proper tenant for it, and one not of a *too political party man*, or one that would make himself too busy in parochial matters or a dissenter.' Lord Aveland (formerly Sir G.J. Heathcote) recommended a candidate who, the Grimsthorpe agent was glad to say, met the requirements: 'From what I can learn he is a steady young man and attends the Church of England. I believe his father is an independent, but is also a

[16] Northumberland County Record Office, Middleton of Belsay MSS., B 16/xiii/1-12.

[17] YARB 9 (letter books, 1846-57).

very steady man, and at the late election supported Sir John Trollope with his vote.'[18] The Willoughby tenantry were expected not only to vote tory in 1841 but also to sign protectionist petitions and attend political meetings. The Grimsthorpe agent reported that when Trollope and Turnor came to address a meeting at Bourne the latter had a poor reception. Those who interrupted his speech included three officials of the Bourne Agricultural Society, one of them a steward living on the Grimsthorpe estate. When questioned afterwards, however, they declared that 'nothing more was meant than a little fun.'[19]

It was clear, then, that at least some Lincolnshire landlords gave a fairly wide interpretation to the concept of legitimate influence, and that it was often unnecessary, where the tenants understood what was expected, to issue specific political instructions. There is some danger, however, in taking at their face value the claims of landlords about the docility of their tenants. Country gentlemen liked, when writing to each other, to imply that their tenants would lay down their lives for them if necessary, conveniently forgetting those stresses and irritations which arose from time to time on even the best-managed estates. Still more chary should one be of the statements of stewards and agents, who naturally wished to give the impression that they knew both the general feeling among the tenantry in question, and the best way of dealing with individual recalcitrants.

Evidence from the side of the tenants is less easy to come by, but occasional glimpses suggest that the view of landlord-tenant relations just described was not confined solely to the landlords themselves. On estates where influence was traditionally exercised, tenants were genuinely reluctant to promise their votes without first learning their landlords' wishes. In 1852, to take one example out of many, the tenants of the earl of Scarbrough's Lindsey estate at Glentworth, a few miles north of Lincoln, refused to plump for Cholmeley until the agent communicated to them Scarbrough's wish that they should do so.[20] In South Lincolnshire the Thorold

[18] 2 ANC 7/35/53, 55. The London agent, Lewis Kennedy, was a prominent protectionist.

[19] 2 ANC 7/6.

[20] Bill of professional charges of Thomas Rhodes, Cholmeley's principal election agent in 1852, MON 25/13/1/2/2, f. 19.

estate was one of those where the landlord was consulted in political matters. Thomas Lee of Barkston wrote to Heathcote in 1839: 'I have always consulted and been guided by my landlord on such occasions. But as I have not an opportunity at this time of taking his opinion I hope you will excuse me making any promise at present.'[21] Thomas Lowry, Thorold's agent, sent a similar reply to Heathcote's request for support. 'My votes are entirely under the direction of Sir J.C. Thorold, and if he requires my undivided vote for Mr. Handley he of course must have it.' But another tenant, William Dolby of Marston, was able to send Heathcote more definite information:

> I yesterday met Mr. Lowry, who was receiving Sir J. Thorold's rents here, when he said Sir John would feel obliged to any of his tenants who would give a vote for Mr. Handley, and he would not ask them for the other, leaving them entirely free to please themselves in that respect. I consider every good Landlord ought to direct one of his Tenant's votes, and under the circumstances I shall with much pleasure give you a Vote and also do what I can for your election, and I stated publicly at our dinner table yesterday that I should vote for you, and I am sure you have Mr. Lowry's wishes for your success.[22]

Even these statements of the tenant viewpoint, it might be objected, are professions designed for the eyes of a landlord. According to the Cobdenites,[23] the seeming willingness of tenants to follow their landlords merely concealed the fact that they dared not do otherwise. The tenants-at-will were utterly dependent on their landlords, and they knew that if they were wayward at election times their livelihoods would be imperilled by the risk of eviction from their farms. A leaseholder knew that he had at least a temporary security of tenure; whereas the tenant-at-will, if given immediate notice to quit, might, besides the loss of income, stand also to lose a good deal of the capital that he had invested in his farm. Even when forced to admit that in England cases of political eviction were extremely rare, the Cobdenites would still maintain that the pressures on the average tenant to conform

[21] 3 ANC 9/14/351. [22] 3 ANC 9/14/384-6.

[23] See, for instance, Henry Ashworth, *Recollections of Richard Cobden . . .*, 1879, pp. 147, 171, 282; J. Morley, *The Life of Richard Cobden*, 1896, i. 304.

were enormous. A recent historian, moreover, has endorsed this view of landlord-tenant relations as being determined by 'psychological coercion'. H.J. Hanham considers that 'even on the best-managed estates the "free association" of landlord and tenant was based on coercion.'[24]

The trouble with this explanation of tenant voting is that it can neither be proved nor disproved by the available evidence. A glance at one Lincolnshire estate, however, suggests that the Cobdenites did not know, or (as in the case of Cobden himself) chose to ignore, the economic facts of farming in the mid-nineteenth century, and that Professor Hanham leaves out of account a great deal of what went on in tenant farmers' minds at that time.

The Brocklesby tenants who voted so uniformly for Cholmeley in 1852 were not all wealthy exponents of wold farming at its most highly capitalized, but they included a number who were men of consequence in northern Lindsey. Of at least one, a pioneer of turnip husbandry in the early nineteenth century, it was said that he retired with a fortune of £80,000.[25] Even the succeeding generation, who farmed in times of higher rents and lower prices, were mightily prosperous. In 1836 it was calculated that a tenant of 1,020 acres made a clear annual profit of £1,390, exclusive of housekeeping, and of the interest of £6,000 invested in the farm.[26] Such a tenant could afford to drive to market in his gig and keep a very well-supplied table. He might breed his own hunters, and would almost certainly appear, well mounted and resplendent in scarlet, at the meets of the Brocklesby Hunt. He would be on easy social terms with his landlord, at least in the days of the first baron and first earl,[27] and in his own parish he might be looked up to as if he were its squire. He might even exercise the political as well as the social

24 H.J. Hanham, *Elections and Party Management in the time of Gladstone and Disraeli*, 1959, p. 11.

25 Samuel Sidney, *Railways and Agriculture in North Lincolnshire*, 1848, p. 72, referring to George Nelson of Gt. Limber.

26 YARB 5/3.

27 For a memorial erected at Brocklesby to a 'tenant and friend' of the first baron Yarborough, see Nikolaus Pevsner and John Harris, *The Buildings of England: Lincolnshire,* 1966, pp. 200-1.

privileges of such a position, and influence the votes of those dependents who were electors.[28]

The Brocklesby tenants were often recruited from the substantial yeomanry of the county, men whose families had held 500 or more acres in Lindsey for several generations. A good example is Henry Healey, who farmed at Little Limber, near Brocklesby, in the 1830s, and whose family had been landowners in the Frodingham neighbourhood, over by the Trent, since the sixteenth century. The Skipworth family, which supplied Brocklesby tenants in the nineteenth century, was a widely-ramified clan, one branch of which set up as gentry at South Kelsey, near Caistor. Tenants also rose directly into the landowning class, purchasing estates in open parishes along the borders of the estate. One sitting tenant, William Wright of Wold Newton, bought the whole of that parish from the third earl of Yarborough in 1870, for over £100,000.[29]

These men were not likely to quail before an overbearing agent, or go in fear of reprisals if they spoke their minds.[30] Nor was their outlook narrowly confined to the estate. They had their own position in the county, and their own family alliances. They travelled widely, and had plenty of opportunity to form their own political opinions. In religious matters, moreover, they were quite likely not to be pillars of the Church of England in their respective parishes. Whatever Willoughby might require or expect, Yarborough had to bear in mind that a large proportion of the people on his estate were Methodists.[31]

Nevertheless, the Brocklesby farmers were tenants-at-will. They held their farms under agreements which gave them no

[28] J.E. Denison wrote to Lord John Russell in July 1852: 'I went on Monday to Louth to give my vote. My chief tenant [Isaac Sharpley of Kelstern] is a sort of king among the wold farmers, and can command ten times as many votes as I can' (P.R.O., Russell MSS., 30/22/10C/930).

[29] *Stamf. Merc.*, 4 Nov. 1870.

[30] It was interesting to note that one Willoughby tenant who in 1839 publicly stuck to Turnor and declined to support Heathcote in South Lincolnshire was Richard Dawson. Although presumably a voter for S. Lincs., he lived at Withcall, near Louth, and was one of those rich wold farmers described above. (3 ANC 9/14/387, Dawson to Heathcote, 11 Sept. 1839.)

[31] YARB 9, Yarborough to Lord Lansdoune, 12 Dec. 1846. The Brocklesby steward was said to have declared, about forty years earlier, that 'the Methodists were some of the best tenants Lord Yarborough had' (George Lester, *Grimsby Methodism. . .*, 1890).

long-term legal security, despite the fact that they were required by those same agreements to lay out large sums to maintain the fertility of their holdings. Small wonder, one might think, that they voted according to their landlord's wishes. It might rather be asked why they ventured to sink their capital in their farms to start with.

The explanation lies partly in the system of compensation for unexhausted improvements that grew up in Lincolnshire in the early nineteenth century. Known as the Lincolnshire Custom, its origin was connected with the spread of high farming. A tenant who took on a recently enclosed upland farm, still in its barren state, would pay a very low rent during the first few years. The rent would be increased when the farm was yielding good white and green crops, and the tenant would then require a greater security for his investment.[32] The Custom worked in this manner. It was reckoned, for instance, that the operation of chalking benefited the soil for a period of seven years. If the tenant left his holding three years after this operation, the incoming tenant would receive four years' benefit from an investment he had not himself made. He would compensate his predecessor, therefore, to the extent of four-sevenths of the original outlay. Arrangements of this kind were sometimes specified in written agreements, but more often tenants put their faith in the Custom, which grew to have almost the force of law. Whilst it was usual for the compensation to be settled between the incoming and the outgoing tenant, there were occasions when farms came on to their owners' hands, and in this case the owner himself had to compensate the outgoing tenant. If a dispute arose, the assessors acting for each side would call in an independent arbitrator.

The Custom grew slowly, however, and was never uniform throughout the county. In the 1840s an allowance for oil-cake fed to cattle in the yard had to be specified in the Brocklesby agreements, since it had not yet become widely adopted as part of the Custom of the county.[33] On the other hand, Yarborough's tenants were not generally allowed part

32 S.C. Agricultural Customs, *Parl. Papers*, 1847-8, vii, 32 (evidence of William Hesseltine of Worlaby).

33 G.M. Williams, 'On the tenants' right to unexhausted improvements, according to the Custom of North Lincolnshire', *Journ. Roy. Ag. Soc.* vi. (1845-6), p. 44.

of the cost of drainage if he provided the tiles. And three years for boning on the Brocklesby estate was rather a slender allowance, particularly compared with the schedules adopted on many Lincolnshire estates later in the century.

The fact, too, that the landlords chanted the praises of the Custom makes one suspect that tenants were not equally happy with it. The landlords favoured a voluntary tenant-right system because it kept down the level of claims. If tenants began to demand more compensation, the landlords would have to raise rents, and sordid bargaining would replace the feeling of mutual confidence between landlord and tenant.[34] Worst of all, thought the landlords, were leases, which would effectively destroy their right to control the management of their own property.[35] For they liked not only to dictate the quantities of manure to be used by their tenants, but also to control their farming activities in other ways. Many Lincolnshire tenants in the 1850s were prohibited from ploughing up even the poorest grassland, and woe betide those who set about exterminating the hares and rabbits which ate up their crops.[36]

The Lincolnshire Custom, therefore, was not enough by itself to make a tenant happier in defying the political wishes of his landlord. More important for his security was the tradition by which sitting tenants were disturbed only in exceptional circumstances. Even a Brocklesby tenant, as already mentioned, might be caught out by his landlord's definition of what circumstances counted as exceptional. But a landlord such as Yarborough would be extremely careful to avoid a precipitate action that might provoke the indignation of the farming community or the malice of political opponents. It was well known, after all, that some farms on the Brocklesby estate had remained in the same families for several generations; and cases were not uncommon of trustees assuming a tenancy during the minority of an 'heir'. Whatever discomforts or unpleasant repercussions

34 S.C. Agricultural Customs, *Parl. Papers,* 1847-8, vii, 441 (questions of Sir John Trollope to William Loft).

35 L.A.O., Massingberd Mundy MSS., MM 7/9/76, Sir C.H.J. Anderson to Charles Mundy of S. Ormsby, 12 May 1847.

36 The 2nd earl of Yarborough set a good example to the county, however, when he gave his tenantry leave to shoot game, so long as they did not disturb the fox coverts (*Stamf. Merc.*, 20 Nov. 1847).

might be the result of 'voting the wrong way', at least the substantial Brocklesby farmer, and probably most other Lincolnshire fifty-pound tenants, knew that the ultimate weapon of 'psychological coercion', the threat of political eviction, was seldom employed and never implemented.

If too much should not be made of the element of psychological coercion, in what other ways can the characteristic pattern of tenant behaviour at elections be explained? D.C. Moore, in a Columbia thesis entitled 'The Politics of Deference', has provided a theory which owes something to recent sociological thought. He describes the political role of the great landowners of England in the nineteenth century as a function of their unquestioned social leadership in the rural counties. The tenant deferred to his landlord in politics because he deferred to him in everything else. For him to presume to think, let along act, independently would be to deny his essentially dependent position in rural society.[37] Norman Gash, in his influential book on early Victorian politics, has written in a somewhat similar vein. 'In the country districts . . . the situation was semi-feudal, and the tenant followed the political tenets of his landlord as a kind of political service due to the owner of the land from the occupier.'[38]

Now there is no denying that most Lincolnshire farming tenants were deferential in their electoral behaviour. But behind a single pattern of behaviour can lie many different motives. It was not simply their desire to fulfil their role in rural society that made the Brocklesby tenants, for instance, vote for Cholmeley in 1852. They were neither so socially inferior, nor so politically ignorant, as the exponents of the theory of deference would have us believe.[39] They voted as adherents of a political interest that was greater than the Yarborough estate, and which extended some way beyond its borders. The second earl of Yarborough could muster only a small number, comparatively speaking, of fifty-pound

[37] D.C. Moore, 'Politics of Deference: a study of the political structure, leadership, and organisation of English county constituencies in the nineteenth century', Columbia University Ph.D. thesis, 1959, p. vii *et passim.*

[38] *Politics in the Age of Peel,* p. 117.

[39] For Walter Bagehot's emphasis on these two elements in political deference see his *English Constitution* (ed. R.H.S. Crossman, 1964), pp. 247 ff.

tenants.[40] But even in 1852, when circumstances were unfavourable to the full deployment of his interest, he was able to carry Cholmeley to the top of the poll in the Brigg, Barton, Caistor, and Grimsby districts.

His influence was in part the result of the large sums which he subscribed to all kinds of local cause and charity. He was, too, a prominent freemason, being Grand Master of the Province from 1849. But his best political investment was the Brocklesby Hunt, whose country extended over most of northern Lindsey above a line from Gainsborough to Louth, and which gave some social cohesion to that vast neighbourhood.[41] As Member for North Lincolnshire Yarborough had consolidated the family interest, not only through local patronage but also by devoting himself to major public undertakings—the passing of the General Inclosure Act of 1845, the creation of the port of Gainsborough, and above all the building of the Manchester, Sheffield, and Lincolnshire Railway.

He was thus able to draw on a feeling of local loyalty that resembled a kind of patriotism in miniature, and that renders Monck's parallel with Queen Victoria not wholly absurd. Particularly in the late 1850s, when Yarborough was lord lieutenant of the county, every occasion was taken in northern Lindsey to show appreciation of his virtues, not only as a good landlord, but also as the wealthiest and most beneficent personage in that corner of the world. His birthday was celebrated at dinners attended by many besides the tenantry; and he received addresses of condolence or congratulation to mark important family events.

His tenants voted in a local as much as a tenurial context. They voted with their neighbours as well as for their landlord; and this gave their votes political meaning, as well as social significance. A vote given simply in deference to a landlord's wishes can hardly be said to represent a political act, although it might have political consequences. But a vote given for a local interest was, in the nineteenth century, a decidedly political act, even though we might now regard the voter's conception of politics as a limited one. To imagine the Brocklesby tenants voting in this latter way (since imagination

[40] See above, p. 33.
[41] See George F. Collins, *History of the Brocklesby Hounds, 1700-1901*, 1902.

must regrettably take the place of direct evidence), surely accords better with what we know about them than to picture them as mere mechanical products of a deferential society.

The Brocklesby estate was, it is true, somewhat exceptional in Lincolnshire, and smaller tenants might be found on smaller estates who conformed more closely to the deferential model. But the conformist behaviour of even these tenants concealed various motives. Gratitude for past favours might be among them, but hope for future favours was often the stronger factor.[42] When Monck's tenants replied to his ponderous communication, they ended their letter on a practical note: 'We are convinced that with Free Trade we must have a continuation of low prices, and that it will require our best energy and economy in the management of our farms aided by your kind assistance in competing with the produce of other countries who are less burdened with taxation than ourselves.' Monck received this letter with satisfaction, and concluded his acknowledgement with an assurance that his kind assistance would not be lacking: 'It shall be my endeavour to assist you in improvements, and, upon the maxim of live and let live, it will always be my desire to have the rents of the estate fixed so that both you and I shall have just share in the profits of active, skilful and commercial cultivation.'[43] In other words, the generous landlord, willing to invest in buildings and drainage, and unwilling to rack his tenants up to fully commercial rents, was also the landlord who might reasonably expect to influence his tenants' votes. In the case of a miserly and unpopular landlord his political influence (if any) might depend simply on his fixing his rents at a sufficiently low figure. An agriculturist from the south of England, visting Lindsey in 1848, commented that there were three principal obstacles to the spread of high farming: lack of landlord capital, over-preservation of game, and 'a desire for political influence in addition to rent'. 'To expect political influence beyond what personal popularity will obtain', he concluded, 'is simply to sacrifice so much rent.'[44]

Tenant farmers also had to bear in mind that their political

[42] S.C. Parliamentary and Municipal Elections, *Parl. Papers,* 1870, vi, 135.
[43] Middleton MSS., B 16/xiii. [44] Sidney, *Railways and Agriculture*, p.83.

record might be looked up when they came to move to other farms. Many landlords, when considering applications for tenancies, must have checked the votes of prospective tenants in the most recent poll book; and naturally they favoured applicants who had been used to voting for the right side. In 1854 the Revd. E.R. Larken wrote to his nephew, William Monson, about a possible tenant: 'R. Morris voted wrong last time I see, but he must reform if you take him of course.'[45] If his old landlord were of the same politics, on the other hand, the tenant might secure a good reference. In 1856 Sir Edward Brackenbury (1786-1864) of Skendleby wrote to William Monson on behalf of an applicant for a farm: 'I have reason to believe that Mr. Joseph Kirkham (Audleby) and Mr. Robert Martin, both great friends of the Liberal cause, would give Mr. Barnes a recommendation.'[46]

Kirkham was a prominent Yarborough tenant and, at this period, an enthusiastic Liberal. One cannot imagine his accepting a tenancy on a tory estate, and we may be sure that his vote for Cholmeley in 1852 was a genuinely 'political' one.[47] Of such people it would not make much sense to talk of A voting for B because he was the tenant of C: it would be nearer the truth to say that A farmed under C partly because he had always been a consistent supporter of B's party.

Whether the landlord chose the tenant or the tenant chose the landlord could depend, other things being equal, on the state of the market. In good times there might be keen competition for farms,[48] but in times of depression the tenant might have the upper hand, and a few poor seasons and a period of low prices could effect a remarkable change in the deferential attitude of the average farmer. The following letter from a Monson tenant dates from the palmy days of the Crimean war:

Your kind circular arrived here yesterday, the purport of which I have communicated to Mr. Starmer, legal agent at Wainfleet, and will not fail to comply with its other requests respecting the correction of the Register of Voters . . . . I also have great pleasure in informing you, that

45 MON 25/13/14. 46 Ibid.
47 For his role in the election campaign of 1852 see below, p. 141.
48 For Brocklesby farms there was at most times a long waiting list (YARB 9, letter books).

Mr. Shelly, late Benniworth, says he is very desirous to remain your tenant, and will not fail (when the time comes) to serve you.[49]

Five years earlier the writer of this letter had been among the signatories of a round robin to Lord Monson from his Lindsey coast tenants, asking bluntly for rent reductions necessitated by Free Trade prices. Monson (a free trader) commented to his son: 'Of course they ask for reductions to make more sure of an abatement at the rent day.'[50] Abatements were granted, but they gave no satisfaction. In October 1851 Monson's agent forwarded to him a letter from Marshall Heanley, his chief tenant at Croft (and a strong tory protectionist), 'begging him [the agent] to instil into me that he does not like to be asking constantly for abatements and he must have a *reduction–instil* into me, is that not a good word . . .?'[51] Earlier that year, having received a very disagreeable letter from another tenant, Monson told his son: 'I only trust that the whole set of tenants are not consorting a strike together.'[52]

By March 1852, when the Liberals were canvassing North Lincolnshire, times had begun to improve, and with them relations on the Burton estate. But Monson warned his son to go carefully: 'You will be careful in canvassing the tenants not to give them any reason to accuse me of coercion–generally I think they will oblige us, but when they do not I should only express regret if I were you.'[53] He drafted a letter for his son to send the Croft tenants, regretting that, through illness, he could not canvass them in person, but saying he would be grateful for any assistance they could render the candidate. Not all tenants, however, were to receive the identical letter.

To Green I should say Dear Sir, to the others whom you know nothing of Sir, and to Green also you must alter the phrase 'every elector on my father's estate' to 'every elector at all connected with my father's estate'. Perhaps the same phrase too would be better to Heanley, who

49 MON 25/13/1/21/1. See also Thompson, *English Landed Society*, p.198.
50 MON 25/10/1/2/4/39, 23 Sept. 1850.
51 MON 25/10/1/3/1/30. Marshall Heanley (c. 1811-84) farmed about 1,040 acres at Croft in the 1860s, 140 of his own and the rest rented from the Monson and Drake families (see *Parl. Papers*, 1867-8, ix, 271). He succeeded to some of William Loft's political influence in the Marshes.
52 MON 25/10/1/3/1/123, 23 Jan. 1851. 53 MON 25/10/1/3/2/79, 4 Mar. 1852.

rents other land besides mine. Whenever you think they are at all pledged to Stanhope, you had better leave out about the second vote, being contented if you can get one to Cholmeley.

Monson's experience with his tenants goes to show that, at least on some estates, the conventions of deference were not enough by themselves to secure political conformity. Monson was a great landowner, and a peer of the realm, but his influence on his tenants waxed and waned with the weather and the price of wheat in Lincoln or Boston market. Part of his trouble lay in the fact that the estate was under-capitalized. He could not afford to be as generous with draining tiles as a Brownlow or a Yarborough. Another part of the explanation lay in the lack of a strong or consistent political tradition on the estate. The sixth baron's predecessor had been a tory.

Some landlords had such a bad reputation with their tenants that, even had they been able to control the weather, they could not have controlled more than a handful of votes. The second baron Yarborough received the following report of politics in Burgh-le-Marsh in 1825:

No parish in the county is less under influence than this . . . . William Cook, esq., [is] the most unpopular squire in the County possessing not the smallest interest among his neighbours. At a meeting of the greater portion of the Burgh Freeholders they had the frankness to declare to Sir William Ingilby that if their Squire voted for him they would not!!![54]

This instance is untypical. But if deference was the more usual attitude among rural voters, it was partly because deference paid. And if there *was* feudalism on some estates, it was feudalism of a very bastard variety.

[54] 'A list of the Freeholders of the County of Lincoln . . .', p. 108.

5

INDEPENDENCE

ROBERT VYNER of Gautby wrote to Joseph Banks of Revesby, on 8 September 1740:

> The gentlemen, assembled at the horse races at Lincoln, judging it proper that some persons should declare themselves candidates for the next election for the county, were pleased to direct Mr. Whichcot and myself to undertake that service. The principles on which we tender our services, setting aside the cant word of the Country Interest, are independency and uncorruption. 'Tis what we both profess, and I verily believe both mean.[1]

Vyner and Whichcot belonged to the category of independent country gentleman, so common in eighteenth-century English county politics, and so lucidly described by Sir Lewis Namier.[2] The concept of independence survived, however, into the following century, and the changing use of the word, with all its ambiguities, may help to explain the politics of 1840 as well as those of 1740.

Independence in politics was primarily a matter of opinion, and only secondarily a matter of economics. Vyner went to parliament to give his votes as a man who thought for himself, rather than as one merely responding to his party's call. If he represented any interest, it was not that of government or even opposition, but that of the county which returned him, and of the landed and agricultural interests of that county. Within the county, it was of the great aristocratic interests that he was independent. Where those interests were whig, as in Lincolnshire, the country gentlemen tended to acquire tory support, though Vyner and Whichcot themselves may be described as whigs.[3]

Sir Robert Heron of Stubton is a good early-nineteenth-century example of the independent whig country gentleman.

1 Spalding Gentlemen's Society, Banks Stanhope MSS., 6/4.

2 Sir Lewis Namier, *The Structure of Politics at the Accession of George III*, 1928, p. 70.

3 Vyner was more independent, and less of a whig, than Whichcot. See Romney Sedgwick, *The House of Commons, 1715-54*, 1970, ii. 501, 533; Sir Lewis Namier and J. Brooke, *The House of Commons, 1754-90*, 1964, iii. 589, 628.

When he stood for Lincolnshire in 1818, it was as an opponent of the compromise by which the whig and tory leaders each held one of the county seats. He condemned 'that system by which the freeholders had been deprived of their rights, that system of settling the election by five or six persons in a private room'. Not a man of great wealth or broad acres, he deplored the notion that 'vast property was an indispensable qualification of a candidate'. Just as he was ready to oppose the party leaders at Westminster, so he was ready to oppose in his own county those influences which upheld the party system. He came forward as the choice of the freeholders, whom another speaker at the same election urged to 'come to a decision with minds unbiased by party spirit'.[4]

Though Heron might not be as wealthy as Pelham or Chaplin, he went to parliament as a man of independent means, and one able to resist the 'captivating allurements of ministers'. Allix, one of his supporters, made it clear what these 'allurements' were, when he attacked the vast number of pensions and places at the disposal of government. Heron's votes would not be given with an eye to any reward he might receive from the Treasury.[5]

The word 'independence' could also be applied to county politics, however, in a way which might cause embarrassment to politicians such as Heron. The yeoman and smallholder could be independent of the squire, the middle and lower classes independent of the aristocracy. The agitation that preceded the first Reform Act had many features which men like Heron could approve. But he was very far from approving the radicalism which it fostered. He had no wish to see tenants voting independently of their landlords, or the farmers and tradesmen of the county choosing their Members independently of the landed interest. He believed, on the contrary, that 'the people of England never have acted, and never will act, with permanent vigour, unless under the guidance of men of rank and consequence.'[6] At the end of his life he opposed the farmers' candidate at the South Nottinghamshire by-election of 1851, declaring that 'it did

[4] *The Poll . . . for the County of Lincoln . . .* , Lincoln, 1818. [5] Ibid.

[6] Sir Robert Heron, *Notes,* printed Grantham, 1850, p. 104.

not become lawyers to aspire to the representation of South Nottinghamshire.'[7]

In the 1830s Holbeach was a leading South Lincolnshire stronghold of the radical independents. Their politics were characterized by an adherence to Reform, and when they formed an 'Independent Electors' Association' in 1835 its members pledged themselves to support only reforming candidates for the county.[8] They were strong in their denunciation of undue landlord influence at elections. In 1832 they required Trollope to write to Lords Exeter and Bristol, begging them not to coerce their tenants. They also asked Trollope to pledge himself not to join any anti-reforming ministry under Peel or Wellington, and on his refusal to do this they withheld their support from him.[9] This matter of pledges brought such men as Heron into direct opposition to the radical independents. Heron might regard himself as a reformer, even to the extent of desiring the introduction of the ballot. But to have his freedom in parliament restricted by a pledge to his constituents, to be bound to vote for men as well as measures, ran contrary to his most deeply-held political principles.[10]

Just as the presence of landlord influence is reflected in the regular voting of close and semi-close parishes, so too the large open parish, relatively free of large landowners, presents a characteristic pattern in the poll book. In South Lincolnshire the contest of 1841 shows Heckington and Swineshead, the first in Kesteven and the second in Holland, to have been among the most independent parishes in the division. The electors cast their votes in the following ways:

	Heckington	Swineshead
Handley (Liberal) plumpers	42	64
Trollope (tory) and Turnor (tory)	16	38
Handley and Trollope	—	29
Handley and Turnor	32	29

[7] *Stamf. Merc.*, 21 Feb. 1851. Col. Tomline, who stood for N. Lincs. in 1881, was perhaps the last of this school of independent politicians.

[8] *Stamf. Merc.*, 3 July 1835. [9] *Stamf. Merc.*, 6 July 1832.

[10] In 1847 the 2nd earl of Yarborough wrote to Cholmeley asking him not to give any pledge on the Maynooth question at the general election. 'I cannot describe to you my horror of the growing want of firmness in candidates to resist the unconstitutional demands of electors who require pledges . . .' (YARB 9, letter books, Yarborough to Cholmeley, 30 July 1847).

Handley, the independent and reforming candidate, gained the largest number of votes in both places. But in Swineshead just under, and in Heckington just over, one-third of the electors split their votes across party lines. They gave one vote to the Liberal as a reformer, and one to a tory as a representative of the agricultural interest. Turnor was the more popular agricultural candidate in Kesteven, and Trollope in Holland (where the voting at Holbeach was similar to that at Swineshead).

Heckington and Swineshead were both rich grazing parishes bordering the fens: their boundaries met at the South Forty-foot Drain. They both lay on the road from Lincoln to Boston, which meant that they were in the way of reforming influences from the latter if not from the former. And both parishes had strong nonconformist congregations. Their tradition of political independence can be traced at least as far back as 1823, when they had large majorities for Thorold despite local landed support for Ingilby.[11] By 1857, however, the tradition was waning. A Swineshead correspondent, writing about the county contest of that year, informed the readers of the *Spalding Free Press* that 'our old independent spirit seems to have left us.'[12] The large graziers were now mostly Conservative. And Swineshead's importance—it had once been a market town—had further declined in the railway age.[13]

In Lindsey it was the towns rather than the villages which harboured the greater proportion of the division's independent electors. But certain villages showed an independent spirit in 1841, particularly Goxhill, Barrow, North Somercotes, Friskney, Sibsey, Coningsby, Saxilby, Haxey, and Scotter. Most of these parishes were strong in Wesleyan and Primitive Methodism, and Coningsby had a Baptist tradition. All were large and generally scattered villages without large estates. Goxhill, Barrow, North Somercotes, and Friskney were marsh villages, and the latter two in particular had rich grazing grounds. The fenside parish of Coningsby voted independently in 1841, as did those of Friskney, Sibsey, and Stickney. But in the Axholme region the pattern was less marked.

11 For this contest see below, p. 93.

12 *Lincs., Boston and Spalding Free Press,* 24 Mar. 1857.

13 The farmers still met once a week at one of the inns, however, for entertainment and conversation (*White*, 1856).

That there was some link between the grazing interest and the independent interest, among both landlords and farmers, appears from the foregoing to be very probable. But what constituted that link is not easy, at least for the historian of the period after 1832, to explain. Landlords connected with the grazing interest were not always men of lesser substance than the owners of broad arable domains. Sir Joseph Banks and Sir John Thorold (the ninth baronet), perhaps the leading independent politicians of the county at the end of the eighteenth century, and both supporters of the grazing interest, had sizeable estates by any standards, and were men of the first consequence in the county. Perhaps it was that landlords of pastoral estates felt themselves to be of the same interest group as their tenants, whereas arable landlords were more inclined to think of themselves as the 'landed interest', a group apart from and above the tillers of the soil. Certainly landlords like Banks and Thorold could take a personal interest in sheep-breeding, and maintain their own flocks on part of their estates. Such activities would of course bring them into close contact with their tenants and neighbours, who themselves might be well-known sheep-breeders and men of wealth and social standing.[14]

At Westminster the Member connected with the grazing interest would naturally act independently of his party when speaking or voting on issues such as the wool trade. Thorold, more vocal than many county Members, spoke three times during the parliament of 1784-90, and on each occasion the subject was the propriety of allowing a limited export of wool.[15] Sometimes the representatives of the wool growers would act in concert with the cloth manufacturers' lobby, although there was not always harmony between the two interests.[16] There were close economic connections, furthermore, between the grazing and the barley-growing interests, and the barley growers' demand for the repeal of the malt tax had a great attraction for independent politicians,

[14] Some owners of grazing estates, such as the Trollopes of Casewick, had risen from the yeoman class.

[15] Namier and Brooke, *House of Commons, 1754-90,* iii. 526; James Bischoff, *A Comprehensive History of the Woollen and Worsted Manufactures*, 1842, i. 207. Banks wrote a pamphlet on the subject in 1782 (*D.N.B.*). See also Sir Francis Hill, *Georgian Licoln,* Cambridge, 1966, p. 116.

[16] As Lord Milton found when M.P. for Yorkshire (Bischoff, op. cit., i. 409).

first of the gentlemanly and later of the radical variety.[17]

The independent voting of tenants in grazing districts was often, of course, a reflection of the politics of their landlords. To take the case of Heckington, Henry Handley had a personal interest in the parish. His father, in fact, had bought the manor from the Heron family. But this does not explain the tendency of the graziers towards radical independence in parishes such as Holbeach. Perhaps the most that can be said with any confidence is that the grazier was less dependent on the soil, and less tied to the local market, than his fellow members of the agricultural community. His chief investment was his stock, and both his rent and his labour bill were smaller items, comparatively speaking, than in the case of the arable tenant. What he produced was an industrial raw material. At the beginning of the nineteenth century most of the Lincolnshire graziers produced a long wool that went to supply the worsted manufactures of the West Riding.[18] In particular the grazier was only secondarily, if at all, a wheat grower, and thus unlikely to be a staunch protectionist.[19]

In the parish community independence in politics was associated, very naturally, with independence in religion, and both graziers and shepherds may well have inclined more to nonconformity than the agricultural classes as a whole.[20] But this is a large question, and the evidence produced by Lincolnshire poll books is disappointingly insubstantial. When the spirit of independence declined after 1830, it was probably in those parishes with strong nonconformist traditions that its spirit lingered longest.

It would be wrong to claim, however, that the independent part of the Lincolnshire constituency always gave its votes in accordance with settled political principles. Those not under the influence of a landlord might respond to an influence less readily detectable from the poll book, and one which was difficult to anticipate without detailed local knowledge on

[17] See below, p. 103.

[18] See John James, *History of the Worsted Manufacture in England,* 1857; Herbert Heaton, *The Yorkshire Woollen and Worsted Industries from the Earliest Times to the Industrial Revolution*, 2nd edn., Oxford, 1965.

[19] For the Conservative connotations of Protection see below, p. 107.

[20] For shepherds' religion see W.H. Hudson, *A Shepherd's Life,* 1936 (Everyman edn.), pp. 37, 105, 244. Shepherds have, of course, been Liberal ever since Shakespeare's day.

the part of a district agent or his assistants. Thus the Louth agent reported to the principal Liberal agent for North Lincolnshire in 1869: 'The voters of this district are composed mainly of small freeholders, and how they might cast their votes at an election would depend very much on the influences brought to bear on them at the time, as their politics amount to nothing at all.'[21] In such districts as the Marsh and the Isle, the canvass was of great importance, and it was impossible to predict, from a knowledge of landed influence alone, how North Lincolnshire would behave at the polls. In 1841, for instance, the following canvassing instruction was issued by the Liberal central committee: 'It is of the greatest importance to secure all the small freeholders who do not attend the market towns, and are apt to give their votes to the first person that solicits them. If any have been missed in the last week's canvass, do not let the other party get them first.'[22]

[21] L.A.O. Stubbs Deposit, I/29, F. Sharpley to Messrs. Hett, Freer, and Hett, 7 July 1869.
[22] STUBBS I/14/1/80.

6

POLITICS AND RELIGION

For most of the period 1832-85 the diocese of Lincoln consisted of the counties of Lincoln and Nottingham. It had once been much larger, but was still, in the mid-nineteenth century, one of the largest in England. Lincoln, before the coming of the foundries, was essentially a cathedral city, and its numerous clergy played an important part in its politics. But the bishopric was not a rich one, and its incumbents exercised comparatively little influence in county politics after 1832. Bishops Kaye (1827-52) and Jackson (1852-69) ruled with mildness and discretion, qualities, however, which were lacking in their successor, Christopher Wordsworth (1869-85).

Of the three Parts of the shire, the Church was strongest in Kesteven, where the first earl Brownlow put himself at the head of a large body of tory squires and parsons. Except in the towns, they encountered little nonconformist opposition. In Holland the situation was less simple. It had several very rich livings, and resident incumbents could provide the social leadership which in Kesteven was more the prerogative of the squire. The Revd. Dr. William Moore (1785-1866) was described after his death as having been the 'potentate of Spalding'.[1] He was incumbent of Spalding and Moulton, which together yielded not far short of £2,000 a year, and a prebendary of Lincoln. He was for some years chairman of Holland quarter sessions, and was related by marriage to two other leading Holland families, those of Johnson (of Spalding) and Tunnard. Other rich Holland clergymen, however, were not always resident, and in times of depression their tithes were grudgingly paid and keenly resented. The worse case was Holbeach, where the vicar drew £1,000 a year from the parish and the absentee lay rector £5,000. Some of the large parishes also had charitable endowments which provided fuel for sectarian animosities.

[1] *Stamf. Merc.*, 16 Mar. 1866.

Lindsey too had its rich livings and influential parsons, particularly in the Marsh and in the Isle of Axholme. For many years the leading Conservative politician of the Isle was the Hon. and Revd. Charles Dundas, rector of Epworth from 1843 to 1883. His example of sitting on election committees and publicly supporting Conservative candidates was one enthusiastically followed and emulated by many of the Lindsey clergy, and one as common in the 1880s as it had been in the 1830s.

But the clerical politicians were not all tory. A characteristic of Lindsey, and one no doubt related to its large Wesleyan body, was the readiness of the Church and nonconformity to unite on certain issues. Chief of these was the supposed threat to Protestantism from the Church of Rome. The Maynooth grant and the papal aggression crisis aroused much protestant feeling in Lindsey.[2]

Rural broad churchmen and the less militant nonconformists were also united in their opposition to the new high churchmanship of the Puseyites and ritualists. Sir Culling Eardley Smith (1805-63), founder of the Evangelical Alliance, was a Lindsey landowner.[3] In 1847 the Lincolnshire branch of the Alliance was supported not only by churchmen but by Wesleyans and Independents.[4] Of course, hatred of popery was more likely to make a Wesleyan vote Conservative than a churchman Liberal. But Lindsey had a vocal minority of low churchmen who, besides giving their support to such things as temperance and mechanics' institutes, also worked for the Liberal party. Such men were the Revd. C.J. Barnard of Bigby, the Revd. C.F. Newmarch of Pilham, the Revd. E.R. Larken of Burton, and the Revd. J.M. Holt of Fulstow.[5]

2 For these issues generally see Norman Gash, *Reaction and Reconstruction in English Politics, 1832-52,* Oxford, 1965.

3 His estate at Nettleton, near Caistor, was sold before 1868. A Liberal, he sat for Pontefract (1830-1). He took the name of Eardley in lieu of Smith in 1847.

4 *Stamf. Merc.*, 19 Mar. 1847.

5 For Barnard see below, p. 142; for Newmarch and Larken, p. 148 f.; and for Holt, p. 68. Among the laymen of the Church who supported both the temperance movement and the whig party in Lindsey were Sir Henry Dymoke, James Whiting Yorke of Walmsgate, and Sir Edward Brackenbury of Skendleby. Yorke and Brackenbury lived in an independent part of Lindsey, and Brackenbury was related to R.C. Brackenbury (1752-1818), the Methodist squire of Raithby.

On Sunday 31 March 1851 the following numbers of worshippers in Lincolnshire attended the most popular service of the day:

	Number	% of total population
Church of England	51,789	13·00
Methodists (all connexions)	58,650	14·00
Wesleyans	38,760	9·50
Primitive Methodists	16,923	4·00
Other Methodist connexions	2,967	0·50
Independents	5,142	1·25
Baptists (all connexions)	5,043	1·25

The Wesleyans were particularly strong in Lincolnshire. In England as a whole they formed only 4 per cent of the total population, and among rural counties the figure for Lincolnshire (9·5 per cent) was exceeded only by those for Bedfordshire (13 per cent) and the East and North Ridings of Yorkshire (16 per cent and 19 per cent respectively). The Primitive Methodists were also numerous in Lincolnshire, and their number of worshippers added to that of the Wesleyans was greater than that of the established Church.

The following table shows that within the county the various sects were unevenly distributed:

	% of population		
	Lindsey	Kesteven	Holland
Wesleyan	11	5	8
Primitive Methodist	5	1	3
Independent	1	1·5	2
Baptist	1	1	4

The Methodists were strongest in Lindsey, but the old dissenting connexions, the Independents and Baptists, had their stronghold, if such it can be called, in Holland.[6]

The role of Methodism in English nineteenth-century politics has not yet been fully elucidated, and the following observations are only the roughest sketch of a very complicated subject. It is probable that local studies may to some degree correct the impression given by the pronouncements of the Wesleyan Conference, and the part it played, or claimed to play, in national politics.[7] The Conference

[6] *Parl. Papers*, 1852-3, lxxxix, 81-5.

[7] For Lincolnshire see especially James Obelkevich, 'Religion and Rural Society in South Lindsey, 1825-75', Columbia University Ph.D. thesis, 1971.

represented the Wesleyan ministry but not its laity, and the Conservative politics of Bunting and other leaders were not necessarily those of the rank and file of the connexion.[8] At the general election of 1841 the Wesleyan ministers appear to have supported Peel, but it is significant that in Lincolnshire at this time there was discontent in some societies with their own ministers. A Boston Wesleyan was expelled by his superintendent for writing letters to the *Stamford Mercury* signed 'A Hater of Priestcraft'. The Louth Wesleyans were angry with their ministers for claiming an exclusive right of admitting members. And in the following year, 1842, the Grantham society was reported to be anxious to get rid of its superintendent, 'an incessant stickler for the supremacy of the sacerdotal office'.[9]

This is evidence from the great urban centres of Lincolnshire Methodism, however, and peace was no doubt better preserved in the country districts.[10] There were many parts of the county where the village societies were indebted for their survival to the toleration of the squire, who might grant a site for a chapel, and the patronage of some large farmer, who might contribute much of the cost of building it. Farmers such as Stephen Bourne of Ashby Puerorum or Francis Sowerby of Aylesby were pillars of rural Wesleyanism, and often exerted a religious influence over their labourers.[11] Nor were the Methodists in the villages always murmuring against the squire and the parson. With respect to the former, they often followed Wesley's own dictum, 'You have nothing to do but save souls', and were content if they were allowed to go their ways in peace. If the parson were non-resident, or

8 For a recent study of the internal and sectional politics of Methodism see Robert Currie, *Methodism Divided: a Study in the Sociology of Ecumenicalism,* 1968.

9 *Stamf. Merc.*, 6 and 13 Aug. 1841, 1 Apr. 1842.

10 Robert Currie (op. cit., p. 49) quotes Dr. William Small of Boston (the 'Hater of Priestcraft' above-mentioned) as showing that 'comparatively few' Wesleyan laymen were Conservatives. This was undoubtedly true in Boston, later a vigorous centre of Wesleyan Reform, but probably far from true as far as the rural districts of Lincolnshire were concerned.

11 For Sowerby see *A Memorial Sketch of Francis Sowerby, of Aylesby, Grimsby,* n.d. For Bourne see John E. Coulson, *The Peasant Preacher: Memorials of Mr. Charles Richardson,* 2nd edn., 1866. Bourne plumped for Ingilby (independent whig) in N. Lincs., 1832 and 1835, and Worsley (the only whig candidate) in 1841. But he appears to have plumped for Stanhope (independent Conservative) in 1852. Sowerby split between the tory and the whig in 1832, 1835, and 1841, and split between the two *Conservatives* in 1852.

neglectful of his duties, the Wesleyans might be the only effective religious influence in the parish. But a hard-working, evangelical priest seldom met with sectarian opposition. The rural Methodist regarded himself as a nonconformist rather than a dissenter.[12] And there were many who should more strictly be described as partial conformers, those who attended morning church and evening chapel. The practice of religious bilaterality was so common in Burgh that in 1843 the vicar proposed to exclude all chapel-goers from church in order to discover where he really stood.[13]

In the towns there was probably a more clear-cut division between church and chapel. The chapel became the focus of at least part of the social life of a small market town. At Caistor, for instance, there were few social events not organized by the Wesleyans in the 1860s, and complaint was made of the 'dearth of unsectarian entertainments' in the town.[14] At Cleethorpes, originally a Methodist fishing village in an otherwise Anglican parish, the Methodists ran many of the boarding houses which swelled the place into a seaside resort, and for many years kept their hold on the town council.[15]

In the 1830s, and later in the 1850s, church-rate controversies must have forced many Wesleyans to choose between Church and dissent, and in the 1830s there is evidence that in Lincolnshire they generally chose the latter. J.B. Sharpley[16] of Louth, in the north of the county, and William Whitsed of Crowland, in the south, were Wesleyans who led opposition to rates for the upkeep of the parish church and its services. At Horncastle, where there was little old dissent, a church rate was defeated in September 1836, by 270 votes to 242. Of 24 voters in this poll whose names can be traced in Wesleyan baptismal registers for the Horncastle circuit, 19 opposed the rate and only 5 supported

12 In accordance with this distinction I have reserved the word 'dissenter' for members of the Baptist and Independent connexions.

13 *Stamf. Merc.*, 30 June 1843 (presumably Burgh-le-Marsh).

14 Eileen H. Mumby, *Methodism in Caistor*, Caistor, 1961, p.18.

15 Frank Baker, *The Story of Cleethorpes and the Contribution of Methodism through Two Hundred Years*, Cleethorpes, 1953, pp. vi, 93.

16 John Booth Sharpley (1800-72), corn merchant, was the leader of the Wesleyans in Louth, and was later, though reluctantly, to join the Wesleyan Reform movement. The 'town Sharpleys' were Liberal upon the whole, the 'country Sharpleys' tending towards Conservatism (information of B.A. Sharpley, Esq., of Louth).

it.[17] At Gainsborough, however, where the Unitarians and Independents led the parochial opposition, the Wesleyan minister and his leading laymen preserved an uncomfortable neutrality in the 1830s.[18]

Church-rate contests, however, are not always a reliable guide to voting behaviour at parliamentary elections. In parish politics the Church of England might be the enemy, but in national politics the Wesleyan, like the low churchman, seems to have been more concerned to oppose the Church of Rome. In 1845 the Wesleyans were among the angriest of Worsley's constituents when he refused to oppose the Maynooth grant, and throughout the country they joined with fervour in meetings to denounce the encouragement of popery. Much public indignation in the county also greeted the 'papal aggression' of 1850, although by this time the Wesleyans, engaged in internecine conflict, seem to have been paying less attention to public affairs. On the other hand, the Wesleyans joined with the dissenters to oppose the education clause in the factory bill introduced by Graham in 1843, although, in Lincolnshire as elsewhere, they supported Russell's education bill of 1847.[19] The truth seems to be that the connexion was unreliable in politics, and that, as the spirit of Reform declined in the 1840s, it became increasingly hard to rally its members to the Liberal cause.

The politics of Lindsey were, to a far greater extent than those of South Lincolnshire, influenced by the Wesleyan vote. Although in 1849 there were only 14,000 or so members of Wesleyan societies in the division,[20] their influence was greater than their mere number would suggest. For one thing, they were strongly represented in the farming class, which in its turn was strongly represented in the electorate.[21] It seems to have been the general rule, though no doubt one to which there were many exceptions, that farmers tended to be Wesleyans and farm labourers Primitive Methodists.[22] For

[17] *An account of persons assessed to the Poor Rate, in the parish of Horncastle, and of the manner in which they voted at the poll for a Church Rate of Sixpence in the Pound, commencing on Friday, 2 September, 1836 . . .* , pr. Jas. Babington, Horncastle (Lincoln Public Library, Local Collection); Methodist registers, Horncastle circuit. The sample is perhaps too small to be of great significance.
[18] *Stamf. Merc.*, 29 May 1840.
[19] *Stamf. Merc.*, 1843-7, *passim.*
[20] *Minutes* of the Wesleyan Conference, 1849. [21] See below, p. 78.
[22] See E.P. Thompson, *The Making of the English Working Class*, 1963, p. 297.

another thing, the sect was strongest in the independent parts of the division, and among those voters who were least affected by landed influence. Its principal strongholds were in the towns of Lincoln, Grimsby, Louth, and Horncastle. And in the rural districts societies were most thickly clustered in the Marsh, from Spilsby in the south to Barton in the north.[23] The Fens, where the parochial system had failed to assimilate the newly drained areas, were also full of Methodists. In the Isle of Axholme, on the other hand, they were not quite so strong or vocal.

Both parties in North Lincolnshire made appeals to the Wesleyans, the whigs on independent, and the tories on agricultural grounds. The whigs made the most of church-rate and education controversies, and in particular emphasized the friendly disposition of the house of Brocklesby towards the connexion. An election handbill of 1841, for instance, addresses itself to the 'Wesleyan Electors of Lindsey', and the author signs himself 'A Wesleyan and a Freeholder'. It points to the political activity of tory parsons, who are opposed to popular education and religious freedom: Worsley, on the other hand, is 'one of the unflinching supporters of the RIGHTS and LIBERTIES of an Enlightened People'. The proof?—one has but to notice 'the appearance of so many chapels along the range of the vast estates of Earl Yarborough'.[24] During the contest the whigs of Brigg and Barton sent circulars to the ministers, leaders, and trustees of Wesleyan chapels in their districts, having been advised by 'some of the most influential members' of the Barton society that they would be 'of great service to his lordship'.[25] These circulars were probably copies of the bill just quoted. In registration matters, too, an effort was made to get Wesleyans on to the register, although an attempt to qualify some of them as trustees of chapels met with no success.[26]

But the tories too were not without hopes of Wesleyan support. In the 1830s Sheffield and Corbett were careful not to alienate them. But the most striking case is that of

[23] The Revd. Edwin H. Tindall, *The Wesleyan Methodist Atlas*, [1878]. Circuit membership figures as returned to the Conference are difficult to use, because of the nature of the circuit boundaries and their frequent alteration.
[24] STUBBS I/14/11. [25] STUBBS I/14/1/55.
[26] *Stamf. Merc.*, 7 Oct. 1842; STUBBS I/11/1.

Banks Stanhope, the independent Conservative candidate in 1852. Despite his own strong churchmanship he was prepared to subscribe to Wesleyan chapel funds, and to take one of his Methodist tenants round the constituency with him during his canvass.

What has been said about the independent vote in Lindsey, however, applies also to the Methodists. Many of them lacked strong commitment to either party. The election bill quoted above, though admittedly with an ulterior purpose, emphasized the freedom of the Wesleyan layman to vote according to his own conscience, undirected by his connexional leaders.

Your preachers are of both sides in politics, some are tories, but I should say (and I have mixed with them half my life time) the majority of them are whigs. They are however altogether a class of men who are moderate in their views, interfere very little with politics, and leave their members to exercise their own judgment in the choice of their parliamentary representatives.[27]

That judgement was sometimes affected by material considerations. In 1841 the superintendent and stewards of the Gainsborough circuit wrote to Brownlow, offering their votes for Christopher and Cust in exchange for a chapel site at Torksey. But, whether because they disapproved of the request, or because it was refused, the majority of the Gainsborough Wesleyans were reported to have plumped for Worsley.[28]

In 1852 the Primitive Methodists of Wrawby, who were building their chapel, approached Cholmeley with a request for a subscription:

We cannot [wrote their spokesman] do anything in return to enrich you, but what we can do we will, we will heartily thank you and pray for you: I have a small parcel of ground which entitles me to a vote which I have promised your canvisers a plumper. My father and brother supports you in the same way, we have several of our connection giving you the same support.[29]

At the same election Cholmeley's Horncastle agent advised him to comply with a similar request from Horncastle, since 'the Primitives were almost to a man his supporters.' The principal agent, however, advised Cholmeley not to send a subscription until after the election, 'lest his motives be

[27] STUBBS I/14/11.
[28] *Stamf. Merc.*, 16 July 1841. [29] STUBBS I/10/3/107.

misrepresented'.[30] Unlike the Wesleyans, the Primitives seem to have been reliable supporters of the Liberal party, and it is significant that in Lincolnshire they seem in many places to have had closer relations with the Baptists and Independents than with the original Methodist connexion.[31] But, being strong principally among the labouring classes and small tradesmen, they were in all probability an insignificant proportion of the county electorate.

The Baptists were the most consistent Liberals among the Lincolnshire nonconformists, but, like the Methodists, their militancy varied according to the local environment. The town with the largest number of Baptists in 1870 was Spalding, but in politics it was the Boston brethren who took the lead in the county. In Bourne and Holbeach the Baptists, though numerically weaker than the Wesleyans, were a large enough proportion of the nonconformist population to make their influence felt. At Louth they were a large body, but the Wesleyans through sheer weight of numbers had the greater influence on the public life of the town. In Holland it was the southern part, that nearest to the dissenting counties of Bedford and Cambridge, which had the greatest concentration of Baptists. But in the middle years of the century they made progress in the country between Spalding and Boston, and also founded several churches in Kesteven, which, apart from Bourne, had been almost empty of the sect in 1840. Similar progress was not made, however, in the open villages of Lindsey, where the place of old dissent was often taken by Wesleyan Reform after 1850.[32]

It was not until about 1818 to 1824 that Independency appeared in Lincolnshire in its most distinctive form.[33] It originated largely in Lindsey, but by 1860 had congregations in most of the towns, though few of the villages, of Lincolnshire. Around 1850 it was strongest in Boston, Brigg,

30 MON 25/13/1/2/2, f. 17f.

31 At Brigg, for instance, the Primitive Methodists, but not the Wesleyans, co-operated with the Independents. It was a rare thing to see a Wesleyan minister at a Primitive gathering (*Stamf. Merc.*, 7 May 1847, 16 Nov. 1849).

32 *Parl. Papers,* 1852-3 lxxxix, 81-5; *The Baptist Hand-Book for 1870.*

33 The Revd. J.T. Barker, *Congregationalism in Lincolnshire*. But the Dissenters' Certificates (among the diocesan records in the Lincolnshire Archives Office), to which Mr. Michael Lloyd has called my attention, reveal several small congregations flourishing in the eighteenth century.

Gainsborough, Lincoln, Grantham, Sleaford, and Stamford; in most of these places, however, its numbers were vastly inferior to those of the Methodists. In those towns where it was the more numerous of the old dissenting sects—Brigg, Gainsborough, Lincoln, Grantham, Sleaford, and Stamford—it may partly account for the lack of spirit often shown in the conduct of local politics.[34] The Independents acted with the other nonconformists in the 1830s, over questions such as church rates, but they declined in both numbers and militancy in the 1840s, and it was not until the late 1870s that they re-emerged as a political force in the county. At Brigg, partly owing to the fact that the town was not an ecclesiastical parish, its leading merchants and professional men seem to have supported the Independent chapel. But its register in the middle years of the century is a sorry tale of internal disputes and wrangles, fostered in part by the structure of discipline within the connexion.[35] Although there was a Lincolnshire association of Independent churches from 1844, individual congregations continued to lead an isolated existence compared with the Baptists and Methodists.[36]

Finally, there was a small but important body of Roman Catholics, principally in Lindsey. They were strongest in the Rasen neighbourhood, where they were supported by the landowning families of Heneage, Constable-Maxwell, and Young, and also at Lincoln, Louth, Barton, and Brigg (where the Elwes family was, and is, the leading Catholic influence). There were also a few Irish settlers in the Isle. Most of the Catholics in the county were moderate in politics, and in 1850, for instance, were careful publicly to dissociate themselves from papal policy. Nevertheless, as G.F. Heneage found, Catholic connections virtually excluded even the most respectable gentleman from standing for the county. The Lincolnshire Catholics appear to have been Liberal in politics in the middle years of the century, but by 1870 it is possible that many of them had followed V.D.H. Cary-Elwes into the Conservative party.[37]

34 At Gainsborough the Unitarians were the leaders of the dissenting and reforming party.

35 Brigg Congregational Church, Minutes (from 1857).

36 *The Congregational Year Book for 1846*; Barker, op. cit.

37 W.J. Battersby, *The Complete Catholic Directory*, Dublin, 1846; John Denvir, *The Irish in Britain*, 1892, pp. 412-14; *Lincs. Chron.*, 15 and 29 Nov. 1850.

7

THE MECHANICS OF RURAL POLITICS

(i) FARMERS' MEETINGS

UNTIL the late 1870s the political life of Lincolnshire was very closely related to the character and habits of the farming class. Tenant farmers, said George Skipworth of South Kelsey in 1844, were, 'from their habits and pursuits, adverse to party and political warfare'.[1] In April 1868 his son, G.B. Skipworth, wrote to the secretary of the North Lincolnshire Liberal Association: 'I confess that according to the present aspect of political affairs, there seems almost as much occasion for a *medium* or *neuter* society as one of a more decided character . . . . The truth of it is I should like to know my man as well as his politics, perhaps even *before them.*'[2]

When the farmers were compelled by the state of their pockets to enter into a political agitation, they were conscious of their weakness *vis-à-vis* their great enemy, the industrial and manufacturing interest. In 1849 the protectionists of Holbeach lamented that

> the merchants, manufacturers and traders of this country (living as they do chiefly in populous places), possess the power of assembling with ease by thousands within their own towns, and of obtaining thousands of signatures to their petitions; whilst farmers, on the contrary, are scattered over the whole face of the country, at considerable distances from each other, and cannot, without the consequent difficulties, meet even in small numbers . . .[3]

Even had it been practicable, on the score of expense, to flood the countryside with literature, and to employ lecturers to agitate the villages, the farmers would have resented the disturbance of their rural quiet more than they would have welcomed the dissemination of protectionist propaganda.

These attitudes were closely related to the pattern of the farming year. At certain seasons the farmer had no time for

1 *Stamf. Merc.*, 2 Feb. 1844.
2 STUBBS I/29. 3 *Stamf. Merc.*, 25 May 1849.

anything but the task in hand. It was impossible to conduct a political campaign during harvest. And the ordinary working farmer had little spare time during the week for the recreation of organized politics. But, for all except the smallest farmers, there was one regular weekly function which combined business with social intercourse, and that was the market. There the farmer not only sold his corn, but met his friends to talk over the news of the day.

Particularly in Lindsey, the market ordinary was an important social and political phenomenon. Having conducted their sales, the farmers would repair for the ordinary to one of the inns of the town; and there, over the cheap but substantial meal, they would, according to the state of the market, become expansive and convivial or grumbling and tendentious. They could provide an easy audience, once the cloth was drawn and the liquor circulated, for a county Member come to pay them his respects. But they could also, when none of the gentry was present, foment plans for independent political action.

Often the company was of mixed politics, but with the co-operation of the chairman, generally a respected and well-established local farmer, an ordinary could be expanded or converted into a party meeting. Thus in 1837 the tickets for an ordinary at Horncastle were issued by the local tory agent, and a whig who had nevertheless contrived an entrance was ejected from the room.[4] More usually an ordinary would convert itself not into a party meeting but into a meeting of the local protectionist society. The chairman of the ordinary, in these cases, was generally also the chairman of the society, and in this double role could exercise much influence. Such a man was William Skipworth of South Kelsey,[5] a substantial yeoman farmer, who played an important part in the revival of protectionism in North Lincolnshire in 1849-50.[6] At the same period the City Arms ordinary at Lincoln was used for political purposes by the Lincoln and Lindsey Agricultural Protection Society. This society, when projecting an agitation in all the major market towns of North Lincolnshire, determined as a first step to communicate with the chairmen

4 *Stamf. Merc.*, 8 Sept. 1837.
5 Brother of George Skipworth of Moortown Ho., S. Kelsey.
6 See below, p. 127

of the various ordinaries.[7] As late as 1863 J.R. Kirkham of Audleby, William Skipworth's successor as chairman of the Angel ordinary at Brigg, led a revival of the malt-tax movement in his neighbourhood by raising the subject with his fellow farmers over luncheon.[8]

By this date, however, the ordinary had waned as an influence in constituency politics. Members and candidates did not enjoy their tours of the markets. In 1853 Sir Montague Cholmeley wrote to William Monson, chairman of the North Lincolnshire Liberal Association, about the advertisement of his programme: 'I should be glad to receive the list to revise it before it goes to the papers, as really six consecutive ordinary dinners eating every day with Christopher yellow pudding is more than human nature can stand in this hot weather.'[9] Another group of objectors to the practice were the tradesmen of the town, who on market day were tied to their shops and hence deprived of a chance to hear their Member.[10] Although the doors were sometimes opened when dinner was over, so that the speeches might reach a larger audience, there was not always room for many additional people, and the price of admission could be high. There was also a growing number of temperance advocates in the constituency, including not only tradesmen who could not, but also farmers who would not attend the ordinaries. The Revd. J.M. Holt of Fulstow attended a Louth dinner for Worsley in 1841, where 'he perceived from what he saw around him (eyeing the alcohol) that that would be an improper time for him to give them a teetotal lecture.'[11]

A Lincolnshire Agricultural Society, intended to foster good farming throughout the county, was founded in 1819. But its sphere of influence seems never to have extended far beyond Lincoln and Sleaford, and it faded away in the 1840s. In the middle years of the century the most influential body of its kind in the county was the North Lincolnshire Agricultural Society, founded by the first earl of Yarborough in 1836. It was held in turn at all the major towns of Lindsey, and in its early years catered both for the

[7] *Stamf. Merc.*, 7 Dec. 1849. [8] Ibid., 13 and 20 Nov. 1863.
[9] MON 25/13/14. [10] *Stamf. Merc.*, 11 July 1851.
[11] Ibid., 29 Oct. 1841.

exhibition of stock and machinery and also for ploughing competitions to encourage skill in the labouring class.

Yarborough's motives in taking the lead were not perhaps purely agricultural. The society covered his son's constituency, and was bound to contribute to the strength of the Brocklesby interest. But rule 1 of its constitution forbade the introduction of subjects 'connected with any legislative enactment' at its meetings.[12] If Yarborough could not use the society's platform for political speeches, at least his political opponents lay under the same edict.

In the absence of a restraining influence, however, the edict came to be honoured more in the breach than the observance. Sir Montague Cholmeley, who should have known better, was one of the earliest offenders, at the Brigg show in July 1849. 'He knew it was difficult to avoid politics on an occasion of this sort, owing probably to the few opportunities there were for Members and constituents to meet: If he trenched a little on the forbidden ground, he hoped he should be forgiven.'[13] In June 1851, at a heated period in Lindsey politics, two leading tory farmers proposed that the rule should be amended by adding the words 'save and except such as directly and exclusively relate to agriculture'. But the movement failed, probably owing to the vigilance of the second earl of Yarborough.[14]

Speaking at the old Lincolnshire Agricultural Society in 1834, Henry Handley, then M.P. for South Lincolnshire, hoped that 'although the Reform Bill had divided the county into two parts, . . . they would ever co-operate for the protection and advancement of the interests of agriculture'.[15] But the leading tory supporters of the Lincolnshire society, Colonel Sibthorp, Charles Chaplin, and the Hon. A.L. Melville, were not keen to merge it with Yarborough's North Lincolnshire society. In South Lincolnshire stock was exhibited at autumn meetings in the various market towns, those held at Grantham being the most important.[16] It was not until 1868 that a South Lincolnshire society was formed, and then it was

12 See the printed *Annual Reports.* 13 *Stamf. Merc.*, 27 July 1849.
14 STUBBS I/16, North Lincs. Agricultural Society, secretary's letter book.
15 *Stamf. Merc.*, 8 Aug. 1834.
16 The South Lincolnshire stock shows did not prohibit political discussion, which appears to have saved the M.P.s for that division from the trouble of attending ordinaries (except at election times).

only as a preliminary to the formation of a new Lincolnshire Agricultural Society, covering the whole county, later in the same year.

The amalgamation of the South and North Lincolnshire societies in the united county body was in part a reflection of the improved railway connections available between the market towns, and of the belief that, now the county was divided by the second Reform Act into three divisions, its agricultural divisions made even less sense than before. But the movement was initiated by two tory gentlemen, Sir John Trollope and Henry Chaplin, and it registered a stage in the decline of the Yarborough interest. The third earl Brownlow, leading supporter of the Grantham society, was made patron of the amalgamated body, the third earl of Yarborough taking second place as president.

Rule 20 of the new Lincolnshire Agricultural Society prohibited the introduction of 'any question of a political tendency'.[17] But the ascendancy in county politics achieved by the tories in the 1870s was soon reflected in the annual speechmakings at the society's shows. In 1879 Sir John Astley, Conservative Member for North Lincolnshire, delivered a blunt protectionist speech, and in the following year he transgressed further by making references to his recent defeat at the general election. In the autumn of 1880 Edward Heneage, then Liberal Member for Grimsby, led a counter-movement, objecting to the heavy consumption of alcohol at the annual dinners, and defending his right to toast 'other denominations' as well as 'the bishop and clergy'.[18]

From 1846 the North Lincolnshire society confined itself to stock and machinery, and the ploughing competitions were delegated to local societies in the market towns of Lindsey. The ploughing meetings were held in the autumn, after harvest and before the autumn sowing. It was a time when the gentry who patronized these gatherings were likely to be in residence on their estates, and when M.P.s could report to their constituents on the events of the preceding session.

[17] *Rules of the Society and Annual Report*, 1869.
[18] *Stamf. Merc.*, 29 Oct. 1880. For Edward Heneage see p. 163 n.16 below.

Colonel Weston Cracroft-Amcotts, M.P. for Mid Lincolnshire, put the matter concisely when addressing his local ploughing meeting in 1871: 'He knew perfectly well that they liked to see their members at this time of the year, to take their measure, and judge how the parliamentary session had agreed with them, and whether they were fit and worthy to represent their constituents in the future.'[19] At the Caistor meeting in the same year, William Torr 'ventured to express the opinion, which he had held for a quarter of a century, that agricultural Members best consulted their own happiness and the wishes of their friends by frequently coming amongst their constituents'.[20] In 1869 H.G. Skipworth (of Rothwell) had remarked at a similar function: 'If it were not for those local ploughing meetings they would rarely have an opportunity of hearing the opinions of their representatives on any questions in Parliament which affected the interests of the farmers.'[21]

It was to the farmers, therefore, and not to the mainly unenfranchised labourers, that the remarks of the speakers were principally addressed. Although the rules of the local societies prohibited 'purely party politics',[22] they allowed, unlike the stock shows, the introduction of political matters of concern to the agricultural interest. In Lindsey at least this meant frequent references to Protection. The ploughing meetings were, after all, arable affairs, and they took place at a season when the farmer could begin to assess the profit or loss brought him by his recently harvested wheat and barley.

It is not surprising, therefore, that in the 1830s and '40s the local agricultural societies were closely associated in many towns with the agricultural Protection societies formed to conduct political agitations. At Boston, for instance, the two organizations appear to have been identical. The duke of

19 *Stamf. Merc.*, 3 Nov. 1871.

20 Ibid., 24 Nov. 1871. William Torr (c. 1808-74) farmed at Riby (under Colonel Tomline), Aylesby, and Rothwell, and took over the famous Aylesby rams and shorthorns from a branch of the Skipworth family. He was elected to the council of the Royal Agricultural Society in 1857. A Conservative (his younger brother, John Torr, was Cons. M.P. for Liverpool, 1873-80). (*Journ. Roy. Ag. Soc.* 2nd Ser. xi (1875), p. 303.)

21 *Stamf. Merc.*, 26 Nov. 1869.

22 William Loft, speaking at the Alford Society (*Stamf. Merc.*, 29 Oct. 1847).

Rutland's Waltham Agricultural Society circulated protectionist petitions in addition to arranging ploughing meetings. In some cases the careless nomenclature used by speakers and newspaper reporters adds to the historian's confusion.[23]

In the 1870s some of the local meetings followed the county society in 'trenching on the forbidden ground'. Henry Chaplin, who inherited the presidency of the Alford Society from Nisbet-Hamilton, condescended to treat his rustic audiences to rehearsals of his parliamentary speeches on foreign and constitutional policy. In the 1880s, however, the autumn meetings began to die out, the result, as will be shown, of political as well as economic factors.[24]

The corollary to the rise of the agricultural gathering was the decline of the county meeting. It was bound to disappear along with the type of independent politics for which it had been such a suitable vehicle. And in Lincolnshire its demise was hastened by the division of the county in 1832. It did not die at once, however. In 1841, for instance, the high sheriff was made to summon two county meetings, one for Lindsey at Lincoln and the other for the southern division at Sleaford. Politically important county meetings were held again in 1842 and 1850, although both were party manoeuvres rather than the expression of county opinion. By 1850 it was becoming rare to consider the expedient except in times of political crisis.

(ii) THE POLLING DISTRICT

The creation of polling districts in 1832, designed to reduce the travelling, and hence the expense, involved in county elections, was delegated in each division to the magistrates in quarter sessions. But the boundaries of the districts, at least in Lincolnshire, were founded not on petty-sessional divisions but on market regions. In Lindsey, for instance, the polling places chosen in 1832 were the major market towns, that is, the towns which supported a flourishing weekly corn market, drawing on a neighbourhood within an approximate radius of eight miles—Barton, Brigg, Epworth, Gainsborough, Grimsby, Horncastle, Lincoln, Louth, Market Rasen, and

23 *Stamf. Merc.*, 29 May 1835, 4 Dec. 1840, 12 Jan. 1844.
24 See below, p. 229 f.

103.

Spilsby.[25] Between 1835 and 1841 three more towns were made polling places, minor market towns with a radius of approximately four miles—Alford, Caistor, and Wragby. In the 1850s three more such towns were added to the number—Kirton, Wainfleet, and New Bolingbroke. These minor markets often lay on what had been the borders of the original polling districts. Thus Kirton was eight miles from both Gainsborough and Brigg, Caistor the same distance from Brigg and Rasen. Saltfleet, in 1856, was the first village to be created a polling place for Lindsey, though it had formerly been a market town, and still had an annual stock fair. It was not until 1872, in connection with the Ballot Act, that villages were made the centres of a significant number of polling districts.

The case was slightly different in Kesteven, where the market towns of Sleaford, Grantham, and Bourne had areas of about ten miles in radius. In northern Kesteven a lack of market towns meant that two villages had to be made polling places: Swinderby,[26] eight miles south-west of Lincoln, and Navenby, eight miles due south. Both these places went to the mid division in 1868, however, leaving the new division of South Lincolnshire with only market towns as its polling places—Sleaford, Grantham, Bourne, Boston, Donington, Spalding, Holbeach, and Long Sutton. They all had major markets, except Long Sutton, which had originally been included in the Holbeach district, and Donington.

The central town of each district was not only where the electors polled but also where the electoral register was annually revised. It was the task of the overseer in each parish to prepare list of electors already qualified, to receive fresh claims for inclusion in the lists, and to receive notices of objection to old electors or new claimants. It was then, however, the duty of the overseers to attend a special court at the polling town, to which they brought their lists of electors and claimants, and which was presided over by a barrister appointed for the purpose. The barrister received the lists, heard evidence with respect

[25] This can be deduced from details of carriers to and from the market towns in *White*, 1842, etc.

[26] The polling took place not in the village but at Swinderby Halfway Houses, a hamlet on the Newark Road.

to disputed qualifications, and conveyed the corrected lists to the clerk of the peace, to be considered as the register then in force.

It is well known that there were many inaccuracies in and omissions from the registers. Persons dead or removed from the district remained on the register unless objected to by the overseer himself or some interested party. Claims had to be accepted by the revising barrister unless objected to, and names objected to were struck off unless adequately defended. At the parochial level the political parties relied on 'correspondents', whose duty was to ensure that newly qualified persons sent in claims to vote, and that the names of unjustified claimants were objected to when appropriate. But it was often deemed inadvisable to provoke party strife by unjustified or even justifiable objections. And, on the other hand, claims could be made in cases where the qualification was known to be insufficient, in the hope that no objection would be made, or that the voter objected to would feel a healthy indignation towards the agents of the opposite party.[27]

A good correspondent would have sufficient local knowledge to ensure that most of the eligible electors in his parish belonging to his party came on to the register. But the most satisfactory arrangement was that the correspondent should himself be the overseer, and thus acquire direct access to the rate books. The office was often filled by a farmer, and its duties, for which there was no remuneration, were not always conscientiously carried out. But an overseer might have his sense of duty supplemented by the knowledge that his landlord was interested in the state of the register.

Even so, the parochial officer or correspondent might lack the legal knowledge which the operation of the registration machinery required, and which could be contributed only by the legal agents retained in each district. The agent, aided by one of the several manuals of election law, could ensure that the forms of claim were properly completed, and that both claims and objections reached the overseer within the appointed time. But his most important work was that of supporting claims and objections before the revising barrister.

[27] Registration papers for the Brigg district, Liberal subagency, in STUBBS I/11; Francis Newman Rogers, *The Law and Practice of Elections, Election Committees, and Registration,* 1847, etc.

In order to defend a claim it might be necessary, for instance, to produce documents establishing a title to some property in the claimant's ownership, or to present evidence to prove that an elector claiming in respect of a farm had been in occupation of that farm for the required length of time. If the claimant were the agent's own client the defence of the claim would of course be all the easier.

What kind of man was the district agent, and how did he fit into the pattern of rural politics? A good example to take is that of John Hett (1803-78) of Brigg, for many years an agent of the Liberal party in North Lincolnshire. At the time of the general election of 1852, when he acted as district agent for Sir Montague Cholmeley,[28] he was the senior partner of Messrs. Nicholson, Hett, and Freer.[29] The firm was the leading one of the Brigg neighbourhood, and must have maintained a large office and clerical staff. Perhaps its local standing was similar to that of the firm described by George Eliot in her *Scenes from Clerical Life*:

> Pittman and Dempster were the popular lawyers of Milby and its neighbourhood, and Mr. Benjamin Landor, whom no one had anything particular to say against, had a very meagre business in comparison. Hardly a landholder, hardly a farmer, hardly a parish within ten miles of Milby, whose affairs were not under the legal guardianship of Pittman and Dempster.[30]

Some of the firm's influence came from its connection with the Yarborough interest, which brought it a good deal of business. But more important were the numerous public offices held by the partners. John Hett, besides a number of lesser clerkships, held the responsible posts of clerk to the Brigg magistrates and clerk to the Brigg board of guardians. Through this work he became inevitably acquainted with most of the resident gentry and large farmers of the district.[31] No

[28] See below, p. 142.

[29] *Law List; Kelly and White; Stamf. Merc.*, 6 Dec. 1878; Marjorie J.F. Hett, *A Family History*, pr. Horncastle, 1934. I am grateful to Mr. Michael Lloyd for drawing my attention to the last-named.

[30] Virtue's edn., ii. 57.

[31] Robert Toynbee, a Lincoln solicitor, wrote to William Monson in 1860, about securing the post of clerk to the Lindsey magistrates: 'The overseers of the poor, surveyors of highways, churchwardens, etc. are sworn in before the magistrates. The clerk necessarily forms an acquaintance with them, and it is really impossible to over-rate the advantage of such an acquaintance in attending to the registration, canvassing at an election and in other matters' (MON 25/13/18).

wonder that he and his kind were 'a powerful, knowing body'. They knew enough of enough people's business to be aware of the best quarters for the exercise of political influence, and the best way to exert it. They themselves, indeed, might have a strong pull over some of their smaller clients, a pull which they were not reluctant to use for political purposes. 'A rich solicitor', wrote the second earl of Yarborough in 1853 to William Monson, 'can do a good deal by the power he obtains by lending out his money.'[32] It was but a step from drawing up a mortgage for a smallholder to becoming the mortgagee. That Hett had such influence is suggested by the following letter from a small freeholder during the contest of 1852.

> Sir, I received your letter respecting voteing for Sir Montague Cholmeley. I have been well canvist but never promised no one aney thing of the sort. Should have wrote before but been in bed ever since Thoresday. I shall have very great pleasure in doeing aney thing for Mr. Hett that lyes in my powr that is a plumper.[33]

Solicitors of this kind tended to be Conservative, which gave that party an important advantage in country districts. They could always, as one politician bluntly put it, 'be bought' for the other side.[34] But they might prove an expensive commodity. Where the buyer was an influential magnate such as Yarborough, the agent might be content with the knowledge that he was a recognized dependent of the Brocklesby interest, and that he would be remembered when it came to the dispensation of local patronage such as county-court clerkships. But an agent working in a region beyond whig influence, one where some of his clients might be leading local tories, was more inclined to exact his price when a contest occurred.[35] The more the agent was obliged to work against the party supported by his leading clients, the less work he would do, and the more he would charge for it.[36]

[32] MON 25/13/14, 11 July 1853. [33] STUBBS I/10/3/81.
[34] 2 TD'E H/26/58, J. Drakard (proprietor of the *Stamford News*) to Charles Tennyson d'Eyncourt, 24 Jan. 1836.
[35] Agents were normally retained for a comparatively small sum—£10 a year in the case of the North Lincolnshire Liberals—to attend to the registration. But this was an earnest of more substantial profits in the case of a contested election.
[36] See also below, p. 145

There were, on the other hand, attorneys attached by principle to the Liberal party, and able to exert influence of quite a different kind. Richard Dawson of Epworth, Liberal agent for the Isle of Axholme in 1852, belonged to the class of expensive attornies just described. But his successor, Josiah Merrils, was a genuine Liberal. Larken would have liked to retain both as agents for the North Lincolnshire Liberal Association. He wrote to William Monson in April 1854:

I should be inclined to recommend Merrils being secured as agent, if not to the *exclusion* of Dawson in *conjunction* with him. It is evident he is popular with the independent body, Wesleyan, etc., and all the unfettered politicians of the Isle, as Dawson is *not* most decidedly . . . . He would be reliable among the thinking and Dawson among the mechanical portion of the voters.[37]

Hett was not as expensive as Dawson (though his bill in 1852 was large enough), but he could exhibit those professional jealousies which often interfered with party loyalties. The weekly corn market at Kirton in Lindsey was revived in September 1849, following the opening of railway communication with Gainsborough, Sheffield, and Manchester in the previous year. And in 1852 a separate committee was formed to canvass its neighbourhood. For registration purposes, however, it remained part of the Brigg district; and Hett and the Gainsborough agent, who stood to lose a few parishes from their respective districts, objected to the creation of a separate Kirton polling district in 1854. They resented the contraction of their spheres of influence, and did not wish to see another attorney going round what they regarded as part of *their* districts. It was necessary for William Monson to send Hett the following letter, significantly dated from Manby Hall, Yarborough's seat near Brigg.

This application [to the magistrates for the creation of the new district] has . . . been agreed to with the perfect concordance . . . of the North Lincolnshire Liberal Association who retain your services for the district of Brigg, and who therefore will expect your co-operation and assistance in this matter. I need scarcely add that this motion has the entire approbation of *all the leading Liberal families* in this division of the county.[38]

[37] MON 25/13/14. [38] STUBBS I/12; MON 25/13/8.

(iii) THE REGISTER

Lincolnshire was said to have had about 5,000 freehold electors in the middle of the eighteenth century.[39] By the early nineteenth century the figure was reckoned at about 9,000, and it rose further during the period of fen drainage and enclosure.[40] In 1836-7 the total number of Lincolnshire electors registered in respect of freehold qualifications was 11,681. By 1864-5 the total had risen to 14,869. In that year there were also 5,366 persons who qualified as occupiers of lands or premises at a gross estimated rental of fifty pounds and above. A further 1, 397 leasehold, copyhold, and other voters brought the total registered electorate of the county to 21,632.[41] This numerous body returned only four Members to parliament, whereas the Lincolnshire boroughs, with a total constituency of under 6,000 returned nine.

Comparatively large though the county electorate was, during the period 1832-67, it was only twenty-five per cent of the adult male population of Lincolnshire. It was a largely rural electorate. In 1855-6 there was only one municipal borough of over 10,000 inhabitants which was not separately represented in parliament. That was Louth, which contributed 408 voters to the North Lincolnshire register. Lancashire had thirteen such towns, contributing a total of 4,794 county electors. Again, in 1864-5 only 1,679 county voters in Lincolnshire qualified in respect of property within parliamentary boroughs, compared with 11,424 in Lancashire.[42]

As might be expected, the farming class was strongly represented in the Lincolnshire county electorate. Around 1850 farmers comprised one-tenth of the adult male population of the shire, but nearly one-half of the electorate.[43] And the parish-by-parish arrangement of the poll books serves to emphasize the fact. In a small parish there might be

39 Namier and Brooke, *House of Commons, 1754-90,* i. 324. Nobody knew for certain, since the land-tax returns, the only basis on which estimates could be be made, were quite unreliable. Registration was finally introduced in 1832.

40 *The Poll for the County of Lincoln, 1807;* J.D. Chambers, 'Enclosure and the Small Landowner in Lindsey', *Lincs. Historian,* i (1947), pp. 15-20.

41 *Parl. Papers,* 1865, xliv, 549 ff. For tables based on this and other returns see below, Appendix B, p. 255.

42 *Parl. Papers,* 1857-8, l; 1864-5, lvii, 18.

43 A calculation based on the poll book for the North Lincolnshire election of 1852, which gives the occupations of a proportion of those who voted.

a mere handful of electors—five or six farmers, perhaps a tradesman or craftsman, and the parson (who might himself be counted as an agriculturist if he farmed his glebe). Only in good-sized villages of five or six hundred inhabitants might tradespeople and others form an appreciable part of the electorate; and only in the most populous parishes might trades be represented on the register by small groups rather than individuals.

In 1864-5, a year for which comparatively detailed figures are available from parliamentary returns, the forty-shilling freeholders formed three-quarters of the total county electorate of Lincolnshire.[44] The large number of freehold and copyhold electors on the register, per thousand of population, was probably related to the fact that Lincolnshire had a high proportion of *agricultural* properties, that is, estates of one acre and above, as opposed to estates of under one acre.[45]

Registration Counties	Estates one acre and above as percentage of total number of estates (1873)	Freehold and copyhold voters as percentage of adult male population (1864-5)
Lincoln	53	18·0
Cambridge	49	14·0
Nottingham	32	12·0
(English average)	28	11·5
Lancaster	14	8·0

The highly industrial county of Lancaster had, relatively to its population, a small number of freehold electors, despite its numerous small urban properties. Among the rural counties the number of smallholders in Lincolnshire must have contributed to its exceptionally large total of forty-shilling freeholders. It is dangerous, however, to generalize from a small sample, and a complete table for the English counties might not tell such a simple tale. Much depended on the amount of attention paid to registration, for instance, and the numbers of freeholders with county votes qualifying in respect of property within the boundaries of parliamentary boroughs.

44 *Parl. Papers,* 1865, xliv, 549 ff.

45 The table is drawn from the summary of the return of owners of land (1873), *Parl. Papers,* 1876, lxxx, and the registration returns for 1864-5.

Under the first Reform Act the freeholders were joined by a group of fifty-pound occupiers, whose numbers, like those of the freeholders, varied appreciably from county to county. One factor was the proportion of the larger farmers (with gross estimated rentals of fifty pounds and upwards) who owned their holdings, and who could, therefore, have qualified previously as freeholders.[46]

Registration County	Owner-occupiers as percentage of £50 farming tenants	Registered £50 tenants as percentage of adult male population
Rutland	12	7
Lincoln	27	6
Cambridge	35	3

But this is a small sample from predominantly rural counties. In Lancashire, where agricultural holdings accounted for less than a third of the fifty-pound tenants, the size and ownership of farms could play only a minor part in determining the relative number of rental electors on the register.

Turning from Lincolnshire as a whole to its county divisions in the period 1832-67, it seems that the boundary commissioners were confronted with no very difficult problem in 1832. The size of the shire made it an obvious case for division, and nothing could be simpler than to divide it into Lindsey on the one hand, and Kesteven and Holland on the other. Lindsey, or North Lincolnshire, was by itself a large constituency. Indeed, it had the most numerous electorate of all English rural and semi-rural county divisions. Its total of forty-shilling freeholders was exceeded only in South Lancashire, Middlesex, and the West Riding. Its total of fifty-pound tenants, however, was exceeded, even among the more rural divisions, by North and South Devon.

Nor was South Lincolnshire, though smaller, an insignificant constituency. Among the more rural divisions it was exceeded in electorate only by South Devon, West Gloucestershire, and East Somerset. And its total of fifty-pound tenants was not far short of Lindsey's. Within South Lincolnshire, the freeholders and copyholders contributed 78 per cent of the electors in Holland, but only 65 per cent in Kesteven. The

[46] *Parl. Papers,* 1866, lvii, 510; 1861 census.

figure for the whole division was 72 per cent, compared with 76 per cent for Lindsey.

There were significant fluctuations in the registers of the two divisions between 1832 and 1867.[47] The state of the register is not a reliable guide to the relative positions of *parties* in any division. In the period 1853-7, for instance, when the Liberals made steady gains in North Lincolnshire, there is little in the registration figures to indicate their activity. The new claims substantiated by the Liberal agents must be set against their success in purging the register of objectionable Conservative electors. The register does, however, provide a guide to periods of relative political activity in the county. It tended to rise at times of excitement, and then gradually decline in the succeeding calms. Thus there was considerable activity in South Lincolnshire between 1835 and 1842, followed by stagnation between 1843 and 1856. In North Lincolnshire the periods of expansion were 1834-6, 1840-2 and 1851-3.

In South Lincolnshire it was the Holland register which increased more appreciably than the Kesteven one in the periods of expansion, a fact probably related to the higher proportion of freeholders in Holland. As a rule, it was difficult to get small freeholders to take the trouble to register. But this meant that they were a fallow field from which, by a determined campaign of registration, a rich political harvest might be reaped. That there were many unregistered freeholders in South Lincolnshire in 1867 is suggested by the number of twelve-pound occupiers who were enfranchised by the second Reform Act. As many as 2,662 of them appeared on the register of 1868-9, whereas a total number of only 2,686 *non-owning* twelve-to-fifty-pound occupiers had been returned in 1866.[48]

Under the second Reform Act, passed in 1867, the county electorate was swelled by the addition of some 7,000 electors qualifying under the twelve-pound ratable-value franchise. This brought the total electorate of the county to 28,600 in 1868-9, but these voters were apportioned by the boundary commissioners into three new divisions. Admin-

47 See below, Appendix B, Table I, p. 255.
48 *Parl. Papers*, 1868-9, l, 113; 1866, lvii, 510.

istrative county boundaries were ignored, and a mid division was formed out of southern Lindsey and a portion of northern Kesteven. The new South Lincolnshire was the largest of the three divisions, but it was exceeded in electorate by thirteen other county divisions, including suburban and semi-rural ones as well as the great new constituencies in Yorkshire and Lancashire. The boundary commissioners made no proposals for extending the boundaries of any Lincolnshire borough in 1868.[49] But the Lincoln suburb of Bracebridge remained the only suburb of a represented borough to contribute appreciably to the county electorate. Most of the new voters, in fact, seem to have been agricultural occupiers.[50] In South Lincolnshire there were thirty parishes in 1868 with thirty or more twelve-pound occupiers, and only nine of those parishes were urban or suburban in character. In rural counties the number of newly-enfranchised electors in 1868 was, at least theoretically, related to the number of occupiers of holdings worth between twelve and fifty pounds a year who did not own those holdings, and who therefore could not previously have qualified as freeholders. But calculations on this basis are put out by the fact that, whereas the freeholders and fifty-pound tenants had to take the trouble to register themselves, the register of twelve-pound occupiers was compiled by the overseers directly from the rate books. The total of twelve-pound electors, therefore, included some owner-occupiers who had not previously registered as freeholders.[51] Thus in Cambridgeshire 65 per cent of occupiers in the twelve-to-fifty-pound range did not own their holdings, but 70 per cent of those occupiers came on to the register for 1868-9. Lincolnshire, however, does not follow even this pattern, for whereas, as in Cambridgeshire, 65 per cent of these occupiers did not own their holdings, only 58 per cent of them, a lower proportion, came on to the register. This was due at least partly to the inefficiency of some of the overseers, who,

49 *Parl. Papers,* 1867-8, xx.

50 In Lincolnshire a five-acre holding was on average sufficient to confer the new franchise. The twelve-pound voters were most numerous in the Fens, where fewer small farmers owned their holdings than in the Marsh or the Isle of Axholme.

51 30 & 31 Vict., c. 102, s.30; Rogers on *Elections*, 11th edn. (1868), p.129.

through informalities in their returns, effectively disfranchised the whole of the twelve-pound electors in several parishes.[52]

If the second Reform Act was the important one for the boroughs, there is no doubt that the third Reform Act, passed in 1884, had its major impact on the counties. Whereas in 1871 34 per cent of the adult male population of Lincolnshire was enfranchised, in 1891 the proportion was 85 per cent. The clause of the 1884 act giving the vote to householders in the counties seems to have been effective in Lincolnshire, for in that county 98 per cent of the householders were enfranchised in 1891. The total county electorate rose from 31,366 in 1883-4 to 72,824 in 1885-6, whilst the borough electorate rose only from 21,061 to 21,704.[53] Lincolnshire was redivided into seven divisions, with electorates ranging from 9,741 to 11,597. These constituencies were of course much smaller in area than the old county divisions of the period 1832-84. But they had a similar number of electors, and were single-Member constituencies. The ratio of electors to Members was therefore altered from roughly 5,000 to one to 10,000 to one. Moreover, the local centres of each division were now, in 1885, some forty or so villages, whereas previously they had been ten or so market towns. Registration and boundary changes were thus by themselves enough to ensure that 1885 was the inaugural year of a new type of politics in the rural English counties. The 1867 act had been moderate enough in its effect not to disturb the essential unity of the period 1832-85, whereas the acts of 1884-5 were the start of an epoch in rural politics which, in many parts of England, continues to the present day.

[52] *Stamf. Merc.*, 25 Sept. 1868. [53] Stamford was disfranchised.

8

THE COUNTY PRESS

THE LIBERALS were strong believers in the enlightening influence of the press. In 1836, when only a handful of newspapers circulated in the county, the editor of the *Lincoln Gazette* wrote to Charles Tennyson d'Eyncourt: 'The source of all our evils is the confounded newspaper stamp duties—the disinclination to read is of itself a sufficient obstruction to keep the farmers in bigotry and servility.'[1] The duty was reduced in that year, but it was still unrepealed in 1852, when Stanhope (according to an opponent) gulled the electors in benighted Lindsey villages 'where a newspaper might enter only once a week.'[2]

But from 1854 there was a great expansion of the cheap weekly press in the county. One of the successful newspapers dating from that period was the *Grantham Journal*, to which a Liberal of the borough paid the following tribute in 1868: '[The *Journal*] may not be with us or against us in expression, yet, while such admirable reports of speeches and public meetings are given to us by the reporter of that paper now present, I say [it] is a great aid to the cause of Liberal progress in this county and neighbourhood.'[3] In 1873 a letter from 'a marshman' informed the readers of the *Stamford Mercury* that even the labouring classes now kept up with the news: 'Now we working men generally gets [sic] to know what is going on all over the country, through the papers, as well as anybody else'.[4]

A closer look at the county press, however, suggests that, after as well as before the 1850s, it was no great buttress of the Liberal cause. In the *Lincoln, Rutland, and Stamford Mercury* the county enjoyed the oldest, and for most of the

[1] 2 TD'E H/26/7, E.B. Drury to Charles Tennyson d'Eyncourt, 30 Jan. 1836.
[2] J.R. Kirkham at a North Lincs. Liberal dinner, *Lincs. Times,* 17 Mar. 1857.
[3] *Grantham Journ.,* 7 Oct. 1868.
[4] *Stamf. Merc.,* 22 Aug. 1873. The letter was probably a fabrication, but none the less significant for that.

nineteenth century probably the largest, of the English provincial weeklies. It was never a cheap paper. Its price had been almost prohibitively high in the early years of the century, but it survived to benefit from the reduction of the 'taxes on knowledge' after 1836. In that year its price was reduced to 4½*d*., and there were further reductions to 3*d*., in 1861 and 2*d*. by 1868. In 1852 its circulation averaged 12,060 copies weekly, through a large district which included Lincolnshire, Rutland, and much of the neighbouring counties. Its nearest rivals among the newspapers read in parts of Lincolnshire were the *Doncaster Gazette* (Liberal) with 2,270 copies weekly, the *Hull News* (Liberal) with 2,900, and the *Nottingham Journal* (Liberal-Conservative), with 2,570. The only newspapers, apart from the *Mercury*, which circulated chiefly within Lincolnshire at the same date were the *Lincolnshire Chronicle* (Conservative), with 1,540 copies weekly, the *Boston Herald* (Conservative), with 450, the *Lincolnshire, Boston, and Spalding Free Press* (Liberal), with 400, and the *Lincolnshire Times* (Liberal), with 300. The *Mercury* carried a great deal of district intelligence and many advertisements throughout the period, and around 1870 it was reckoned to make £10,000 a year for its proprietors, the Newcomb family.[5]

The *Mercury* was, in general tone, a Liberal journal in the 1830s, and so it remained in the 1880s. Richard Newcomb junior, its editor and proprietor from 1834 to 1851, was a Liberal churchman and an opponent of Lord Exeter's interest in Stamford. After his death, when the property passed to a nephew, the new editor John Paradise ran the paper on very similar lines. But the *Mercury*, as it described itself in 1856, was 'more strictly speaking, a general *news*-paper, than a political journal'. There were no leading articles, though the editor would sometimes write letters to himself over the pseudonymous signature of an 'Observer', 'A Freeholder', or 'An Elector of Lindsey'. The local correspondents, often men of substance and influence in their respective neighbourhoods, were allowed a fairly free hand in their weekly reports. Some,

5 The *Newspaper Press Directory*; return of newspaper stamps, *Parl. Papers*, 1854, xxxix, 479; James Grant, *History of the Newspaper Press*, 3 vols., 1871-2, iii. 335; information of David Newton, Esq., research editor, East Midland Allied Press.

such as John Noble of Boston, adopted a radical tone at times,[6] and the reporting of church-rate controversies in the 1830s, and Wesleyan dissensions around 1850, generally leaned to the progressive side. But by the early 1880s some correspondents, notably those for Caistor, Brigg, and Gainsborough, were taking a decidedly Conservative attitude.

The *Mercury*, whatever its role in Stamford politics, had always been conscious of its largely agricultural readership as a county paper. Its usual line in county contests, when a clear line is discernible, was the advocacy of Liberal unity behind whig or moderate candidates such as Cholmeley or Packe.[7] In 1868, 1874, and 1880 there were letters giving prominence to the advocacy of non-party tenant farmer candidates. And in 1874 the reporting was distinctly favourable to the farmers in their battle with the labourers' unions. Though branded as a free-trading paper by its Conservative contemporaries, it opened its columns to protectionist sentiment during the great Lindsey contest of 1852.

In the 1830s the Yarborough interest in North Lincolnshire had its mouthpiece in the *Lincoln Gazette*, which was sufficiently tame, at least before 1836, for Ingilby to dub it the 'Brocklesby Gazette'.[8] But it was discontinued in 1841. In 1847 William Gresham founded the *Lincolnshire Times* to cover Lindsey in the Liberal interest. But it was firmly reforming and free-trading, and showed little enthusiasm for the whig Cholmeley. It was purchased by the Conservative journalist E.R. Cousans around 1856 and discontinued in 1861. In 1859, however, the *Lincoln Gazette* was refounded by the Liberal J.E. Brogden, who ran it on independent principles until 1871. In that year it was taken over by E.R. Cousans, but under his son H.E. Cousans it supported the Liberal party in North and Mid Lincolnshire from 1878. The Isle of Axholme was covered for the Liberals by the *Doncaster Gazette*, founded in 1794, whilst northern Lindsey was covered by the *Hull Advertiser* and later by the *Hull and Eastern Counties Herald.*

[6] See his obituary, *Stamf. Merc.*, 17 Aug. 1866.
[7] See, for instance, the 1868 election, p. 169 below.
[8] 2 T D'E H/34/76, Charles Pelham to Charles Tennyson d'Eyncourt, 28 Sept. 1836.

After the failure of *Drakard's Stamford News* in 1834, the division of South Lincolnshire was dependent for some years on the *Stamford Mercury* for its Liberal news. The *Lincolnshire, Boston, and Spalding Free Press* was founded by Henry Watkinson in 1847 as a reforming organ for the division, and played some part in the contests of 1857 and 1868. By the latter date, however, it had become very moderate in tone, and after Watkinson's death or retirement in 1875 it leaned towards the Conservatives.

For those farmers who wished to read the newspapers and yet remain bigoted and servile there was always the *Lincolnshire Chronicle*. Founded by a group of gentry, solicitors, and others in 1833, its object was to advocate Protestant and protectionist opinions in the county, and its ambition to counter the influence of the *Stamford Mercury*. In the first few years of its existence it nearly burst itself in trying to emulate the grand scale on which the *Mercury* was conducted;[9] but under Henry Bellerby, editor from about 1840 to 1858, it became moderately prosperous and achieved a wide circulation in the county. Assisted by the *Boston Herald*, the *Doncaster Chronicle*, and the *Hull Packet*, it lent all its weight to the protectionist campaigns which culminated in the elections of 1852. But thereafter it decreased in influence. E.R. Cousans purchased it in 1862 and removed its offices from Stamford to Lincoln, where he edited it until his purchase of the *Gazette* in 1871.

The *Chronicle* was not the first Conservative county paper. James Amphlett, later the distinguished editor of the *Shrewsbury Journal* and *Staffordshire Advertiser*, founded the *Lincoln Herald* around 1828. In 1832 he moved it to Boston, where it was successful in opposing a rival journal sponsored by Newcomb.[10] Amphlett left the county soon afterwards, but under Thomas Fricker the *Boston Herald* became influential in Holland and eastern Lindsey. It became the *Lincolnshire Herald* in 1854, and was taken over in 1866 by Henry Farrow, a former *Herald* man who had founded the successful *Boston Gazette* in 1860.

The burgeoning of the penny press failed to have the political impact which might have been expected. Many of

[9] *Stamf. Merc.*, 13 Jan. 1837. [10] James Amphlett, *Recollections*, 1860.

the cheap weeklies in the later 1850s were one-man affairs with minute circulations. And most of them preserved the political neutrality essential to the success of a small market town newspaper. There were a few exceptions. Grimsby had its Liberal organs in the *Grimsby Guardian*[11] and the *Grimsby News*.[12] The latter had district reports from northern Lindsey, and paid some attention to the county contests of the period 1880-5. The *Louth Times*, founded in 1872, supported the North Lincolnshire Liberals from 1878, and may well have contributed to their success in 1880. By 1885, however, it had apparently been taken under the wing of the *Boston Guardian*, the leading Liberal journal of that borough since 1854. All these newspapers presented a consistently Liberal viewpoint, but their coverage and circulation, like those of their Conservative rivals, were essentially urban and municipal, and they did not regard county politics as their special mission.[13]

[11] 1855-71.

[12] Founded 1874, a Liberal paper under J. Bainbridge from 1876.

[13] The *Sleaford Gazette*, founded in 1854, was the only Conservative penny journal not published in a municipal borough.

PART TWO

NARRATIVE

9

PARTY POLITICS AND THE AGRICULTURAL INTEREST, 1832-1846

(i) THE UNDIVIDED COUNTY, 1741-1831

BETWEEN 1741 and 1761 Lincolnshire was represented by two independent county gentlemen, Robert Vyner of Gautby and Thomas Whichcot of Harpswell. But in 1761 the Ancaster interest, which had been powerful earlier in the century, was revived. Lord Brownlow Bertie was returned with Whichcot, and an independent opposition, led by Vyner and Sir John Thorold (eighth baronet), collapsed before the day of nomination. There followed a period of thirty-five years in which one whig and one independent held the county seats. Bertie retired in 1779, to be succeeded as senior whig member by Charles Anderson Pelham (later first baron Yarborough). Sir John Thorold (ninth baronet) held the second seat from 1779 to 1796. In the latter year, however, he was succeeded by Sir Gilbert Heathcote (fourth baronet), a ministerialist whig, and in the following years the independent interest in the county languished.

The Napoleonic war period saw the emergence of a body of tory sentiment among the Lincolnshire gentry. At the general election of 1802 Heathcote was joined by the tory Charles Chaplin, and for the next twenty-nine years the whig and tory interests divided the county between them. Chaplin and many of his supporters were not strongly partisan politicians, and having secured one seat they were not anxious to establish a claim to the second. They believed in the 'peace of the county', and, at a time when patriotic causes made heavy demands on their purses, they had no desire to incur the enormous expense of county contests. These attitudes persisted into the post-Reform period, and were to be especially evident in the North Lincolnshire contests of 1832 and 1835.

Heathcote retired in 1807, to be succeeded by Charles Pelham (later second baron and first earl of Yarborough).

A group of militant tories, led by the first baron Brownlow, made this election the occasion of the first county contest since 1724. They put forward Richard Ellison, the Lincoln banker, and Member for that borough since 1796, to challenge Pelham. Ellison attacked the whigs for their assault on the royal prerogative, and raised the cry of 'the Church in danger'. Some of the freeholders, not for the last time, responded to the beat of the Protestant drum. But, apart from the Brownlow interest, Ellison had little landed support, most of the gentry preferring to split between Chaplin and Pelham. The result (in a low poll) was

Chaplin	1,589
Pelham	1,162
Ellison	948[1]

In 1818 Sir Robert Heron launched an independent opposition to Charles Chaplin the younger, then coming before the electorate for the first time. But Pelham and Heathcote gave him little encouragement, and he received solid support only from Sir John Thorold (tenth baronet) and Viscount Milton (later fifth earl Fitzwilliam).[2] The voting was

Pelham	3,693
Chaplin	3,069
Heron	2,623

There was a direct conflict between the Brocklesby interest and the independent party in 1823, when Pelham succeeded his father and went to the House of Lords. He wished Heathcote to accept the vacant county seat,[3] but on his refusal brought forward instead Sir William Amcotts Ingilby (1783-1854), of Ripley Castle, Yorkshire. Ingilby was a choice of desperation, acceptable to Yarborough principally as a means of keeping Heron out of the seat. And, as events transpired, it would have been better for the Brocklesby interest had Yarborough made his peace with Heron. Ingilby had succeeded through his mother to the Amcotts property at Kettlethorpe (near Gainsborough) and in the Isle of Axholme. But he was not well known in the county. Eccentric

1 *The Poll for the County of Lincoln,* 1807.

2 Heron, *Notes*, pp. 74-97; *The Poll for the County of Lincoln,* 1818.

3 ANC 13/B/4; 3 ANC 9/10/2, 4; Yarborough to G.J. and Sir Gilbert Heathcote, Oct. 1823.

in politics as in manners and appearance, his antecedents were tory, and he was later to veer towards the radical party.

Thorold was persuaded to stand against Ingilby at the by-election in December 1823, and he was supported both by Heron and by a more reforming group of independent politicians led by General Johnson.[4] Thorold, Heron, and Johnson were all Kesteven landowners, and the contest became partly one of Kesteven versus Lindsey and Holland. The tories of the Grantham neighbourhood gave their interests to Thorold as a local man and an opponent of the Yarborough interest. But he received only fragmentary support in Holland and southern Lindsey, and the northerly wapentakes of Lindsey were all but unanimously behind Ingilby. Thorold was beaten by 3,816 votes to 1,575.[5]

The contest was followed by a division in the independent camp, Heron and Thorold refusing to endorse the choice of Johnson as a possible candidate for the next general election.[6] In 1826, in fact, Ingilby and Chaplin were returned without opposition. But the reformers' day came in 1830, when at the general election Ingilby announced himself a convert to their cause. Chaplin opposed the second reading of the Reform Bill in March 1831, but at the general election in May he resigned rather than face the certainty of a contest. Charles Anderson Worsley Pelham (eldest son of the second baron Yarborough) came forward as an advocate of 'fair, just and constitutional reform', and was returned unopposed with Ingilby.[7]

Chaplin's retirement bears witness to the strength of Reform feeling in the county, but exactly how strong it was is difficult to judge. Before the end of 1830 agitations were under way in Lincoln and Boston, and local tory interests were encountering growing opposition at Grantham and Stamford. In the early months of 1831 the movement spread from the boroughs to the market towns of the county, and even in some of the larger villages there were 'Free and Easys' at which the progress of the Bill was discussed and the

[4] W.A. Johnson (1776-1863), of Witham-on-the-Hill, near Bourne, owned about 2,500 acres in Kesteven. M.P. for Boston, 1821-6; Oldham, 1837-47.
[5] *The Poll for the County of Lincoln,* 26 Nov.-6 Dec. 1823.
[6] Heron, *Notes,* pp. 134 ff. [7] *Stamf. Merc.,* 13 May 1831.

circulation of petitions organized.[8] But in Lindsey, at any rate, no general ferment swept the countryside. Ingilby had his radical supporters at Gainsborough and Louth, but they do not seem to have wished to see him returned with another radical colleague in place of Chaplin. Elsewhere—at Brigg, Horncastle, and other small market towns—a feeling in favour of more moderate Reform prevailed. The situation in Kesteven and Holland was different, for there Chaplin was better known than Ingilby, and the feeling against the former was much stronger than the feeling for the latter. Here, perhaps, was Johnson's chance. Supported by the reformers of Bourne and Holbeach,[9] he came forward for the county on Chaplin's retirement, only to be obliged to retire in his turn when Pelham appeared. The independent reformers of Lincolnshire were strong enough to remove Chaplin, but not to prevent Pelham from succeeding him. Pelham no doubt calculated on that, and so probably, mindful as always of the peace of the county, did Chaplin.

Thus Lincolnshire returned two Members whose votes contributed to the eventual triumph of Reform. But when Chaplin and his fellow tories declined a contest in 1831 they were thinking in terms of local as much as of national politics. They were already looking beyond the enactment of the Bill, and were husbanding their resources for the battles over the divided county that were to come.

(ii) NORTH LINCOLNSHIRE, 1832-7

When the county was divided in 1832, both its Members became candidates for the northern division, comprising the Parts of Lindsey. The tories were reluctant to oppose Pelham, whose vast personal interest made his position seem almost unassailable.[10] But they were not prepared to concede the

[8] *Stamford News,* 1831, *passim.*

[9] For their Reform associations see *Stamf. Merc.,* 15 and 22 Apr. 1831.

[10] 'It could not be denied', declared John Wilks in the Commons in January 1832, 'that by the division proposed, the interest of [Yarborough] would, in the division of Lindsey, completely prevail, and that any effort by an independent candidate to resist his nomination would be in vain' (*Parl. Deb.* 3rd Ser. ix, 822, 24 Jan. 1832). In fact Brocklesby had little chance of controlling both seats, and it never attempted to do so. But it was true that the division of the county favoured the whigs.

other seat to Ingilby, whose lukewarm protectionism and radical opinions rendered him, in their opinion, unfit to represent an agricultural constituency. In particular they were annoyed by his recent conversion to the ballot, which they considered 'a sort of acting in the dark, out of character with Englishmen, and calculated to create suspicion and distrust between parties where the best understanding ought to exist'.[11]

They had difficulty, however, in finding a champion. Chaplin, whose interest had been cut in half by the division of the county, was not to be coaxed from his retirement, and he had no heir to succeed to his interest.[12] A candidate was eventually found, however, in Sir Robert Sheffield. Like Chaplin he was a popular landlord and magistrate, and like Chaplin again he was not a dedicated party politician: he had supported Pelham's father in 1818. But his estates lay a good distance from Brocklesby, and one of his chief assets as a candidate was his property and influence in the Isle of Axholme.

Faced with this opposition, Pelham and Ingilby campaigned on a broad reforming platform, and appeared together at festivals held at Lincoln, Alford, Gainsborough, and Grimsby to celebrate the passage of the Bill. The demonstration at Lincoln was chaired by Yarborough, and attended by contingents from many parts of the county. Ingilby, Charles Tennyson, G.F. Heneage, Sir Montague Cholmeley, and Major Handley[13] were among the speakers.[14] Sheffield, while standing primarily as an agricultural candidate, was also at pains to show the independent electors of the division that he could respond to the spirit of the times. He advocated retrenchment, tax reductions, and the reform of government patronage. On one issue dear to the nonconformists, that of the abolition of slavery, he was more enthusiastic than the ministerialist Pelham.

[11] The words were Sheffield's at the nomination. (*The Poll . . . for the Northern Division of Lincolnshire,* p.7.)

[12] He told a Sleaford meeting in 1837: 'If he had been fond of a seat in the House, he would have had reason to complain of the Reform Bill; but it gave him the opportunity of seeing more of the Lincolnshire farmers, and he had been happier ever since' (*Stamf. Merc.*, 13 Oct. 1837).

[13] Benjamin Handley of Pointon, *c.*1784-1860, M.P. for Boston, 1832-4.

[14] *Stamf. Merc.*, 16 Nov. 1832.

It was to no avail. The result of the poll in December 1832 was

Pelham	6,554
Ingilby	4,748
Sheffield	3,858

In every polling district the largest number of electors was that which split its votes between the two successful candidates. The combination was favoured by the great whig interests of the county—Heneage, Cholmeley, Anderson, Scarbrough, St. Albans, and Fortescue—as well as by the reformers of Lincoln, Gainsborough, Spilsby, Alford, and Horncastle. In contrast, the only important tory interests to plump for Sheffield were those of Brownlow and Turnor, much as had been the case in 1823. Sheffield did well only in the Lincoln district, where he had the support of Sibthorp, Ellison, and the Church party, and in the Isle, where his personal influence was supplemented by that of the parsons. In both districts, however, he had to contend with the appeal of Reform to the independent electors. Elsewhere in the division the tory gentry, following the example of Chaplin himself, split their interests between Sheffield and Pelham.[15]

The tories could take comfort, nevertheless, from the substantial gap between Pelham's poll and Ingilby's, and from the cracks that had already begun to appear in the whig-radical front. In November 1831 Yarborough had absented himself, pleading a 'chronic effusion of the liver', from a county meeting at which Ingilby had demanded the reform of the Upper House.[16] At the nomination in December 1832 Heneage, though willing to propose Ingilby, deprecated his attacks on the Church; and Ayscough Boucherett, who proposed Pelham, exchanged angry personalities with Ingilby's leading supporter, Charles Tennyson.[17] During the contest Pelham avoided coalition with Ingilby, and they maintained separate committees. Had most of the whig interests plumped for Pelham, Ingilby would have been left with little landed support, and little popularity outside the larger towns.

15 See the poll book for details of voting. 16 *Stamf. Merc.*, 25 Nov. 1831.
17 Ibid., 21 Dec. 1832. At Tennyson's request William Brooke omitted the altercation from the report which he published in the poll book (2 TD'E H/37/80).

He did nothing to strengthen his position as Member for Lindsey during the following two years. His performances in the House were fiascoes, and his attempts to prove himself a dedicated agricultural Member were frustrated by what he publicly described as 'a parcel of rotten whigs'.[18] In his dealings with his constituents he was guilty of that familiarity which quickly earns the contempt of the rural elector,[19] and he spent little–and could afford to spend less[20] –on building a permanent electoral organization.

Significantly, the movements which led to his downfall were begun, not by the tories, but by the right wing of the whig party. Encouraged by Ayscough Boucherett, George Heneage deserted his Lincoln constituents on the dissolution of parliament in December 1834, and offered himself for the county.[21] It was not to be the last time that a member of the Heneage family aspired to the title of Member for North Lincolnshire, and not the last time that Hainton and Brocklesby failed to act in concert. Heneage came forward at least partly, as Ingilby divined, 'from an idea of the almighty power of Pelham'.[22] But Pelham had no wish to precipitate a contest by an open rupture with the radicals. Heneage, feeling the ground slipping from under him, then appealed to the independent and nonconformist vote–a role in which, considering the Catholic connections of his family, he was unlikely to succeed.

This development finally decided the tories, until then reluctant to move, to produce a candidate of their own. Chaplin, after an injudicious flirtation with Heneage,[23] decided that this time it would be necessary to oppose Pelham as well as Ingilby. He found a sufficiently uncompromising candidate in T.G. Corbett of Elsham (d. 1868),[24]

18 *Stamf. Merc.*, 15 Nov. 1833.

19 It was a criticism of one of Ingilby's addresses that it did not 'sustain the decorum of rank and influence' (2 TD'E H/26/7, E.B. Drury to Tennyson d'Eyncourt, 30 Jan. 1836).

20 He appears to have been always short of cash, and was reduced to borrowing large sums of money from Tennyson (2 TD'E H/30/5, Ingilby to Tennyson, 15 Feb. 1827).

21 Ipswich and E. Suffolk R.O., HA 53/359/42, Boucherett to Angerstein, 23 Dec. 1834.

22 2 TD'E H/29/3, Ingilby to Tennyson, 30 Dec. 1834.

23 Brownlow was enraged at his 'preposterous conduct' (Massingberd MSS., 1/154, Brownlow to the Revd. F.C. Massingberd of S. Ormsby, 8 Jan. 1835).

24 5,000 acres in Lindsey, later increased to over 8,000. Stood for Lincoln (independent), 1826; sat (Cons.) for N. Lincs., 1835-7.

who, with only a few days to go to the nomination, issued an address firmly supporting the royal prerogative and praising the tories as the upholders of agricultural Protection. On Corbett's appearance Heneage withdrew.

In the resulting three-cornered contest, which took place in January 1835, the poll was

Pelham	4,479
Corbett	4,450
Ingilby	3,984

Corbett not only vanquished Ingilby but came near to ousting Pelham at the top of the poll. His success was the more remarkable in that his campaign had been very short, compared with Sheffield's in 1832. He also lacked the strong personal interest which Sheffield had brought to bear. His estate was not, by Lindsey standards, a large one, and it was rather too close to Brocklesby for comfort. He benefited from a rise in the number of tory plumpers and a fall in the number of tory votes split with Pelham, although it is worth noticing that this movement took place more among the farmers than among the gentry of the division. Chaplin, Dymoke, Brownlow, and Turnor plumped for Corbett, but Sheffield was among those who split with Pelham.[25]

Among the whigs, Anderson and Cholmeley were the only prominent supporters of Pelham not to withdraw their support from Ingilby.[26] Boucherett plumped for Pelham, and Heneage split between Pelham and Corbett. His example was followed by a number of farmers in the Caistor and Rasen districts, on the outskirts of the Brocklesby interest, and in retaliation the Tennyson tenants were asked to plump for Ingilby.[27] The reformers of Lindsey had not greatly diminished in numbers since 1832. But they were poorly organized. And in their anger at Pelham's failure to give them positive support some were ill-advised enough to split between Ingilby and Corbett. The latter, it is fair to add, modified his toryism so far as to angle for the nonconformist vote, and his declaration on the hustings that 'the Church and Dissent must stand or fall

25 See *The Poll for the . . . Lindsey Division of Lincolnshire, Jan. 1835.*

26 Cholmeley attempted to mediate between Ingilby and Heneage, and Yarborough may at one stage have held him in reserve as a compromise candidate (*Stamf. Merc.*, 25 Dec. 1835; 3 ANC 9/14/239, Cholmeley to G.J. Heathcote, Dec. 1834).

27 2 TD'E H/4/16, John Thorpe to Tennyson, 17 Jan. 1835.

together' may have conciliated some of the Wesleyan farmers.[28]

If Corbett had benefited from the reaction against Ingilby, he himself was soon the victim of a similar phenomenon. He became unpopular in the division in 1835 for voting against the malt-tax motion, and later for not voting at all. Agriculture began to recover from the depression in which it had languished in 1834, and the reformers recovered their spirits as a wave of church-rate contests swept the county. In 1834 there had been controversies in Boston, Lincoln, and Louth;[29] but in 1835 the agitation spread to rural parishes such as Marshchapel and Hogsthorpe in Lindsey, and Bicker and Sutton St. James in Holland. The reformers of Lincoln and Boston extended a helping hand to their comrades in the county, and the passing of the Municipal Corporations Act stimulated the Reform party in what had formerly been the tory town of Louth.[30]

Ingilby at first took courage from these hopeful signs, but in August 1836 he announced that he would not stand again. He did not feel equal to the expenditure of money and energy on the reconstitution of his party, and saw no reason to hope that Pelham would enter into a substantial treaty of agreement with him. Pelham, like many whigs who had done badly in 1835, was now showing a renewed enthusiasm for the cause of Reform. In the session of 1837, for instance, he declared himself in favour of the abolition of church rates.[31] But this did not necessarily mean that he would be prepared to coalesce with Ingilby in registration and election work. Ingilby was perhaps unduly cynical in believing that Lord Yarborough's conversion to 'the People' was 'D--- stuff and nonsense'.[32] But its effect was certainly to cut the ground from under the feet of the radical baronet.

Ingilby's retirement was precipitated by Corbett's decision, after the 1836 session, to make way for a new tory candidate at the next election. R.A. Christopher, a Scotsman who had inherited large Lincolnshire property through his wife, owed

28 In this, however, he was merely following the precedent set by Peel (see N. Gash, *Reaction and Reconstruction in English Politics, 1832-52*, Oxford, 1965, p.70).

29 See *The Law, Practice and Principles of Church Rates, being the . . . Report of a Vestry Meeting at Louth,* 1834.

30 *Stamf. Merc.*, 1835, *passim.*

31 *Parl. Deb.* 3rd Ser. xxxvii, 212, 296, 10-13 Mar. 1837.

32 2 TD'E H/117/18, Ingilby to Tennyson d'Eyncourt, n.d.

his introduction to Lindsey politics to Chaplin. His principal seat in the county, Bloxholm, was not far from Chaplin's seat at Blankney. But the bulk of his Lincolnshire property was in Lindsey, and his seat at Well, near Alford, was well placed to influence an important body of Lindsey electors, the farmers of the Marsh. A strong party politician, and devoid of charm, he was what Macaulay would have called a 'loud and acrimonious tory'. Unlike Chaplin, he had no family tradition of friendship with the Brocklesby interest.[33]

No third candidate appeared, and at the general election of 1837 Pelham, now Lord Worsley,[34] and Christopher were returned unopposed. There was no spirit of compromise, however. Both sides formed committees and were ready for the emergency of a contest. Worsley was supported by reformers as well as whigs, and went so far as to announce his conversion to the ballot. Christopher waxed wroth on the church-rate question, and did his best to rally those agriculturists who had been disappointed in Corbett. The election, despite the lack of a contest, marks the entry of both the whig and the tory parties of Lindsey into the post-Reform era of party politics. Brocklesby and Blankney had kept their leadership of their respective sides, but one had done so at the cost of radical concessions, the other at the cost of an adherence more to men and less to measures.

(iii) SOUTH LINCOLNSHIRE, 1832-7

Two reformers, G.J. Heathcote and Henry Handley (1799-1846), were returned unopposed for South Lincolnshire, the division comprising the Parts of Kesteven and Holland, in 1832. Heathcote was a very moderate whig, and left his seat for Boston to come forward for South Lincolnshire only when it appeared that an expensive contest was almost certain at the former, and very unlikely in the latter. Neither the town nor the county cherished a strong regard for him personally, but he had at least the weight of family tradition, political connection, and a numerous tenantry to support his claims.

33 He had, however, in the large expense he had incurred in purchasing the Well estate, a strong enough reason for hoping to avoid a contest. (Scottish Record Office, Biel Muniments, GD/6/976).

34 His father was created earl of Yarborough and baron Worsley in Jan. 1837.

Handley, in contrast, had a personal interest and not much else. The son of a wealthy and influential banker at Sleaford, he was a gentleman farmer who took a progressive interest in agricultural affairs. He had married into the whig nobility, but his father-in-law, the second baron Kensington, had no Lincolnshire connections. Handley himself was an independent reformer rather than a whig in politics: at a slightly later date he may be described more simply as a Liberal.[35]

The basis of Handley's successful candidature was his ability to bring together the old and new traditions of independence. He was respectable enough to secure the approval of Heron, who, though now by no means a radical, disapproved of such faint hearts as Heathcote. And he was radical enough to win over those whose sympathies inclined more to Johnson than to Heron. Supported by his cousin, Major Handley, and by Charles Tennyson, Handley gathered to him former Johnson supporters at Boston and Stamford. And even Richard Healy and the radical independents of Holbeach were at length won over.

The absence of a contest does not mean that the voters of South Lincolnshire were united behind Heathcote and Handley in 1832, nor that there was insufficient feeling to produce a rival candidate. The election was, in fact, preceded by a lengthy period of manoeuvres and canvasses. The first prospective candidate to take the field, in the early months of 1831, was Johnson, and his candidature soon produced a tory opponent in Sir John Trollope.[36] Johnson's weakness, however, was revealed by his abortive candidature for the whole county. The reformers turned to Handley, and the whigs, who might well have preferred Trollope to Johnson, now felt able to launch their own candidate. Trollope thereupon retired. But, as in the case of Pelham and Ingilby, there was no coalition between Heathcote and Handley. The latter feared, indeed, that in the event of a contest the

35 As Member for the cloth-manufacturing town of Heytesbury from 1820 to 1826 he had not voted consistently with the opposition, as Stanley later reminded him (*Parl. Deb.* 3rd Ser. lviii, 1036, 2 June 1841). Trollope described him to Milton in September 1832 as 'a renegado tory. . . , now a professor of radicalism', in short, as another Ingilby (Casewick MSS.).

36 A Conservative, perhaps, rather than a tory. Until 1831 he had been an adherent of the Fitzwilliam interest in Northamptonshire, and at first he was hopeful of whig support in South Lincolnshire.

Willoughby and Heathcote tenants might have been asked for plumpers, even though Handley's own supporters were prepared to split their votes with Heathcote.[37]

Heathcote and Handley were again returned unopposed in 1835 and 1837, but by the latter year only Handley could claim that he still held the confidence of a substantial body of the electors. Though never committing himself to the ballot, he deplored the exercise of undue influence by landlords. And in December 1834 he delighted a Holbeach audience by condemning tithes as 'a tax upon the capital, skill and industry of the occupiers of the soil'.[38] He was also careful to give his votes in the Commons for the reduction of taxation and the abolition of church rates. But above all he contrived to win and keep the confidence of a good number of his farming constituents—particularly the graziers among them.[39]

Heathcote meanwhile had lost any popularity he may have had with the reformers. After the election of 1835, when Pelham was busy trimming his sails, Heathcote fell from grace by opposing the abolition of church rates. In 1837 he received the following reprimand from William Stanger of Fleet, a strongly nonconformist parish near Holbeach:

> You must be aware that the great body of dissenters are feelingly alive to the settlement of that [the church-rate] question, and as it has been stated in the house that numbers of them are indifferent to it, I think you and other candidates will be convinced on your canvass that such a statement is decidedly incorrect.[40]

At the same time the tories, who as late as 1835 were prepared to see Heathcote returned as a man of very moderate views,[41] at length decided that a 'Conservative Association' should be started in the division. Chaplin gave his blessing to the formation of the organization in August 1836, but the prime mover was that bigoted tory, the ninth earl of Winchilsea (1791-1858), who had recently inherited the Haverholme estate near Sleaford.[42] In 1837 it was proposed to start Winchilsea's relative Christopher Turnor, of Stoke

[37] *Stamf. Merc.*, 6 and 13 July 1832. [38] *Stamf. Merc.*, 12 Dec. 1834.

[39] The *Stamford Mercury* made a point of noting the interest he took in such questions as the tallow duty and the proposed removal of Smithfield market to Islington.

[40] 3 ANC 9/14/306, William Stanger to Heathcote, 27 June 1837.

[41] 3 ANC 9/14/228, Brownlow to Heathcote, 3 Jan. 1835.

[42] 3,700 acres. His aunt Harriet had m. Sir J.W. Gordon, bart., of Haverholme.

Rochford, as tory candidate. But he had not been sufficiently brought before the electorate,and Chaplin may have feared retaliation against Christopher in Lindsey if an opposition were started in South Lincolnshire.[43]

(iv) THE AGRICULTURAL INTEREST AND PROTECTION, 1830-7

In 1830 the farmers of Lincolnshire were more concerned with the malt-tax question than with the agitation for Reform. In January Handley chaired a county meeting at which the repeal of the malt and beer duties was demanded. The barley growers reasoned (their grasp of economics being none too strong) that the removal of the duties would allow them to stand out for higher prices, and that the demand for second-quality barley would be stimulated once the maltsters found themselves able to afford to use it. (The effect of the tax was, or was said to be, that the maltsters found it worth while to use only the finest grain.) The abolition of the tax was advocated chiefly by whigs and independents, but Colonel Sibthorp was among the tories who viewed the movement with favour. Chaplin, on the other hand, threw cold water on it, and thought the farmers would be better advised to concentrate on defending the corn laws.[44]

Agricultural politics were lost sight of in the excitements of the following year, but during the election campaigns of 1832 the subject of Protection was elevated to an important position by both landowners and farmers. 'Depend upon it,' declared Corbett when nominating Sheffield, 'the very first question that will be agitated in the reformed parliament will be the repeal of the corn laws.'[45] And in South Lincolnshire leading farmers gave their support to Trollope as a protectionist. Richard Dawson wrote to Heathcote on 28 July 1832: 'As you express yourself decidedly determined to support the present Corn Laws and the Agricultural Interest generally, I wish you may be successful, in conjunction with Sir John Trollope . . . . Free Trade would be the ruin of this Nation.'[46]

[43] 3 ANC 9/14/309, J.W. Dudding of Saxby to Heathcote, 27 June 1837.
[44] *Stamf. Merc.*, 15 Jan. 1830.
[45] Ibid., 21 Dec. 1832. [46] 3 ANC 9/13/34.

As if to fulfil Corbett's gloomy prophecy, the session of 1833 was not far advanced before W.W. Whitmore, radical Member for the manufacturing town of Wolverhampton, gave notice of a motion in favour of a fixed duty on foreign corn, to replace the sliding scale that had been in operation since 1828. Lincolnshire agriculturists hastily met to voice their protests. A meeting was held in Lincoln by the Lincolnshire Agricultural Association, a body formed to promote the political interests of the farmers and fostered by Sibthorp and Chaplin. Only a small minority, led by J.W. Dudding, a large farming tenant of Lord Scarbrough's at Saxby, declined to defend the sliding scale and advocated a continuation of the anti-malt-tax movement. The Kesteven Agricultural Association, a similar body meeting at Sleaford, was less firmly protectionist, and quite a large minority spoke against the malt tax, including Johnson and Healy.[47]

Encouraged by the radicals and independents at Westminster, Ingilby seized an opportunity to move for a reduction of the malt tax in April 1833. After a quaint speech he divided the House, and managed to secure a majority of ten.[48] But four days later another vote reversed the decision, after the whig leaders had threatened to introduce a property tax to make up the lost revenue. The other three Lincolnshire Members had all given their votes for Ingilby's motion, but of them only Handley gave a second independent vote consistent with his first. Heathcote and Pelham answered their party's call.[49]

Before the session of 1834, with farmers suffering from a depression in wheat prices, the protectionist agitation in the county assumed much more formidable proportions. The Lincolnshire association took the lead, and endeavoured to promote district committees in all the major market towns of the county. By April committees had been formed

47 *Stamf. Merc.*, 19 and 26 Apr. 1833. The chairman of the Kesteven association was J.C.L. Calcraft, for whom see above, p. 29.

48 *Parl. Deb.* 3rd Ser. xvii, 689. Ingilby, in a speech blending the principles of the independent country gentleman with those of Cobbett, wanted to know why the landlord should be taxed more heavily than the fundlord. 'While the landlord had his carriage, his horses and his servants, for all of which he was highly taxed, the fundlord might have nothing but an old woman and a cat, for neither of which was he taxed at all (A loud laugh)' (*Stamf. Merc.*, 3 May 1833).

49 *Parl. Deb.* 3rd Ser. xvii, 758 ff., 30 Apr. 1833.

throughout Lindsey and Holland, but the Kesteven association refused to merge itself in the movement, and kept aloof from the organizers at Lincoln. The principal business of the committee at Lincoln was to get petitions signed and circulated, but it was also to send delegates to the London meetings of a national Agricultural Association, modelled on a body formed for a similar purpose in the 1820s.[50]

Corbett was chairman of the Brigg association, and was aided by at least some of the protectionist organizations of Lindsey in the election contest of 1835.[51] Apart from Corbett there were at least three other tory chairmen of district protectionist organizations—Sheffield at Winterton, Thomas Gee, the banker, at Boston, and George Chaplin, a relative of Charles, at Louth. At Alford, to show that farmers as well as squires were prominent in the movement, the leaders were William Loft and Robert Cartwright of Well. The association at Grimsby, however, and to a lesser extent those at Barton and Caistor, were Brocklesby affairs. Boucherett was chairman at Market Rasen and Anderson at Gainsborough, though both associations had tory elements. Of course the political organization of central and district committees was closely paralleled by the agricultural. The 'Lincoln and Lindsey' association, as the Lincolnshire had by now renamed itself, also had a nobler model before it, when it referred to its meetings with delegates from the districts as the 'Lincolnshire Agriculturists' House of Representatives'.[52]

At the nomination in January 1835 Sheffield, proposing Corbett, urged the farmers to 'return a strictly independent man to watch over their interests'.[53] But Corbett soon revealed his lack of independence by voting against the Chandos malt-tax motion in the session of 1835. It was a vote of which Pelham, now enjoying the greater freedom of the opposition benches, made the most. As corn prices rose, divided counsels again prevailed in the agricultural interest. Before the session of 1836 both Handley and Sibthorp were attracted to schemes for currency reform. But Heathcote and

50 *Stamf. Merc.*, 14 Feb.-16 May 1834.

51 One of his first actions as Member was to write to the associations, expressing eagerness to keep in touch with them and readiness to present their petitions. (*Stamf. Merc.*, 27 Feb. 1835.)

52 *Stamf. Merc.*, 1834-5, *passim.*

53 *The Poll Book for . . . the Lindsey Division,* pp. 295 f.

Pelham, with their party now back in power, followed the advice of Chandos to concentrate on the local taxation question.[54]

Why did Protection, rather than the malt tax, become the dominant agricultural issue in Lincolnshire politics in the years 1832 to 1835? Economic factors were clearly important, the chief of them being the prevailing low price of wheat.[55] Arable farmers naturally took the state of their local markets, and the weekly intelligence from Mark Lane, the London exchange, as the readiest means of reckoning their prosperity. And when wheat fell below fifty shillings a quarter for longer than one season they would begin to demand that something be done about it. Being of the opinion that, if left to itself, the home market would normally obey the laws of supply and demand, they blamed its frequent failure to do so upon foreign competition. If a poor season were not followed by high prices, it was clear—at least to them—that cheap imports were the cause of the mischief. Hence their demand for Protection, which meant, roughly speaking, a guaranteed minimum price for wheat in the home market.[56]

In the early 1830s two further economic factors served to concentrate the attention of agriculturists on the price of wheat. Sheep and barley prices remained relatively stable. And, a development particularly noticeable in Lincolnshire, wheat was rapidly outpacing barley in importance as an arable crop. Upland regions such as the Wolds, which grew barley in the early years after enclosure, could now support crops of wheat as part of a more intensive agriculture. And the drainage of the fens had been followed by a great increase in the wheat acreage and a decline in the acreage devoted to pasture.[57]

With the decreasing economic importance of the grazing interest, and the elevation of wheat to a position of primary importance in the local agricultural economy, it is not

54 *Stamf. Merc.*, 20 Nov. 1835. 'Local taxation' meant primarily the poor rates, which were assessed principally on land and generally paid by the occupier rather than the owner. But the phrase was sometimes used to include the less onerous burdens of the county rate and the land tax.

55 See below, Appendix C, p. 257.

56 See also Derek Walker-Smith, *The Protectionist Case in the 1840s,* Oxford, 1933.

57 This was a point stressed in the evidence of Lincolnshire witnesses to the Select Committee on Agricultural Distress; see *Parl. Papers,* 1836, viii, Part i. 306, 421, 430-1; Part ii. 20.

surprising that farming politics saw a shift in emphasis from the malt tax to Protection.[58] But the concentration of this change into the few years after 1830 was the result as much of political as of economic factors. Just as the anti-malt-tax agitation had attractions for independent politicians,[59] so the protectionist programme tended to find its adherents among the more conservative elements in rural society. Protection was a demand not for change but for stability, and one which united, rather than divided, the interests of landlord and tenant. (Urban radicals preferred to say that it was a landlords' cry in which, by specious arguments, their tenants were induced to join.) And it implied more than a protection of farmers' prices, or through them of landlords' rents. It came to symbolize the resistance of traditional rural society to the politics and philosophy of Manchester and Birmingham.

It is significant in this connection that the period under analysis was the first few years of the Reform era. Despite the Chandos clause and the redistribution of seats, the agriculturists regarded the Reform Act as a threat to their political influence. Corbett told the Lindsey electors in 1835: 'Whatever good effects may have arisen from the Reform Bill, I am afraid it is but too evident that the agricultural interest has not that preponderating weight in the House of Commons that it formerly possessed.'[60] The fact that it was the whigs who had passed the Bill, and the whigs who remained in power during most of the following years of agricultural depression, had important consequences for rural party politics. In 1830 the tory Sibthorp could still parade his independence in matters of agricultural policy. At the general election of that year he was actually encouraged, by Healy and a member of the Thorold family, to stand for the county in opposition to Chaplin, on the strength of his greater enthusiasm for the repeal of the malt tax.[61] Two years later there could be no doubt that Healy and Sibthorp stood on opposite sides.

[58] Even the graziers had more cause for being protectionist in 1830 than they had in 1800. By 1830 they probably produced more fine wool than long wool, and the fine wool was beginning to suffer competition from Spanish and Saxon imports.

[59] See above, p. 53. [60] *The Poll Book . . .*, p. 290.

[61] *Stamf. Merc.*, 13 Aug. 1830.

In the same way it became harder for the whigs to convince the farmers of their sympathy. Heathcote and Pelham succeeded for a time by their firm pronouncements in favour of Protection. Pelham wisely encouraged the Lindsey associations in 1834, preventing them from coming entirely under tory control. Ingilby, however, considered the agitation to be a tory job, and with characteristic unwisdom wrote to the Lincoln and Lindsey Agricultural Association and told it so.[62] Handley steered a middle course. The carefully-phrased address which announced his candidature in 1832 advocated a Protection for the farmer 'fully commensurate with the heavy burdens exclusively imposed upon him'. Thereby he hoped to conciliate such supporters as Healy, who considered that Protection would no longer be necessary once those burdens were removed.[63] In 1834 it was probably under his guidance that the Kesteven Agricultural Association resisted the take-over planned by the Lincoln and Lindsey. It decided that, in view of Althorp's assurance to Handley in the House that no measure to alter the corn laws would be introduced that session, there was no need for a full-scale agitation.[64]

(v) NORTH LINCOLNSHIRE, 1837-41

Corn prices recovered in the later 1830s, and indeed by 1839 Lincolnshire farmers were discovering that prosperity could bring its own political dangers. The high price of food in the manufacturing towns resulted in the formation of the Anti-Corn-Law League, and the agricultural interest was quick to take alarm at the mass meetings and mob oratory by which its agitation was promoted. Meetings were held in Lincolnshire in January 1839 in anticipation of trouble in the coming session. All four Members for the county were at pains to emphasize that they would never vote for Free Trade. The whig Members were nevertheless regarded with suspicion by Christopher, Corbett, and Sibthorp.[65] But the decision of the Melbourne ministry during 1839 to make the corn laws on open question eased the position of Worsley,

62 Ibid., 16 May 1834.

63 See his correspondence with Lord Milton, published in the *Mercury* of June and July 1832.

64 *Stamf. Merc.*, 18 Apr. 1834.

65 *Stamf. Merc.*, 1 Mar. 1839.

Heathcote, and Handley. The tories could not now attack them as followers of the ministry on the corn question without exposing themselves to charges of seeking party advantage by their 'factious' conduct.

The situation was altered, however, by the budget of 1841. Baring's proposals to reduce the sugar and timber duties, followed early in May by Russell's conversion to the principle of a fixed duty, gave the tories the chance to rally the agriculturists to their side.[66] It was one thing, they argued, to support a government which had declared its neutrality on the Protection question, but quite another to contine to give votes in support of a government that had taken a significant step towards Free Trade. At a county meeting for North Lincolnshire, held on 21 May 1841, Corbett, Christopher, and Winchilsea delivered broad attacks on the Melbourne government. And Thomas Brailsford of Toft Grange, who had taken a leading part in the Lincoln and Lindsey Agricultural Association from its inception in 1834, attempted to get Worsley to declare that the government had lost his confidence. Worsley, while making plain his opposition to the fixed duty, expressed himself ambiguously on his general attitude to the ministry.[67] And when, on 4 June, Peel carried his motion of no confidence, Worsley voted on the government side. There was a bitter exchange between him and Christopher during the preceding debate.[68]

The dissolution speedily followed, and there were soon rumours afoot of an opposition to Worsley in Lindsey. Sir John Beckett (1775-1847) was the favourite in the Gainsborough neighbourhood, and indeed his Axholme connections might have rendered him a strong candidate had he been sufficiently well known elsewhere in the division.[69]

66 The proposal for a fixed duty of 8*s*. 0*d*. a quarter was intended to do away with the undoubted weaknesses of the sliding scale, and, less convincingly, to stabilize prices around 56*s* 0*d*. a quarter.

67 *Stamf. Merc.*, 28 May 1841.

68 *Parl. Deb.* 3rd Ser. lvii, 828-35. Worsley afterwards told a Lincoln ordinary that 'during the ten years he had been in that House, he had never before heard one county Member address another as Mr. Christopher addressed him' (*Stamf. Merc.*, 25 June 1841).

69 Sir John Beckett, of Somerby (near Gainsborough) owned 4,380 acres in Lindsey. M.P. (tory) for Cockermouth, 1818, 1820-1; Haslemere, 1826-32; and Leeds, 1835-7. Elder brother of Edmund Beckett Denison (M.P., Yorks. W.R., 1841-59), and the Revd. George Beckett, sometime rector of Epworth.

Around Spilsby there was hope that Lord Willoughby, who had deserted the whigs on the corn question, might find a candidate. But strongest was the feeling at Louth, where the yeomen, after failing to secure a local protagonist, began to talk of sending to London for a candidate.[70]

Chaplin and Christopher, remembering the lesson of 1835, had so far been reluctant to encourage the movement. But the events at Louth were considered to have cleared the gentry of 'any set against Lord Yarborough',[71] and it was no doubt decided that a respectable local man had better be produced before the embarrassing arrival of some carpet-bagger from London. No champion arose, however, from the ranks of the gentry, the lack of time and the certainty of a large expenditure no doubt discouraging the few possible candidates. In this situation Chaplin was unable to resist the offer of Lord Brownlow to start his grandson, the Hon. C.H. Cust.

Cust was little known in the division. He was a soldier by profession, and a younger son of Viscount Alford. He was not, it is true, an ordinary younger son, since he was to inherit the Hume estates on the death of his grandfather, including a large estate in Lindsey. But there was no seat on the Lindsey property, and when Cust made a brief personal appearance in the division he was discovered to have little grasp of politics and no skill at public speaking. The whigs, remembering the previous excursion of the Cust family into county politics in 1816, were predisposed to judge him harshly, and Chaplin himself viewed the candidature with something less than enthusiasm.[72]

The result of the contest was

Worsley	5,401
Christopher	4,522
Cust	3,819

Despite the embarrassments of the preceding months, Worsley

[70] They had hoped for George Tomline, who, however, stood for Shrewsbury (Ipswich and E. Suffolk Record Office, Pretyman-Tomline Deposit, T 99/123, Disraeli to Tomline, 31 May 1841).

[71] L.A.O. Anderson MSS., 5/2/2, diary of C.H.J. Anderson, p. 296.

[72] Scottish Record Office, Ogilvy of Inverquharity MSS., GD/205/Portfolio 15, Chaplin to Christopher, 17 Sept. 1841. (William Cust, younger brother of the first earl Brownlow, came forward on the death of Charles Chaplin the elder in 1816, and only reluctantly gave way to Charles Chaplin the younger in 1818.)

did better than he had in 1835. He benefited, of course, from the absence of a radical candidate, from his personal popularity, and from a united whig interest. He was supported by Anderson, Boucherett, and Vyner; and Heneage, who had split with Corbett in 1835, now gave a straight party vote. Two large Lindsey landowners, moreover, who had been accounted tories in 1835, now brought their interests behind Worsley. Angerstein helped to consolidate the whig position in the Market Rasen district. And Elwes, though like Angerstein a non-resident proprietor, brought several influential men in the Brigg district into the whig camp.[73] But Worsley also received the support of the nonconformists, including for once a probable majority of the Wesleyans. And in the towns—principally at Lincoln and Gainsborough—he received the votes of professed free-traders, who may, however, have done him more harm than good.

Most of the tory gentry, including Tomline and Sheffield, split between Christopher and Cust. Around Alford and in the Isle many loyalties were divided between Christopher and Worsley. But in the Louth and Spilsby districts there were strong votes for the two tories, despite Cust's comparative lack of appeal to the independent portion of the electorate. Christopher did not improve his total poll between 1835 and 1841, and the performance of Cust in the latter year did not even equal that of Ingilby in the former. But the tories had reason to find comfort in the straight party votes given by the farmers of the division, who were now more willing to accept the party of Sir Robert Peel as the political friend of agriculture.[74]

(vi) SOUTH LINCOLNSHIRE, 1837-41

Heathcote and Handley had been unmolested in 1837, but soon after the general election of that year the South Lincolnshire Conservative Association held a grand demonstration at Sleaford.

> Lord Winchilsea took the chair beneath an arch of dahlias; a mixture of which too formed a crown and a bible of immense size over his head:

[73] Principally the Rev. C.J. Barnard of Rigby, who chaired Worsley's Brigg committee.

[74] The percentage of the electorate which gave straight party votes was 58 per cent in 1832, 41 per cent in 1835, and 75 per cent in 1841.

he gave 'the Queen', 'the Queen Dowager', with eyes half starting from their sockets, cheeks of the hue of burning charcoal, and a voice half-choked with extreme excitement.[75]

Trollope made a vigorous defence of the House of Lords, and Chaplin congratulated the yeomanry on taking the lead in the formation of the association—rather implausibly, in view of the formidable array of peers and gentry on the platform. A registration fund had been started in 1835, the leading tories contributing ten or twenty pounds apiece to a total subscription of about £140 a year. Trollope was treasurer, and also supervised the work of the district agents. Finally, in 1839, it was decided to launch a requisition to Christopher Turnor. He was adopted at a meeting of politicians connected with the division at the Carlton Club, Exeter and Brownlow agreeing to put down £500 each in the event of a contest.[76]

Turnor was not a man of great personal influence or political ambitions, and his principal qualifications were presumably his marriage connection with Winchilsea and his wealth. But the mere fact of the appearance of a prospective tory candidate in the division had an important effect on party alignments. In particular it rallied the tories of the Grantham neighbourhood, where the influence of the whigs and independents had formerly been of some account.[77] But the time was not well chosen for a tory agitation, as was revealed by the results of the canvass for signatures to Turnor's requisition. Handley still held the confidence of the independent farmers of Holland,[78] and in Kesteven Heathcote's position looked better than it had for some years. Developments in Rutland, where the Exeter interest was threatening old Sir Gilbert Heathcote's seat, roused his son to exert himself for his party, and his conduct won the approbation even of Heron.[79] Willoughby, moreover, agreed to rally the Grimsthorpe interest in his relative's favour.[80]

75 *Stamf. Merc.*, 13 Oct. 1837. 76 Casewick (Trollope) MSS.
77 An important seceder was Thomas Manners, the Grantham agent for Lord Dysart, who had previously acted for Heathcote, but who now declared that he would support Turnor as 'a neighbour and a personal friend'. Heron wagered him ten guineas that Heathcote would beat Turnor, but to no avail (3 ANC 9/14/378-9).
78 Casewick (Trollope) MSS.
79 3 ANC 9/14/344, Heron to Heathcote, 20 Apr. 1839.
80 3 ANC 9/14/363, Willoughby to Heathcote, 2 July 1839.

As in Lindsey, however, the tories of South Lincolnshire were quick to protest against the budget of 1841. Chaplin called a county meeting at Sleaford, which Heathcote and Handley were prevented by their parliamentary duties from attending.[81] The *Lincolnshire Chronicle* began a fierce campaign against them, and was suitably outraged by their failure to oppose the government on the motion of no confidence. Handley, like Worsley, came under attack from Christopher during the debate, and was obliged to publish the text of his speech after a garbled version appeared in the *Morning Chronicle*.[82]

At the dissolution both Heathcote and Handley suddenly announced their retirements. Heathcote's reasons are not far to seek. Willoughby, as already noted, repented of his transient enthusiasm for the whigs, and had taken the opportunity of the events of the 1841 session to transfer his allegiance to the tories. As a staunch and indubitable protectionist he had some colour of justification for his conduct.[83] But Heathcote was pulled rather than pushed out of his seat. Willoughby would scarcely have mounted a campaign against his son-in-law, but he was saved embarrassment by the latter's decision to succeed his father in Rutland, where there was every possibility of a contest.

On Heathcote's retirement Trollope came forward to join Turnor as second tory candidate. He was now a much more formidable politician than when he had first come out in 1832. His personal interest was strong, and he could be sure of a substantial following in the Bourne, Stamford, and Spalding neighbourhoods, assisted by the much increased interest of Lord Exeter in that part of the division. He had, moreover, connections with the grazing interest, and a link, through his trusteeship for Thorold, with the old independent party.

It was Trollope's emergence that decided Handley to follow Heathcote into retirement. He probably calculated that Trollope would take some of his agricultural support, leaving

81 *Stamf. Merc.*, 21 May 1841.

82 *Parl. Deb.* 3rd Ser. lvii, 1318 and 1403 (30 Apr. and 3 May 1841); *The Speech on the Motion of Sir Robert Peel. . ., 2 June 1841, by Mr. Handley, M.P. for South Lincolnshire.*

83 He sent a letter to the Sleaford meeting forecasting that rents would fall by one-third under the fixed duty (*Stamf. Merc.*, 21 May 1841).

him little to hope from the reformers, who were now much weaker than in Lindsey, and less from the disintegrating whig party. But personal inclination also prompted his decision. He had not enjoyed the recent political storms, and lacked the whig zest for tightrope walking. Nearer his heart was the Royal Agricultural Society, in whose foundation he had assisted in 1838, and whose president he became in 1841. As in the case of other politicians connected with the Society,[84] his protectionist convictions, which he continued to affirm to his constituents, had probably cooled. In 1834 he had encouraged the Kesteven Agricultural Association to put its faith in self-help rather than government protection.[85] And by 1838 he was ready to quote Cobden on the need for scientific improvement.[86]

The spirit of independence was not yet dead in South Lincolnshire, however, and at the nomination Handley was proposed, in his absence and apparently without his knowledge, by Ingilby, and seconded by Thomas Cooper of Swineshead, a yeoman farmer. Committees were hastily formed at Sleaford and Boston, and the Fortescue, Clifford, and other interests were engaged for Handley. At the polls there was a good number of plumpers for him in the Boston and Long Sutton neighbourhoods. But around Sleaford and Grantham the tories did well. They were supported by the full weight of local tory landed interests; and many of the independent voters split between Handley and Turnor, rather as the Lindsey independents had split between Ingilby and Corbett in 1835. Handley received one of their votes as an independent reformer, and Turnor received the other as a local man and staunch protectionist. In the southern parts of the division there were many split votes between Handley and Trollope, and both the Heathcote and the Thorold interests were divided between those two candidates. The votes cast were

Turnor	4,581
Trollope	4,563
Handley	2,948

84 Earl Spencer, for instance. 85 *Stamf. Merc.*, 18 Apr. 1834.

86 Henry Handley, *A Letter to Earl Spencer (President of the Smithfield Club) on the Formation of a National Agricultural Institution,* 1838. Part of the letter discusses the comparative merits of fermented and unfermented dung.

Even had Handley attempted to rally the farmers and to prepare for a contest with an efficient committee, it remains doubtful whether he would have held his seat. He lacked the one thing that Worsley in his division enjoyed, and that was a whig landed interest of sufficient size to awe the tory gentry. With its head, Lord Willoughby, removed, the whig party of South Lincolnshire could do no more than wag its feeble tail in 1841.

(vii) THE LOSS OF PROTECTION, 1842-6

The Peel administration of 1841-6, like that of 1834-5, was not slow to offend the agricultural interest, but this time it remained in office long enough to reap the consequences. In October 1841 Christopher acted as Peel's 'pilot balloon' when, in a constituency speech that was reported in the national press, he suggested an amendment of the sliding scale.[87] Under his scheme foreign wheat would pay 5*s.* 0*d.* when its price was 65*s.* 0*d.* a quarter and above, sliding to a maximum of 20*s.* 0*d.* at 50*s.* 0*d.* and below. The intention was to stabilize prices between these limits, and eliminate the opportunities for speculators caused by the uneven graduation over a wider range of prices under the scale of 1828. With wheat below 40*s.* 0*d.* in the Continental markets in the autumn of 1841, it was hoped that the farmers would be grateful for an assurance that prices would not fall below 50*s.* 0*d.* in the English market. The assurance could not be given with much confidence, but at least the 20*s.* 0*d.* offered by Peel might be compared advantageously with the 8*s.* 0*d.* offered by Russell.

The Lincolnshire farmers, however, were most indignant. The old scale had given a duty of 36*s.* 8*d.* with wheat at 50*s.* 0*d.*, and now the 'farmers' friends' were proposing to reduce it to 20*s.* 0*d*. Lord Willoughby convened the Bourne Agricultural Association to condemn the tory scheme, and the Boston association, despite Christopher's willingness to

[87] Peel did not, as far as I know, encourage Christopher to make the speech, but he certainly applauded it; and there was a correspondence between Christopher and Gladstone at his instigation (*Lincs. Chron.*, 29 Oct. 1841; Ogilvy of Inverquharity MSS., Portfolio 16, Peel to Christopher, 3 Nov. 1841, and Gladstone to Christopher, n.d.; Addit. MSS. 44, 358, f. 213, Christopher to Gladstone, 9 Nov.). Ballooning was in vogue at the time.

discuss the matter with them, would accept nothing below a duty of 25*s*. 0*d*. on wheat at 50*s*. 0*d*.[88]

At the start of the session of 1842 Peel introduced a measure similar to that propounded by Christopher, and both Christopher and Turnor voted for its third reading. Christopher, it is true, had moved an amendment for a maximum of 25*s*. 0*d*., but had been advised by the duke of Richmond to withdraw it when it received support from the opposition.[89] The budget of that year, with its income tax and its reduction of the duties on imported livestock, caused another outcry in Lincolnshire. A county meeting was called at which Sheffield condemned the income tax and Chaplin attacked the altered duties: 'The foreigner, when he found the English market no longer prohibited to him . . ., would send in his live cattle, living himself economically upon frogs' legs and rare dishes of that sort, of which he was so fond.'[90]

The Lincolnshire Liberals were no idle spectators of these events. Worsley got the Caistor and Grimsby associations to condemn the sliding scale. And later, in 1843, he was a prominent critic, inside and outside the House, of the Canadian Corn Bill, which he claimed gave a loophole by which foreign corn could evade the full import duties.[91] Handley recovered his zest for politics in 1842, when he voiced the alarm of the Kesteven graziers about the tariff.[92] And in 1843 there appeared to be a revival of radical independence in the county. The malt tax was again trundled out on agricultural platforms, and at a county meeting in April 1843 there were demands for lower rents. At Grantham Healy condemned the Conservative landlords of the division for exerting their influence to secure Handley's defeat, and claimed that Russell would after all, have proved a better friend to the farmers than Peel.[93]

88 They would have preferred a maximum duty of 30*s*. 0*d*. on wheat at 45*s*. 0*d*. (*Stamf. Merc.*, Jan.-Feb. 1842).

89 *Parl. Deb.* 3rd Ser. lx, 1139; *Stamf. Merc.*, 1 Apr. 1842.

90 *Stamf. Merc.*, 8 Apr. 1842.

91 For the debates on the bill see *Parl. Deb.* 3rd Ser. lxix, 600, 747, 948, 1251, 1576. Worsley moved the rejection of the second and third readings.

92 He was well received by a meeting of graziers at Bourne, at which Willoughby, somewhat repenting of his late conduct, took the chair. (*Stamf. Merc.*, 8 Apr. 1842.)

93 *Stamf. Merc.*, 28 Apr. 1843.

These portents were not lost on the three Conservative Members for Lincolnshire. Trollope was the first to break with Peel, voting against the third reading of the Corn Importation Bill in 1842. Next year Turnor joined Trollope in opposing the second reading of the Canadian Corn Bill, on which Christopher abstained. In the county this important development was apparent when, in January 1844, the Lincoln and Lindsey association was encouraged by Christopher and Chaplin to hold a series of protectionist meetings. There was no further legislation on the corn question in 1844, however, and the agitation quickly subsided. But it had served to re-establish the Conservative leadership of the county protectionist movement. There was reluctance to accept the guidance of the Lincoln and Lindsey association only at Bourne and Caistor, where the district bodies preferred to communicate directly, rather than through Lincoln, with the Agricultural Protection Society lately formed in London.[94]

While Peel remained in office, however, the position of the Lincolnshire Conservatives was a difficult one. The Lincoln and Lindsey decided to make a stand in defence of the corn laws as they then stood . But, since many of its members had condemned the 1842 measure at the time of its passage, it was difficult to work up much enthusiasm for this programme. It also went against the grain to argue that they were satisfied with the prices they were getting under the act, although in 1844 the market began to recover. Besides, it was difficult to know what Peel would do next, and hopeless to try to stop him, as they found in the Repeal crisis of 1845-6.

That crisis was accompanied by no dissolution of parliament, and no resignations of Lincolnshire Members, all of whom voted against the third reading of the Corn Importation Bill in May 1846.[95] Christopher had been the first, early in January, to dissociate himself publicly from Peel's ministry. He told a Lincoln meeting that

> he would not join any political party, but associate with those Members who would form in the House what might be termed the country party,

[94] Ibid., Jan.-Mar. 1844.

[95] For the division lists see *Parl. Deb.* 3rd Ser. lxxxv, 265; lxxxvi, 721. Only four Liberal county Members, of whom Worsley was one, opposed Repeal on this division.

> and who, keeping aloof from all faction, would maintain that bold and determined front which would prevent any ministry, no matter whether Sir Robert Peel's or Lord John Russell's, from carrying out any diminution of protection to the native industry of this country.[96]

Worsley accepted this proof of Christopher's independence, and agreed with the Conservative protectionists of the division that a 'bold and united stand' should be made in defence of the agricultural interest. At the same time he declared in the House, no doubt too pessimistically for some of his constituents, that 'he was not one of those who would delude the farmers . . . with the idea that they could get back again the protection which it was now proposed to be taken from them.'[97] In South Lincolnshire Trollope attacked Peel as a man 'false to his friends, his principles and his country'.[98] Turnor was more subdued, and was reported to have paired for the second reading of the bill in March, but he voted with the protectionists in May. The only Lincolnshire peers to vote for Repeal were Ripon and Bristol on the Conservative side, and St. Albans, Scarbrough, Fortescue, Lindsey, and Monson on the Liberal.[99] But none were prominent county politicians.

The session in which the long-dreaded, loudly denounced repeal of the corn laws took place passed with very little agitation among the Lincolnshire farmers.[100] It was the same in other parts of England, and its strangeness was remarked upon at the time.[101] The causes were part political, part psychological, and part economic. As has been shown, the farmers of the county could do little to affect the issue. The Lincoln and Lindsey circulated petitions, but that was a proceeding more effectively exploited, and indeed rendered ridiculous, by the Anti-Corn-Law League. The politicians of the county presented a united front which left no room for party quarrels. Besides which the farmers were tired of agitating, and appeared to accept the inexorable triumph of

96 *Stamf. Merc.*, 9 Jan. 1846.
97 *Parl. Deb.* 3rd Ser. lxxxiv, 436-67, 2 Mar. 1846.
98 *Stamf. Merc.*, 16 Jan. 1846. 99 *Par. Deb.* 3rd Ser. lxxxvi, 1405.
100 They even failed to get a county meeting. (*Lincs. Chron.*, 13 Feb. 1846.)
101 'Wherever we turn our eyes, whether to Gloucestershire, Shropshire or Cambridgeshire, we find the same symptoms—disorganisation and dissension among some country gentlemen, indifference on the part of others; whilst the great body of the tenant farmers appear wholly unconcerned, or very lukewarm in the Protection cause' (*The Times*, 11 Feb. 1846).

the free-traders with characteristic fatalism. Their detachment, moreover, was encouraged by the fact that, as in 1839, they had benefited by the circumstances that had led to the crisis. By the middle of 1846 corn prices had fallen from their famine level, but the Lincolnshire farmers were still doing very well. Their feeling was for settling the question, and allowing the markets a time of quiet in which to adjust themselves.

Whatever the case in Essex or Sussex, there is little evidence from Lincolnshire of tenants' urging on their landlords in 1846.[102] Even Healy, formerly not reluctant to give the landlords their marching orders, now waited to receive the orders that failed to come. He appeared at a Grantham meeting in January 1846

> to represent and support the tenantry—a tenantry who only wanted the stimulus of their landlords' support to set the question in dispute at rest,—a tenantry who were good soldiers but bad officers, who, if their landlords would only . . . say 'Come on', would shew themselves with an iron front, and maintain their ground in spite of a thousand Leagues.[103]

But the battle, at least in Lincolnshire, had already been fought, in 1841, and the county Members had acknowledged the victory of the farmers in 1842-3.

D.C. Moore, in an article entitled 'The Corn Laws and High Farming', has put forward an economic and sociological interpretation of the Repeal crisis.

> The crux of the rural problem lay in the dialectical opposition between those customs and policies on the one hand which served to reinforce the hierarchical structure of rural society and the cohesion of the rural interest group, and, on the other hand, the exigencies of agricultural prosperity in an era of high farming.[104]

It is true that Protection did to some extent 'reinforce the hierarchical structure of rural society'; and it could be plausibly argued that high farmers were less likely to be deferential than low ones. The error is to suppose that the

102 See Mary Lawson-Tancred, 'The Anti-League and the Corn Law Crisis', *Hist. Journ.* iii(2) (1960), pp. 162-83.

103 *Stamf. Merc.* 16 Jan. 18. He was now more of a protectionist than he had been in the 1830s.

104 D.C. Moore, 'The Corn Laws and High Farming', *Econ. Hist. Rev.* 2nd S., xviii (1965), p. 551. (For a more balanced view see Betty Kemp, 'Reflections on the Repeal of the Corn Laws', *Vict. Stud.* v (1961-2), p. 189.)

higher the farmer, the less strongly he was attached to Protection. The Lincolnshire evidence points, if anything, the other way. Yarborough's tenants did become restive in the early 1840s, but that was because they suspected him of wavering in his allegiance to Protection. In December 1842 he made an indiscreet speech in the Isle of Wight, dwelling on the distress caused in the manufacturing districts by the high price of corn.[105] And in G.M. Williams he appointed an agent who, with his free-trading views and emphasis upon Improvement, caused offence among the leading Brocklesby farmers.[106] H.G. Skipworth, who had a disagreement with Williams during 1844, chose Yarborough's birthday dinner in 1845 as the occasion to make a speech advocating rent reductions.[107]

High farmers, in fact, had most to lose by low prices, and it was a frequent question at agricultural dinners, how the cultivation of the Wolds and Heath, and the costly drainage of the Fens, could be maintained in an era of Free Trade. Nor was this argument used only by landowners. Samuel Vessey of Halton Holegate used it at a Spilsby meeting in 1844 where 'there was scarcely a landlord in the room'.[108]

The agricultural societies of the 1830s and 1840s, the stock shows and the ploughing meetings, were manifestations of the spirit of Improvement, and were, it is true, often promoted by whig aristocrats with only a lukewarm attachment to Protection. But agricultural societies were often, at least in Lincolnshire, used as protectionist platforms. And the act of spreading another layer of bones over their fields did not increase the zest with which the farmers looked forward to Free Trade. Rather they did it because they feared it might be their only chance of survival.

105 *Stamf. Merc.*, 6 Jan. 1843. 106 Ibid., 13 Jan. 1843.
107 Ibid., 16 Aug. 1844, 15 Aug. 1845.
108 Ibid., 9 Feb. 1844. Vessey occupied land under Willoughby, but he also had land of his own, and was lord of the manor of Halton (*White,* 1842).

10

MID-CENTURY POLITICS, 1846-1857

(i) NORTH LINCOLNSHIRE, 1846-52

THE FIRST earl of Yarborough's diplomatic vote against Repeal was his last political action. He died in September 1846, and Worsley, translated to the Lords as second earl of Yarborough, was at once faced with the problem of finding a candidate for his county seat. His choice fell on Sir Montague Cholmeley.

Cholmeley was not widely known in the Lindsey division, residing mostly at his principal seat near Grantham. He was no longer a young man, did not enjoy good health, had never been a good speaker, and had ceased since the early 1830s to take a keen interest in politics. But for Yarborough the choice of Cholmeley had compensating advantages. He was apparently prepared to accept the seat more or less on Yarborough's terms, and agreed to meet half the cost of any contest.[1] In politics he regarded himself as a middle-of-the-road whig of the Melbourne school.[2] He was moderate enough to please the old-fashioned whigs of the division, but the reformers, or some of them, may have remembered his activity in the period 1831-2. He was, in short, a good compromise candidate. (His attempt at mediation between Heneage and Ingilby in 1834 has already been noticed.)

Yarborough no doubt hoped that the end of Protection would serve to strengthen his interest and render the division more manageable. But in 1846 the 'peace of the county' rested on the basis of a united opposition to Repeal. Cholmeley's task as Member was to preserve that peace as long as possible. Yarborough had inherited, along with the title, a number of debts and obligations. He wished to devote as much spare income as possible to improvements on the estate, including the building of more cottages and schools

[1] There is no specific record of their agreement, but never does Cholmeley appear to have taken his own way, independent of Yarborough's advice and approval, in the period 1847-52. For the election expenses see below, p. 146.

[2] *Stamf. Merc.*, 14 May 1852.

for his labourers,[3] and he had no desire to provoke another contest as expensive as that of 1841. Cholmeley's position was, in short, that of a seat-warmer. His function, as he himself stated, was to 'fill a gap in the stable',[4] and to keep the seat safe until Yarborough's heir should come of age.

When coming before the constituency in January 1847, therefore, Cholmeley said as little as possible, reaffirming his commitment to Protection, and refusing, on Yarborough's advice, to pledge himself on the Catholic question.[5] At that by-election, and again at the general election of July 1847, he was returned unopposed. In truth, Christopher's instincts as well as his own were for the continuation of the compromise. The tories had also spent a great deal, and to less effect, in 1841. And in July 1847 the new protectionist group in the House of Commons, to which Christopher belonged, had not yet been organized by Lord George Bentinck into a party worthy of the name. Wheat prices were again at famine level in the early months of 1847,[6] and little capital could be made out of the corn question, although Christopher was careful not to lower the protectionist flag below half-mast.

Although the Corn Importation Bill had been passed in 1846, it was not until 1 February 1849, when the duty was finally reduced under the provisions of the act to a nominal shilling, that England became a free-trading country as far as grain was concerned. By that time corn prices had fallen a good deal since July 1847, despite a poor harvest in 1848. Lincolnshire farmers began to complain in the early months of 1849, and by April Lord Henry Bentinck could write, somewhat optimistically, to Disraeli:

> I hear that Lord Yarborough's great wealthy tenants are cracking—one is already gone and rumours are very rife about several others. The banks are smelling out the rat and beginning to shorten their accounts. I expect a few more such failures in the best-farmed land in England will settle Free Trade.[7]

[3] YARB 9, Yarborough to Lord Lansdowne, 12 Dec. 1846.
[4] *Stamf. Merc.*, 6 Aug. 1847.
[5] YARB 9, Yarborough to Cholmeley, 30 July 1847. The current issue was the government endowment of Roman Catholic schools.
[6] *Stamf. Merc.*, 13 Aug. 1847. A quarter of wheat had fetched 100*s.* 0*d.* at Gainsborough in May.
[7] Hughenden (Disraeli) MSS., B/XXI [cf. p. 124, n. 10] /B/354, Henry Bentinck to Disraeli, 7 Apr. 1849.

The county took little interest in Disraeli's motion praying for a reduction of the burdens on land at the beginning of the session of 1849.[8] But the failure of that motion reminded agricultural politicians of the lesson they had learnt in 1846, that without a dissolution of parliament they could not significantly increase their weight and influence in the House of Commons. At the end of March James Banks Stanhope took the lead in Lindsey, by getting Dymoke to summon the Horncastle Protection Society. Stanhope himself moved the principal resolution, favouring a return to Protection rather than a persistence with the local taxation campaign.[9]

He was also active in the Boston neighbourhood, where he took over the presidency of the protection society from Thomas Gee. There was considerable feeling against Sir James Duke, the free-trading Member for the borough, whom Stanhope may at one stage have hoped to succeed. Corn prices were lower at Boston than at markets such as Lincoln and Grantham, which were nearer to the large consumer markets of the Midlands. And the graziers, with whom, as an heir of Sir Joseph Banks, Stanhope had a special connection, were also suffering, in 1849, from exceptionally low wool prices. Allied with the farmers and graziers were the ship-owners, who were strongly against the repeal of the Navigation Laws. They feared increased competition from foreign vessels, just as the farmers feared competition from the foreign grain carried in those vessels.

On 1 May 1849 the National Association for the Protection of British Industry and Capital was inaugurated in London. Its object was to unite the agricultural, shipping, and colonial interests in a vaguely-expressed protectionist programme, and to obtain a dissolution of parliament so that protectionist Members could be returned at the following elections. Among its leading supporters was the fourth earl Stanhope, uncle and guardian of J.B. Stanhope. And its secretary was the shipowner G.F. Young.

In May the Lincoln and Lindsey society met to consider the desirability of agitating for a county meeting. But they were dissuaded by Chaplin, no doubt with Christopher's full

[8] *Parl. Deb.* 3rd Ser. ciii, 424 ff., 8 Mar. 1849. [9] *Stamf. Merc.*, 6 Apr. 1849.

concurrence. The leaders of the parliamentary protectionist party had not given their support to the National Association, and in the local context the tory gentry were, as always, reluctant to move against the Yarborough interest. By the autumn of 1849, however, the position, both national and local, had altered. The protectionist leaders had been obliged to make conciliatory gestures towards the strong protectionists in the party, with Christopher acting as peacemaker between Disraeli and Young.[10] In Lindsey, as Christopher knew, the farmers were becoming increasingly militant as prices dropped forty shillings after the harvest. They were starting, moreover, to find in Cholmeley and Yarborough a focus for their indignation. Cholmeley had proved a lazy and ineffective Member, neglecting both his parliamentary duties and his agricultural constituents. And it was well known that Yarborough, although he had never renounced his former protectionism, had *de facto* accepted Repeal and desired no further agitation on the subject.[11]

A further meeting of the Lincoln and Lindsey society was held on 30 November, when Christopher took the chair.[12] It marked the first round of the assault on the Yarborough interest. Thomas Greetham of Stainfield complained of Cholmeley's absence from farmers' meetings, and William Skipworth of South Kelsey, a good indicator of farming opinion on the fringes of the Brocklesby estate, urged the farmers 'not to be too nice as to what were the views of Lord Yarborough or any other nobleman in the county'. Chaplin and Christopher still moved cautiously, however. Only after a meeting for the city of Lincoln had been held, at which a certain amount of protectionist feeling among the tradesmen was evinced,[13] was a county meeting ventured upon.

Yarborough declined to attend the county meeting, held on 25 January 1850. But the protectionists were successful in extracting from him a statement of his views on the corn

[10] Hughenden MSS., B/XXI/H/77, Christopher to Disraeli, 8 Oct. 1849. See also B/III generally.

[11] See for instance his speech on the Address, *Parl. Deb.* 3rd Ser. xcv, 14 ff., 23 Nov. 1847.

[12] *Stamf. Merc.*, 7 Dec. 1849.

[13] *Stamf. Merc.*, 21 Dec. 1849.

question. 'I believe', he wrote in a published letter to Boucherett,

I believe that those who encourage the farmers to expect relief from the re-imposition of protective duties are only deceiving themselves and others . . . . I am satisfied that the present low prices of corn and livestock are not wholly caused by the abolition of the duties on those articles of consumption.[14]

This made things very difficult for Cholmeley, who was obliged to attend the meeting. He made a short and mumbled speech, and then had to sit through a protectionist tirade from Heneage, who was at this time flirting with Lord Stanley's party.[15]

Despite this skirmish, however, the protectionists of Lindsey were subdued during the session of 1850. Slowly rising prices put farmers in a better temper as harvest approached, and when the North Lincolnshire Agricultural Society met at Louth on 25 July Yarborough as chairman was able to prevent party politics being raised.[16] Christopher in fact delivered a very moderate speech on the local taxation question. Perhaps his reassuring experience at that meeting gave Yarborough a false confidence, for it was probably on his advice that Cholmeley, at the Caistor ploughing meeting in October 1850, ventured to blow colder on Protection than he had yet done in a public speech.

While expressing his opinion that protection was requisite for the British farmer, . . . he felt bound to tell his constituents he feared there was no hope of its being restored, and that those who buoyed them up with anticipations that there would be a return to the old system, inflicted upon them a serious injury.[17]

Christopher replied in the following month from the platform of the Alford Agricultural Society:

[14] Ibid., 18 Jan. 1850. Major William Beresford, one of the protectionist whips, had written to Disraeli about the meeting: 'This will be a considerable annoyance to that arch humbug and agricultural impostor Lord Yarborough. Poor George Bentinck used to say to me that the greatest object he had was to face Lord Worsley before the assembled farmers of Lincolnshire, that he might convict him in their presence of imposition and treachery' (Hughenden MSS., B/III/87, 21 Dec. 1849).

[15] *Stamf. Merc.*, 1 Feb. 1850. Beresford's letter quoted above was written at Hainton.

[16] *Lincs. Chron.*, 2 Aug. 1850. [17] *Stamf. Merc.*, 8 Nov. 1850.

> On the part of the leaders of the great Country Party, he told them *Protection was not dead* . . . . They were more than ever convinced, from their experience of Free Trade, that it was a failure and a delusion.[18]

Cholmeley was careful not to recant his principles, although, with Yarborough, he clearly believed that they were no longer worth much in practical political terms. Christopher, on the other hand, while apparently advocating the revival of Protection as a party programme, did not promise to stick to his principles further than the next general election. He followed Derby's strange policy of allowing the electorate to dictate to the Conservative party what its principles should be. But these subtleties were lost on the farmers of Lindsey, who saw the question in much simpler terms. Prices were again falling after the harvest, and Christopher seemed much more disposed to come to the aid of the suffering agriculturist than Cholmeley.

The Lincoln and Lindsey society met before the session of 1851, and agreed to launch 'a committee to attend to the registration of protectionist electors throughout the county'.[19] But it was not until after Derby's failure to form a government in February that the society finally entered the realm of party politics. On 15 April it met to plan for the dissolution that was now the only way to secure a protectionist ministry. With Boucherett in the chair, it was agreed to start a requisition for Stanhope, who was to unseat Cholmeley and ensure that Lindsey returned two genuine protectionist Members at the general election.[20]

The society would not have committed itself in this way without the agreement of Chaplin and Sibthorp, who no doubt preferred Stanhope to the tenant farmer candidate who might otherwise have arisen. But, apart from Boucherett, who was not a man of great means or influence, none of the leading tory gentry of the division gave active or enthusiastic support to Stanhope. The squire of Revesby was undeniably well connected, and had both the money and the ability to conduct a long campaign. But it must have seemed to many,

[18] Ibid., 22 Nov. 1850.

[19] *Lincs. Chron.*, 10 Jan. 1851. Sibthorp, Chaplin, and Christopher each subscribed £20.

[20] Ibid., 18 Apr. 1851. Delegates from the district societies were present.

Chaplin among them, that it was premature to disturb the peace of the county, and particularly to disturb it by an agitation directed largely at Lord Yarborough. 'Sir Montague,' thundered the *Lincolnshire Chronicle* in May 1851, 'you are but a shadow of the Lord of Brocklesby . . .; you are not a protectionist in your heart of hearts . . .; you are a doomed man.'[21] Such was the tone of a campaign that might last several months. One of Stanhope's leading advocates was Henry Healey, of Ashby, a former Brocklesby tenant, who stirred up the Isle of Axholme with a vengeance fed, it was said, by a personal feud with Lord Yarborough.[22] Christopher certainly gave no countenance to the movement. Much discouraged by Derby's failure to form a government, he was even thinking of retiring from politics altogether.[23]

Whatever the views of Chaplin or Christopher, however, Stanhope received strong support from several of the local protection societies. William Skipworth had done good work in the Brigg region, although many farmers in that neighbourhood appear to have drawn the line at a direct conflict with Brocklesby. But the men of the Isle, once aroused, could set at nought the traditional interests of the division. Here, for once, is an ordinary yeoman farmer speaking his mind at a protectionist meeting, and furthermore, being reported at length in a county paper:

They had been struggling with this Free Trade for four or five years, and they were now tired out, for there was no use in a farmer spending his time and his money if his business would not pay . . . . The free traders told them to look to reduced taxation as a remedy, but what reduction of taxation could compensate the farmers for the loss of one pound a quarter on their wheat? The burthen the farmers now had to bear was intolerable, and to get rid of it they must send men to parliament in whom there could be no mistake . . . . Turncoats were of no use to them; they did not want men who were protectionists on the hustings and in the newspapers, but who, when wanted in the House, were either asleep on the benches, or out of the way, or else voting on the wrong side. They had got a pledge from Mr. Stanhope and if he did not do his duty they could turn him out, for it was the farmers who were bringing him in, and not the great landlords.[24]

[21] Ibid., 16 May 1851.
[22] MON 25/13/1/10/3, George Maxsted of Winterton to Yarborough, 28 Mar. 1853.
[23] Hughenden MSS., B/XXI/N/85, Christopher to Disraeli, 1 Mar. 1851.
[24] George Cocking, a yeoman farmer of Crowle and a founder member of the Isle of Axholme Protection Society, speaking at Epworth in January 1852 (*Lincs. Chron.*, 16 Jan. 1852).

It is remarkable that with such a strong faith in parliament should go such a profound ignorance of party politics.

Stanhope agreed to stand if presented with a well-signed requisition, and by August the district protectionist committee had collected nearly 4,000 signatures. Faced with this demonstration of support, he could hardly now withdraw, and on 15 August he issued an address formally announcing his candidature.[25] He may, however, have felt less optimism than he had in April. Protectionist feeling had waned to some extent in the meantime. And so had the anti-Catholic fervour he had exploited earlier in the year. Cholmeley, moreover, had returned from abroad on the news of the movement for Stanhope, and had since then done something to restore his reputation in the constituency. Early in June he met Yarborough in London, where they discussed the position with Thomas Rhodes, Cholmeley's principal agent.[26] It was decided that Cholmeley should partially recant his statement at Caistor the previous autumn. He issued an address, perhaps one written for him by Yarborough, emphasizing his independent votes for Disraeli's motion in 1849[27] and against the repeal of the Navigation Laws, and claiming that it was still possible to be both a whig and a sincere protectionist.[28] He followed this up by attending agricultural meetings in the summer and autumn, and in November issued an address announcing his decision to stand again. By this time some of those who had signed the requisition for Stanhope had recanted, and even Heneage seems to have returned to the fold.

Before the session of 1852 it seemed that the Russell government could not survive much longer, and, nationally and locally, the protectionists girded up their loins for the struggle of the anticipated general election. Early in the new year the Lincoln and Lindsey held a secret conference. No record of its proceedings has survived, but it is probable that Christopher let it be known that he had no intention

[25] *Stamf. Merc.*, 22 Aug. 1851.

[26] MON 25/13/1/2/2, bill of particulars of Thomas Rhodes, f. 2.

[27] See *Parl. Deb.* 3rd Ser. ciii, 779, 15 Mar. 1849.

[28] Loft, at a protectionist dinner at Brigg, demanded to know what a Liberal protectionist was: 'He was told they were a sort of half-and-half people—a mixture very well in beer but not in politics' (*Stamf. Merc.*, 11 July 1851).

of coalescing with Stanhope.[29] The latter may have then accounced his wish to retire, but if so he was dissuaded by the representatives from the Isle, who forced him into taking up a position more independent of party than he had probably envisaged in April 1851.[30] At any rate, he attended a large gathering at Epworth on 8 January 1852, where he pledged himself to resign his seat if he supported any government which should 'in any way follow or maintain the doctrines of Free Trade'.[31] A canvass soon began in the Isle, but Stanhope did not inaugurate a general canvass of the division until 14 February, when the government was expected soon to go to the country.

The following events served to emphasize the gulf between Stanhope's position and that of Christopher. Russell resigned on 14 February, but there was no dissolution. Derby formed a government, and on 27 February announced in the Lords that Protection, together with the general election, was indefinitely postponed. Christopher accepted office under Derby as Chancellor of the Duchy of Lancaster. He assured his constituents that his principal consideration was his faith in Derby's protectionist principles. But he prevented any canvass for him on the occasion of his re-election for the division in March, and appeared in his public statements to prefer Cholmeley to Stanhope as his colleague or prospective colleague in parliament.[32]

This lack of party spirit, so unbecoming in a Conservative junior minister, was of course dictated by his wish to avoid a contest, if not at the dissolution, at least at the by-election. He calculated not only on the absence of influential gentry support for Stanhope, but also on the new moderation shown by Cholmeley. The Liberal committee, under Heneage's chairmanship, had started a canvass in response to Stanhope's campaign at the end of February. But it had been conducted with conspicuous lack of zeal and obvious lack of success. Cholmeley had not worked half as hard as Stanhope in paying

29 Christopher wrote to Chaplin on 4 January: 'I beg to thank you for not committing me to any coalition in the approaching contest' (Scunthorpe Museum, Sheffield MSS., F/1/1/2).

30 A rumour to this effect was reported in the *Mercury* of 16 Jan.

31 *Lincs. Chron.*, 16 Jan. 1852.

32 Helmsley (Anderson) MSS., diary of Sir C.H.J. Anderson, vol. 6, 26 Feb. 1852.

those personal visits on market days which were such a necessary part of the canvass. The emphasis was placed on Stanhope's disturbance of the peace of the county, and where plumpers could not be obtained the committees were advised to secure split votes between Cholmeley and Christopher. Heneage had no enthusiasm, and was chiefly concerned in his candidature for the City of Lincoln, which meant pleasing the Conservatives in order to beat the radical candidate Charles Seely. Indeed, when the canvass results had trickled in, early in April, Heneage advised Cholmeley to retire.[33]

At this point, however, Yarborough intervened. He was no doubt exasperated by Cholmeley's inability to steer a middle course. First he had ruined his standing with the farmers, and now he was alienating any genuine Liberal support that he still retained. Yarborough should have reflected—perhaps he did—that the position in which he had placed Cholmeley was a very uncomfortable one. At least, however, the announcement of Cholmeley's retirement was prevented, the party organization put under new direction, and the canvass restarted.[34]

When Cholmeley resumed his visits to his constituents late in April, he began to pay attention to such parts of the division as Alford and Spilsby, and to sprinkle his orations with references to the malt tax, church rates, and 'the old Blue cause'. Ingilby appeared, more eccentric than ever, to exclaim 'Vote for my boy!' And by early June a band of Liberals felt brave enough to march on Epworth, from which, however, they were repulsed with some loss of blood.[35] A second general canvass, begun in May by the Liberals in consequence of another dissolution scare, was conducted with more spirit, and met with better success, than the first.[36]

The effect, however, was to draw Christopher and Stanhope closer together. Christopher saw that he would lose more than he had gained by continuing his policy of conciliation with Cholmeley. Besides which, Stanhope's supporters had from the first canvassed for Christopher also, rather as the radicals

[33] MON 25/13/1/2/2, Rhodes's bill, ff. 9, 17, 21. [34] Rhodes's bill, ff. 21-5.

[35] See R.J. Olney, 'The Battle of Epworth, 3 June 1852', in *Lincolnshire History and Archaeology*, vol. 1, no.5 (1970).

[36] See Rhodes's bill, and, for the Brigg district, p. 144 below.

in 1832 had canvassed for Pelham as well as Ingilby.[37] Christopher could not object to Cholmeley supporters splitting their votes with him. But it would go badly with him if the independent protectionists began in large numbers to give their first vote to Stanhope and their second to Cholmeley.[38]

Stanhope for his part probably knew that his movement was steadily losing way as corn prices at last began to move upwards in the early months of 1852. In consequence he began to emphasize more the revenue and less the protective aspect of his proposed corn duty, and to concentrate less on his independence and more on his toryism. On 15 June Christopher finally announced his formal coalition with Stanhope, and Loft at Alford led the way in forming joint committees.[39]

The closing stages of this long campaign produced yet another shift of position. Christopher began to indicate in his speeches that he entertained doubts as to the desirability of the total repeal of the Maynooth grant. Cholmeley had sinned grievously in the eyes of the Wesleyans, when, during the session of 1851, he had supported the motion to grant a sum for the repair of the Roman Catholic college at Maynooth. And it was the strength of Wesleyanism among the Lindsey farmers, combined of course with their economic grievances, that had helped to make Stanhope's movement such a strong one. Now, in late June and early July, with the corn question less urgent, the religious issue was revived with fresh gusto. Cholmeley, who was still lagging behind the Conservatives, did his best to underline his opposition to the grant and to explain, or explain away, his previous vote. He was supported by prominent broad churchmen in the division, including the Revd. J.C. Barnard of Bigby and the Revd. Andrew Veitch, an old enemy of Stanhope's.[40] Whether Cholmeley's blunt Protestantism similarly pleased the Baptists and Independents of Lindsey, as well as the Wesleyans, is not clear. But then

37 Rhodes's bill, f. 9.

38 Boucherett had written to Sheffield earlier in the year that Stanhope's party was strong enough to place Christopher either at the top or at the bottom of the poll if it chose (Sheffield MSS., F/1/1/3-6).

39 *Stamf. Merc.*, 18 June 1852.

40 Veitch had been dismissed by Stanhope from the curacy of Revesby.

they were a much less significant portion of the electorate. There was one group which did, however, take offence, and that, of course, was the Catholics.[41]

The long-awaited election took place in July 1852, and the result was

Christopher	5,585
Stanhope	5,579
Cholmeley	4,777

If the poll had been taken in October instead of July, Cholmeley might have retained his seat, given a continuing recovery in the price of grain. But in July it seemed that his defeat was the almost inevitable nemesis of the whig party in North Lincolnshire. The farmers had never got over his free-trading tendencies in 1850. And before that he had offended them by his absences from the division and from parliament. He also failed to built up a strong personal influence to protect him from the charges of being Yarborough's nominee.

Equally he had failed to conciliate the urban Liberals, who were more numerous, and more vocal, in Lindsey in 1852 than they had been in 1841. Dissent had prospered in the towns, and even Wesleyanism had thrown up a militant Reform movement which affected some rural societies as well as most of the urban ones.[42] As in 1841, moreover, but more evidently and embarrassingly for Cholmeley, the urban Liberals were mostly for Free Trade. Both at Lincoln and at Grimsby the borough Liberals did little effective work for Cholmeley among the county voters. And this is not surprising, when it is realized that Cholmeley, even in the latter part of his campaign, had no ready-made reforming programme with which to unite his party and revive the 'old Blue cause'. The field had been allowed to remain in fallow for too long, and even at places like Alford and Spilsby memories of the 1830s had faded.

Yarborough himself was not free from blame for the débâcle. He had provided plenty of opportunities for his enemies and detractors, by his incautious public utterances

41 William Constable Maxwell, of Everingham, Yorks, lord of the manor of West Rasen, publicly withdrew his support from Cholmeley (*Stamf. Merc.*, 12 Mar. 1852).

42 In 1852, however, internal dissensions still absorbed much of the Wesleyan movement, to the exclusion of national politics.

and somewhat austere attitude towards the management of his estate.[43] He had been led to neglect his local interests by his involvement in railway business. And his chairmanship of the Manchester, Sheffield, and Lincolnshire Railway failed to prevent Manchester and Sheffield's domination of the company, at the expense of the Lincolnshire end of the line.[44]

(ii) NORTH LINCOLNSHIRE, 1852–A POLL BOOK ANALYSIS

The poll book on which this analysis is based was published by Thomas Fricker, the Boston proprietor of the Conservative *Lincolnshire Herald.*[45] The commentary is, not surprisingly, a partisan production. But care was taken to copy the poll clerk's lists as accurately as possible, and the figures which resulted did not differ materially from those of the official return.[46] The poll book is interesting as being the last record of open voting in North Lincolnshire, which did not poll again until 1880. And it is of wider significance, not least because for some polling districts it gives details of voters' occupations. According to a recent study it is the latest poll book to give a satisfactory occupational sample for an English county division.[47]

The poll was a remarkably high one. A calculation based on the poll book information gives an average poll of 85 per cent in the division, with a variation of only 6 per cent in the various polling districts. If the duplicate entries of the register could be systematically excluded the figure would be higher.

The following table gives the proportion of the electorate which voted in each of four principal ways:

43 In February 1852 Yarborough caused trouble in Lindsey by declaring in the Lords that 'from personal observation he could state that he never saw such an amount of drainage being carried out as he had seen this winter', implying that the farmers were not in fact as depressed as they made out (*Parl. Deb.* 3rd Ser. cxix, 56, 3 Feb. 1852). He also caused uneasiness among his tenantry in the spring of 1852 by calling in a respected Nottinghamshire agriculturist to revalue his farms, although the result was on balance a reduction in rents (YARB 5, estate rentals and correspondence).

44 See George Dow, *Great Central,* vol. 1, 1959, pp. 111, 121, 140-1.

45 *Poll Book of the North Lincolnshire Election, Taken in July 1852, with a History of the Election, etc.*, ed. Thos. Fricker, Boston, 1852.

46 Ibid., Introduction.

47 J.R. Vincent, *Pollbooks: How Victorians Voted,* Cambridge, 1967, p.2.

Polling District	Plumpers for Cholmeley %	Voters splitting between Christopher and Stanhope %	Cholmeley—Stanhope %	Cholmeley—Christopher %	Others %	Total %
Alford	29	45	4·0	18	4·0	100
Barton	39	34	11·0	9	7·0	100
Brigg	43	38	6·0	10	3·0	100
Caistor	42	25	20·0	10	3·0	100
Epworth	24	62	9·0	3	2·0	100
Gainsborough	28	49	10·0	9	4·0	100
Grimsby	50	33	7·0	9	1·0	100
Horncastle	26	55	12·0	4	3·0	100
Lincoln	26	49	4·0	17	4·0	100
Louth	27	52	8·0	9	4·0	100
Market Rasen	49	28	13·0	8	2·0	100
Spilsby	25	57	11·0	6	1·0	100
Wragby	32	58	0·5	9	0·5	100
TOTAL	34	45	9·0	9	3·0	100

Each district had its distinctive pattern of voting, and none of them, with the possible exception of Gainsborough, approximated closely to the average pattern of the division as a whole. One factor in regional variation was landed influence. It was only in those districts where such influence was predominantly in Cholmeley's favour that he received sufficient plumpers to bring him to the top of the poll. In the division generally, however, there was no very rigid conformity of tenants to their landlords' politics. There were about 65 close parishes in Lindsey in 1852, and of these only 25 showed absolutely regular voting. Of 45 major landowners in the division (that is, owners who held, or whose descendants held, over 3,000 acres in 1873), only 27 secured absolutely regular voting in one or more parishes on their estates.[48]

More remarkable is the number of voters who gave cross-party votes, splitting either between Cholmeley and Christopher or between Cholmeley and Stanhope. Christopher and Stanhope had no need of such votes, and indeed the solidity of the Conservative party vote is striking, especially in the important districts of Epworth and Spilsby. But if Cholmeley had not picked up a number of cross-party votes he would have trailed his opponents far more ignominiously than in fact he did. Sometimes a high proportion of such votes indicates a conflict of rival allegiances, as on the fringes of the Yarborough estate; sometimes a genuine independence, as in a few of the open parishes. Occasionally there was the example of a landowner who had his own reasons for not giving a straight party vote.

Another variable, which the foregoing table fails to reveal, is the differing political behaviour of town and country. In the thirteen market towns of the division which acted as polling places there were more Cholmeley plumpers (698) than voters who split between the two Conservatives (572). But Cholmeley, with his lukewarm Liberalism, could not hope to recover in the towns the votes that he lost in the countryside. Only at Grimsby did he have a decent majority of the votes cast, and that was partly due to influence.[49] At

[48] Poll book; *White,* 1842.

[49] The Yarborough candidate for the borough, Edward Heneage, was defeated.

Epworth, Horncastle, and even Lincoln itself, there were more Christopher–Stanhope than Cholmeley voters.

In 9 out of the 13 districts there are a number of parishes for which the poll book provides details of occupations for over half the voters. A sample has been taken covering 44 per cent of the total number of voters in the division.[50] Fortunately it is fairly representative in party allegiance of the division as a whole.

	Cholmeley	Christopher–Cholmeley	Christopher–Stanhope	Others	Total
Sample %	30	10	48	11	99
Whole division %	31	9	48	12	100

The following classification of occupations, based on the poll book descriptions, has been adopted:[51]

i. The gentry and their servants, the clergy, and the professional and administrative classes.
ii. Farmers, yeomen, cottagers, and labourers.
iii. The liquor interest.
iv. Merchants, jobbers, and dealers.
v. Manufacturers.
vi. Millers and maltsters.
vii. Craftsmen, including smiths, tailors, carpenters, and shoemakers.
viii. Retail tradesmen, including grocers, butchers, bakers, and drapers.
ix. Miscellaneous, including carriers, watermen, auctioneers, castrators, well-diggers, etc.

The following table gives the voting of the various classes:

	Cholmeley %	Christopher–Stanhope %	Others %	Total %
i.	31	51	17	99
ii.	27	56	17	100
iii.	29	42	28	99
iv.	48	31	21	100
v.	45	34	21	100
vi.	31	40	29	100
vii.	35	31	32	98
viii.	33	31	36	100
ix.	53	23	24	100
TOTAL	30	48	21	99

[50] Within the 9 districts, voters have been taken only from those parishes for which details of occupation are given in the case of over 50 per cent of the electors voting.

[51] My classification is designed to correspond to the main occupational groups in a largely rural constituency, and differs to some extent from that adopted

The agriculturists emerge predictably as the most Conservative class in the electorate, followed by the gentry and professional groups, and supported by the millers, maltsters, and innkeepers. The craftsmen, tradesmen, merchants, and manufacturers, on the other hand, leaned towards the Liberal party. In class ix the strength of nonconformity among the sailors and fishermen was probably the weightiest reason for the strong Liberal vote.

Within each group there are some interesting variations:

	Cholmeley voters	Christopher-Stanhope voters
Clergy [Class i]	26	98
Dissenting ministers [i]	3	0
Farmers [ii]	567	1,260
Yeomen [ii]	42	44
Labourers [ii]	45	50
Publicans [iii]	3	13
Brewers [iii]	9	6
Shoemakers [vii]	44	28
Tailors [vii]	25	12
Blacksmiths [vii]	13	33
Drapers [viii]	10	5
Butchers [viii]	15	22
Grocers [viii]	14	21

If there is one determining factor, it would appear to be the amount of dependence of each group upon the agricultural economy. Thus butchers and blacksmiths were more Conservative than tailors and drapers. The publicans were sometimes also farmers; but the brewers, on the other hand, should perhaps be classed with the manufacturers.[52] An important subsidiary factor was, of course, religious allegiance. The Conservative affiliations of the Established clergy are striking, although their economic interests in many cases must have increased their willingness to vote with the *rural* party. Shoemakers were well known for their nonconformist views. And perhaps those farmers who described themselves as yeomen leaned more to nonconformity than the farming class as a whole.

by Dr. Vincent (op. cit., pp. 51-54, 140-1, 179-81). But there are many difficulties, particularly in distinguishing between craftsmen and tradesmen.

52 The samples in classes iii and iv are, however, too small to be of great significance.

It is noteworthy that butchers and grocers voted in a similar way, contrary to what a recent study by J.H. Vincent, weighted as it is towards medium-sized urban constituencies, would lead one to expect.[53] It can also be observed that it was the craftsmen and tradesmen who were the classes most prone to cross-party voting. There is no doubt that farmers were not above attempts to influence their tradesmen by threats of 'exclusive' or 'party' dealing,[54] and a vote split between Cholmeley and Christopher or Stanhope and Cholmeley may have been an attempt either to satisfy the claims of both customers and conscience, or merely to satisfy as many customers as possible. But it may also have been the village shoemaker or shopkeeper who kept alive what was left of the independent tradition, deserted as it now was by most of the farming community.

Within the polling districts the voting of the occupational groups was to some extent affected, as indeed one would expect, by patterns of local influence. In every class the proportion of electors who plumped for Cholmeley in the Barton district, for instance, was higher than the proportion in the more Conservative district of Louth. Within the farming class there were further variations reflecting the relative strengths of Liberal and Conservative landed interests in each district. In Caistor, Grimsby, and Wragby districts the farmers were more Liberal than the electorate as a whole. Over the whole division the rental voters were more Conservative than the freeholders. Of the freeholders 33 per cent plumped for Cholmeley, and of the tenants only 26 per cent. But this cannot be taken as an indicator of the strength of Conservative landlord influence. The figures reflect rather the higher proportion of farmers among the fifity-pound tenants than among the freeholders.[55]

The voting at Louth, for which a good occupational sample can be given, reveals a divergence between town and country with the same polling district.

[53] Vincent, *Pollbooks,* pp. 61-3.
[54] *Lincs. Chron.*, 7 June 1850.
[55] The farmers formed about one-quarter of the freeholders, but over three-quarters of the tenants on the Lindsey register in 1852.

Class	Louth parish		Louth district	
	Cholmeley voters	Christopher–Stanhope voters	Cholmeley voters	Christopher–Stanhope voters
i	28	29	39	60
vii	33	26	42	39
viii	13	11	14	18

The urban 'gentlemen' or 'esquires' of Louth were clearly a different set of men from the gentry of the polling district.[56] The craftsmen were more Liberal in the town than in the country. But most striking is the case of the tradesmen, who were Liberal for the major part in Louth and Conservative for the major part in the district as a whole. They would have been even more Liberal in Louth had it not been for the butchers, who voted, this time in accordance with Dr. Vincent's analysis, predominantly Conservative.

(iii) MID-CENTURY ELECTIONEERING: THOMAS RHODES OF MARKET RASEN, CHOLMELEY'S PRINCIPAL AGENT

Thomas Rhodes (*c*.1791-1879) was a well-established solicitor at Market Rasen. He numbered Heneage among his influential clients,[57] and it was probably this connection which brought him the principal whig agency in 1841, when Heneage chaired Worsley's election committee. Thereafter Rhodes acted first for Worsley and then for Cholmeley, and by 1852 he could place a thorough knowledge of the division at the latter's service, though his ideas of electioneering were by then a little old-fashioned.

During 1851 he had kept Cholmeley informed of movements in the constituency, and his presence at the London conference of June in that year has been noted. The address which Cholmeley then issued was printed by Rhodes's direction, and circulated to the sub-agents, generally solicitors like himself, whom Cholmeley retained in each polling district.[58] When Cholmeley began a series of visits in the division, it was Rhodes who made the arrangements and saw to their

56 See Dr. Vincent's remarks, *Pollbooks,* p. 54.

57 Or so I have assumed from various references in letters in the Monson MSS., none of which, however, affords positive proof.

58 The following paragraphs are based mainly on Rhodes's bill of particulars, MON 25/13/1/2/2, a large and elaborate document, which, despite its nature as a *pièce justificative*, provides a wealth of generally reliable detail.

advertisement in the county papers. It was sometimes necessary to ensure that sufficient tenants of Liberal landowners were present at ordinaries and farmers' meetings to ensure that the Member got a decent reception. In November Rhodes had to dissuade Cholmeley from attending a ploughing meeting at Owston, after receiving reports from Richard Dawson, the Epworth agent, that a rough greeting would await him.

In December 1851 and January 1852 the preliminary steps towards forming an election machine were taken. It was agreed that Heneage should again take the chair of the central committee at Market Rasen, and Rhodes took his advice as to the appointment of district chairmen. It was necessary to alert the district agents and to replace any that were known or feared to be disaffected.

On 13 February 1852 Cholmeley instructed Rhodes to open the campaign. He went at once to Heneage, who sanctioned the assembly of the central committee on the 17th. This committee consisted of the various district chairmen, who then returned to their districts to form committees with the assistance of their respective local agents. It was not until 21 February, however, that Heneage, on receiving news of Russell's resignation, sent instructions to set the canvass in motion. Rhodes wrote to the district agents (with whom he was henceforth in regular contact), forwarding to them advice on the law of corrupt practices, canvass books, and literature for distribution.

As the canvass returns came in from the districts they were analysed by Rhodes in consultation with Heneage. Where committees had apparently been guilty of inefficiency, from a comparison of their figures with the poll of 1841, they were exhorted to do better. And where it transpired that landowners had failed to communicate their wishes to their tenants they were urged, in suitable cases, to do so. Cholmeley had already written personally to influential landlords on Rhodes's suggestion. But where they were non-resident a specific request or, more usually, a statement of how the landlord would himself vote, was necessary before the tenants would commit themselves, or before the agent would cease working for the other side.

Meanwhile Cholmeley was touring the market towns. Rhodes supplied local enthusiasts with bands and flags where desirable. He also made sure that Cholmeley's speeches were accurately reported in the papers, even correcting the proofs before they went to press. Cholmeley, like the district agents, had to be kept within the law, particularly in the matter of subscriptions to Primitive Methodist chapels and other worthy causes.

When, early in April, Heneage advised the abandonment of the campaign, Rhodes summoned the central committee as requested. But he also had the sense to write to his old employer Lord Yarborough, whose intervention in the conduct of the canvass speedily followed. From then on Rhodes took his orders from Cholmeley and Yarborough rather than Heneage. Yarborough engaged an active and genuinely Liberal tenant, J.R. Kirkham of Audleby, to assist in the arrangement of meetings. Finally, in the last fortnight of the contest, Heneage was officially superseded as chairman of the central committee by a 'deputation' of Yarborough adherents–William Hutton of Gate Burton, the Revd. C.J. Barnard, Weston Cracroft,[59] and the Hon. William Monson, the young and capable heir of the sixth baron. One of the principal functions of the deputation was to prevent excessive expenditure by the local committees, which Heneage lacked the interest, and Rhodes the authority, to check.

During the last days of the campaign Rhodes was fully occupied in negotiating an agreement over refreshment tickets with the Conservative agents, and communicating with the district agents about out-voters. Rhodes had to arrange the journeys of these voters to the districts in which they qualified, and for which, regardless of residence, they therefore had to vote. When the day of nomination arrived he laid on a special train to take supporters to Lincoln, where it was considered important that Cholmeley should win the show of hands. During the two days of the poll Rhodes and his clerks worked 'until late in the evening' at the central committee rooms, sending and receiving reports of the state of the poll to and from the districts. The battle was fought

[59] Weston Cracroft (1815-83), son of Robert Cracroft (1783-1862) of Hackthorn, by Augusta, 2nd dau. of Sir John Ingilby, of Ripley, was M.P. (Lib.), Mid Lincolnshire, 1868-74. He and his father took the additional name of Amcotts on the death of Sir William Amcotts Ingilby in 1854. Colonel Amcotts owned 6,847 acres in Lincolnshire in 1873.

and lost. But consolation might be derived from the fact that his account with Cholmeley already stood at over £360.

(iv) MID-CENTURY ELECTIONEERING: THE WORK OF A DISTRICT AGENT, JOHN HETT OF BRIGG

The ideal of a district committee was that it should be chaired by an influential landowner, guided by a core of enthusiastic and experienced gentlemen, and composed of a body of canvassers representing every parish and township in the district. In the case of the Brigg committee in 1852 the ideal was far from realized. The chairman was the Revd. C.J. Barnard, who represented the Elwes family locally but who was not himself a very powerful figure. The core consisted of three or four respectable inhabitants of Brigg, more experienced than enthusiastic. And as far as the canvassers in the villages were concerned, they were mostly well-to-do Elwes and Yarborough tenants, which meant that there was no shortage of them where they were not really needed, in the close parishes east of Brigg, and a serious lack of them where they *were* needed, in the open parishes and Conservative-influenced places west of Brigg.

In these circumstances the energetic services of the agent, John Hett, were of the greatest importance to Cholmeley's cause in the district.[60] Having first written to the outlying parishes, enclosing canvass books for each parish, Hett and his partner Freer called in person on friends in the parishes nearer to Brigg. As the canvass progressed they found time to visit the more distant places as well, making sure that the larger open villages were thoroughly worked over. Hett also received reports from his more enthusiastic lieutenants. Edwin Empson of Bonby, a Yarborough tenant, wrote describing his canvass of the neighbouring village of Worlaby.

> I am afraid you will consider the result of my canvass very unsatisfactory, but those who have not promised will not pledge themselves to anyone else. They wish to wait and hear a little more before they finally decide, and if Sir Montague *comes out* a Protectionist and opposed to Maynooth I think we may calculate on three or four plumpers, and the others

[60] For Hett see above, p. 75. The following paragraphs are based mainly on material in the Stubbs deposit (STUBBS I/10), together with Hett's bill of particulars (MON 22/A/50).

divided with Mr. Christopher . . . . I have told Thomas Walker, who gives a plumper, to use his influence and secure the small free holders if possible, and he promises to do so.[61]

Much of Worlaby was owned by a non-resident proprietor, who exercised no influence. It is interesting that Walker, the carpenter and wheelwright, stood more chance than Empson, the substantial farmer, of securing the small freeholders.

Besides his visiting, Hett had much to do in his office in Brigg. He had to extract from the register a list of non-resident voters, that is, electors qualifying in his district but residing in another. These had to be canvassed where they resided, which meant corresponding with the agents of the districts concerned. And of course other agents wrote to him respecting their non-resident voters. There were also the out-voters, that is, voters living beyond the boundaries of the division, but qualifying in the Brigg district. Hett sent out circulars to seventeen such voters, first forwarding them to Barnard for his signature.

In the later stages of the campaign it was the larger open villages upon which efforts were concentrated. At a meeting of the committee at Brigg on 6 July it was decided to order a quantity of flags, ribbons, and rosettes, and to engage a band. The expense was considerable. The ten bandsmen—Hett made sure that they were non-voters—were each engaged for six days at ten shillings a day, and the eight flag bearers for the same period at 'five shillings per day, without any extras'.

But the principal task of the committee meeting of 6 July was to arrange for the conveyance of voters to the poll. For this purpose Hett made the meeting as large as possible, and most of the full committee were present. Conductors, that is, persons willing to provide transport and to see that all the known Liberal voters went to the poll at Brigg, were appointed for each parish. For some of the places west of Brigg, where there were no residents able to provide conveyances, a few of the Brocklesby tenants volunteered to drive over and shepherd the Liberal flocks. Conducting was of vital importance in the open villages lying some miles from Brigg. Few of their inhabitants had the political enthusiasm to walk to the poll, or to arrange their own transport. But many were ready to

[61] STUBBS I/10/3/21.

take advantage of a free ride, with the prospect of refreshment and entertainment at the end of it. On 10 July Hett received a report on the state of parties in Ashby township.

'Old Drury they had persuaded to turn, but I turned him again, as I promised he would have his 3/6 refreshment ticket . . . . Smith was not for going to poll at Brigg until I told him they would all go in a cart together. Got a plumper from Richard Wright but promised to find him a gig . . . .'[62]

The parish conductors were mostly volunteers, but as the time for the contest approached Hett engaged a large number of paid helpers. Refreshment ticket distributors, and men to guide the voters to their correct polling booths, were engaged after consultation with the Conservative agent for the district, Robert Owston. For each of the two booths Hett appointed an inspector, a check clerk, a messenger, a posting clerk and a committee clerk. There was also a special messenger whose duty it was to run to the telegraph office at Brigg to telegraph the state of the poll to Barnetby, whence it would be conveyed by special train to Market Rasen.

The number of electors who plumped for Cholmeley in July 1852, in that part of the Brigg district directly under Hett's supervision,[63] was 194. The first canvass in March had produced an estimate of 143 plumpers, and the June canvass one of 172. The figures reflect not only the increased efficiency of the second canvass, but also the steady improvement in Cholmeley's position during the campaign.

The poll book, however, confirmed Brigg's reputation as an 'equivocal' district.[64] The eastern sector, including several Yarborough parishes, voted well for Cholmeley. But in the western sector there was a very marked falling away of Liberal support. In 1841 eleven of the western parishes had returned majorities of Liberal plumpers, but none did so in 1852. The western sector, indeed, voted rather like the Epworth district, the eastern sector similarly to the Caistor district. The principal impression is of a topographical recession of the Yarborough interest.

[62] STUBBS I/10/3/113. Before the poll it was agreed that the refreshment tickets should be worth 5*s*. 0*d*. for a plumper and 2*s*. 6*d*. for a split vote.

[63] A separate committee was formed for the neighbourhood around Kirton Lindsey. It took over responsibility for the canvass of certain parishes in the Brigg and Gainsborough districts.

[64] The epithet was E.B. Drury's, in a letter to Charles Tennyson of 19 Dec. 1832 (TD'E H/111/93).

(v) THE NORTH LINCOLNSHIRE LIBERAL ELECTION ACCOUNT, 1852-6

For the Liberals the North Lincolnshire election of 1852 was a very expensive failure. There had been no financial committee to keep a close watch on expenditure from the central committee room at Market Rasen, and the district committees had conducted their campaigns with varying degrees of extravagance. The case of Epworth was a particularly bad one. The total expenditure for that district reached the immense sum of £1,738, or four guineas for each split vote or plumper for Cholmeley. These figures included the agent's bill, the refreshment ticket account, and the general district expenses. This last item, totalling about £1,000, included printing and advertising, the hire of a band and flag bearers, the employment of messengers and conductors, and various items of refreshment for the voters by way of treating. Gross extravagance occurred also at Lincoln, where the general expenses included £68. 11*s*. 0*d*. for 'men engaged on nomination day', £5 subscribed to the restoration of a city church, and £130. 8*s*. 7*d*. spent, or so he alleged, by the landlord of the White Hart.[65]

It need not be conjectured that Cholmeley's supporters set out deliberately to spend as much of his (and Yarborough's) money as they could. In a large district, let alone a large county division, it was almost impossible to enforce general and uniform principles of economy. It was traditional to conduct elections with saturnalian enthusiasm, and bands were hired, flags waved, and favours distributed, unless the candidate issued specific orders to the contrary. In certain districts, such as Barton, Louth, and Lincoln, the venal influence of the corrupt boroughs of Hull, Grimsby, and Lincoln probably made itself felt in a greater than average amount of treating. Added to these factors there was the operation of that electoral principle by which the level of expenditure moved in inverse proportion to the popularity of the candidate. In the Epworth district, to take the obvious example, Cholmeley's supporters no doubt resorted to treating as the only way of gaining votes. In cases where tradesmen and solicitors felt they had lost custom, moreover, by working

[65] MON 25/13/1/2/4, 7 and 16.

for the unpopular side, they were liable after the election to recoup their losses by sending in extortionate bills.

Cholmeley and Yarborough demonstrated another electoral principle, by which the willingness of the candidate to pay his bills was, naturally, related to his success or unsuccess in the contest. After Cust's defeat in 1841 there had been trouble among the Conservatives over the settlement of their election account,[66] and now, in August 1852, it was the turn of the Liberals to have an unpleasant *post mortem* inquisition.

Cholmeley began by appointing a finance committee under Heneage, the job of which was to inspect the bills as they were forwarded from the district committees and agents and to decide whether or not they should be paid in full.[67] This was in fact the normal procedure. But it did not satisfy Yarborough, who feared that Heneage would advise the payment of the bills in full to conceal his own want of management.[68] Besides, it was not Heneage's money. Yarborough and Cholmeley had agreed to meet half the expenses each, and both stood to be mulcted of about £5,000. But Yarborough had a further motive for reducing the bills as far as possible. If a precedent for extravagance were once established it would prove difficult to destroy, and no candidate other than a member of his own family would venture to contest the seat.

Soon after the election Yarborough was in communication with Edward Ellice, the whig party manager, who referred him to the parliamentary agent Joseph Parkes. Though now retired from active party management, Parkes was still consulted on matters of election expenditure, in regard to which he was well placed as a taxing master in Chancery.[69] Rhodes was asked to forward the district bills to Parkes, who looked them over in January 1853 and advised several large reductions, particularly in the innkeepers' demands. Yarborough accordingly explained the position to the local party leaders at a meeting at Brocklesby in February, and Rhodes was instructed to proceed with the payment of the

[66] Scottish Record Office, Ogilvy of Inverquharity Muniments (GD/205), portfolio 15, correspondence between Christopher and Chaplin, 1841.
[67] Rhodes's bill, ff. 47-54.
[68] MON 25/13/14, Yarborough to Monson, 18 May 1853.
[69] See Norman Gash, *Politics in the Age of Peel,* pp. 418 ff.

bills, with suitable deductions, in co-operation with the district committees.[70]

It must be admitted that Rhodes's position was difficult. To carry out Parkes's recommendations would be to invite a series of court cases and cause offence and irritation among many local pillars of the party. As it was, the innkeepers caused some trouble. At Barton a publican secured a compromise settlement after enlisting the sympathy of the district committee. The landlord of the White Hart at Lincoln threatened to take Cholmeley to court if not paid in full, with what outcome is unrecorded.[71]

The next stage was the payment of the district agents, who on Parkes's advice were asked to send in bills of particulars that could be taxed if necessary. Yarborough hoped that Parkes himself would undertake the settlement of the accounts. On his refusal Monson and Hutton were appointed to supervise Rhodes's negotiations with the agents, with whom, if left to himself, he would undoubtedly have been too lenient.[72]

Some haste was desirable, since the still unpaid agents were unlikely to exert themselves in registration business, and since Cholmeley had no desire to be met by their black looks when he made his proposed summer tour of the market towns.[73] But it was not until 13 August that the unobjectionable bills were paid; and the objectionable ones led to a series of unpleasant exchanges. Dawson of Epworth and Hett of Brigg were able to secure compromises, which were due to the reluctance of Monson and Hutton to lose their services.[74] In only one case, that of William Andrew of Lincoln, did the bill go for taxation. But before judgment was passed Heneage, who needed Andrew's goodwill in Lincoln city politics, got Cholmeley to agree to a settlement out of court.[75] Lord Monson commented to his son: 'The fact is that Cholmeley is not up to the mark in head. He is the best man we can get taking the pocket into consideration and that is all that can be said. As for Heneage I think he is a very loose fish indeed . . . .'[76]

[70] Rhodes's bill, ff. 54-9. [71] Ibid., ff. 61-4.
[72] MON 25/13/1/24/11, Yarborough to Monson, 11 July 1853.
[73] MON 25/13/1/10/7, Hutton to Monson, n.d. [74] MON 25/13/1/9 and 11.
[75] MON 25/13/1/12. [76] MON 25/10/1/3/3/4, 13 Dec. 1853.

At the beginning of 1855 there was still one large account outstanding, and that was the charges of Rhodes himself. He had been superseded by this date as principal registration agent, and was probably more than a little disgruntled. He was slow to produce his claim, and eventually did so in the form of a prodigious bill of particulars, totalling about £600, although Monson and Hutton had not requested a full account.[77] Rhodes of course knew his ground, and felt quite safe in challenging the committee to tax him if they dared. Monson, advised by Parkes, took a high line, with complete unsuccess. Rhodes stood on his professional dignity, and claimed that the matter was one between himself and Cholmeley. Parkes finally turned the matter over to James Coppock, the Liberal agent, who advised a compromise. Cholmeley settled the account in March 1856, by paying Rhodes only £50 less than he claimed.[78]

The election account was now closed at a figure exceeding £10,000. It marked the end of an era, for Monson calculated that under the Corrupt Practices Act of 1854, mild though it was, no future contest for the division would cost more than £6,000.

(vi) THE NORTH LINCOLNSHIRE LIBERAL ASSOCIATION, 1853-7

On 25 April 1853 the Liberals of Lindsey assembled to launch the first regular political association to be formed in the division. Its chairman was William Monson, assisted by a central committee including Hutton, Cracroft, and Sir Henry Dymoke. And its secretary was the Revd. E.R. Larken, rector of Burton-by-Lincoln, Monson's uncle by marriage, and a man of Liberal views and some ambition.[79] Committees had already been formed in most of the polling districts, their principal function between elections being to assist the registration agents. The district committees were entitled to send representatives to confer with the central committee at regular intervals. Membership of the association was open

[77] The largest items were £245 for over 1,350 letters at 3*s*. 6*d*. each, and £179.13*s*.3*d*. for travelling expenses.

[78] MON 25/13/1/4 and 6.

[79] His zeal in the work of the association was at least partly fed by the hope of preferment from the hands of grateful ministers, but in this he was disappointed.

to anyone paying the minimum subscription of one shilling a year.[80]

The association, the idea of which may have been suggested to Yarborough by Parkes, was intended to broaden the basis of Liberal support in the division. The party was henceforth to embrace not merely a coterie of major landowners, but also those middle-class and urban politicians whose aid Cholmeley had largely failed to enlist in 1852. Efforts were made to include leading townsmen on the district committees, particularly those of Lincoln, Gainsborough, and Boston. At Lincoln Larken endeavoured to unite the Seely and Heneage parties. And at Gainsborough another political priest, the Revd. C.F. Newmarch of Pilham,[81] got a prominent local radical[82] to be secretary of the committee.

Yarborough's aim, however, was to provide the appearance, rather than the reality, of a democratic organization. It was he who appointed the central committee, and he who controlled the association. The rank and file of the membership might be useful in routine constituency work. But it was not intended that the association should dictate to the party in matters such as election policy or the choice of candidates.[83] Indeed, the funds of the association, augmented though they were by subscriptions from the large landowners, seem to have amounted only to about £200 a year. This was adequate to cover registration expenses, but was not intended for election purposes.

Yarborough was chiefly concerned to remove the immediate responsibility for the running of the party from the shoulders of the inefficient Cholmeley, and give it to a small group of eager but extremely respectable men who could be relied on to work under general guidance from Brocklesby. When Member for the division, Yarborough had himself devoted considerable time to supervising and encouraging the district

80 MON 25/13/1/24/7.

81 Newmarch was Yarborough's chaplain, and like Larken was fond of Mechanics' Institutes and other good works among the urban working classes. He was soon afterwards promoted to the rich living of Leverton, near Boston.

82 John Hyde, a retired tax collector and a Unitarian.

83 Similarly the West Riding Reform and Registration Association, one of the models of its kind, was confined to registration work. But in that division there had long been pre-election meetings at which district delegates were consulted. See F.M.L. Thompson, 'Whigs and Liberals in the West Riding, 1830-60', *Eng. Hist. Rev.* lxxiv (1959), pp. 214 ff.

agents, and to maintaining local committees of voluntary helpers.[84] Cholmeley had allowed this organization to run down, neglecting to pay the agents their yearly retaining fees and losing contact with the local party workers. Now Monson and Larken were between them to take on most of this work. This also meant superseding Rhodes as principal agent, as far as registration work was concerned, although it was agreed that he would continue to act as Cholmeley's election agent if the latter decided to stand again. The district agents were retained where they were willing to work for the new organization, but Yarborough probably hoped that the party would in future cease to be so dangerously dependent on their uncertain zeal. It was also hoped that those who had indulged in excessive treating in 1852 would turn over a new leaf. A circular of June 1853 to the district committee members took an unprecedentedly moral line: '. . . the Elective Franchise is a solemn trust, with which they are invested, not for their own personal or pecuniary benefit, but for the advantage of the whole community, and particularly those who, at present, are excluded from political power.'[85]

In its immediate objective, the improvement of the Liberal position on the register, the association had some success. Larken claimed 128 gains in 1856, 149 in 1854, 172 in 1855, and 186 in 1856.[86] The total gain in these four years was 635, only 173 short of the difference between Cholmeley's and Christopher's poll in 1852. In October 1855 Larken wrote to Monson: 'In a few more years the register alone would give us a majority. With what we have gained, and the change of opinion relative to Christopher, we may fairly calculate that we shall have *one* next time.'[87]

The principal credit for the registration gains must go, however, to the district agents. It is doubtful whether their committees were a great deal of assistance to them. In some districts, indeed, it was not until long after the inauguration of the association that committees were formed at all. Monson had to write to Brackenbury in January 1855 to

[84] STUBBS I/11/8. [85] STUBBS I/11/10.
[86] MON 25/13/1/25/15, Larken to Monson, 22 Nov. 1856.
[87] MON 25/13/14, 20 Oct. 1855.

make him take the lead in the Spilsby district.[88] And in February of the same year it was discovered that correspondents had been appointed for only 4 of the 23 parishes in the Caistor district.

In this situation it was impossible for the central committee to reduce what Parkes called their 'standing army' of attornies. Indeed, their principal worry was the necessity for restoring the morale of disaffected agents and replacing those who resigned. A few solicitors with genuinely Liberal views—Robert Toynbee of Lincoln (a connection of the Monsons'), Josiah Merrils of Epworth, and Edward Johnson of Barton—replaced older members of their profession who had been particularly expensive in 1852. But recruitment was not made easier by the less attractive financial prospects which political agency now afforded. The agents of the association were retained at £10 a year in the 1850s, as they had been by Worsley in the early 1840s. But elections would in future be less profitable. And the incidental profits of being connected with the Yarborough interest were less than when the heir himself had held the seat.

The Corrupt Practices Act of 1854 curtailed the polling at county elections from two days to one, and placed restrictions on the conveyance of voters to the poll. In consequence the Lindsey Liberals pressed for the creation of new polling districts. But they ran into difficulties first with the Bench, whose duty it was to change the district boundaries, and who were predominantly Conservative;[89] and secondly with the agents, who disliked the disturbance of their spheres of influence. For at least one new district, that of Kirton, the Liberals had to fall back on an attorney whose politics had been suspect in 1852.[90]

88 MON 25/13/1/19/4, Brackenbury to Monson, 25 Jan. 1855. Brackenbury's excuse for inaction was that the local influences (Willoughby and Christopher) were tory, and that Liberal farmers and tradespeople did not care to risk giving offence by having their names published as members of a committee, particularly between elections.

89 Of 86 Lindsey J.P.s whose votes can be traced in the 1852 poll book, 48 split between Christopher and Stanhope and only 17 plumped for Cholmeley. The bench included many parsons, and there had for years been a tory lord lieutenant.

90 Letter books of Joseph Howlett of Kirton, Liberal sub-agent 1841-52 and 1855-8, inspected by kind permission of Messrs. Burton and Dyson, of Gainsborough and Kirton.

If the association had failed on the one hand to emancipate itself from the system of professional agency, it failed on the other to win the complete confidence of the radical and dissenting wing of the party. To them Yarborough's central committee seemed to be composed either of Yarborough's creatures or of men with very lukewarm opinions. The Revd. C.J. Barnard, who would have been a good intermediary between the two sections of the party, was not asked to join the central committee until 1855.[91]

The urban Liberals of Lincoln and Gainsborough had joined the association in 1853 in the hope that at the next election it would bring forward a second, and more radical, candidate, together with Cholmeley.[92] At first the central committee made some attempt to find a running partner for Cholmeley, if only to hasten a compromise by frightening the other side. But none of the gentry had the means of financing his own candidature, and it was soon apparent that nobody would subscribe adequately, particularly since a contest would thereby have been made inevitable. Cholmeley himself, indeed, muttered in 1853 about a subscription for himself, and at first wondered if he should stand at all.

By 1855 the townsmen seem to have abandoned their campaign for a second candidate. Their weakness in the division had been revealed in the previous year, when the Reform question was briefly revived. The abortive Reform proposals of 1854 were supported in Lincoln, Gainsborough, and Louth. But elsewhere in the division there was little enthusiasm. The association held a Reform meeting in Lincoln in April 1854, but the gentry failed to arrive, and Seely chose the occasion to deliver one of his attacks on Heneage, whom Monson then had to mollify.[93] Cholmeley, Dymoke, and others welcomed the decline in party spirit that came with the Crimean war, and the radicals turned their attention to another round of church-rate contests.

The fall of the Aberdeen coalition in January 1855 found Yarborough and Monson well prepared for the possibility of a dissolution. Yarborough and Cholmeley had reached agreement about possible election expenses. Cholmeley

[91] MON 25/13/14, Larken to Monson, 22 May 1855.
[92] *Lincs. Times*, 3 May 1853. [93] MON 25/13/1/23.

would pay half the bill, the other half being met as far as possible by subscription, with Yarborough supplying the difference.[94] Larken circularized the whig landowners of the division, who had promised £1,300 by the end of May, thus saving him the further trouble of sending begging letters to the middle classes.[95] The generosity of the gentry was prompted by the knowledge that in all probability their money would not be called for. The Conservatives would probably concede the second seat, and there seemed no serious likelihood of a second, independent, Liberal candidate.

Christopher had fallen from grace with his constituents in the autumn of 1852, when the government of which he was a member had bowed to the will of the country and abandoned Protection. Stanhope remained true to his principles, voting against Palmerston's as well as Villiers's motion in the autumn session.[96] Since then Yarborough's political interest in the division had recovered, as the memories of the depression receded. His standing improved particularly in Grimsby, which began to feel the benefit of the new docks and railway, and which gratefully returned the young Lord Worsley in 1857. It was known, furthermore, that there was a feeling among several of the gentry in favour of a compromise.

Christopher appears at one stage to have suggested that Stanhope, as the younger Member, should retire. But early in 1856, using the occasion of his succession to the Scottish Nisbet-Hamilton property, he intimated to the Liberals, through Dymoke, that he would not stand again.[97]

The circumstances of the general election in March 1857 favoured the one-and-one return in North Lincolnshire. There was no great amity between Cholmeley and Stanhope, who took issue with each other on the question of Palmerston's bellicose foreign policy. But the constituency itself was at peace. The farmers had enjoyed exceptionally high prices during the Crimean war, and neither side had any desire to raise the ghost of Protection. Nor was there much interest in the Reform question, so that Cholmeley could well afford to

[94] MON 25/13/1/19/9, Cholmeley to Monson, 9 Mar. 1855.

[95] MON 25/13/1/20/20, Larken to Monson, 21 May 1855.

[96] *Parl. Deb.* 3rd Ser. cxxiii, 696 ff. Christopher opposed Villiers's free-trading motion, but followed the Conservative leadership in supporting Palmerston's compromise motion. During the debates he was sarcastically attacked by Bright.

[97] MON 25/13/1/25/1 and 3.

conciliate the radicals of the division by references in his public speeches to church-rate abolition and the extension of the franchise.[98] Had there been an opposition Yarborough would probably have brought forward a second candidate in Weston Cracroft Amcotts. But the election passed off without incident, and Cholmeley and Stanhope were returned unopposed. Thereafter, though it continued to function in registration matters, little was heard of the North Lincolnshire Liberal Association.

(vii) SOUTH LINCOLNSHIRE, 1846-57

Handley, who had been for some time in poor health, died on 29 June 1846. There was no obvious successor to his interest—nobody, that is, with the ability, the means, or the inclination to challenge the entrenched tory interests of the division. Heathcote had perhaps the means, but he had no wish to stir up an opposition; and he was given at least some colour of an excuse by the fact that his relative Willoughby had acted since 1844 with the Conservative protectionists.

Turnor (the junior Conservative Member) retired from his seat in 1847, and Chaplin had some difficulty in finding a suitable successor. He hoped to produce a candidate from the Grantham region; but, after being unsuccessful in that quarter, he agreed with some diffidence to promote Lord Burghley,[99] the young heir of the marquis of Exeter. An inexperienced and wholly unimpressive politician, Burghley's militia duties connected him with Northamptonshire rather than South Lincolnshire; and there was some disgruntlement at his candidature in those parts of the division which were unaccustomed to bow the knee at the name of Cecil. He was nevertheless returned unopposed with Trollope.

During the bad times of 1849-51 there was no strong protectionist movement in South Lincolnshire comparable with that in the northern division. There was of course no Cholmeley against whom to mount an independent opposition. Burghley became unpopular in Holland, where his abstentions

[98] *Stamf. Merc.*, 13 Mar. 1857.

[99] The 3rd marquis of Exeter (1825-95) was M.P. for S. Lincs., 1847-57, and N. Northants., 1857-67.

from agricultural meetings were particularly resented; but Trollope managed to prevent the politicians of Holbeach and Long Sutton from going to the length of launching a tenant farmer candidate. Part of the secret of Trollope's own influence was his devotion to the local interests of his division, and his frequent appearances among his constituents. But he also contrived to secure and retain the adherence of part of the old independent interest.

In March 1852 he was made president of the Poor Law Board in Derby's government. But his nomination speech, when he stood for re-election for South Lincolnshire, was more like that of an old-style independent country gentleman than that of an office-holder. He looked forward to the settlement of the Protection question at the forthcoming general election, and advocated legal reforms and even reductions in public salaries. He was nominated by Thorold, who from about 1849 must be considered a Conservative.[100]

There was no opposition to Trollope's return in March 1852. Nor was there any contest in July, when he was again returned in company with Burghley. This time Trollope's nomination speech was decidedly ministerialist in tone, encouraging the farmers to look to a general reform of taxation rather than a return to Protection. He was seconded by Healy, whose politics now appeared to be of a very moderate nature. 'Mr. Chaplin [he said] . . . had saved them a great deal of trouble in selecting the Members; but they had generally turned out better than was expected.' Even Burghley was forgiven, a sure sign that the farmers' bank balances were in a healthier state. The election passed off with the least possible excitement, the Spalding correspondent of the *Mercury* commenting that the farmers had 'merged their political principles into love for their own order . . . . There has prevailed an almost unanimous desire to strengthen the hands of those who are thought to be the most friendly disposed to the interests of the soil . . . .' With the return of two protectionists assured, the agriculturists turned their mind to other things; and when the candidates visited Spalding market shortly before the nomination, they found more interest in the election of poor-law guardians than of parliamentary representatives.[101]

[100] *Stamf. Merc.*, 19 Mar. 1852, 19 Oct. 1849.
[101] *Lincs. Chron.*, 13 Apr. 1852; *Stamf. Merc.*, 16 and 23 July 1852.

Trollope, like Christopher, voted for Palmerston's motion in November 1852, and Burghley, like Stanhope, opposed it. But Trollope, with his general record as a good agricultural Member, was able to ride out the storm; whereas Burghley, by his neglect of his constituents, was soon the less popular of the two. By the autumn of 1856 Trollope, tired of apologizing for the absence of his colleague at agricultural meetings, was willing publicly to encourage those who wished Burghley to retire, and he even intimated that he would not be averse to having a whig returned as his colleague at the next general election.[102]

In this situation Heathcote, who had been raised to the peerage by Palmerston in February 1856, taking the title of Baron Aveland, was at last roused to action. He brought forward his distant relative George Hussey Packe, of Caythorpe, a Liberal of a mild and whiggish kind, who had stood unsuccessfully for Newark in 1847. No attempt was made to enlist the support of the urban Liberals of the division, who considered Packe's views on Reform and church rates to be extremely tepid. Nor was any attempt made to prepare for a contest. Packe and his supporters were therefore considerably embarrassed when Burghley retired at the general election of 1857, only to be replaced by a stronger Conservative candidate in Anthony Willson, of South Rauceby. Willson was the son of Anthony Peacock, senior partner in the bank of Peacock, Handleys, and Peacock at Sleaford.[103] But he had established himself as a country gentleman, and took a prominent part in local and agricultural affairs. In politics he was a moderate Conservative rather than a tory.

Packe, after some hesitation, decided to go to the poll in March 1857. With a poor organization and an unfavourable register he knew his hopes were small.[104] But in fact he did somewhat better than Handley had done in 1841. The votes were

Trollope	4,020
Willson	3,636
Packe	3,188

[102] *Stamf. Merc.*, 17 Oct. 1856.

[103] Anthony Peacock jun. (1811-66), of whom we treat, took the name of Willson in lieu of Peacock in 1851.

[104] Leicestershire County Record Office, Prestwold (Packe) MSS., Box 700, E/8. Until he succeeded his brother in 1867 Packe was not, by county standards, a wealthy man, and could not afford to spend much on paid agency.

Packe benefited from the exercise of a certain amount of influence by Aveland, Dysart, Cholmeley, and others. Willoughby de Eresby asked only one vote for Trollope, and quite a number of voters in the Bourne neighbourhood split between Trollope and Packe. At Grantham Packe's chairmanship of the Great Northern Railway brought him further votes. And he was also assisted by the expansion of the Baptist and Wesleyan Reform connexions in some of the more populous places in Holland and southern Kesteven. But there was little left of Handley's former interest. The banking influence at Sleaford now went to Willson.[105] And there was a marked decline in independence and a swing to the Conservatives in Heckington, Swineshead, and the grazing parishes near Boston. Packe's whig support, combined with a small though growing urban and dissenting vote, served in fact to conceal the declining appeal of Liberalism to the agricultural voters.

105 The *Mercury* (10 Apr. 1857) estimated that it was worth 200 votes.

11

THE SPREAD OF RURAL CONSERVATISM, 1857-1874

(i) PARTY POLITICS AND THE REFORM QUESTION, 1857-66

AT THE general election of 1857 the Lincolnshire Liberals had recovered one of the four county seats. In 1859 they recovered a second, and with the unopposed return of Packe for South Lincolnshire they were now represented in both the county divisions for the first time since 1841. Perhaps a new epoch in county politics was beginning, one in which the Liberals would maintain and strengthen themselves in the rural districts. After all, those districts were beginning to be opened up by the railways and civilized by the influence of a cheaper press. The towns were growing, and so were Liberal and dissenting influences in them. The countryside was being brought closer to the towns, or so it might be expected, than ever before. The great issue which had divided urban and rural interests, that of Free Trade, was, according to general opinion, 'for ever laid to rest'; and the farmers had in recent years been given some reason for imagining that Free Trade was not the evil they had feared. All that was now needed was a Reform agitation to stir memories of the period 1826-32, and revive in the farmer those Liberal sentiments which had for so long remained dormant.

But any Liberal who indulged himself with such speculations sadly misconstrued the signs of the times, and was due for much disappointment in the succeeding few years. In the first place the two 'Liberals' returned in 1859 were simply milk-and-water whigs, who were promoted at least partly with a view to securing the 'peace of the county', and allowed by the tories to take their seats for pretty much the same reason. If the North Lincolnshire election of 1857 had been a truce between the two parties, that of 1859 was more in the nature of a treaty. Despite their party voting in the Commons, Cholmeley and Stanhope had no serious differences on Reform or foreign policy. The former, though still willing to be described as an 'old reformer', took a very moderate tone on the hustings, and was proposed by Heneage, whom the Lincoln Liberals regarded as a Conservative to all intents and purposes.[1] In South Lincolnshire Willson announced that since his opinions were not radically different from those of the other two candidates he would not be justified in agitating the division. His conduct was certainly approved by Trollope, who in the previous year had told a Grantham meeting that 'it did not much signify what a man's politics were. They generally meant the same thing–the good of the country.'[2]

Neither Packe nor Cholmeley voted consistently with the Liberals during the ensuing parliament. They opposed Baines's bill to extend the borough franchise in 1861; and Packe, though not Cholmeley, voted against a bill to abolish church rates in 1863. They were again returned without a contest in 1865. On the North Lincolnshire hustings Cholmeley was proposed by Amcotts in what the *Chronicle* called 'an excellent Conservative speech', arguing that neither party in the division could hope to return both Members, 'excepting under very strong political excitement'. Stanhope was equally conciliatory, expressing the belief that 'moderate men of both sides were drawing closer together.'[3]

Both the Liberal Members were becoming Conservative in their old age, and both were encouraged in this by the state of their respective parties. Cholmeley's position had been weakened by the death of the second earl of Yarborough in 1862, the succession of his less able and less politically-minded son, and the consequent weakening of the family interest both in the county and at Grimsby. In South Lincolnshire Packe was largely dependent on the support of Aveland, whose opinions were becoming more Conservative even than those of Packe himself.

It was not, however, a mere question of strategy. The one-and-one returns in 1859 and 1865 represented a widespread feeling in the county in favour of political peace and

[1] *Stamf. Merc.*, 15 Apr. 1859.
[2] Ibid., 30 July 1858. The failure of the Conservative ministry of 1858-9 made men like Trollope support Palmerston in order to keep out the radicals (Helmsley [Anderson] MSS., Trollope to Anderson, 18 May 1858).
[3] *Lincs. Chron.*, 21 July 1865.

quietness, and the opinions of the Members returned reflected the growing mood of Conservatism in the electorate. If Liberalism and dissent were making headway in the larger towns, the effect seems to have been to widen rather than to narrow the gulf between town and country.[4] Countrymen may have become more familiar with the towns, but they did not necessarily like what they saw and heard. Farmers who had once championed the Liberal cause in North Lincolnshire were now reluctant to be classed with that 'turbulent demagogue', as H.G. Skipworth called John Bright.[5] It is significant that in religion, as ever, closely connected with politics, there was a parallel movement. Conflict between Church and dissent subsided in the later 1850s, and after 1860 urban parishes which had previously held out against church rates began voluntarily to grant them. The Established Church began to regain some of its lost ground in the country-side, and the spread of harvest festivals and the church-restoration movement were symptoms of its revival.

At political meetings the unity of the agricultural interest began to be the dominant theme, partisan speeches being increasingly unwelcome. At the North Lincolnshire Show in 1864 William Torr proposed the health of the County Members in these words: '. . . although represented in the House of Commons by gentlemen holding entirely different opinions, yet in questions affecting the common weal they were one. He believed no county in England was more thoroughly represented than Lincolnshire in the agricultural interest.' Replying, Cholmeley recalled that Torr had once been 'one of his strongest opponents', and was glad to think that he had lived down the ill feelings of 1852.[6]

This meant two things. One was that farmers were not after all so happy with the state of their industry as they had seemed a few years before. In the early 1860s they were becoming increasingly worried by production difficulties and

[4] Between 1861 and 1891 the number of places in Lincolnshire with over 1,000 inhabitants fell from 78 to 69, but the proportion of the population living in those places rose from 54 per cent to 59 per cent. Thus while the larger places grew larger the smaller grew still smaller.

[5] J.R. Kirkham declared at a Caistor meeting in November 1866: 'Mr. Stanhope used sometimes to call him a radical, but he had a horror of Mr. Bright' (*Stamf. Merc.*, 23 Nov. 1866).

[6] *Stamf. Merc.*, 5 Aug. 1864.

falling profits. Secondly, they felt themselves vulnerable to continuing attack by the manufacturing interest, particularly as regarded their waning influence in parliament. Hence their failure to be swept along by the Reform enthusiasm of the early 1860s. In 1859 Stanhope had declared that 'he would not willingly assent to any measure that depresses the agricultural interest, already insufficiently represented in the House of Commons.'[7] And Cholmeley opposed the extension of the borough franchise in 1861, because he felt, with other rural county Members, that any Reform measure must be accompanied by a redistribution scheme that gave more seats to the counties.[8]

In 1866 Cholmeley voted for the second reading of the Liberal Reform Bill. He had intended to abstain, but the strong feelings of some members of the North Lincolnshire Liberal Association, probably combined with some party pressure at Westminster, made him change his mind.[9] He started voting with the opposition during the committee stage, however, and helped to defeat the government on Dunkellin's amendment of 18 June.[10] But the reforming section of the North Lincolnshire Liberals was not strong enough to give an impressive demonstration of its displeasure, and there was a marked lack of excitement in the constituency, compared with the period 1830-2. The Association was paralysed by internal division, and decided not to hold a meeting or circulate petitions in April 1866.[11] In October a Reform demonstration was held at Lincoln to which deputations went from Rasen, Brigg, and Louth. But it was largely a working-man's affair.

Packe deserted his party with more alacrity than Cholmeley, voting for Grosvenor's amendment of 12 April, which asked for a redistribution scheme to be harnessed to the franchise proposals. It is significant that the Hon. G.H. Heathcote (then sitting for Rutland) was in the same lobby on that division. If the Reform Bill of 1866 had reached the Lords, Aveland

7 *Stamf. Merc.*, 15 Apr. 1859. 8 *Parl. Deb.*, 3rd Ser. clxii, 410, 10 Apr. 1861.

9 The Brigg committee of the N.L.L.A. sent a telegram to Cholmeley urging him to vote for the bill (STUBBS I/12, Larken to Hett, Freer, and Hett, 12 and 25 Apr. 1866).

10 See *Parl. Deb.* 3rd Ser. clxxxiii, 152 ff; clxxxiv, 536; F.B. Smith, *The Making of the Second Reform Act,* 1966, pp. 84, 103-8.

11 STUBBS I/12.

would most probably have been counted among its opponents;[12] and it must have been with Aveland's concurrence, if not his advice, that Packe voted with the opposition on the second reading. There was an outcry at Spalding; and Sleaford, Bourne, and Holbeach also expressed their indignation with their Member. But the reformers were even weaker in the southern than they were in the northern division, and their protests came to nothing. When Packe and Trollope visited the farmers in the autumn of 1866 they found them still preoccupied with the cattle plague.

(ii) THE REDISTRIBUTION OF SEATS AND THE GENERAL ELECTION OF 1868

When the Conservatives introduced their Reform Bill in 1867 Cholmeley and Packe returned to their party fold, and it was the turn of Stanhope and Trollope to reconcile the claims of conscience with those of party. Trollope seems to have taken little part in the debates on parliamentary strategy within the Conservative party. But Stanhope played an important role in bringing the county Members behind the leadership. He saw the hopelessness of going to the country on an anti-reforming platform; and his acceptance of household suffrage for the boroughs must have been influenced by the carrot of a favourable redistribution of seats, which Disraeli assiduously dangled before the rural county Members.[13]

The scheme of redistribution, as set out in Schedule D of the Reform Bill of March 1867, proposed to double Lindsey's representation by making it into two constituencies. The line of division was to run east to west, confining the Yarborough interest in the North Lindsey constituency. Nisbet-Hamilton and Stanhope proposed certain modifications to the scheme, but they did not oppose it on principle. They did not believe that their party could carry more than two of the four Lindsey seats, and their main concern was to avoid contests by ensuring a balance of power in each division.[14]

12 F.B. Smith, op. cit., pp. 107-8.

13 Hughenden (Disraeli) MSS., B/XX/T/85A, Stanhope to Colonel Taylor, a Conservative whip, 13 Mar. 1867.

14 Hughenden (Disraeli) MSS., B/XI/J/94, Dudley Baxter to Montague Corry, 16 Mar. 1867; *Parl. Deb.* clxxxvi, 293, 21 Mar. 1867.

During the committee stage in July, however, the government decided that Lincolnshire, being a county of over 300,000 inhabitants, should be divided more or less equally into three two-Member constituencies. A new mid division was to be formed from part of southern Lindsey, with the addition of the two northernmost wapentakes of Kesteven.[15] From the point of view of Nisbet-Hamilton and Stanhope this rearrangement, though leaving the political map less tidy than they would have liked, had its advantages as well as disadvantages. Cholmeley's seat of Norton Place fell within the new northern division, where Yarborough's remained the dominant influence. Amcotts and Edward Heneage[16] would belong to the mid division, where, however, they would now be balanced not only by Stanhope and Nisbet-Hamilton themselves but also by the young Henry Chaplin, whose Kesteven seat at Blankney was included in Mid Lincolnshire. Trollope was not so happy. He disliked having to lose Chaplin, and feared the voting strength of the new twelve-pound occupiers of Holland in the southern division.[17]

At first Stanhope intended to stand for Mid Lincolnshire, but in November 1867 he told Nisbet-Hamilton of his willingness to stand down in favour of Chaplin.[18] The claims of the latter to a county seat were exceptionally strong, and his adoption as candidate would certainly forestall any Liberal designs on the second seat.

Henry Chaplin (1840-1922) succeeded his uncle Charles in 1859. A keen sportsman, he was master of the Burton and later of the Blankney hounds. His racing enthusiasm brought him national as well as local fame when he won the Derby in 1867. And he had already won public sympathy at the time of the elopement of his intended wife, Lady Florence Paget, with the marquis of Hastings. Although a mere esquire, he

15 *Parl. Deb.* 3rd Ser. clxxxviii, 1285; Boundary Act 1868, 31 & 32 Vict., c. 46.

16 Edward Heneage (1840-1922), who s. his father G.F. Heneage in 1864, was M.P. (Lib.) for Lincoln, 1865-8, and Grimsby, 1880-92 and 1893-5. Chancellor of the Duchy of Lancaster, 1886; cr. baron Heneage, 1896.

17 When the boundary commissioners visited the county in the autumn of 1867 he tried to persuade them to give part of Holland to Mid Lincolnshire (*Stamf. Merc.*, 18 Oct. 1867).

18 Hughenden (Disraeli) MSS., B/XXI/S/531, Stanhope to Disraeli, n.d.

was a member of high society, and well placed to begin a successful career. He knew the Prince of Wales, and was a member of the Jockey Club, two avenues to political influence, though he was also to find them avenues to financial ruin. He had, moreover, a distinguished Conservative pedigree. His uncle had been a highly respected and influential county Member, and he himself became a friend of Lord Henry Bentinck and a protégé of Disraeli.[19] Unfortunately his attempts at Disraelian oratory were sustained by something less than Disraelian wit, and his total lack of humour blinded him to the mirth he caused in others.[20] Nevertheless he was to establish a certain position as a Conservative spokesman on agricultural affairs, and held minor office in the ministries of 1885, 1886-92 and 1895-1900.

His views in the 1860s placed him in a newer school of Conservatism than Stanhope and Nisbet-Hamilton. In 1865 he proposed Stanhope on the Lindsey hustings, perhaps somewhat to his discomfort, as a man 'amenable to constitutional progress and reform'. He was not above cultivating the working-class voters of Lincoln, which lay at the centre of the new mid division of Lincolnshire; and in October 1867 he presided over the formation of a Constitutional Registration Association for the city.[21] A similar organization for the mid division was contemplated in April 1868, when Chaplin was launched as a candidate.[22] But Nisbet-Hamilton probably thought it unnecessary to proceed with it in the absence of any Liberal bid for both seats.

Hamilton was right in supposing that moderate counsels would prevail in the Liberal party. The candidate from that side who had the strongest claim to represent the division was Amcotts. He was a man of substantial means, active in local and agricultural affairs, and of well-known, if moderate, Liberal views. Both sides knew that if he came forward with Chaplin a contest would be avoided, and this outcome was encouraged by Hamilton from the one side and William Monson, who had succeeded his father as seventh baron in 1862, on

19 See Chaplin's Introduction to Lord Henry Bentinck's *Foxhounds, and their Handling in the Field,* 1922.

20 Henry W. Lucy, *A Diary of the Salisbury Parliament,* 1886-92, p. 139; A.G. Gardiner, *Prophets, Priests and Kings,* new edition, 1914, pp. 212-19.

21 *Stamf. Merc.*, 4 Oct. 1867.

22 *Spalding Free Press,* 28 Apr. 1868.

the other.[23] Monson's only problem was Edward Heneage, who had been returned for Lincoln in 1865, but who was ambitious to become a county Member. Though more of a Liberal than his father, Edward Heneage was an equally shifty politician, and Monson no doubt wished to avoid those complications in Lincoln city politics which would inevitably follow Heneage's candidature for the county.[24]

Both Heneage and the Lincoln Liberals had to be conciliated, however, and the result was the creation of the Mid Lincolnshire Liberal association. Heneage took the chair at its first meeting in the spring of 1868. And Robert Toynbee, Monson's solicitor and former Lincoln agent for the North Lincolnshire Association, used what remained of the old machinery to circulate a requisition for Amcotts. The latter agreed to stand in July, when Heneage chaired a public meeting at Horncastle to present the requisition. Amcotts explained his views, and was then formally adopted. He stressed that he would support Gladstone's plans for the Irish Church, and declared himself willing to enter parliament as 'one of the rank and file of the Liberal party'.[25] All this was mere window-dressing, perhaps, but it served its purpose, and at the general election at the end of 1868 Chaplin and Amcotts were returned unopposed.

Sir Robert Sheffield had died in 1862, and Corbett, long inactive in county affairs, was to die in August 1868. Anderson and Nisbet-Hamilton were left, therefore, as the surviving leaders of the older generation of Conservatives in northern Lindsey.[26] Old-fashioned in their attitude to local politics, they exaggerated the declining power of the Yarborough interest, and were content to bring forward only one candidate for the new constituency of North Lincolnshire.

Their choice was, like that of Chaplin for the mid division, calculated to reduce the chances of a contest. Rowland Winn

[23] MON 25/13/14, Amcotts to Monson, 28 June 1868.
[24] Compare G.F. Heneage's desertion of his Lincoln constituents in 1834, p. 97 above.
[25] MON 25/13/18, Robert Toynbee to Monson, 17 July 1868; *Stamf. Merc.*, 24 July 1868.
[26] Nisbet- Hamilton owned no property in the new North Lincolnshire, but as former senior Member he was always deferred to in constituency matters.

(1820-93) of Appleby, near Brigg, was the son of Charles Winn of Nostell Priory, near Wakefield. An able business man, he had redeemed the family fortunes, and had had experience of party management in the West Riding of Yorkshire.[27] Once in parliament he was to prove a hard-working, if somewhat uninspiring, organizer and whipper-in for his party.[28]

Henry Chaplin, whose Tathwell estate lay in the division, H.R. Boucherett, the son of Ayscough Boucherett, and probably Winn himself all considered that a bid should be made for the second seat. Boucherett saw himself, indeed, as Winn's partner. But Anderson and Hamilton had their way. They did agree, however, to the formation of a Conservative Registration and Election Association. As its name implied, it was not just a mere registration machine, but was to have, ostensibly at least, 'the sole direction and management of all matters connected with the representation of the division'.[29]

Cholmeley had been absent from the local agricultural meetings in the autumn of 1866, and rumours of his retirement had begun to spread. By the early months of 1868, however, he had recovered some of his interest in politics. He brought his son out for Grantham in March, and around April appears to have agreed to stand again for North Lincolnshire.

In July a second Liberal candidate was under consideration for a few weeks. He was no urban radical, however, but a Liberal of more uncertain tone than Cholmeley. Colonel Tomline, a tory in 1841, had crossed by the Free Trade bridge into the Liberal camp. But his politics were mainly those of an independent agricultural Member, though he never achieved his ambition of a county seat for Suffolk or Lincolnshire. His Lindsey seat of Riby Grove lay near Grimsby, in which he built up an independent interest that had generally been opposed to those of Yarborough and Heneage.[30] In 1868, however, Yarborough turned to Tomline for help in throwing

[27] Nostell Priory (Winn) MSS., A/1/8/1, letters of Rowland to Charles Winn, 1838-73.

[28] He was a lord of the treasury, 1874-80, and on his retirement from active politics in 1885 was cr. baron St. Oswald.

[29] L.A.O., Burton Deposit, BS13/2/1/1.

[30] L.A.O., Daubney Deposit, IV/4. Grimsby, as the largest town and the only represented borough, was of considerably greater importance in the new than it had been in the old northern division of the county.

out the sitting Member for Grimsby. And Tomline, with at least half an eye on the county, had been putting himself forward for some months, mainly through the columns of the *Mercury*, as a champion of the farmers. He was a strong advocate of Chambers of Agriculture and county financial boards, and had secured the goodwill of at least two leading farmers and Brocklesby tenants in his neighbourhood, J.R. Kirkham and H.G. Skipworth.[31] But Edward Heneage was able to put a stop to Yarborough's machinations at Grimsby, probably by threatening an opposition,[32] and no doubt Cholmeley jibbed at the idea of running in harness with Tomline in North Lincolnshire. By the middle of July it was agreed, at a conference at Brocklesby, that Cholmeley should stand alone.[33]

It had probably been Monson's wish to keep the old North Lincolnshire Liberal Association as the organization for both the new north and mid divisions. But Yarborough did not wish to have anything to do with Mid Lincolnshire, and a new association was therefore started for the north.[34] Yarborough agreed to subscribe £50 a year, Angerstein and Cholmeley £21, Amcotts 10 guineas, and Lords Monson and Scarbrough £10. But from the start it was a half-hearted affair. Messrs Nicholson, Hett, and Freer went to work as principal agents. But their zeal was probably tempered by the knowledge that Yarborough was lukewarm, and that the Elwes family had become Conservative. The latter was a blow all the harder since Brigg was the polling town of the division. The district agents sent in gloomy reports of a lack of political feeling in the constituency, and indeed it was not surprising, when there was only one candidate standing, and that candidate Sir Montague. Had this state of affairs been known to the Conservatives there might have been renewed pressure on Anderson and Nisbet-Hamilton to agree to a contest. But, as it was, the election went off quietly, and Cholmeley and Winn, a rather incongruous pair, were unopposed.

31 STUBBS I/29, minutes of the North Lincolnshire Liberal Registration Association, 2 July 1868.

32 Heneage put on Yarborough what Tomline described to his Grimsby agent as 'irresistible pressure' (Daubney Deposit, IV/4/29, Tomline to W.H. Daubney, 6 July 1868).

33 STUBBS I/29, William Birkett (Yarborough's agent) to Thomas Freer, 11 July 1868.

34 STUBBS I/29, Yarborough to Hett, 16 Apr. 1868.

Packe, who had disappointed the reformers of South Lincolnshire in 1866, angered them in the spring of 1868 by his abstention on the Irish Church resolutions. In September 1868 he issued an address declaring his willingness to stand again. But he was known to be against Irish disestablishment, and the vagueness of his address suggested that he might be willing to vote against a Gladstonian government on that point. In answer to representations by the Liberals of Boston and Spalding he declared merely that he would support his party on 'all material points of a Liberal policy', and that only if it came to a question of confidence in the government would he positively vote in favour of Irish disestablishment.[35]

It was clearly Packe's design to conciliate his opponents more than his own more radical supporters. No preparation was made for a contest, and the association which had been formed to ensure Packe's return in 1859 had been allowed to become moribund. The Boston Liberals attempted to launch a new organization in September 1868, but it was too late to attend to that year's registration. Rather than launch a second Liberal candidate, therefore, most of those who remained dissatisfied with Packe nevertheless agreed to support him, rather than risk losing both seats to the Conservatives. Packe calculated upon this feeling, and also upon the timidity of some of his leading opponents. Trollope, who had retired to the Lords as Baron Kesteven in April 1868, was as usual reluctant to join battle. He and his successor to his seat, William Earle Welby,[36] agreed in July, at a meeting at Kesteven's London house, that only one candidate, Welby himself, should be brought forward at the general election. The Conservative whips expostulated to Stanhope and Hamilton, but they declined to interfere; and even a letter from Disraeli himself, complaining of 'the apathy and general want of energy, among our leading friends in your great county', had no effect.[37]

Both Packe and Trollope, however, had reckoned without the third earl Brownlow, a keen young Conservative politician,

35 *Spalding Free Press,* 22 Sept.-20 Oct. 1868.

36 W.E. Welby (1829-98) was M.P. for Grantham, 1857-68, and S. Lincs., 1868-84. He took the additional name of Gregory when he s. his father in 1874.

37 Casewick (Trollope) MSS., Disraeli to Kesteven, 29 June 1868; Hughenden (Disraeli) MSS., B/IX/G/59, Stanhope to Gerard Noel, 13 Nov. 1868.

who had succeeded his brother the previous year.[38] He arranged for H.F.C. Cust to take over Edmund Turnor's seat at Grantham, leaving the latter free to come forward as Welby's colleague for the county. Henry Chaplin almost certainly encouraged the movement, perhaps to atone for the lack of a contest in his own division.

Turnor was held back, however, until the day of nomination, when the emergence of a so-called second Liberal candidate gave the Conservatives the pretext they needed to start a canvass against Packe. The second Liberal was in fact no Liberal at all. He was John Taylor, a London solicitor with family connections in south Holland, who came forward at the last minute as an independent farmers' candidate. He was proposed by William Hunt, a leading farmer in Deeping Fen. In that area there was disgruntlement among the farmers, who were facing an exacerbated labour problem following the recent legislation on agricultural gangs. They also felt that with the retirement of Trollope the constituency would be represented by Kesteven residents who had few contacts with Holland.[39] Taylor was seconded, however, by a Spalding radical[40] who had remained unconvinced by Packe's Liberal protestations.

Taylor withdrew shortly after the nomination, but the Conservatives were already in full cry. Packe was left with the certainty of losing his seat, and lamented bitterly that he had been opposed by no fewer than three Conservatives. The decision of Kesteven's conference in July had been informally communicated to him, and he now maintained, supported by the Liberal press, that his opponents had been guilty of a breach of faith.[41] But in truth he had only himself to blame. He came a bad third in a low poll.

Welby	4,514
Turnor	4,078
Packe	2,714

The Conservative candidates both did better than their predecessors in 1857, and there was much more consistent

38 The 3rd earl (1844-1921) was M.P. for N. Salop, 1866-7. He s. Aveland as lord lieutenant of Lincolnshire in 1867.
39 *Spalding Free Press*, 13 Oct. 1868.
40 Charles Brett, a builder and a Wesleyan Reformer.
41 The *Daily News* took up his case.

party voting on the Conservative side. Welby headed the poll in all districts, and in no district did Turnor trail him by more than 100 votes, despite his late candidature and lack of strong personal influence.

Packe also benefited to some extent from the decline in cross-party voting. In the Bourne and Spalding districts he received plumpers from some of those Liberals who had split with Trollope in 1857. And at Heckington and Sleaford former Willson-Packe voters now voted for Packe only.[42] But if Packe benefited from the removal of these local influences, he found that his own local influence had very sadly declined. He lost votes in his own neighbourhood, where both Welby and Turnor had some local pull; and at Bourne he was said to have fallen from grace through his failure to bring a railway to the town from Sleaford. At Holbeach and elsewhere there were probably Liberal abstentions among the nonconformist electorate.

There was a significant increase in the Liberal vote at Spalding, which had seen more political activity in the 1860s than ever before, and which was conscious of its new importance as the returning town for the South Lincolnshire division. But this trend was not exhibited by the small market towns, such as Bourne and Holbeach. Nor did the borough Liberals of Grantham and Boston rally to the Liberal cause in the county. Grantham had possessed a Reform League since 1866, and in 1868 returned two Liberals unopposed. Nor were these Liberals—Hugh Cholmeley and the Hon. F. Tollemache—strangers to the county, but on the contrary men of considerable local connections. Yet Grantham parish produced only two plumpers for Packe, and nothing was done about canvassing the surrounding villages. The Grantham Liberals probably considered Packe tantamount to a Conservative, and did not see why they should stir a finger for him. The Liberals also did badly at Boston, where the Conservatives had by far the superior organization.

In the rural districts the decline of independent voting noticed in connection with the contest of 1857 had

[42] Of 23 Willson-Packe voters in 1857 who can be traced in the poll book of 1868, 16 plumped for Packe and only 3 split between Welby and Turnor. The other 4 split between Welby and Packe.

continued in the 1860s. The remains of the old Handley party in the urban parishes of Sleaford and Boston appear to have split between Packe and Welby. But, particularly in the grazing parts of the Bourne, Boston, and Holbeach districts, there was a swing to the Conservatives. Welby, like Trollope before him, took care to cultivate the graziers.[43]

Landed influence was as strong in the division in 1868 as it had been in 1857. But this time no landlord influenced his tenants to give cross-party votes. Of the 51 close parishes which voted regularly in 1868, 48 were Conservative and only 3 Liberal. Aveland exercised no influence, and the voting on his estate showed a Conservative tendency. Cholmeley, Nevile of Stubton, and the earl of Lindsey did what they could, but it was very little. The Conservative landlords, led by Brownlow, were most formidable in the Grantham region, and some of them, including both Turnor and Welby-Gregory, had increased their estates by purchase in the middle years of the century.

The new twelve-pound occupiers turned out to be less Liberally inclined than Lord Kesteven and others had feared. Indeed, only 29 per cent of them plumped for Packe, compared with 31 per cent of the whole electorate. This difference must be accounted for at least partly by registration peculiarities. In Kesteven tory landlords took care to get their small tenants on the register. In Holland many of the new voters abstained, and others were more Conservative in their voting than the freeholders and tenants, perhaps because they contained a larger proportion of farmers. In the open villages the new voters followed the pattern set by the old; and in the parishes under landlord influence the twelve-pound occupiers were just as regular in their voting as the fifty-pound tenants.

(iii) THE AGRICULTURAL INTEREST, 1857-68

The growing concern of Lincolnshire farmers with the local and national representation of their interests, in the

43 He regretted the failure of the Metropolitan Cattle Market bill of 1868, which he described, at a meeting at Benington, near Boston, as a measure designed to give 'more protection to the grazier' (*Boston Gazette*, 3 Oct. 1868).

years after 1859, was related to the difficulties through which their industry was passing at that time. The good times of the Crimean war period were not sustained in the later 1850s, and in 1859 low yields, low prices, and rising labour costs had combined to drain the capital of arable farmers. Prices improved in 1860 and 1861, but yields were again unsatisfactory. In 1863 an abundant crop raised the hopes of farmers that they would be able to recoup some of their losses. But an expensive harvest was followed by an autumn during which wheat prices ranged as low as 40*s*. 0*d*.

It was at this time that an agitation for the repeal of the malt tax began in Lincolnshire. Speeches on the subject were made at agricultural meetings in the autumn of 1863, and before and during the session of 1864 petitions were circulated in the Grantham neighbourhood, in the Isle of Axholme, and around Louth. At this latter place the Louth Agricultural Society was in communication with the Central Anti-Malt Tax Association in London. Marshall Heanley, of Croft, a leading man in the Louth society, put himself at the head of the Lindsey farmers, and several substantial wold farmers, including Brocklesby tenants, lent their support to the movement. Stanhope, who had been lukewarm on the subject in 1863, took care to keep abreast of feeling on the malt tax in 1864 and early 1865, and for a few months Lindsey saw something reminiscent of the farmers' movement of 1850-2.

There was certainly a fall in barley prices at this period, and in many Lincolnshire markets the demand for inferior barleys became particularly slack.[44] But the sheep and barley farmers of Kesteven, buoyed up by good stock and wool prices, did not lead the agitation of the 1860s as they had that of the 1830s. Indeed, many farmers supported the anti-malt tax movement who themselves grew little or no barley. In November 1863 Thomas Campbell, at the Owston Agricultural Society, spoke up for the suffering farmers of the Isle.

> They had hoped this year to make up somewhat for previous unfavourable seasons, but the low prices, both in wheat and potatoes—the staple commodities of the district—had doomed them to disappointment. The

[44] *Stamf. Merc.*, 27 Nov. 1863 (market intelligence).

abolition of the Malt Tax would not affect the farmers of the Isle so much as many others, not much barley being grown with them in comparison with other produce, but still if it would do them any good they would be thankful. And he was inclined to think they must be benefited even by a modification of the duty.[45]

The farmers wished to find a focus for their discontents. They liked to be against something, and it was no longer practicable to be against the Corn Laws. At first the question of the malt tax was raised by Liberals, such as Thomas Campbell himself, but in 1864 the movement was taken up by former protectionists. Indeed, some of the large farmers would have liked to hold forth on the Corn Laws had they dared, and their remarks on the malt tax had a distinctly protectionist savour. At the Caistor ploughing meeting in 1863 William Skipworth complained of the fiscal injustice whereby the English farmer paid a heavy excise duty on barley, whilst the foreigner could send cheap wheat into the country duty-free.[46] In November 1864, again at Caistor, T. Richardson of Winterton (a Conservative) spoke out for a duty on imported barley. He received some support from G.B. Skipworth of Moortown, despite Cholmeley's conviction that 'such a motion would be laughed out of the House'.[47]

Urban Liberals such as Charles Seely, who had once recommended the farmers to agitate for the repeal of the malt tax, now thought of good reasons why it should be retained. When R.L. Everitt, the Suffolk farmer and champion of the barley growers, came to lecture to Lincoln on the malt tax, he had a poor reception. One of his audience, 'a man who appeared as if he had just left the forge', attacked the cant of the farmers about cheap and wholesome beer. 'He did not believe they cared a straw whether the poor man had a shoe to his foot or not.'[48]

All four Lincolnshire Members supported the malt-tax resolution in the session of 1864,[49] and they found themselves once more in the same lobby in 1865, when they opposed the second reading of the Union Chargeability Bill. Again there was a conflict of interest between town and country, but this time the country was very much on the

[45] *Stamf. Merc.*, 27 Nov. 1863. [46] Ibid., 13 Nov. 1863.
[47] Ibid., 18 Nov. 1864. [48] *Stamf. Merc.*, 16 June 1865.
[49] *Parl. Deb.* 3rd Ser. clxxiv, 988 ff., 14 Apr. 1864.

defensive. The purpose of the bill was to make the poor of each union chargeable to the whole body of ratepayers in that union, instead of, as formerly, only to the ratepayers of the parish in which the pauper was settled. By this means it was hoped to remedy the system by which farmers and landowners kept their parochial burdens to a minimum, chiefly by neglecting to build adequate housing for their labourers. Instead they employed casual labour from neighbouring towns and open villages, whose ratepayers were then obliged to support large numbers of unemployed men when the farmers had no work for them.

Lincolnshire had many examples of this system, particularly on the Wolds and Heath and in parts of Holland such as Deeping Fen. And in several places the poor rate had been causing friction between town and country, especially in Holland. At Boston a rate-payers' association had been formed to campaign for greater urban representation on the board of guardians. The inhabitants of the town did not see why they should pay a rate of four or five shillings in the pound, while many surrounding rural parishes paid one shilling or less.[50]

The union chargeability movement was easily turned by Bright, Villiers, and others into a broad attack on the agricultural interest. Farmers were denounced not only for failing to build or repair cottages, but also for the low wages paid to labourers, and for the gang system whereby women and children were employed to perform operations such as weeding and stone-picking. Lincolnshire farmers indignantly rebutted the charges of the radicals. Under union chargeability, it was suggested by Cholmeley and others, farmers would cease to keep on labourers in winter, and would have less interest in keeping aged and deserving servants off the parish.[51] But these considerations, or rather threats, did not impede the passage of the bill.

The agricultural interest had a more encouraging experience, in terms of its parliamentary influence, in connection with the cattle plague agitation of 1865-6. Lincolnshire was not one of the worst-affected counties, but its farmers and

[50] S.C. Poor Law Administration, *Parl. Papers,* 1862, x, 327 ff.; *Parl. Deb.* 3rd Ser. clxxviii, 277 ff., 27 Mar. 1865; *Stamf. Merc.*, 19 Dec. 1862.

[51] *Stamf. Merc.*, 11 Nov. 1864, 21 July and 17 Nov. 1865.

graziers suffered heavy losses, particularly in Holland and the Lindsey Marshes.[52] Representatives went from the North Lincolnshire and Louth agricultural societies to a large London meeting on 8 February 1866. It demanded tighter restrictions on cattle movements and compensation for compulsory slaughter, and both demands were, in substance, conceded by the Cattle Diseases Prevention Act passed later that month. Stanhope claimed that the rapid passage of this legislation revealed the agricultural body, when they chose to unite, as 'a strong power in the country and in the Legislature'.[53]

The agitation also revealed that the farmers had no permanent machinery by means of which they could exercise pressure on parliament at the national level, or gather information and circulate petitions at the local. When the North Lincolnshire Agricultural Society met at Lincoln to hear a report of the London meeting, T. Richardson 'condemned that want of unanimity which prevented landlords and tenants binding themselves together for mutual protection'.[54]

The North Lincolnshire society had not been intended to participate in movements of this kind, and the Lincoln meeting was more reminiscent of the old Lincoln and Lindsey Agricultural Protection Society. The collapse of that body had been due not so much to the final expiry of the protectionist cause in 1852, as to the fact that in promoting Stanhope it had turned itself into a party organization. Its local societies had become, in effect, district election committees. Of them only the Louth society had survived, and that because it had been founded in May 1851, just too late to be involved directly in Stanhope's candidature. Even so, it became dormant in 1853, but was revived in 1860. Since then it had kept its political as well as agricultural character, and its role in the anti-malt tax movement has already been noticed.[55]

The national and county Chambers of Agriculture were intended to fill the void left by the failure of the old

52 Report of the Veterinary Department of the Privy Council, *Parl. Papers*, 1867-8, xviii, 219 ff.

53 *Stamf. Merc.*, 16 Nov. 1866.

54 Ibid., 23 Feb. 1866.

55 Heanley boasted in January 1865 that the society had funds to the sum of £1,500 (*Stamf. Merc.*, 3 Feb. 1865).

protectionist organizations. But, in Lincolnshire at least, the movement got off to a slow and feeble start. When the Lincolnshire Chamber was formally launched in June 1867, the farmers of the county, now enjoying better grain prices, took a less than enthusiastic interest. As a result the gentry who attended it, principally Amcotts, Stanhope, and Edward Heneage, had things very much their own way, and the proceedings were tame. There was no dominating issue to fill the place of Protection as a rallying cry, and the county Chamber was not supported by an adequate number of local committees in the market towns.[56]

At the general election of 1868 the chief agricultural questions discussed by the Lincolnshire candidates were the malt tax and county financial boards. But the malt tax movement had died down early in 1866. And the farmers were not greatly eager to be associated with the magistrates in levying the county rate. Some of the agriculturists—notably the few Liberals among them—had something to say on the theme of 'no taxation without representation'. But the county rate itself was one of the least of the farmers' financial worries. And Liberal magistrates such as Heneage were sensitive to aspersions cast on their administrative abilities. It is noteworthy that Amcotts, first chairman of the Lincolnshire Chamber of Agriculture, was perhaps the most tepid of all the county candidates in his views on both county boards and the malt tax.

(iv) CONSERVATIVE ASCENDANCY, 1868-74

In North Lincolnshire the Conservative Registration and Election Association quietly but efficiently went to work. The subscription list was headed by Winn, with £40, and Sheffield,[57] with £20, other landowners contributing smaller sums. The principal agent was J.F. Burton of Lincoln, whose

56 The Lincolnshire Chamber was slow in starting despite the efforts of John Algernon Clarke (1828-87), of Long Sutton, secretary to the Central Chamber in London. (For Clarke, who was later editor of *Bell's Weekly Messenger*, see his obituary in *The Times* of 19 Nov. 1887; also J.A. Scott Watson and May Elliott, *Great Farmers*, 1937, at p. 251.)

57 Sir Robert Sheffield (1824-86), 5th bart. The finances of the Sheffields, like those of the Winns, benefited considerably from the Frodingham and district ironstone developments.

family business had for many years held the principal Conservative agency for the whole county. District committees were formed to assist the sub-agents in registration work and the collection of subscriptions. A surviving registration return, compiled by Burton in 1869, shows impressive gains, particularly in the Isle of Axholme, where parochial as well as district committees had been established.[58]

In some quarters, however, there was dissatisfaction with the policy pursued by the party leaders. The Louth agent wrote to Burton in July 1870: 'As it appears from what happened at the last election that our leaders have no intention of fighting we do not pledge ourselves to continue our subscription to the fund.'[59] The grumblers were appeased in 1872, however, when a delegates' meeting of the association agreed to launch a second candidate at the next election. The favoured candidate was J.B. Astley, of Everley, Wiltshire, son-in-law of the late T.G.Corbett. But Astley was too poor, and too lacking in political enthusiasm, to risk the possibility of a contest.[60] When both he and Cary Elwes declined, the association adopted H.R. Boucherett.

The Liberal organization in the division presents a sad, and an instructive, contrast. The subscription list shrank until by 1873 the association could not have carried on without Yarborough's £50 and Cholmeley's £20. The district agents, whose salaries had been cut in 1870, ceased to earn even their reduced wages; and the secretary, Edward Peacock of Bottesford, deserted to the Conservatives. After the general election of 1874 Yarborough allowed the association to collapse altogether, and from then onwards Thomas Freer of Brigg, the principal agent, did no further registration work.[61]

Instead of finding a second candidate to meet the Conservative challenge in 1872, Yarborough failed to find a replacement for Cholmeley, who was anxious to retire. Late in 1873 J.R. Kirkham informed Freer that Viscount Melgund, son of the third earl of Minto, was thinking of coming

58 L.A.O., Burton Deposit, BS 13/2/1/2; Taylor, Glover and Hill Deposit, TGH/4/Box 1.

59 BS 13/2/1/10, T.F. Allison to J.F. Burton, 22 July 1870.

60 He had not yet succeeded to his father's Wiltshire estates, and he held the Elsham estate in trust for his son. What money he had he spent on horse-racing (Sir. J.D. Astley, *Fifty Years of my Life*, 1894, ii, 91-2).

61 STUBBS I/29.

forward.[62] But after making a few enquiries he wisely changed his mind.

Cholmeley died suddenly in January 1874, and the Liberals of Louth and the Isle were indignant to learn that Yarborough had ready no successor. Cholmeley's death was followed almost immediately by the dissolution of parliament. Astley changed his mind about standing, now that there was the likelihood of a walk-over, poor Boucherett agreed to stand down, and Winn and Astley were returned unopposed at the general election.

The abdication of the whig party in the north division was paralleled by a similar débâcle in the mid. Amcotts became increasingly out of sympathy with the Gladstone government of 1868-74. He abstained on the third reading of the Ballot Bill in 1872, and after the session informed the Liberal association of his wish to retire from parliament at the next dissolution. He thought that Heneage might like to fill his place, but that gentleman withheld his assistance. Nor would Monson come to the aid of the association.[63]

Amcotts meanwhile had notified the Conservatives of his decision to retire, and they proceeded to adopt a second candidate. The obvious choice was the Hon. Edward Stanhope, second son of the fifth earl Stanhope, and adopted heir of James Banks Stanhope.[64] He was already known to the county through his work as one of the assistant commissioners on the employment of women and children in agriculture. He and Chaplin, like Winn and Astley, were returned unopposed in 1874.

In the southern division of the county Welby proved himself an active agricultural Member, somewhat in the style of Trollope, though lacking those opportunities for private Members which had been available in Trollope's time. Turnor, on the other hand, did not distinguish himself either by his activity in parliament or by his amiable condescension towards his constituents. But it could not be denied that he

62 Melgund (later, as 4th earl of Minto, Governor-General of Canada and afterwards Viceroy of India) had retired from the army in 1870, and hunted the Brocklesby country for a time.

63 *Stamf. Merc.*, 13 and 20 Sept. 1872.

64 Edward Stanhope (1840-93) was M.P. for Mid Lincs., 1874-85, and the Horncastle division, 1885-93. He held various government posts from 1875, principally that of Secretary of State for War, 1887-92.

was a good practical agriculturist, and a ready participant in local and county affairs.

There was no association to support Welby and Turnor. But there was an efficient registration committee, well served by district agents, and handsomely oversubscribed by the numerous Conservative nobility and gentry of the division.[65] The Liberals, on the other hand, lacking influential support and energetic leadership, failed to put their rickety house in order after the defeat of 1868. The Boston Liberals, who had themselves suffered a setback in 1868, were even less inclined than usual to assist the county movement, and Spalding by itself could do nothing. The consequence was that with an unfavourable register and a non-existent organization, no Liberal candidate could be attracted to the constituency in 1874.[66] Thus in the south as well as the north and mid divisions the Lincolnshire Conservatives were triumphant.

This triumph was in spite of the Ballot Act, which its more radical advocates had hoped would weaken the power of the tory landlords in the agricultural districts. Since there were no contests for the Lincolnshire divisions in 1874, it is hard to assess the effect of the measure. But, to judge from the elections of 1880 and 1885, it did little to undermine the traditional patterns of tenant voting. In 1872 it neither dismayed the Lincolnshire tories nor noticeably heartened their opponents.[67] Its principal effect was probably to increase the disapproval with which the Liberal landowners regarded the Gladstone administration, and encourage them to withdraw their active support from the party at the following general election. Along with the ballot came a proliferation of polling districts, but the Lincolnshire Liberals lacked the organization to take advantage of any help this might have given them.

The Conservatives were also favoured by another corollary of the ballot, the abolition of the ceremony of public nomination. In times past—in South Lincolnshire in 1841,

65 Casewick (Trollope) MSS., registration accounts for 1872-3. In these years the income was about £480 and the expenditure only £180. Aveland's name appears among the leading subscribers.

66 *Stamf. Merc.*, 30 Jan. 1874.

67 Amcotts was surprised that he had received no petitions on the subject. Neither had Chaplin (*Stamf. Merc.*, 11 Nov. 1871).

for instance—last-minute candidates had emerged to challenge the choice of the party leaders. Such movements were rarely successful, but after 1872 they became even less of a substitute for the carefully planned and organized campaign.

In 1874 the dissolution came suddenly, catching the Liberals unawares, but even if they had been prepared with candidates for the Lincolnshire divisions they would have met with scant success. The farmers were too preoccupied with the labour problem to spare much thought for party politics. In 1872 the urban movements for higher wages and shorter hours had spread to the villages of Lincolnshire, and an outbreak of local strikes had been followed by the emergence of extensively organized union movements. By January 1874, their courage raised by good wheat prices and a greater abundance of labour, the farmers were about to hit back. For the time being, however, the question had little impact at the level of parliamentary politics, largely because so few labourers had the vote. True, the union leaders were beginning to demand household suffrage in the counties, but the threat to the electoral predominance of the farmers was still a distant one. Farmers like H.G. Skipworth saw no inconsistency between their anti-unionism and their Liberal principles.[68] In some counties the harassed agriculturists may have resorted to the promotion of independent tenant farmer candidates to defend their interests.[69] But movements of that kind were probably fostered as much by feeling on the tenant-right issue as by the labour question. In Lincolnshire there was little interest in proposals for tenant-right legislation. And over the strikes and lockouts the landlords generally supported the farmers against the labourers, if not always as firmly as the farmers would have liked.[70] Besides which, although tenant farmer candidates were supposed to be non-party, it is hard to imagine one of them standing against two tories in any of the Lincolnshire divisions.

68 He was among the large wold farmers who organized a lockout in the spring of 1874. Earlier he had been surprised to find disaffection among his own men (*Stamf. Merc.*, 19 Apr. 1872).

69 E.g. the candidatures of George Storer for South Nottinghamshire, and B.B. Hunter Rodwell for Cambridgeshire in 1874.

70 Heneage, like some other Liberal landowners, was publicly in favour of a compromise in 1874. But it was reported that privately he had taken measures against the union movement (*Labourers' Union Chronicle*, 18 July 1874).

The Conservatives of Lincolnshire carried off a prize in 1874 that might have been theirs in 1868, had their leaders at that time been less concerned with the peace of the county and less frightened of the twelve-pound occupiers. But, apart from personalities and tactics, the victories of 1874 did no more than reflect an almost universal Conservative feeling among the farmers and landowners of the county, a feeling that had been gathering strength since the early 1860s, and which, despite appearances, was to persist to a great extent in the countryside during the following years.

12

THE SPREAD OF URBAN LIBERALISM, 1874-1885

(i) THE LIBERAL REVIVAL IN NORTH LINCOLNSHIRE 1874-80

THE THIRD earl of Yarborough died in 1875, leaving as his heir a boy of sixteen. The chief political influence on the young earl was that of his step-grandfather, Lord Monson, who brought him up as a Liberal, and secured his election to Brooks's Club while still an undergraduate at Cambridge. He did not come of age until July 1880, but, on Monson's advice, he made his début in Lincolnshire politics in April 1879, when he attended a meeting of the Grimsby Liberal Association.[1] The chairman of the meeting was Edward Heneage, who announced his return to active politics after four years of semi-retirement, and who made it clear that the meeting had reference to county as well as borough politics. He promised to 'assist to the utmost of his power to bring about an alteration in the representation of the northern division of the county', and even offered to stand himself if no other candidate could be found. Yarborough's brief speech made a good impression: 'His ancestors he said had been Liberals, and he considered it only his duty . . . to belong to the same party, and to do everything in his power to support that party.'[2]

In September 1879 delegates from various parts of the division met at Grimsby to appoint a registration agent, and to send a deputation to Heneage inviting him to stand.

Heneage, however, had already given up the Liberal cause in North Lincolnshire as a bad job. Late in April he had gone to address the Liberals of Louth on agricultural politics, but had been received with little enthusiasm. And it became apparent that the revival of the Brocklesby interest inaugurated at the Grimsby meeting had faltered and failed. He wrote to Wintringham, his Grimsby agent, in July 1879:

[1] MON 25/13/21. [2] *Stamf. Merc.*, 21 Apr. 1879.

As regards North Lincolnshire I think it is quite hopeless to attempt to fight it, though it might be worthwhile to start a candidate and see what came of it; the electors seem to have gone to sleep and the Brocklesby interest broken; the farmers do not care two pins for party politics and are playing a waiting game; I am given to understand that the Brocklesby tenants and farmers do not desire a contest at the *next* election, and advise Lord Yarborough to keep quite still.[3]

Heneage, who was brother-in-law to the third earl's widow, was aware that all was not well on the Brocklesby estate. Lady Yarborough herself had no strong political feelings. The trustees, who were Sir Charles Anderson, her brother, and herself, had no desire to revive the old interest. And they had made themselves unpopular by an unwise exercise of their power of distraint. There was more bitterness in the autumn of 1879, when some of the tenants lost their shooting rights to Sir John Astley.[4]

Heneage was not the only pessimist among the old guard of the Lindsey Liberals. When Monson wrote to G.C. Uppleby of Barrow in December 1879, inviting him to assist in the reorganization of the division, he replied: 'No one can object to the present government more than I do, but in all North Lincolnshire I don't know of half a dozen men who are not either Tories or Jingos or are totally indifferent to politics.'[5]

Uppleby and Heneage must have been surprised when, in April 1880, the Liberal party recovered one of the North Lincolnshire seats. The victory was the culmination of a movement which owed next to nothing to whig leadership or agricultural support. Its character from the first was largely urban and nonconformist.

Louth and Gainsborough were the first towns to form Liberal Associations after the general election of 1874. C.R. Farmer, an ironfounder and merchant, was made president of the Gainsborough association, and its first meeting was chaired by Charles Shipham, a miller and corn merchant.[6] At Louth the lead was taken by Dr. Sharpley, W.R. Emeris, and Saville Smith, veterans of municipal

[3] L.A.O., Heneage MSS., 2 HEN 2.

[4] 2 HEN 2, Heneage to J. Wintringham jun., 19 Feb. 1879; *Stamf. Merc.*, 12 Sept. 1879, 23 July 1880. Professor Hanham has no justification for saying (*Elections and Party Management*, p. 27) that during the minority the estate 'fell into the hands of strong opponents of the Beaconsfield government'.

[5] MON 25/13/1/27/5.

[6] *Stamf. Merc.*, 12 June, 2 Oct. 1874.

politics, whom Heneage considered were 'of *no* influence at all', but who were in fact widely respected in the division.[7]

In 1879 further associations were formed at Rasen, Barton, and Brigg. The Rasen body was started with assistance from Louth, and its chairman was Joseph Wilson, a tradesman and the chairman of the Local Board. Amcotts, Angerstein, and Heneage were invited to the inaugural meeting, but none of them came.[8] At Brigg the lead was taken by George Jackson, the printer, and J.H. Sergeant, of A.M. Sergeant and Co., brewers and maltsters. At Barton the leading men were a carrier, a solicitor, and a chemist. They appear to have received encouragement from the Liberals of Hull.[9]

It was the Grimsby Liberal Association, however, which endeavoured to unite the party in the division. It had been reorganized in 1878 by the blue party in the borough, and its inception had owed nothing to Heneage. Its meeting in April 1879 was not inspired by Heneage, and indeed he was at first suspicious of it.[10] Likewise the delegates' meeting in September was not a revival of the old North Lincolnshire Liberal Association, but an assembly convened by the Grimsby party and representing the several associations of the division.

Since 1876 the nonconformists of Lincolnshire had been increasingly active in politics. Most of the towns of the northern division held meetings to protest against the Turkish atrocities in 1876,[11] and in 1877 the burials question excited sectarian feeling. The temperance movement, after a lull from 1872 to 1876, found a new lease of life, and from 1877 speakers from the Liberation Society found ready audiences in Lindsey, especially in Louth and the nearby villages in the Marsh.

As elsewhere in the country, it was the Wesleyans and Congregationalists as well as the Baptists who became more militant in the late 1870s, and this had an important effect on North Lincolnshire politics. C.R. Farmer of Gainsborough came of a strongly Wesleyan family. Joseph Bennett of

[7] 2 HEN 2, Henage to J. Wintringham jun., 19 Feb. 1879; *Stamf. Merc.*, 4 Dec. 1874, 14 and 21 Mar. 1879.

[8] *Stamf. Merc.*, 21 and 28 Mar. 1879.

[9] *Stamf. Merc.*, 13 June 1879.

[10] 2 HEN 2, Heneage to Wintringham, 27 Mar. 1879.

[11] For which see R.T. Shannon, *Gladstone and the Bulgarian Agitation*, 1963.

Louth, who around 1880 became a prominent figure in Lindsey politics, was a Wesleyan circuit steward.[12] J.H. Sergeant of Brigg was the leading Congregationalist of the town. The only village in the division to have a Liberal association at this time was Goxhill, a stronghold of the Primitive Methodists.

Developments in the Wesleyan connexion, since they affected the farmers' vote in North Lincolnshire, deserve particular attention. Christopher Wordsworth, who became bishop of Lincoln in 1868, did much to worsen the relations of the Wesleyan Methodists with the Established Church. In 1873 he issued a pastoral which professed to desire the reunion of the Wesleyans with the Church, but it was couched in terms that they could not but find offensive.[13] The Revd. William Hudson, a Wesleyan minister of Lincoln, published a reply, in which he stated: 'If this "pastoral" drive the Methodists into active and avowed dissent, the fault will not lie at their door'.[14] The following year Wordsworth was involved in a widely-noticed controversy touching the burials question. He upheld the action of the vicar of Owston in refusing to allow the title of reverend to be used on the tombstone of a Methodist preacher's daughter.[15]

In 1879 the *Mercury* carried a large correspondence about the persecution endured by the Wesleyans of Bag Enderby, near Spilsby, from the squarson of their parish. The case suggests that there was some substance in contemporary Wesleyan claims that 'bigotry and intolerance' were often met with in rural parishes.[16]

Heneage did not give a definite refusal to the North Lincolnshire Liberals in the autumn of 1879, and as late as March 1880 they still hoped that he would come out for the county. But on the dissolution of parliament in the latter month, he decided to stand for Grimsby, and they found

12 M.P. for the Gainsborough division of Lincolnshire, 1885-6 and 1892-5. His family had a timber merchant's business at Grimsby.

13 Christopher Wordsworth, *A Pastoral to the Wesleyan Methodists, with a Friendly Appeal on the Owston Epitaph,* Lincoln, 1875.

14 Revd. William Hudson, *An Answer to Bishop Wordsworth's Pastoral*, 3rd edn., Lincoln, 1873.

15 Owston had a strong Liberal and nonconformist tradition.

16 *Stamf. Merc.*, 23 May 1879; [Thomas Hayes], *Methodism: a Review,* 1879, pp. 93-114.

themselves in consequence without a candidate. There was a series of consultations among their leaders, in which Saville Smith, Joseph Bennett of Louth, his brother Henry Bennett of Grimsby, and Charles Shipham of Gainsborough appear to have taken the leading parts. But it was not until the day of nomination that they were finally successful in finding a champion.[17]

Robert Laycock (1833-81) was not a Lincolnshire resident, nor did he come from the class from which that county had been accustomed to choose its representatives. He was the son of a rich Northumberland coal owner, and lived at Wiseton, near Bawtry, in Nottinghamshire. But Wiseton was not far from Gainsborough and the Isle of Axholme, so that he was not a complete stranger in all parts of North Lincolnshire. And he was a man of some political experience. He had stood for North Nottinghamshire in 1872, and it was probably after his failure to be adopted as Liberal candidate for that division in the spring of 1880 that he decided to cross the county border. His politics were firmly Gladstonian, and he advocated the usual programme of an extension of household suffrage to the counties, the creation of county boards, and the reform of the land laws.[18]

He brought with him his agent G.W. Hodgkinson, who, in co-operation with the new associations of the division as well as the old professional agents, appears to have made good use of the few days between the nomination and the poll. The Conservatives, on the other hand, were reported to have let their organization run down.[19] Winn was too busy in the whips' office, and Astley, who had proved himself a singularly incompetent, not to say fatuous, Member, took little interest in party business. The result, though close, was an humiliation for both of them:

Laycock	4,151
Winn	3,946
Astley	3,856

Laycock received the blessing of Yarborough, Heneage, Angerstein, St. Albans, and others. Heneage himself was too

17 *Louth Times*, 10 Apr. 1880.

18 *Retford, Worksop, Isle of Axholme and Gainsborough News*, 6 Apr. 1880; William Saunders, *The New Parliament*, 1880.

19 *Lincs. Chron.*, 16 Apr. 1880.

busy at Grimsby to be of much assistance. But care was taken to let it be known that Brocklesby was on the Liberal side. Yarborough wrote to Monson on 8 April: '. . . I am sure it is well known here that our sympathies are with Mr. Laycock, . . . and from what I hear I should say that Mr. Laycock and Sir John Astley will be returned, and Mr. Winn turned out.'[20] At a Caistor meeting C.M. Nainby of Barnoldby-le-Beck declared from the chair that

> he had always supported and backed up the Yarborough interest, which had been Liberal for generations past. He had heard very gratifying accounts of the canvass on behalf of Mr. Laycock, and the present Lord Yarborough had assured him that if he had the power to vote he should have supported the Liberal candidate.[21]

But apart from Nainby, who had in any case always been a Grimsby rather than a county politician, there was little sign of Liberal enthusiasm from the Brocklesby tenants. H.G. Skipworth and J.R. Kirkham, who might have rallied them, were dead. Many may have split between Laycock and Astley, the local favourite.[22] One leading tenant, William Frankish of Great Limber, certainly made no bones about his Conservatism. At another Caistor meeting, this time for the Conservatives, J.W. Dixon 'congratulated his party upon the security of their present position in this locality, which was formerly a hot centre of their opponents'.[23]

Among the leaders of the Lindsey farming community there was scarcely one who spoke out for Laycock, excluding those who, like John Hay of South Reston, supported him at least partly on religious grounds. Where good Liberal village meetings were reported in the local press, they were generally in Methodist parishes, such as Haxey and Epworth in the Isle of Axholme; Messingham and Scotter near Gainsborough; and marsh villages near Louth, such as Covenham, Grainthorpe, and North Somercotes. But the real strength of Laycock was his support in Gainsborough, Grimsby, and Louth. Liberalism was particularly strong at Louth at this election, and its co-operation with Grimsby was of great importance in the

[20] MON 25/13/21, Yarborough to Monson, 8 Apr. 1880.

[21] *Stamf. Merc.*, 16 Apr. 1880. Professor Hanham takes this speech too nearly at its face value, and is followed by Dr. T. Lloyd (Trevor Lloyd, *The General Election of 1880*, Oxford, 1968, p. 71 n.).

[22] *Doncaster Gazette*, 16 Apr. 1880.

[23] *Stamf. Merc.*, 2 Apr. 1880.

contest.[24] Scunthorpe was not yet a large town, and its iron industry had recently suffered in the general economic depression. But it sent representatives to the Liberal committee at Brigg, and at least one of its ironmasters gave active support to Laycock.[25]

The labourers in the country districts were mostly unenfranchised, as already stated. But between 1874 and 1880 their union organizations had turned to political rather than economic agitation. They brought Liberal politicians from outside the county to the platforms of large labourers' meetings at Market Rasen and elsewhere, and they brought to the villages that political education and commitment which had formerly been the virtual prerogative of the towns. It was reported in 1880 that those North Lincolnshire labourers who did have the vote were overwhelmingly Liberal.[26]

(ii) AGRICULTURAL DEPRESSION AND NORTH LINCOLNSHIRE POLITICS, 1876-81

A run of poor seasons and expensive harvests, unaccompanied by compensating rises in the price of corn, began in 1875. In the autumn of 1876 the large Lincolnshire landowners began to make rent remittances, and by November Edmund Turnor could tell an agricultural audience that 'he feared they were now only beginning to experience the full operation of the free trade measures which were carried thirty years ago.'[27] Little improvement took place in 1877, and the harvest of 1878, on which many farmers had put their hopes of financial recovery, proved a bitter disappointment. By the end of September best red wheat was fetching only 38*s.* 0*d.* at Spalding, and 'immense quantities' of grain were reported to be on their way from America.

During this autumn a protectionist correspondence began to appear in the columns of the *Mercury*. One of the first farmers to speak out was William Chatterton of Hallington, a Chaplin tenant, at the Louth Christmas Fatstock Show in December. He thought that 'something ought to be done at once to protect our native industry.'[28]

[24] *Gainsborough News*, 13 Apr. 1880; *Louth Times*, 17 Apr. 1880.
[25] *Grimsby News*, 9 Apr. 1880. [26] *Louth Times*, 17 Apr. 1880.
[27] *Stamf. Merc.*, 24 Nov. 1876. [28] Ibid., 20 Dec. 1878.

The harvest of 1879 was again difficult to secure and poor in yield, the wheat crop on the cold lowland clays being a disaster. Near Market Rasen the last of the corn was still ungathered when the first snow of the winter fell early in November. Protectionist speeches were well received at the Lincolnshire Agricultural Society in July and later in the autumn at Louth. More significant, however, was the speech of William Frankish of Great Limber at the Grimsby fatstock show in December, in which he combined a sympathy with tenant farmers' grievances with an openly expressed desire for the return of Protection. It could not escape Chaplin's notice that Frankish was a leading tenant of the Yarborough trustees, under whom he held almost 1,900 acres in two large farms. The case of Frankish suggested that the wold farmers were in difficulties as well as the lowland ones, and that sheep and barley were not profitable enough to offset the losses on corn. Frankish had already attracted wide attention by his advocacy of an import duty upon barley to replace the malt tax, and of the compulsory slaughter of all foreign cattle at the ports of entry, in order to protect the home breeder from the importation of disease.[29]

Chaplin also had his eye on another aspect of the rural problem. He wrote to Disraeli on 15 August 1879:

> There is a large district in my own county, commencing with the Isle of Axholme, and extending pretty well all through the Marshes from the Humber to the Wash, where many old estates have been sold and broken up and are now replaced by an infinite number of small holdings and an incredible number of small freeholds, with no game, no resident proprietors, no large places or estates, and in fact where Mr. Bright's 'beau ideal' is in existence already. I have had it partly surveyed on my own account already, and the result of my private enquiries, which are not yet quite completed, lead me to believe that we can shew the system to have 'utterly broken down'. The freeholders are mortgaged up to their eyes, and one of my informants writes this morning, 'hundreds of them must fail and be sold up this year'.[30]

The men of the Isle were depressed in spite of the absence among them of those legal restrictions on the transfer of property which were a favourite theme of the radicals.

29 Iddesleigh MSS., Addit. MSS. 50,052, f. 88, Sir Stafford Northcote to Rowland Winn, 23 June 1875; *Stamf. Merc.*, 19 Dec. 1879; *Parl. Papers,* 1881, xvii, pp. 652 ff.

30 Hughenden (Disraeli) MSS., B/XXI/C/155.

Moreover, the Axholme smallholders could prove a point in county as well as national politics, as Chaplin had learnt long ago from his mentor J.B. Stanhope.

On 30 May 1879 the Lincolnshire Chamber, despite the advice of its president Lord Ripon,[31] voted to support Chaplin's Commons motion on agricultural depression. On 4 July he moved in the House for the appointment of a royal commission on the subject, arguing that there was sufficient evidence of distress to give pause for thought to the most convinced free trader. 'The business of farming', he stated, 'is at present apparently ceasing to pay', and he referred to 'many persons I know' who had become converts to reciprocity or 'fair trade'.[32] After his speech it could be said that Protection, at least in his own party, had become an open question. At Alford, in November 1879, he went so far as to suggest that if American imports continued to grow 'the question of Protection would again have to be seriously considered.'

> No country situated as England was could afford to be dependent on foreign countries for its people's food . . . . The cry of cheap food was a most misleading one, and . . . food so cheap that it could only be bought at the expense of home cultivation would be about the dearest and most ruinous commodity which this country could buy in the markets of the world.[33]

Having secured the royal commission, however, Chaplin could not very well anticipate its conclusions, and at the time of the general election it had not yet begun to report its evidence. At the annual meeting of the Lincolnshire Chamber in January 1880 he contented himself with a speech in favour of a barley duty and a registration duty on corn. And in April he took a very moderate line on the Mid Lincolnshire hustings. Neither he nor Stanhope wished to excite an opposition. And Chaplin had a further reason for caution, in that his brother was standing for the largely free trading constituency of Lincoln.

Winn and Astley, on the other hand, were not afraid to utter the word Protection. Astley in particular spoke his mind,

31 George Frederick Samuel Robinson (1827-1909) was M.P. (Lib.) for Hull, 1852-3, Huddersfield, 1853-7, and Yorks. W.R., 1857-9. He s. his father as 2nd earl of Ripon in 1859, and was cr. marquis of Ripon in 1871. 7,102 acres in Lincs., 1873; seat Nocton, near Lincoln.

32 *Parl. Deb.* 3rd Ser. ccxlvii, 1425.

33 *Stamf. Merc.*, 21 Nov. 1879.

and his address announced that he would 'hail with satisfaction any proposition that may tend to impose a moderate duty on foreign produce, so long as the price of the poor man's loaf will not be raised thereby.' He had already told the Lincolnshire Agricultural Society, in July 1879, that he could see no cure for the depression other than 'having a duty imposed on corn'. Winn was more cautious, and his references to the plight of agriculture were meteorological rather than political. But even he declared that, 'though not absolutely condemning free trade, he thought it fostered many perils that might be avoided by a wise legislative restriction, as for instance on the introduction of American pork and other articles which had occasioned disease and danger amongst many people of this country.'[34]

After the general election the prompt legislation by the Gladstone government on the malt tax and ground game somewhat subdued the Lincolnshire Conservatives. In the first six months of 1881, with slowly rising wheat prices and good harvest prospects, the county Chamber of Agriculture returned to a consideration of local problems—railway rates, fen drainage, cattle disease, and tenant-right valuation. But the harvest was delayed by treacherous weather, and corn yields were lighter than expected.

It was at this juncture, in August 1881, that the sudden death of Laycock was announced. The divisional Conservative association, which had been remodelled after the general election, met at Brigg, and, after failing to secure a local man, entrusted Winn and Chaplin with the task of finding a candidate.[35] Their choice was James Lowther (1840-1904), second son of Sir C.H. Lowther, third baronet, and a distant cousin of the Lowthers of Cumberland and Westmorland, earls of Lonsdale.[36] They were no doubt glad to find a seat for a former minister who had been put out of parliament at the general election. But Chaplin, who knew Lowther socially and through the turf, was also eager to launch him as a thinly disguised protectionist.[37] Since the general election the royal

[34] *Stamf. Merc.*, 2 Apr. 1880. [35] Ibid., 26 Aug. 1881.
[36] M.P. for York, 1865-80, N. Lincs., 1881-5, and the Isle of Thanet, 1888-1904; Chief Secretary for Ireland, 1878-80.
[37] Rt. Hon. J.W. Lowther, *A Speaker's Commentaries*, 1925, i. 137, ii. 84.

commission had published some of its evidence; William Frankish had told the commissioners his tale of woe;[38] and one of the assistant commissioners, S.B.L. Druce, had prepared a report on the Isle of Axholme which fully confirmed Chaplin's conclusions.[39] Lowther's principal interest in politics was the fiscal question, and he had stood for East Cumberland in February 1881 as a strong advocate of 'fair trade'. Chaplin, after consultations with the Louth committee of the North Lincolnshire association, was able to assure him that he would be well received.[40]

Lowther arrived in the constituency not long before the day of nomination, but he made a brisk and spirited tour of the principal market towns. At Rasen he came out firmly for a 'reasonable' duty on corn. At Louth he was not so outspoken, but his chief supporter, W.L. Mason the auctioneer, followed him with a strong protectionist speech. At Caistor, significantly enough, he urged Protection for the barley growers, and Chaplin gave the slogan 'Vote for Lowther and fair trade and no diseased cattle'.

Meanwhile the earl of Yarborough had come of age. He took his seat in the Lords, and was asked by Granville to second the address at the start of the session of 1881, the proposer being Lord Carrington, another Lindsey proprietor.[41] On 26 January 1881 a grand banquet was held at Grimsby to inaugurate a new Liberal association for North Lincolnshire. Yarborough spoke in praise of recent government legislation with reference to burials, game, and the malt tax. And among the distinguished company were St. Albans, Monson, Carrington, Heneage, and Laycock.[42]

The prime mover had been Monson, whose object was to revive the old Yarborough interest in the division, and to replace in whig hands the leadership of the Liberal movement in Grimsby, Louth, and elsewhere. At Grimsby, of course, it was necessary to secure the goodwill of Heneage. But Monson's work was assisted by the fact that Heneage was settled in parliament and no longer a possible county candidate, as well as by the fact that Heneage's high shrievalty, which he had

[38] *Parl. Papers,* 1881, xviii, pp. 652 ff. [39] *Parl. Papers,* 1881, xvi, pp. 386-94.
[40] *Stamf. Merc.*, 26 Aug. 1881.
[41] MON 25/13/21, Yarborough to Monson, 30 Dec. 1880.
[42] *Stamf. Merc.*, 28 Jan. 1881.

taken in 1880, precluded him from much participation in county politics. The foundation of the reconstructed Liberal party in the division was thus a Grimsby alliance between the Yarborough, Heneage, and blue parties. Elsewhere the whig revival had not been so successful. On Monson's advice Yarborough had written to invite Amcotts and Sir Hugh Cholmeley to attend the banquet, but both had declined. The former was now a Conservative, and the latter had ceased to interest himself in Lindsey politics. The duke of St. Albans and Lord Carrington were not figures of much local influence, being connected chiefly with other counties.

Laycock, himself very far from being a whig, must have found his position an uneasy one, whilst his tenure of the North Lincolnshire seat no doubt increased Monson's difficulties in reviving the Yarborough interest. But Laycock's death in August 1881 presented an opportunity of appeasing those moderate and 'agricultural' Liberals who had declined to exert themselves at the general election.[43] In particular it was felt necessary to soothe the Brocklesby tenants. Hence, when the North Lincolnshire Liberal Association assembled under Heneage's chairmanship on 19 August, it was decided to invite Colonel Tomline to stand.

On 29 August Tomline received a deputation at the Yarborough Hotel in Grimsby. He declared himself in favour of county financial boards and an extension of the county franchise, and in reply to a question from Saville Smith of Louth said that he was not in principle opposed to Local Option or Sunday closing. Difficulties emerged, however, when Heneage enquired whether he would give Gladstone a 'thorough, consistent and hearty support'.

Tomline: I will support his policy, with the insertion of the word independent.
Heneage: What you mean is that you will not be an extreme man.
Tomline: No, I never was extreme.
Heneage: You will understand that we desire, as far as possible, to unite all sections of the Liberal party in this county. We have got men of all shades of opinion, and therefore we must be satisfied.
Tomline: I have lived long enough in the world to learn to give and take.[44]

43 Heneage, writing to Wintringham on 6 Sept. 1881, described Tomline as 'a purely agricultural Liberal' (2 HEN 2).
44 *Stamf. Merc.*, 26 Aug. 1881.

This was a bad start. The townsmen discovered that he was lukewarm on the Irish question (as indeed were Heneage and Yarborough), and that on county government and the county franchise his views were barely distinguishable from those of, say, Rowland Winn. The agriculturists were even less favourably impressed. At Brigg he welcomed the repeal of the malt tax as a measure to encourage retrenchment in public expenditure, making no reference to a duty on barley. And at Caistor he put the final nail in his coffin by asking 'How could they expect to revert to protection? The party who suggested it would have a majority of 150 against them in the House of Commons, and would raise civil war in Manchester and Sheffield.'[45]

Toynbee was appointed Tomline's central agent, and attornies such as Freer of Brigg were once again active on the Liberal side. But, although Tomline had the advantage of an early start, he needed more than that for success in the poll. The result was

Lowther	4,200
Tomline	3,729

After the contest Freer analysed the causes of the defeat in a report to Toynbee:

As far as I am able to judge, I consider it is to be attributed mainly to the fact that a great number of the voters who are owners and occupiers of land and persons dependent upon them were induced to vote for Mr. Lowther on the faith of his promises about 'fair trade' or 'protection'. After the speech which Mr. Lowther made at Market Rasen on the subject I believe that the minds of many of the electors were made up to vote for a Conservative rather than a Liberal as the most likely means of obtaining relief from the present agricultural depression. The class of electors in my district favourable to Colonel Tomline consist chiefly of Tradesmen, Small Freeholders and Small Farmers, many of whom are Dissenters, and those against the Colonel were the largest landowners and farmers, and the Clergy and persons under their influence. In many instances the clergyman of the parish was an active canvasser as well as an elector.[46]

Freer was right to emphasize the strength of the protectionist vote in the countryside, although he omitted to mention that it had also been important in 1880. But more significant than

[45] *Stamf. Merc.*, 2 Sept. 1881.

[46] STUBBS I/15. According to Toynbee the canvass reports had much exaggerated Tomline's strength.

the rise in the Conservative was the fall in the Liberal poll. Freer's own canvass results reveal many abstentions in the Scunthorpe district, and Brigg had no more than a small Liberal majority. Clearly Tomline had not been a success with the urban Liberals. Nor did he recover from the Yarborough interest those votes which he lost in the towns. The house of Brocklesby conspicuously failed to pull together. The earl, on holiday in Switzerland, endeavoured without success to get his agent to sit on Tomline's committee. The dowager Lady Yarborough had recently married J.M. Richardson, the son of a former farming tenant and a Conservative.[47] After the election the *Grimsby News*, the 'official' Liberal organ of the borough, accused Richardson of having exercised influence against Tomline, and Heneage felt it necessary to go over to Brocklesby and ascertain the truth of the rumours. He was assured that neither Richardson nor Lady Yarborough had taken any part in the contest, and that they had been surprised and annoyed to hear that some of the tenants had canvassed openly for Lowther. Richardson admitted, however, that most the tenants were 'more or less Conservative', their favourite newspaper being the *Yorkshire Post*.[48] Heneage concluded sadly in a letter to Wintringham: 'the old story is true, it is far easier to teach people to go wrong, than to get them to retrieve their steps.'[49]

(iii) SOUTH AND MID LINCOLNSHIRE, 1874-80

In 1879 Edmund Turnor announced that he would not stand again for South Lincolnshire. He wished to devote his energies to the management of his estate in the difficult years that he anticipated were to come.[50] And his decision was probably hastened by the knowledge that a good candidate was ready to succeed him, one who might forestall any contemplated opposition. This was John Compton Lawrance, of Dunsby, near Bourne.[51] He was a successful barrister, had

[47] See Mary E. Richardson, *The Life of a Great Sportsman, John Maunsell Richardson, with an Introduction by Victoria, Countess of Yarborough,* 1919.

[48] That organ informed the northern farmers in its issue of 25 Mar. 1880 that 'Liberalism is essentially antagonistic to agricultural interests.'

[49] 2 HEN 2. [50] *Stamf. Merc.*, 25 July 1879.

[51] The Rt. Hon. Sir John Compton Lawrance (1832-1912) was M.P. for S. Lincs., 1880-5, and the Stamford division of Lincs., 1885-90; a High Court judge, 1890-1912.

taken silk in 1877, and had recently been appointed Recorder of Derby. In county politics he was a protégé of Trollope's, having seconded him on the county hustings as far back as 1859; but his chief asset in South Lincolnshire was the fact that he was the son of a farmer and grazier, and had at one time farmed himself. He had championed the farmers in the great lockout of 1874, and in 1879 he was prepared to pose as a tenant farmers' candidate. He advocated compulsory tenant-right at the Bourne Agricultural Society in October 1879; and in March 1880, at a Farmers' Alliance meeting at Spalding, he showed himself quite willing to discuss the need for reform of the land and game laws.[52]

The announcement of Lawrance's intended candidature in July 1879 found the Liberals of the division without an association and without a candidate, and they were still in that position in March 1880. They were split in two ways. Spalding and Sleaford could not agree with Boston and Grantham, and the urban Liberals could not agree with the rural. W.J. Ingram, Member for Boston, and J.W. Mellor and Charles Roundell, the candidates for Grantham, were prepared to take an interest in the county representation; their attitude was in contrast to that of their predecessors in 1868. But their preference was for a good Gladstonian Liberal. They had the sympathy of the more advanced Liberals in Spalding, who at one stage favoured the adoption of Sir F. Lycett, a retired glove manufacturer and a Wesleyan. But the prospect of Lycett did not appeal to Colonel Moore, who led the moderate party in the division, and whose leading supporters were G.F. Young, of Wisbech, J.M. Cole, of Roxholme, near Sleaford, Henry Tatam, of Moulton, and Dr. Edward Morris, of Spalding. Of these only Tatam was primarily a farmer. But they all represented the older generation of Liberal politicians in the division, and their wish was for a local candidate with moderate views and rural connections.[53]

They found their man in Charles Sharpe, the Sleaford seedsman. At first sight it might appear a strange choice. The squires of the division regarded him as a mere tradesman. And the farmers were not inclined to embrace commercial

52 *Stamf. Merc.*, 16 Oct. 1874, 31 Oct. 1879, 12 Mar. 1880.
53 *Stamf. Merc.*, 2 and 23 Jan. 1880; *Lincolnshire, Boston and Spalding Free Press*, 30 Mar. 1880.

gentlemen who made fortunes as suppliers to the agricultural industry. In the bad old days—and not such old ones at that—seed merchants had often occasioned heavy farming losses by selling adulterated products.

But Sharpe was no ordinary seedsman. His business was a widely known and respected one, not merely in the county but in England and even abroad.[54] In 1868 he had led a national movement to improve standards in the trade, and was largely responsible for the Adulteration of Seeds Bill which Welby introduced in 1869.[55] Furthermore, he was not only a landowner and occupier himself, but had many relatives farming in the county. In politics he was the inheritor of what was left of the Handley tradition of independent agricultural Liberalism. His friend and solicitor was Charles Rodgers of Sleaford, whose firm provided a direct link with the Handley era.

Sharpe had a farmer's dislike of political agitation, and a business man's instinct of caution. He and Rodgers were well aware of the state of the party in the division. The expenses of a contest would probably have to be met largely from Sharpe's pocket. The fight was certain, and the outcome dubious. But having gone so far he could not easily draw back, and on the presentation of a requisition, circulated by the Spalding association, he agreed to stand.[56] He was defeated, but the result was certainly encouraging for the South Lincolnshire Liberals.

Lawrance	4,518
Welby-Gregory	4,290
Sharpe	3,583

Sharpe's poll was over 800 votes higher than Packe's in 1868, despite Sharpe's failure to make an intensive canvass and his lack of ability as a public speaker. Several factors were in his favour. The Conservatives did not show much spirit, and they suffered from a lack of good platform speakers. Turnor gave little assistance, and Welby-Gregory, abroad for the sake of his health, merely sent an address from Algiers congratulating the Disraeli administration on its

54 Records of Charles Sharpe and Co., Ltd., Sleaford, order books, 1868-72.
55 *The Times*, 16 Mar. 1869; *Parl. Deb.* 3rd Ser. cxcvi, 1916 ff.; ibid., cxcvii, 965 ff.
56 *Spalding Free Press*, 23 Mar. 1880; *Sleaford Gazette, 3 Apr. 1880.*

agricultural legislation. Sharpe, on the other hand, was well supported by neighbouring borough Members and candidates; and to Sleaford came his friend James Howard, the agricultural implement manufacturer, fresh from his triumph in Bedfordshire. Nor were townsmen the only people who graced his platforms. Carrington and Childers remembered, or were reminded, that they owned estates in the Spalding neighbourhood. And there were actually a few farmers, mostly Methodists as far as can be told, who took the chair at village meetings.

Nevertheless, with all these advantages, Sharpe failed to beat Welby-Gregory to second place, and the reasons for his failure are instructive. He fell between two stools, one might almost say between the counter stool and the milking stool. Although we may conjecture that he was, if not a Wesleyan, at least of Wesleyan sympathies and connections, he was lukewarm on issues such as Sunday closing, and refused to launch into attacks on the Established Church. Nor did he regale his urban audiences with radical speeches on county boards and the extension of the county franchise. There was little excitement at Grantham and Boston on polling day, and even from Spalding there were disappointing reports.[57]

On the other hand, Sharpe had little to offer the farmers, at whom his campaign was principally directed. He sympathized with them in their recent difficulties, but dared not advocate Protection. He was sure that 'intense foreign competition' was largely to blame for the low prices, but all he ventured was a hope that the shilling registration duty on imported corn might be restored. For the rest, like Colonel Moore, he emphasized the need for a reform of local taxation, though that subject was now wearing a little thin. He could, like Howard, have taken up tenants' grievances, such as tenant-right, excessive rents, and ground game. But on these themes he was reticent, perhaps because he knew that they did not go down very well with the farmers themselves, however much they appealed to urban sympathizers.[58] He promised to be independent of party where agriculture was concerned, but there was little *radical* independence in his speeches:

[57] *Sleaford Gazette,* 17 Apr. 1880.; *Spalding Free Press.* 20 Apr.

[58] Following a meeting at Spalding in March 1880 a Lincolnshire branch of Howard's Farmers' Alliance was formed, but it was reported to have had a membership of three (*Stamf. Merc.*, 12 Mar. 1880).

There was no landlord, if the matter were put to him properly, who would not be glad to embrace the opportunity of getting some good business man to assist them to represent the agricultural interests . . . of this country . . . . This was not a tenant farmers' question only, it was equally a landlord's question, and a public one also . . . .[59]

On the whole, the farmers were not impressed. The *Sleaford Gazette*, in its analysis of the poll, reported that 'the feeling of many of the tradesmen seemed to be for the Liberal candidate, but the farmers generally seemed more inclined to hold to the Conservatives; there were however a great many exceptions in both cases.'[60] Sharpe confessed himself puzzled. He told a Stamford meeting in June 1881: 'There is a great deal of Conservatism amongst tenant farmers in the county of Lincoln, and I cannot find any reason why this is so. I fail to see what return the Conservatives have made for the agricultural support they have received.'[61] Part of the reason could be given in one word, as Sharpe himself was to admit four years later.

There was no contest for Mid Lincolnshire in 1880. The Liberals of Alford held a meeting and endeavoured to find a candidate, but they received little encouragement from Lincoln. The division had never been contested. Heneage was busy elsewhere. Amcotts had turned Conservative, and Monson must have been daunted by the prospect of trying to revive the old party machinery. The two Conservative Members, moreover, were exceptionally strong candidates. Stanhope and Chaplin were important figures in the Conservative party, although it was felt, particularly in Stanhope's case, that he might with mutual benefit spend more of his time in the constituency. Furthermore, neither of them cared to excite an opposition by provocative speeches on the fiscal question. Chaplin, as already noticed, had his own reasons for caution. And Stanhope's position was that of a ministerialist rather than an independent agricultural back-bencher. He thought there was no hope of a reimposition of the old taxes on food.

59 *Stamf. Merc.*, 12 Mar. 1880.

60 *Sleaford Gazette,* 17 Apr. 1880.

61 *Stamf. Merc.*, 10 June 1881.

(iv) PARTY ORGANIZATION, 1880-4

The changes in the organization of the Conservative party at this period have recently attracted the attention of several historians.[62] In the county constituencies the tendency was away from rural traditions and towards urban methods. Divisional associations were given more influence in policy-making and the selection of candidates; full-time agents were appointed in some cases; and district associations were formed, and integrated into the divisional organizations.

Progress towards this goal was slow and uneven, depending much on local conditions and influences. The Lincolnshire divisions show a varied pattern of development, reflecting differing attitudes towards organization among the Conservative party leaders and managers. In North Lincolnshire Rowland Winn, who succeeded Sir William Hart Dyke as chief Conservative whip in 1880, encouraged the reorganization of the divisional party. The remodelled association, inaugurated in July 1880, provided for district committees on a fairly regular basis, whilst still leaving the direction of registration work in the hands of a part-time agent.[63] But meanwhile local organizations began to spring up in the division. There were associations at Gainsborough and Scunthorpe by 1879, when they sent delegates to the annual conference of the National Union of Conservative Associations.[64] Louth and Brigg had Conservative clubs by 1880. And soon after the general election Brigg took the lead in forming an association for the district as well as the town. It was designed to help with registration and canvassing, of course, but its chief strength was its social role, providing new entertainments for the town, and perhaps even assisting the integration of town and countryside.[65] Winn did not initiate the Brigg association, which grew out of the Working Men's Club, but he encouraged the formation of other similar bodies in the division, particularly in the Isle of Axholme.[66]

[62] The latest contribution, E.J. Feuchtwanger's *Disraeli, Democracy, and the Tory Party* (Oxford, 1968), adds little, concerning county organization, to Professor Hanham's account (*Elections and Party Management*, pp. 17 ff.).

[63] TGH 4/Box 1.

[64] National Union of Conservative and Unionist Associations, conference minutes.

[65] *Stamf. Merc.*, 30 Apr. 1880, 9 Dec. 1881, 17 Nov. 1882.

[66] Ibid., 21 Apr. and 22 Dec. 1882.

Edward Stanhope was one of the Central Committee established by the Conservative party in 1880, and was given special responsibility for county organization. His work in Mid Lincolnshire followed the lines of a report which he and others made to the Central Committee in 1883.[67] Local committees were formed, with the assistance of a worker from Central Office, but it was thought best not to disturb the peace of the division by forming public district associations. Chaplin, however, was not in agreement with this policy, and in 1883 he secured the appointment of a permanent agent to encourage the formation of district associations. His motive was not so much the agitation of the division as the furtherance of his policies in the National Union. The districts could send delegates to the conferences of the Union, and there help to save the party leadership from the threat represented by Lord Randolph Churchill.[68]

The Conservatives of South Lincolnshire were untroubled by the echoes of distant strife, yet they too began to move with the times. In 1880 they formed a divisional association, replacing the private subscription system that had been followed since the collapse of Winchilsea's movement forty and more years previously. The form of organization chosen was similar to that adopted in North Lincolnshire. But in the southern division, where the great landowners were still the backbone of the party, there was no complementary movement to found district associations.

The divisional organizations of the Lincolnshire Liberals in the early 1880s were a sorry contrast with those of their opponents. They received much less assistance from national bodies, and they certainly gave less assistance to local workers in the districts. Lecturers were sent from time to time from the Liberal Central Association and the National Liberal Federation. But the former could not very well interfere with the registration machinery set up by the leading county politicians. And the principles of the latter were inapplicable to rural constituencies. Lincolnshire's distance from London and Birmingham, moreover, discouraged intensive missionary work from those quarters.

67 Revesby (Stanhope) MSS.

68 Christ Church, Oxford, Salisbury MSS., Northcote correspondence, f. 635, Northcote to Salisbury, 19 May 1884.

Despite the reverse sustained in 1881, the North Lincolnshire Liberal Association was not reformed in the following months. Heneage and Monson appear to have thought it sufficient to carry on quietly with registration activity. Few public meetings were held, and nothing was done to encourage new district associations. It was not until April 1884 that a candidate was adopted in place of Tomline.[69] The choice of Sir Henry Meysey-Thompson, a Yorkshire squire with agricultural interests, was made by Heneage.[70] The delegates to the association wished to adopt as a second candidate S.D. Waddy, the Methodist barrister and politician, but Heneage discouraged them.[71]

The Mid Lincolnshire association, responding to pressure from Alford and Horncastle, appointed a committee in December 1883 to consider the adoption of a candidate. But Monson preferred a policy of quietness, and the movement came to nothing. Heneage was absorbed in Grimsby politics, and Ripon was away from home, governing India. A similar spinelessness characterized the southern division of the county. There was now an association of sorts, but it confined itself to registration, and its chairman, Colonel Moore, was becoming increasingly lukewarm in his politics. Sharpe disliked agitation between elections. He was officially embraced as prospective candidate in 1882, but when Welby-Gregory retired in 1884 he allowed the Hon. M.E.G. Finch-Hatton, of Haverholme Priory, to walk over the course.[72]

If the divisional associations, in their leadership and principal functions, looked to the past, the local Liberal movements in the county had their eye on the future. One of the earliest local associations to be formed after 1880 was

69 *Stamf. Merc.*, 11 Apr. 1884.

70 Sir Henry Meysey-Thompson (1845-1929), 2nd bart., M.P. for Knaresborough, 1880 (election declared void on petition), the Brigg division of Lincs., 1885-6, and the Handsworth division of Staffs., 1892-1905. A Liberal Unionist from 1886. Cr. baron Knaresborough in 1905.

71 2 HEN 2, Heneage to Wintringham, 18 Apr. 1884. S.D. Waddy (1830-1902) was M.P. for Barnstaple, 1874-9, Sheffield, 1879-80, Edinburgh, 1882-5, and the Brigg division of Lincolnshire, 1886-94. The son of a former president of Conference, he worked to bring the Wesleyans behind Gladstone in 1880 (Gladstone MSS., Addit. MSS. 44,463, f. 304).

72 M.E.G. Finch-Hatton (1851-98) s. his half-brother as 12th earl of Winchilsea in 1887. M.P. for S. Lincs., 1884-5, and the Spalding division of Lincs., 1885-7. An active agricultural politician in the 1890s.

that at Alford, in October 1881. Its originator was Isaac Nutsey, a Baptist and a leading tradesman in the town. He was determined enough—and presumably rich enough—not to be cowed by the prospect of losing some of his Conservative rural customers. And he saw the spread of local organizations in Mid Lincolnshire as a preparation for the extension of the franchise to the rural workers. He told a meeting at Wainfleet, in March 1883, that 'in view of the large prospective increase in voters by the passing of the County Franchise Bill, it was the duty of all who recognised the importance of politics to do what they could to instruct the labouring classes.'[73] Associations were founded at Wainfleet and Skegness, and in 1883 one was created for the Horncastle district, with the assistance of Francis Otter, the Liberal squire of Ranby.[74]

In the northern division the Louth association kept the Liberal flame burning in the years 1881-3, though without great brilliance. But in 1884 the introduction of the Reform Bill stimulated an unprecedented activity not only in the towns but also in the villages of North Lincolnshire. The Brigg and Gainsborough associations girded up their loins for the task of rural propaganda. In May, for instance, two nonconformist ministers from Brigg went to address a meeting in the new Liberal club room (formerly the Primitive Methodist chapel) in the large open village of North Kelsey. 'The audience of this fine old village abundantly proved that the unenfranchised are alive to the privileges shortly to be conferred upon them.'[75]

Even in South Lincolnshire there was a revival of sorts. Boston, which had been under a cloud since the suspension of the writ after the general election, adopted two Liberal candidates in 1884. One of them, Halley Stewart, took an interest in the Liberal cause in Holland, and helped with the work of forming local associations.[76] During 1884 two such

[73] *Stamf. Merc.*, 6 Apr. 1883.

[74] Francis Otter (1831-95) practised at the Bar before devoting himself to his estate and to local politics. Brother-in-law of George Eliot, and a pupil of Arnold at Rugby, by whom he was much influenced.

[75] *Stamf. Merc.*, 9 May 1884.

[76] Halley Stewart (1838-1937) was M.P. for the Spalding division of Lincs., 1887-95, and Greenock, 1906-10. Son of a Congregationalist minister, and for a time in the same ministry himself. Knighted in 1932.

were inaugurated, at Holbeach and Long Sutton. The Spalding Liberals, though poorly organized, maintained their activities after the 1880 election, and were indignant at Sharpe's failure to contest the division in 1884.[77]

In October 1884 the Lincoln Liberal Association organized a grand county demonstration in favour of Reform. Prominent amongst the assembly were Heneage, Joseph Ruston the ironfounder (now M.P. for Lincoln), Otter, and Sharpe. The crowd of 25,000 was composed largely of Lincoln working men, but deputations were sent from most of the towns of North and Mid Lincolnshire. (Spalding held a rally of its own, attended mainly by agricultural workers, in the following month.) At the time of the Lincoln meeting a conference was held of delegates from all the associations in the county. Halley Stewart, well supported by representatives from Louth and Boston, urged the necessity of a radical reorganization of the Lincolnshire party.[78] But whatever plans were laid were upset in November 1884, when the government reached agreement with the opposition over the redistribution of seats.

Winn disapproved of the compromise negotiated by his leaders, and would have preferred a dissolution on the old franchise. Since, however, the franchise bill would now be allowed through, it was important to secure a satisfactory redistribution. Both Winn and Lowther, from their knowledge of their own division, were strongly for the introduction of single-Member county constituencies. Now that Members and candidates would be expected to visit villages as well as towns, and subscribe to village as well as town clubs and associations, a constituency the size of North Lincolnshire would become an exhausting one to represent, in terms of time, energy, and money. The country gentleman would find politics too nearly a full-time job, and would return to his hunting and shooting, while an undesirable class of London attornies and carpet-baggers monopolized the rural constituencies.[79]

In order to preserve some predominantly agricultural divisions, Winn further proposed a system of extending

[77] *Stamf. Merc.*, 22 Feb. 1884. [78] Ibid., 24 Oct. 1884.

[79] Salisbury MSS., Northcote correspondence, ff. 686, 692, 724, and 726, Northcote to Salisbury, 7 and 21 Oct. 1884, Winn to Lowther, 19 Nov. 1884, and Lowther to Northcote, 20 Nov. 1884.

borough boundaries, or, where this would not serve the purpose, grouping boroughs together. Thus for North Lincolnshire he proposed the grouping of Gainsborough with Lincoln and Louth with Grimsby, leaving a largely rural district which could be divided into two constituencies down the line of the river Ancholme.[80] To the disappointment of Winn and Lowther the grouping system was not adopted for the English boroughs. But there was one final resource left to the Conservative county Members—the proposal of modifications to the draft scheme of the Boundary Commissioners. The political complexion of the Commission left Northcote, for one, somewhat uneasy, but when it went on tour it proved reassuringly amenable to suggestions and objections.[81]

For North Lincolnshire Winn produced his own scheme, which his agent, H.H. Cave of Brigg, persuaded the Commissioners to adopt. The redistribution scheme had envisaged three divisions roughly covering the old northern division. They were to be centred on Gainsborough, Brigg, and Louth, and their boundaries were to follow those of petty sessional divisions. Whilst accepting the principles of the scheme, Cave proposed modifications to separate more satisfactorily the urban from the rural population. He proposed the concentration of the Liberal elements of North Lincolnshire in the new Brigg division, leaving the Gainsborough and Louth divisions comparatively strong in Conservative influences. To effect this the Winterton petty sessional division was to be transferred from Gainsborough to Brigg, and the Rasen petty sessional division from Brigg to Louth. The Louth and Gainsborough boundaries were then to be adjusted in order to preserve an equal distribution of population between the three parliamentary divisions. Despite a protest from Heneage, the Commissioners accepted most of these changes.[82]

Chaplin and Stanhope had no grievance with respect to the dismemberment of Mid Lincolnshire, which was split, roughly speaking, into two constituencies, centred on

80 Ibid., f. 724, Winn to Lowther, 19 Nov. 1884.

81 Ibid., ff. 777 and 789, Northcote to Salisbury, 8 Dec. 1884 and 16 Jan. 1885; Nostell Priory (Winn) MSS., D/3/8/4/2/21, Northcote to Winn, 27 Nov. 1884.

82 *Parl. Papers*, 1884-5, xix, p. 473; *Stamf. Merc.*, 16 Jan. 1885.

Sleaford and Spilsby respectively. The Commissioners adhered to the scheme whereby part of Holland was attached to Sleaford, despite the desire of Moore and Welby-Gregory that the boundary between Holland and Kesteven should be followed throughout its length.[83]

(v) THE NEW COUNTY DIVISIONS AND THE GENERAL ELECTION OF 1885

BRIGG. The division comprised the petty sessional divisions of Winterton, Brigg, and Barton, and half of that of Grimsby, including the parliamentary borough. At a first glance it might be thought that Conservative fears of its being a strongly radical constituency were exaggerated. Liberalism was well established in Brigg, Barton, and the larger villages of the Marsh, such as Barrow and Goxhill. But neither Brigg nor Barton was a large town, and the former was not devoid of Conservative influences. To counteract the Marsh there was a large tract of wold country—true, partly the property of Lord Yarborough—and a substantial group of Conservative estates, chiefly those of Astley, Winn, Sheffield, and Sutton-Nelthorpe. The mining and smelting industries of the Scunthorpe district were rapidly growing, but in the early 1880s Winn seems to have retained some of his local influence there as an employer of labour, and the Liberals were slow to build an organization.

But when all this is said, the fact remains that the Liberals held the seat in 1885, 1886, and 1892. Perhaps their strongest strategic advantage, though one difficult to assess, was the proximity of Grimsby and Hull. Brigg, Barton, and Grimsby were connected by railway with each other, and with Hull by means of the New Holland ferry; and it is worth noticing that at the general election of 1885 both candidates for the Brigg division came from north of the Humber.

The Brigg division was the first of the new Lincolnshire constituencies formally to adopt a Liberal candidate. Meysey-Thompson attended a meeting of delegates at Brigg early in February 1885. Yarborough took the chair, and there was a strong contingent from Grimsby, led by Heneage. Thompson's

[83] *Stamf. Merc.*, 16 Jan. 1885; *Parl. Deb.* 3rd Ser. ccxcvi, 1731-8, committee stage of Redistribution Bill, 14 Apr. 1885.

views were those of a moderate Liberal and tolerant churchman, but he was prepared to advocate the usual Liberal programme for county constituencies—reform of the land laws, local taxation, and local government.[84]

There was some difficulty at first in finding a Conservative candidate. Winn had chosen to stand for the Gainsborough division, and Lowther for the Louth. By the middle of March, however, Winn had found a good candidate in H.J. Farmer-Atkinson. He had no doubt come across Atkinson as candidate for Hull in 1868 and 1880, and knew that he had more recently been considered both for West Cornwall and for a Middlesex division. Formerly a leading merchant and shipowner of Hull, Atkinson also had banking connections with Grimsby and Barton. But his chief advantage as a candidate for the Brigg division was the fact that he was a prominent Wesleyan.[85]

When Salisbury formed his government in June 1885, Winn was not included in it—whether at his own request or not I have been unable to discover—and early in July it was announced that he had accepted a peerage.[86] This led to a contest, the last for the old division of North Lincolnshire, at which Atkinson handsomely defeated Thompson by 4,052 votes to 2,872. Although careful not to damage his future chances by coming out for Fair Trade, Atkinson seems to have been strongly supported by the agricultural part of the constituency. He was reported to have done well not only around Louth and in the Isle of Axholme, but also in the Brigg, Caistor, and Rasen districts.[87]

But at the general election, in November 1885, the position was reversed, Thompson defeating Atkinson in the Brigg division by 5,643 votes to 3,006. Atkinson had lost two of his principal centres of support, the Isle of Axholme to the Gainsborough division and the eastern Marshes to the Louth. But, among the farmers who remained in the constituency, he had if anything improved his position since the spring. His autumn campaign was directed principally at them. He

[84] *Stamf. Merc.*, 6 Feb. 1885.

[85] Ibid., 17 July 1885; Salisbury MSS., Winn/41, Winn to Salisbury, 30 June 1885.

[86] He was cr. baron St. Oswald. At sixty-five he might be considered to have reached retirement age.

[87] *Stamf. Merc.*, 10 and 17 July 1885.

dealt with the need for relieving them of some of their local burdens, and with the need to conduct a further enquiry into the causes of the agricultural depression.

Thompson, on the other hand, was firm in his adherence to Free Trade, and for the rest campaigned on a somewhat more radical platform than had been his wont in the old constituency. He gave full consideration to the allotments question. At Goxhill he declared that 'the labourer, the carpenter, and the shoemaker, and even the shopkeeper in villages, should have a good garden to his cottage, and as much land as would keep a cow through the winter, at the same rent as the large farmers paid per acre for theirs.'[88] He was not a rabid advocate of Disestablishment, as befitted one who retained the confidence of the earl of Yarborough. But he adverted to nonconformist grievances such as Church-controlled education, the difficulty of obtaining chapel sites, the presence of registrars in chapels for marriage services, and so on.[89]

He was well supported in the towns, and by the small tradesmen and shopkeepers in the larger villages. But it is probably true to say that he would not have won the election had it not been for an impressive Liberal vote from the agricultural labourers. Nor would he have received that vote had not the labourers of the division been largely of the Primitive Methodist persuasion. Half the public meetings of the Liberal campaign seem to have been held in Primitive chapels or schoolrooms, and most of the speakers at them were ministers or prominent local laymen of the connexion.[90]

In 1886 Thompson and Heneage became Unionists, and Yarborough went over to the Conservatives. But the rank and file of the Brigg Liberal party remained firmly Gladstonian. When Thompson withdrew they adopted S.D. Waddy as their candidate, and at the general election he was victorious by 3,887 votes to 3,722. The Conservative candidate was John Maunsell Richardson, second husband of the dowager countess of Yarborough.

GAINSBOROUGH. The constituency comprised the petty sessional divisions of Lincoln, Gainsborough, and Epworth. Gainsborough

[88] *Gainsborough News*, 21 Nov. 1885. [89] *Grimsby News*, 9 Oct. 1885.
[90] *Stamf. Merc.*, 30 Oct. 1885; *Grimsby News*, 9 Oct., 13 and 27 Nov., 1885.

and its suburbs represented its chief concentration of population, and the City of Lincoln (with Bracebridge) lay within its boundaries. Gainsborough was connected by railway with Lincoln, Retford, and Doncaster; but the Isle of Axholme lay somewhat beyond convenient reach, in the extreme north-west of the division.

A Liberal association was formed for the division in February 1885, under the auspices of Lord Monson, the only important Liberal landowner in the constituency. At a meeting held at Gainsborough in April, Joseph Bennett of Louth was adopted as candidate.[91] He was neither a country gentleman nor a resident in the division, but he had frequently, since 1882, addressed meetings at Gainsborough and in the Isle, and may perhaps have considered at one time the possibility of standing for the second seat in North Lincolnshire.

Winn was adopted by the Gainsborough divisional Conservative Association in March, being well supported by Anderson, Bacon, Hutton, and others. Winn's retirement, however, was a setback to the Gainsborough Conservatives, and it was not until the autumn that they found another candidate. Major-General C.A. Sim was unknown in the division, and was attacked by Bennett and his supporters as a Jingo and a fair-trader. He had intended to stand for Sunderland, but had withdrawn after a difference with the local party. His candidature for the Gainsborough division was on the recommendation of Captain W.E. Denison of Ossington, near Newark, who had previously declined to come forward himself.[92] General Sim did not conduct a very brilliant campaign, and he was forced to concede the victory to Bennett by 4,955 votes to 3,850.

Bennett's appeal was primarily to the urban vote. He told the inhabitants of Gainsborough that 'if it had not been for the fact that he was convinced that the prosperity of their town had its foundation in the principles of Liberalism, he would never have consented to become a candidate for the Gainsborough division.'[93] And the Gainsborough Liberals were well supported by those of Lincoln. At a Gainsborough meeting in November 1885 a Lincoln Liberal declared that

91 *Stamf. Merc.*, 1 May 1885.
92 *Lincs. Chron.*, 16 and 30 Oct. 1885; *Gainsborough News*, 24 Oct, 1885.
93 *Lincoln Gazette*, 7 Nov. 1885.

'he had come to extend the right hand of fellowship to the electors in Gainsborough. It was sister to Lincoln in manufacture and trade . . . .'[94]

Nevertheless, the Gainsborough voters formed under one-quarter of the constituency, and it was reported that they were by no means solid in their vote for Bennett. The workers at Marshall's foundry supported him, despite the fair-trading views of their managing director. But the tradesmen, relying to some extent on rural custom, tended towards the Conservatives.[95] Despite the Liberalism of the city of Lincoln, moreover, the thousand or so of its residents who had qualifications for the Gainsborough division were said to have been equally divided between Bennett and Sim.[96]

Bennett certainly received few votes from the farmers of the division, and he had made little effort to attract them. Where he scored was with his fellow nonconformists, principally among the labourers of the division. It was the large and medium-sized villages, where Primitive Methodism was well established, which, as in the Brigg division, produced the Liberal majority. Villages like Scotter, Saxilby, and Nettleham might be expected to produce majorities for Bennett. But he also did well in the villages ranged east and west of the Cliff, north of Lincoln.[97] Places such as Normanby-by-Spital had concentrations of agricultural workers—there were no settlements on the Cliff itself—and unionism had spread among them in the 1870s. The Isle of Axholme, on the other hand, was if anything on the Conservative side, although the Liberals, to judge by newspaper reports and surviving canvass returns, did better than they had at the by-election, and better than their opponents expected.[98]

For the general election of 1886 the Conservatives secured a better candidate, Col. H. Eyre, of Rampton.[99] A retired soldier and a country gentleman, he had farmed, near the Trent and not far from Gainsborough, for several years. Bennett, standing as a Gladstonian, lost by 4,123 votes to

94 *Gainsborough News*, 14 Nov. 1885. 95 *Lincoln Gazette*, 28 Nov. 1885.
96 *Louth Times*, 12 Dec. 1885.
97 Ibid. See also Henry Pelling, *Social Geography of British Elections, 1885-1910*, 1967, p. 223.
98 *Gainsborough News*, 12 Dec. 1885; *Lincoln Gazette*, 5 Dec. 1885; TGH/4.
99 Henry Eyre (1834-1904), of Rampton, Notts., was M.P. for the Gainsborough division of Lincs., 1886-92. Strong on the local taxation question.

4,038. Monson had remained loyal to Gladstone, but Ruston's defection at Lincoln caused an upheaval there which left the rival factions little time for county politics.

LOUTH. The Liberals of Louth had some cause to grumble at the peculiarly shaped constituency of which their borough formed the capital. It comprised the Louth and Rasen districts of the old northern division, plus the Wragby district of the old mid division, and stretched twenty-six miles from Bardney on the Witham to Saltfleet on the German Ocean. The Wragby and Rasen areas were separated by the sparsely-populated Wolds from the Louth side of the constituency, although a railway now connected Lincoln and Louth via Bardney, Wragby, and Donington-on-Bain.

Edward Heneage's seat at Hainton fell within the division, and it was he, in consultation with the Louth Liberals, who chose the Liberal candidate in March 1885. Their choice was Francis Otter, who lived only five or six miles from Heneage. Otter was perhaps better known in the Horncastle district, where he had canvassed for Mid Lincolnshire, than at Louth. But he recommended himself to the leaders of the Louth divisional party as a moderate Liberal, and one who would attract support from farmers as well as labourers. They probably supposed that he would have more success than a candidate such as Joseph Bennett in securing the votes of the large wold farmers, despite the fact that those farmers were mostly Methodists and Otter was a churchman.

The campaign that Otter conducted was certainly a moderate one, with the emphasis on agricultural rather than religious grievances. Nevertheless, his opponent, James Lowther, made a more forthright, and undoubtedly more effective, appeal to the farmers of the division, coming out more plainly than Conservative candidates elsewhere in the county for Fair Trade and Colonial Preference. His strongest support at the general election came from the Marsh, where the small farmers and freeholders were suffering particularly badly from the agricultural depression. He also acquired votes from the declining market town of Market Rasen. And even Louth, that Liberal beacon in the old constituency of North Lincolnshire, could be described by the *Grimsby News* as a harbourer of toryism.[100]

100 *Lincs. Chron.*, 27 Nov. and 1 Dec. 1885; *Grimsby News*, 11 Dec. 1885.

But Otter won the election by 4,805 votes to 3,598. Despite his moderation it was reported that he did well on the Wolds and in the Wragby district, and that the Primitive Methodists of the division were 'radical to the core'.[101] Places such as Binbrook, Ludford, and Donington-on-Bain polled well for Otter, though local influences as well as nonconformist allegiance probably played their part in the disposition of the labouring vote. At Donington, for instance, there was a Baptist chapel. But Heneage, Otter himself, and even the Revd. T.W. Mossman, the Liberal high-church incumbent of West Torrington, were well-known and respected in the village.

In 1886 Heneage became a Unionist, and was returned for Grimsby with Conservative help. He may have threatened Otter with an opposition in the Louth division, or perhaps Otter himself, a lukewarm Gladstonian, was reluctant to face an opposition from any quarter. Whatever the cause, he eventually decided to retire, leaving the Louth Liberals at the last minute without a candidate. Lowther had chosen to contest North Cumberland. His successor, A.R. Heath, a London barrister, was returned unopposed in July 1886. In October the Liberals adopted a Methodist candidate in R.W. Perks, who was to hold the seat from 1892 to 1910. But it would be wrong to conclude from his long tenure that the division became a safe one for the Liberal party. Perks's Liberalism was of a moderate and unorthodox variety.[102] He secured the allegiance of the leading Methodists of the division, but it is doubtful if he would have retained it had he not been prepared to vote with the Conservatives on many agricultural questions.

HORNCASTLE. If Louth was a difficult division for the Liberals, in point of shape and composition, Horncastle was well-nigh impossible. Horncastle, the only town of more than 3,000 inhabitants in the division, was connected by railway to Lincoln; and it had tended to look to Lincoln for political leadership when the latter had been the centre of the old mid division. Now it was separated from Lincoln by the easternmost part of the Gainsborough division. Between Horncastle

101 *Louth Times*, 28 Nov. 1885; *Lincs. Chron.*, 4 Dec. 1885.
102 He became a prominent Liberal Imperialist.

and Alford lay the southern portion of the Wolds, and railway communication between the two was slow and circuitous. Spilsby was adopted as the returning town, since it occupied a more central position in the constituency than Horncastle. But Spilsby was in the 1880s a somewhat sluggish market town, not easily to be moved by party feeling. The fen district south of Horncastle and Spilsby was of old a Conservative region, and the only Liberal strongholds lay on the Marsh—Alford, Wainfleet, Hogsthorpe, and Skegness. Even here, as has been seen, the Conservatives stretched the tentacles of their local organization.

Edward Stanhope was early in the field, and, like Lowther, did not consider it necessary to arrange for his adoption at a public meeting. He was confident in his local influence, and in his organization: it was reported that 'lady canvassers and even faded spinsters' were indefatigable in his cause.[103] He was successful in December 1885 by 4,824 votes to 3,959.

His opponent was deficient in both influence and organization. He was William Threlfall (1842-1907), a London barrister and the son of a large Liverpool brewer. He was probably suggested by Alfred Healey, the Horncastle brewer;[104] and he was endorsed by Heneage, the chairman of the divisional association, as the only respectable politician willing to come and spend his money in the division. He was a churchman, and at this date the leading brewing families of the country were not a very radical crew. Nevertheless, he made some effort to capture the tenant farmer vote; and, particularly down in the Fens, he made a certain play with the allotments question.[105]

In such a rural constituency it might be thought that he would be carried home by the labouring vote. But the Primitive Methodists were not as strong here as in the other Lindsey divisions. The major landowners were formidably arrayed behind Stanhope. And the farmers, as usual predominantly Conservative, were especially numerous in the smallholding areas of the Marsh and Fens. It was reported that even Hogsthorpe, that former home of Liberal

103 *Stamf. Merc.*, 11 Dec. 1885.
104 In *Kelly* (1892) he is given as Horncastle agent for Threlfall's Brewery Co. Ltd., maltsters.
105 *Stamf. Merc.*, 24 July 1885.

independence, had powerful tory influences,[106] whilst the fen district 'evidently supplied the majority for Mr. Stanhope'.[107]

He was returned without opposition in 1886.

HOLLAND.[108] Despite its urban concentrations–Boston, Spalding, Holbeach, Long Sutton–the Holland division created in 1885 was predominantly an agricultural one. What makes it of special interest is that it shows, even more clearly than elsewhere in the county, a political division between Conservative farmers and Liberal labourers. The labourers were sufficiently concentrated in towns and large villages, and had a sufficiently vital political tradition by 1885, to make them set the tone of the contest, if not to dictate its result.

Long Sutton is a good example. The labourers, who had preserved their union organization, had for some time been at war with the vicar on the charities question. The vicar wished to continue to appropriate the endowments for his own purposes: the labourers wished to see the charity lands turned into allotments. The vicar, a leading Conservative, was supported by the principal farmers of the parish, who did not see why their men should dissipate their energies by working for themselves as well as for their employers. Agricultural meetings tended to be Conservative occasions. Finch-Hatton, Lawrance, and Halley Stewart visited the Long Sutton Agricultural Society in September 1885, but only the first two were respectfully received. The farmers talked so much among themselves during Stewart's speech that the *Mercury* reporter was unable to follow it. The Liberal meetings on the other hand, were numerously attended by agricultural labourers. Joseph Arch came to address a Reform meeting in October 1884. And Jesse Collings was the chief speaker at a similar occasion twelve months later. He told the labourers that the vote was 'a trust second only to your

106 *Lincs. Chron.*, 11 Dec. 1885. *The Boston Guardian* (7 Nov. 1885) reported that the two leading tories of Hogsthorpe, both farmers and churchmen, had split between Cholmeley and Stanhope in 1852.

107 *Stamf. Merc.*, 11 Dec. 1885.

108 The Conservatives objected successfully to the original proposal to call the division Spalding. Similarly they secured the alteration of 'Brigg' to 'North Lindsey or Brigg', 'Louth' to 'East Lindsey or Louth', etc. A similar attachment to county names also manifested itself in other shires (*Parl. Deb.* 3rd. Ser. ccxcvi, 1738).

religious conviction'. Another speaker at the same meeting recalled that 'in Long Sutton they had fought local battles against local toryism, and although defeated at times they had never been disheartened.'[109]

In 1885 the Liberals adopted Halley Stewart as their candidate. A nonconformist business man, he was already known in the constituency as a strong Liberal. He was too much for Colonel Moore, who, after encouraging Staniland in an abortive movement, turned Conservative.[110] But this did not worry Stewart, who made his principal appeal to the agricultural labourers of the division. He sympathized with them in their wish for allotments on reasonable terms, and advocated the purchase of ground for allotments by the county boards that the Liberals wished to create.

The South Lincolnshire Conservatives met at Spalding in February 1885, and decided to maintain a single association covering the area of the old division. But they also took two steps that they had previously resisted. They appointed an organizing secretary, and instructed him to form not only divisional but also district associations.[111] In June they adopted Finch-Hatton for the Spalding division. He had been reluctant to stand again at the general election. But he was probably persuaded to change his mind on the ground that no other man would be able to carry the constituency against Stewart. Although a trusted friend of the farmers,[112] he did not neglect the labouring vote, and took care to show that there was nothing abhorrent to Conservative principles in the idea of allotments. On general and religious questions, moreover, he followed the moderate lines laid down for him by Welby and Trollope in former days.

He defeated Stewart by the narrow margin of 4,658 votes to 4,580. Stewart did well at Spalding, and at some of the large villages north of Spalding, such as Pinchbeck, Surfleet, and Gosberton. The Liberals also polled well at Holbeach and Long Sutton. But their opponents were strong in the

109 *Stamf. Merc.*, 13 Apr. 1883, 11 July 1884, 10 Oct. 1884, 25 Sept. and 16 Oct. 1885; *Louth Times*, 17 Oct. 1885.

110 *Louth Times*, 31 Oct. 1885.

111 *Stamf. Merc.*, 27 Feb. 1885.

112 At a Deeping St. Nicholas meeting a former Liberal said that 'he had decided to support the best man irrespective of creed, and . . . he believed Mr. Finch-Hatton . . . was the most suitable man to represent the agricultural interests of this division' (*Stamf. Merc.*, 23 Oct. 1885).

Marsh. The farmers exercised strong Conservative influence north-east of Boston, and they were also reported to have done well in the rural parishes of South Holland.[113] It may well have been the votes of the smallholders, both rental and freehold, that tipped the scale in favour of Finch-Hatton.

At the general election of 1886 Finch-Hatton once more defeated Stewart. The figures were 4,561 to 4,273, a slight increase in the Conservative majority. The Liberals were better organized than in the previous year, but the farmers were if anything more solidly behind the Conservatives than before. Again, however, Stewart campaigned on the allotments question, and there is no evidence of a widespread willingness among the labourers of Holland to desert Gladstone and follow Chamberlain.[114]

SLEAFORD. Chaplin must have been pleased with the boundaries of the Sleaford division: they were almost tailor-made for him. They embraced the Lincoln (Kesteven) and Sleaford petty sessional divisions. The former included his Blankney estate, and had, as part of Mid Lincolnshire, been well organized into district associations. And at Sleaford itself—the only town of any size in the new division—he had a not inconsiderable influence, supported by the Hervey and Finch-Hatton interests.

The Liberals, on the other hand, were weak and disorganized. It was not until April that Lord Ripon presided over the formation of a divisional association, and not until October that Sharpe, with some misgivings, consented to become a candidate. Apart from Ripon, who as a peer could not, of course, take an active part in the election, his principal supporters belonged rather to Holland than Kesteven. Even G.F. Young, who was now living at Swineshead and was thus in the Sleaford division, devoted his principal energies to the Spalding contest.[115] In Kesteven Sharpe's local influences were more or less confined to the Sleaford district, and even Sleaford itself lacked a vigorous Liberal movement.

113 *Boston Gazette*, 5 Dec. 1885; *Spalding Free Press*, 8 Dec. 1885; *Lincs. Chron.*, 11 Dec. 1885.

114 It must be said, however, that Stewart, although remaining loyal to Gladstone, had many political views in common with Collings and Chamberlain.

115 Henry Young of Swineshead Abbey, presumably G.F. Young's son, was a Conservative in 1885. And so was J.M. Cole of Roxholme (*Lincs. Chron.*, 18 Sept. 1885; *Boston Gazette*, 21 Nov. 1885).

Chaplin's campaign emphasized the fiscal question, and his advocacy of Fair Trade seems to have gone down well not only with the large farmers on the Heath but also with the small farmers and tradesmen of open villages such as Billinghay and Metheringham. Sharpe, like Chaplin, addressed himself more to tenant farmers than to the labourers. He declared himself willing to enter parliament as an independent agricultural Member, and said very little on religious topics or on the allotments question. Nevertheless, he received support in some of the traditionally Liberal villages—Ruskington, Great Hale, Heckington, and Caythorpe (assisted by Hussey Packe's influence in the last-named).[116] There was a sufficient number of large open villages in the division to have made the contest a much closer one, had the Conservatives adopted a less popular, and the Liberals a more effective, candidate. The result of the poll was: Chaplin 4,761 votes, Sharpe 3,460.

STAMFORD. This division comprised the petty sessional divisions of Grantham and Bourne, plus the parish of Crowland and the Lincolnshire part of the borough of Stamford, now disfranchised. At a first glance the boundaries favoured the Liberals much more than those of the neighbouring Sleaford division. Stamford had a flourishing association, and had returned a Liberal in 1880. Crowland and Bourne also had fairly strong Liberal traditions, whilst in the north of the constituency the borough politicians of Grantham might be expected to stimulate activity in the surrounding countryside.

During 1885 it became clear that some at least of these characteristics were sources of weakness rather than strength. The lead in organization was taken by the Stamford Liberals, who announced that they would henceforth devote themselves to county politics. The earl of Dysart became president of the association, which held its first public meeting on 4 March 1885. Before the end of the month, however, the Stamford Liberals became involved in Rutland politics, where their former Member, Buszard, once more took up the cudgels against the Exeter interest. The Bourne Liberals had at first taken offence at the name of the division, which

116 Packe was at one time considered as a possible candidate (*Lincs. Chron.*, 23 Oct. 1885).

they thought should be taken from their own town and not from Stamford. They were, moreover, as poorly placed as Stamford with regard to railway communication with the Grantham side of the division. The Liberals of Grantham itself, where in 1885 Mellor faced a strong opposition from one of the Welby family, failed to assist the county organization. Worst of all, there was trouble in finding a candidate. Henry Knott of Stamford eventually procured Stevens Cudlip, a glib London barrister with little experience of county politics.[117]

The Conservatives had a much stronger candidate in Lawrance, supported as he was both by the farmers, to whom he offered reforms in local taxation and railway rates, and by the Kesteven aristocracy, whose imposing ranks were led by Aveland, Welby-Gregory, Thorold, and Brownlow.

The result of the contest was: Lawrance 4,647 votes, Cudlip 3,514. The Liberal organization was poor, and Cudlip failed to conduct a thorough canvass. But he was popular in Bourne, Crowland, and (though less evidently) Stamford, and preached the allotments question with some success in the more radical fenside parishes, such as Langtoft and Thurlby. Great Ponton and Colsterworth were Liberal as usual, but elsewhere in the Grantham neighbourhood there was apparently little support for Cudlip.[118]

In the early months of 1885 it almost seemed as if the Reform and Redistribution Acts would introduce no radical changes into Lincolnshire politics. The new constituencies appeared susceptible to the old influences. Landowners such as Lords Dysart and Carrington, who had not taken a prominent part in county politics for some years previously, were encouraged to lend their names to the new divisional associations, and even to take an active part in their foundation. Towns such as Louth and Gainsborough found themselves for the first time the centres of rural constituencies, and representatives of the older generation of town politicians—men such

[117] *Stamf. Merc.*, 13 and 27 Feb., 6 Mar., 5 June, 31 July, 4 Dec. 1885. Cudlip was a Congregationalist (*Boston Guardian,* 28 Nov. 1885).

[118] *Grantham Journal*, 5 Dec. 1885. Great Gonerby and Barrowby were said to have given Liberal majorities, however (*Stamf. Merc.*, 4 Dec. 1885; *Lincoln Gazette,* 5 Dec. 1885).

as W.R. Emeris of Louth and Francis Gamble of Gainsborough—were brought forward to lend an additional respectability to party proceedings.

But the resident upper class of the county—urban and rural—failed to yield an adequate number of parliamentary candidates. All six of the Conservative sitting Members stood for the new divisions. But for the seventh—Brigg—the country gentlemen were constrained to adopt a retired commercial gentleman from Hull.[119] As for the Liberals, Otter was the only candidate to own an agricultural estate in the division to whose representation he aspired. Sharpe and Bennett could be said to represent local commercial interests. But Stewart, Cudlip, and Threlfall were candidates of the carpet-bagging variety. Conspicuously lacking on both sides were new tenant farmer candidates.[120]

Despite the Corrupt Practices Act, politics were still expensive. £1,000 was a great deal to find, especially for those whose interests were involved in the declining fortunes of agriculture. And, at least in 1885, there was no hope of being returned without a contest. It was not so much the expense, however, as the hard work which frightened off possible candidates. Chaplin's fears about the new constituencies were confirmed. Addressing a Spalding meeting in October 1885, he declared that 'the labour of county candidates was now almost as much as was possible to bear.'[121] It was no longer enough to dispense friendly nods in the market place and swallow an ordinary dinner with the farmers. Tradesmen and labourers who were unable to attend ordinaries expected to hear their Members at evening meetings. Men from the more distant villages, moreover, could not easily go even to those meetings. Stanhope, speaking at Horncastle in May 1885, stressed the need for candidates to hold village meetings, 'owing to the increased number of voters who could not be expected to go to the centre of the division to hear their Member'.[122] A village campaign meant a great deal of travelling and a great deal of speaking. Even with the services

[119] And when Winn retired the Gainsborough Conservatives were then without a local candidate.

[120] Such was the dearth of Liberal candidates for county divisions that prospective candidates tended to inspect their constituencies before deciding whether to adopt them, rather than vice versa.

[121] *Stamf. Merc.*, 30 Oct. 1885.

[122] Ibid., 22 May 1885.

of a full-time agent meetings were difficult to arrange, and after struggling through dreadful roads the candidate might arrive to find that his audience consisted of twenty or thirty people (including women and children), huddled in some ill-lit barn or draughty schoolroom.[123]

For the old-style county candidate the work was not only hard but distasteful. Worse than village meetings were the town ones, where heckling and rowdiness were becoming more common. Astley, who had been shouted down at a Brigg meeting in November 1885, reflected on the changing times at a Primrose League meeting at Louth a few months afterwards:

Times are altered, and we have altered so much in our division, and I know the alteration amongst our own neighbours and men is extraordinary . . . . Instead of coming to the squire, the men go on their own ideas, which were put into their heads by men who ought to know better . . . . I may say they really urged their opinions in places of worship, and these are the men who spoil our men and the chance—we had a little—of returning a good Conservative.[124]

Parsons and farmers who had set out to canvass the labourers in their localities had been surprised in many cases at their lack of success. Tom Casswell, grazier, of Pointon, near Folkingham, described his difficulties, in canvassing his own township, to the district agent, Benjamin Smith of Horbling, in November 1885:

I get on badly with the labourers. I never saw such a set of fools as they are. Some say, I don't know yet I want the best for myself, others, I shall not vote at all, others, I have not yet heard both sides. So I expect until Mr. Lawrance has spoken they will not decide.[125]

In February 1891 Henry Winn, parish clerk of Fulletby, near Horncastle, reported, as parish correspondent, to James Gibson, organizing secretary for the Conservatives of the Horncastle division.

It is a most difficult matter to get to know the politics of our labourers. Few of them know the difference between Liberal and Conservative, and the candidate who talks the loudest and promises most is almost sure to secure their suffrage.

[123] This paragraph is partly based on the diaries of Herbert Torr, who on Stanhope's death fought the Horncastle division against Lord Willoughby de Eresby in Jan. 1894. They are in the possession of Mrs. H.N. Nevile, of Aubourn Hall, Lincoln, who kindly gave me access to them.

[124] *Stamf. Merc.*, 4 June 1886.

[125] L.A.O., Smith Deposit, 10/3.

> I have conversed, on the quiet, with most of the men whose cards I return, and few of them manifest any interest in the matter. Some say, I voted last election, and I have never told anyone who I voted for, and I never shall. Some say, I voted for Stanhope last time and he has never done anything for me, as if it were only a personal and individual consideration, and not a matter of National importance . . . . I am sorry to find that those who profess Liberal principles are the most decided.[126]

It was true that the Lincolnshire labourers took a more passive than active part in the general election of 1885. Even when they had made up their minds to vote Liberal, they tended to sit in docile silence through Conservative meetings.[127] They did not throw up forceful politicians from their own ranks, and even Liberal meetings were generally chaired by local tradesmen or—if they could be found—sympathetic farmers. The days of militant agricultural trades-unionism in the county were over, and where the labourers found leaders who spoke their language they were generally not union organizers but Primitive Methodist ministers and class leaders.

It would not do, however, to allow too much credit to the reports of tory farmers and Church people who attempted to canvass the new voters in their parishes. It was in many cases discretion rather than stupidity which tied their tongues. That discretion was necessary can be inferred from the widespread reports of intimidation in 1885, particularly from the Boston district. Few landlords can ever have exercised so much pressure on their tenants as those tenants now did, in many cases, on their work people.[128]

The spread of the Primrose League was an acknowledgement by the Conservatives that the traditional methods of rural canvassing were not getting through to the labourers. In Lincolnshire there were already branches at Horncastle, Spilsby, Alford, and Gainsborough by November 1885. But it was, significantly, the Spalding division which, in the early months of 1886, was the first in the county to have village as well as town 'habitations'.[129]

126 L.A.O., Winn of Fulletby MSS., 1/8, letter book, vol. iii.

127 *Lincoln Gazette*, 7 Nov. 1885.

128 In the Stamford division labourers were observed to tremble at the tables (*Grantham Journal*, 12 Dec. 1885). Several cases of intimidation were followed up in the Holland division, and at least one led to a prosecution (*Stamf. Merc.*, 2 July 1886).

129 For the influence of the League in Norfolk see L. Marion Springall, *Labouring Life in Norfolk Villages*, 1936, p. 111.

The Conservatives retained some advantages in rural electioneering, however, despite the legislation of 1883 and 1884-5. The most important effect of the Corrupt Practices Act in rural counties was the ending of the practice of hiring conveyances to bring up voters to the poll. But it seems that in Lincolnshire the Conservatives found no difficulty in finding volunteers among the farmers to offer rides to their employees and fellow-voters free of charge.[130] The provision of additional polling places by another clause of the act was intended to make it possible for all voters to walk to the poll. But, although the local authorities made further provision for polling places in 1885, it was found at the general election that some labourers were still five or six instead of the regulation three miles from the polling place at which, according to the register, they had to vote.[131]

The abolition of paid canvassing had no great effect on the rural districts, where the canvass was conducted almost entirely by bodies of volunteers, and where the introduction of strangers to make a canvass was seldom successful. Paid agency survived in most Lincolnshire divisions in 1885, and continued to be the most expensive item in a county candidate's account, though the remuneration of individual district agents was reduced.[132] Nor was the system of registration reformed sufficiently either to enable divisional parties to dispense with the assistance of attornies, or to ensure that all the labourers newly qualified to vote were in fact enfranchised.[133]

(vi) THE DECLINE OF THE AGRICULTURAL INTEREST, 1881-5

The reform of local taxation remained the orthodox Conservative panacea for agricultural depression in the early

130 *Lincoln Gazette*, 5 Dec. 1885; *Louth Times*, 8 Dec. 1885. In 1883 Stanhope had written to Salisbury: 'I am strongly of opinion that the prohibition of paid conveyance will be in our favour, except in the case of voters residing out of the county at a considerable distance' (Salisbury MSS., Stanhope/15).

131 The Brigg Liberal Association advocated the creation of more polling districts in 1886 (*Stamf. Merc.*, 22 Oct. 1886).

132 The Gainsborough division agents were paid £20 each in November 1885, not a large sum. But then there were 28 polling districts in the division, and Sim's agency bill came to £502, out of a total expenditure of £1,110 (*Parl. Papers*, 1886, lii, pp. 414-15).

133 As Heneage explained in a letter to the *Stamford Mercury* (14 Aug. 1885),

1880s. The precise remedies were never agreed upon. In December 1881 the Lincolnshire Chamber of Agriculture, at the instigation of the Central Chamber, called an open meeting on the subject. The chair was taken by Edward Stanhope, chairman of the Lincolnshire Chamber for that year, who gave a discourse on the well-worn theme of the differential taxation of real and personal property. But Welby-Gregory and Lawrance favoured the removal of some local charges to the Consolidated Fund.[134] This remedy was also favoured by Lowther, who, despite his Fair Trade views, seldom lost sight of the local taxation question. Addressing the Louth Conservative Working Men's Club in October 1881, he said: 'If there was to be free trade, let it be free trade all round, for the local burdens were equally a tax on the food of the people. They ought to be thrown on the general taxation of the country.'[135]

The recommendations of the Royal Commission on Agricultural Distress, which reported in 1882, were a disappointment to the farmers, and especially to those who attached primary importance to local taxation.[136] But, though not a good year, 1882 did not see a return to the low prices of 1879-80. The Lincolnshire agriculturists, and particularly those of Holland, turned their attention to the need for legislation to check flooding—a very serious problem in the fens at this period. Further measures for the control and eradication of cattle disease were also advocated, including a proposal for a ministry of agriculture to take over the responsibilities of the Privy Council.

Throughout 1883 the Lincolnshire Chamber concerned itself principally with the tenant-right question, and, in so far as the question was one of immediate economic rather than distant political significance, its meetings showed an unwonted independence of spirit. They reflect the stronger position of the tenant, in relation to his landlord, during a time of depression. The incoming tenant could make what terms he

'a very large portion' of the labourers being nonconformists, they seldom saw the notices affixed to the church doors. And few of those on whom objections were served could afford to miss a day's harvest work in order to defend their votes at the revision court.

134 *Stamf. Merc.*, 16 Dec. 1881.

135 Ibid., 14 Oct. 1881.

136 See *Parl. Papers*, 1882, xiv, p. 26, and Chaplin's supplementary memorandum (ibid., p. 37).

chose, and the sitting tenant could use his power of giving notice to quit in order to lower, or at least to prevent an increase in, his rent. It was often held by landlords that the Custom of the county was a matter of arrangement between the outgoing and the incoming tenant, and in practice, during periods of prosperity, this was so. But in bad times, with farms increasingly coming on to their owners' hands, tenant-right questions became rather more often a matter to be settled between the tenant and his landlord.

Since 1873 the Lincolnshire Land Agents' and Tenant Right Valuers' Association had met annually to adopt a schedule of compensation for unexhausted improvements, altered in accordance with farming practice when necessary, and providing a measure of certainty and uniformity previously lacking in the Lincolnshire Custom. For 1879-80 the adopted allowances for liming, marling, and claying, for instance, were all on the seven years' principle.[137]

In the sessions of 1880, 1881, 1882, and 1883 bills were introduced to render compulsory the permissive Agricultural Holdings Act of 1875. To counter such proposals Chaplin introduced his own bills in all these sessions. They merely replaced the system of contracting in, as under the act of 1875, by a system of contracting out. For counties such as Lincolnshire Chaplin's aim was to preserve the Custom from being annihilated by compulsory legislation. The terms of his bill of 1880 provided for the adoption by the contracting parties of a schedule based on that of the Lincolnshire valuers. In 1881, when reintroducing his measure, he modified the schedule to allow ten years for marling. But the county Chamber, whilst preferring his bill to the compulsory one drafted by Sir Thomas Dyke Acland, Liberal Member for North Devon, suggested further amendments, including ten years instead of seven for liming, and fourteen instead of ten for marling. These figures Chaplin adopted when he reintroduced his bill in 1882 and 1883.[138]

The Liberal government's bill which became law in 1883 was a compromise measure, aimed to reassure its own agricultural Members such as Edward Heneage, and to establish

[137] *Stamf. Merc.*, 28 Nov. 1873; *Parl. Papers*, 1881, xv, p. 264.
[138] *Parl. Papers*, 1880, i, pp. 5, 11, 17, 29; 1881, i, pp. 1, 11, 17; 1882, i, pp. 1, 5, 19, 31; 1883, i, pp. 3, 5, 29, 113. See also *Stamf. Merc.*, 4 Mar. 1881.

substantial common ground with Chaplin and other Conservatives. Chaplin gave the measure his general support, although, in his speech on the second reading, he reserved the right to move amendments in committee.[139] The Agricultural Holdings Bill, in the form in which it became law in 1883, introduced compulsory compensation for permanent improvements, but in the matter of temporary improvements–liming, marling, and so on–it allowed landlords and tenants to make special agreements in place of the statutory procedure, provided that they secured a 'fair and reasonable' compensation to the tenant.

The Lincolnshire Chamber proposed that the Custom of the county, as agreed between itself and the valuers, should form the basis of agreements on temporary improvements, in preference to the procedure laid down by the act. The schedule as given in Chaplin's bills of 1882 and 1883 was endorsed by the Chamber, but the valuers thought it too liberal. Before the end of the year a compromise was reached. Where marling was allowed fourteen years in the Chamber's proposals, for instance, and ten years by the valuers, the matter was settled at twelve years.[140] Chaplin adopted the schedule on his own estates, and also took advantage of the clause in the act whereby landlord and tenant could agree in writing on six months' notice, instead of the year's notice otherwise provided for. And probably many other landlords in the county followed suit. Even some of the tenants of Edward Heneage, who had supported the government's bill, elected to continue to hold under the Custom.[141]

There were some farmers in the county who made known their dissatisfaction at the outcome of the government's 'compulsory' legislation. William Hay of South Reston (a Liberal) wished to see an extension of the Lincolnshire Custom that would almost double the agreed allowances, and suggested that in future only one-half of the compensation should be paid by the incoming tenant, the other half being met by the landlord. He also considered, with James Howard of Bedfordshire, that the act failed to protect the sitting tenant from increases of rent in consequence of

139 *Parl. Deb.* 3rd Ser. cclxxix, 1, 110 ff.
140 *Stamf. Merc.*, 5 Oct., 7 Dec. 1883.
141 *Stamf. Merc.*, 21 Dec. 1883, 14 Mar. 1884.

permanent improvements carried out without the landlord's consent. What farmers needed was rent reduction as well as increased compensation.[142] On the other hand, Frankish, who at the beginning of the year had flirted with Farmers' Alliance doctrines respecting security of tenure and land courts, had by the autumn been convinced of the desirability of preserving the Custom.[143] Despite the fact that at Westminster the measure was in part removed from the sphere of party strife, it is hard to resist the conclusion that the Chamber on the one hand, and Liberals like Hay on the other, gave the Lincolnshire debates on the subject a distinctly partisan complexion.

Meanwhile outbreaks of foot and mouth disease, which had given rise to concern in 1880, reached serious proportions. Lincolnshire was one of the worst affected counties in 1883,[144] and one of its Members, Henry Chaplin, was a leading compaigner for the adoption of more stringent remedies by the government. He carried a resolution in the Commons in July 1883, conducted a campaign up and down the country during the autumn, and at the start of the session of 1884 moved an amendment to the address, demanding legislation at the earliest possible date.[145] The amendment was phrased in such a way as to make it a party question, and Heneage and other Liberals who had supported Chaplin in July 1883 voted against him in 1884. The government did, however, introduce a measure; and Chaplin, Heneage, and others combined to make it a little more comprehensive than the government had originally intended.[146]

The Lincolnshire Chamber supported Chaplin's campaign, but compared with the alarms of 1865-6, there was little feeling in the county. When cases of disease appeared there were the usual demands for the imposition of restrictions, followed by the usual complaints that the restrictions were burdensome and ineffectual. Chaplin's campaign, indeed, stressed the difficulties of combating the disease once it had arrived in the country, and emphasized the need to extend the powers of the Privy Council over the importation of live

142 Ibid., 2 Mar. 1883. 143 Ibid., 9 Feb., 5 Oct. 1883.

144 *Parl. Papers*, 1884, lxxxv, p. 415.

145 *Parl. Deb.* 3rd Ser. cclxxxi, 1020 ff. (10 July 1883); cclxxxiv, 203 (7 Feb. 1884).

146 2 HEN 2, Heneage to Wintringham, 4 May 1884.

and dead meat. The demand arose from the dissatisfaction in the Chambers of Agriculture with the previous legislation of 1878, and Chaplin was giving prominence to it at least as early as the North Lincolnshire by-election of 1881. Despite denials that the measures proposed would materially raise the price of meat, there is much to suggest that the protectionist overtones of the contagious diseases agitation were part of its attraction for its supporters.[147]

Soon, however, falling corn prices again forced themselves on the attention of the agricultural interest. The harvest of 1884 was a good one, despite lighter than average yields, but with wheat ranging below 40*s*. 0*d*. it brought little comfort to arable farmers. The gravity of the situation was increased by the fear that with the imminent extension of the franchise farmers would find it harder than ever to force their demands on parliament. In the autumn the county Members addressed farming audiences in a stronger tone than had been used (except by Lowther) since 1880-1. Lawrance and Finch-Hatton told the Long Sutton Agricultural Society that the farmers were entitled to demand compensation for the ruinous foreign competition with which they had to contend.[148] Lowther himself came out firmly for a sliding scale, and Winn sailed closer to the protectionist wind than he had hitherto ventured to do. Chaplin was in favour of an enquiry into the whole fiscal question, and thought it would strengthen the case for a reimposition of the registration duty, and perhaps even a return to some form of sliding scale.[149] At the general election of 1885 there was certainly an idea in the minds of many farmers, though not one openly expressed at political meetings, that a vote for the Conservative party was the only way to assist the return of Protection. Eli Crabtree told a meeting at Morton, near Bourne, in October 1885: 'Now-a-days almost all the farmers had turned tory. Why? One reason was because they were jealous of the labourers' having the vote, and another reason was they were taken with the bait

147 Even Thomas Duckham, Liberal Member for Herefordshire, declared at the Farmers' Club in 1883 that 'the farmers were not justified in tamely submitting to be handicapped with a foreign disease in their flocks and herds while competing with those countries whence the scourge was sent' (*Stamf. Merc.*, 9 Nov. 1883).

148 *Stamf. Merc.*, 12 Sept. 1884.

149 *Stamf. Merc.*, 21 Nov. 1884; *Parl. Deb.* 3rd Ser. ccxciii, 728.

of Protection dangled before their eyes'.[150] Sharpe lamented in the following month that some of his farming friends would back Chaplin—'not that they had an idea in common with Mr. Chaplin's toryism, but owing to the will-o'-the-wisp of Protection'.[151] And it was reported from the Gainsborough division, shortly before the election that 'the greater number of the tenant farmers have attached themselves to the Conservative party, hoping for a return to Protection.'[152]

By the beginning of 1886 wheat was around 30*s.* 0*d.*, and the prices of barley, and of meat and wool, which had until now provided some compensation for the upland farmers, also began to decline. In March 1886 the Lincolnshire Chamber took the bit for once between its teeth and committed itself to Fair Trade, meaning a revenue duty on imported grain, the profits of which were to be devoted to the relief of local taxation.[153] In November Chaplin, at odds with the Conservative leadership on agricultural policy, engineered an elaborate county meeting, the first of its kind to be held in Lincolnshire for many years. Chaplin's tone was cautious, but he was supported by Finch-Hatton, who wished to see a duty on imported flour, and who attempted to link the interests of farmers and labourers, by proposing that wages should henceforth be raised in step with the rising price of corn.[154]

There can be little doubt that there was considerable protectionist feeling among Lincolnshire landowners and farmers in the 1880s. Why then were they so timid in expressing it? It seems that the lessons of the 1840s and early 1850s had been well learnt. It was those who had taken part in the rural agitations of that period who were most reluctant to encourage a new agitation forty years later. Men such as J.B. Stanhope and Colonel Amcotts were convinced that 'the great commercial centres would never consent to have their loaf taxed again.' Lawrance 'did not expect to see a tax on corn again, because that was the first taken off, and it would be the last put on'.[155] Chaplin and

150 *Louth Times,* 17 Oct. 1885. Crabtree, a nonconformist miller of Great Ponton, was a veteran South Lincolnshire Liberal.

151 *Lincoln Gazette,* 14 Nov. 1885.

152 Ibid., 28 Nov. 1885.

153 *Stamf. Merc.*, 5 Mar. 1886.

154 Ibid., 12 Nov. 1886.

155 Ibid., 23 Sept. 1881.

Lowther were less pessimistic, but they believed that for a new protectionist movement to have any success it would require industrial as well as agricultural support. Hence the encouragement they took from the activities of the Fair Trade League in 1881, and from the spread of the depression in the manufacturing districts in 1884. Chaplin's select committee in the latter year was intended to provide material for an alliance of urban and rural interests.[156]

The caution of the protectionists was intensified by the enfranchisement of the labourers. Since the passage of the Agricultural Holdings Act in 1883 the Liberals of the county had paid little attention to the tenant farmers: they were too busy preparing the labourers for their new political responsibilities. One of their constant themes was the importance of preserving Free Trade. Little 'Jimmy Lowther' loaves were sported on poles at public meetings, and aged labourers were prompted to recall their sufferings in the days of dear bread before 1846.

Lord Salisbury, to whom country clergymen were fond of writing, received the following communication in November 1885 from the Revd. W.F. Curtis, of Langriville, near Boston:

> I am canvassing the labourers here in Mr. Stanhope's interest, and find that a Liberal canvasser has been endeavouring to gain their votes with the false assertion that the Conservatives are the enemies of the agricultural labourers, and wish to give the country a dear loaf . . . .
>
> As it is part of my duty to protect my parishioners from false doctrines of all kinds and from the father of lies and his progeny I shall be glad to receive your reply on Saturday so that I may be able to state the truth publicly on Sunday.[157]

The electoral changes were accompanied by equally important changes in the pattern of rural political activity. Whereas previously the farmers had been given frequent opportunities for the public expression of their political views, they now found themselves largely deprived of their customary platforms. Addresses to farmers' ordinaries gave place, as already mentioned, to evening meetings. And the local agricultural societies and ploughing meetings declined both in numbers and in political importance. By 1885 only

156 See also Benjamin H. Brown, *The Tariff Reform Movement in Great Britain, 1881-95*, New York, 1943, pp. 36, 131, *et passim.*

157 Salisbury MSS., general political correspondence, Oct.-Nov. 1885.

the Long Sutton and Alford societies retained their political functions,[158] and most of the other societies in the county had failed altogether. The bad times were partly to blame. But another factor may have been the increasing reluctance of the labourers to be patronized. A train ticket to the nearest urban source of employment was more to be prized than a medal for long service.

[158] The Long Sutton society did not meet the following year, leaving only the Alford, which was under Chaplin's wing.

13

OBSERVATIONS

(i) THE COUNTRY GENTLEMEN

'THE HOUSE of Commons of 1880', recalled Walter Long in the 1920s, 'was the last to contain the "Country Gentlemen Party", as it had existed for many decades.'[1] Whether the country gentlemen had ever formed a party in the strict sense of the word—except perhaps the protectionist party of the late 1840s—may be doubted. But certainly in the rural county constituencies (and Long was thinking mainly of these) the country gentlemen did maintain a near monopoly of the representation until 1885. In January of that year Lincolnshire was still represented in parliament by members of what may be called the hereditary governing class of the county. Lowther, it is true, did not possess a Lincolnshire estate, and Lawrance was not out of the top drawer; but the others—Winn, Stanhope, Chaplin, Finch-Hatton—belonged to families long prominent in Lincolnshire politics. Stanhope, Finch-Hatton, and Chaplin were again returned after 1885. But the country gentlemen were by then adulterated by men such as Bennett, Heath, and Stewart, men who were as little at home on the hunting field as they were at the tables of the great.

Between 1832 and 1885 Lincolnshire had continued to choose its Members from the class that had dominated its representation in pre-Reform days. More precisely, its Members belonged to a small group within a small class. They were the greater gentry, the chief corner-stones of a remarkably stable and traditional rural society. If one were to count up the number of resident country gentlemen with estates of over 6,000 acres in the county, and with London houses, and then deduct from the total those who had no ready money and those who positively hated politics, one would be left with a list of names very similar to that which

[1] Walter Long, *Memories*, 1923, p. 88.

figures in the parliamentary returns. It helped, of course, to be a master of fox hounds or a chairman of quarter sessions (especially the latter), but it was not an essential qualification to understand House of Commons procedure, or to be able to speak audibly in public. There was, in fact, little competition for the honour of representing the county. More often it was a question of impressing his public duty upon some less than willing victim.

Despite the fact that the Lincolnshire electorate was so largely composed of farmers, no working farmer aspired to a county seat between 1832 and 1885. Even the militant farmers' movement of 1850-2 was led by a wealthy and well-connected landowner, James Banks Stanhope. And this was despite the fact that the farming class of the county included not only uncouth and illiterate husbandmen but also a significant proportion of wealthy and articulate agriculturists. Farmers were not dissuaded from becoming candidates solely by the social barriers between them and the gentry, although those barriers were undeniably strong. The principal factor was probably the great expense of contests. A farmer, however rich, could not think in terms of the three or four thousand pounds that a contest might cost. He could, of course, be promoted by his fellow-farmers, but they were not very good at forming organizations and paying subscriptions. A tenant farmer candidate might have arisen at a time of distress in the agricultural community: but that was precisely the time when it was most difficult to collect subscriptions.

The great size of a division such as North Lincolnshire was another obstacle. Even members of county families might be virtually unknown in some corners of Lindsey, and a farmer could rely very little on personal popularity and influence outside his immediate neighbourhood. His political sphere was the market area rather than the county, and it was to the former, by and large, that he stuck.

In the English counties as a whole farmer M.P.s were rarities. Perhaps the four who most accurately fit that description were Edward Ball, who sat for Cambridgeshire from 1852 to 1863, Albert Pell, Member for South Leicestershire between 1868 and 1885, Clare Sewell Read, who represented first East and later South Norfolk from 1865 to 1880, and Thomas Duckham, who was returned for Herefordshire in

1880. Ball, Pell, and Read were all gentlemen farmers, all were Conservatives, and all were men supported by the gentry as well as the farmers of their respective constituencies. All were brought to prominence by particular agitations: Ball by the protectionist movement, and Pell and Read by the cattle-plague and malt-tax questions respectively. Duckham is the odd man out. He was a Liberal,[2] and the only one of the four to be described as 'farmer' rather than 'esquire' in the parliamentary returns. Perhaps in Herefordshire, a grazing county near the Welsh border, there was more militancy among the farmers than in the Midlands and East Anglia—though Duckham himself was no fire-breathing radical.

Sometimes it was members of the legal profession who came to the aid of the tongue-tied agriculturists. It was a retired solicitor, W.H. Barrow, who was returned by the South Nottinghamshire farmers in 1851, and a Queen's Counsel, B.B. Hunter Rodwell, to whom the Cambridgeshire farmers turned in 1874. Like Lawrance, both Barrow and Rodwell, despite their sympathy with the farmers, counted as gentry in the local social context.

There was no social gulf between the gentry and nobility such as there was between the farmers and the gentry.[3] But for a moderately aristocratic county like Lincolnshire it is remarkable how few sons of peers were invited to occupy the county seats. In North Lincolnshire the Yarborough interest was acknowledged by the gentry to have the political tradition and social leadership to justify a claim to one of the seats. But the gentry of South Lincolnshire were not enthusiastic about Burghley's candidature in 1847. And neither division ever welcomed a son of Lord Brownlow, lieutenant of the county though he was. The Cust family was not exactly unpopular. But it was perhaps thought to be more concerned with national than with local politics. Country gentlemen could still remember their ancient title of 'independent', especially when peers joined with party leaders in attempting to influence election policy.

The gentry, then, liked to do things their own way, and that way was characteristic of their class and period. They

[2] He stood as an independent farmers' candidate, but received mainly Liberal support (Lloyd, *General Election of 1880*, pp. 61-2, 83-4).

[3] The gentry, indeed, knew that a long record of service as a county Member was their most likely avenue to the peerage.

thought in terms of connection, relationship, and influence, and their political ardour was sometimes modified by social or personal considerations.[4] The fact, for instance, that the the Cholmeleys and the Welbys were intermarried, though of different political parties, restricted the activities of both in South Lincolnshire politics. More important was the alliance of the daughter of the Conservative Willoughby de Eresby with the whig Heathcotes, which made Willoughby reluctant to play a prominent role in a division where he might have had a strong interest.

The gentry not only selected candidates from among themselves, but their choice often fell on men of moderate opinions and non-partisan popularity, especially where such a choice might lessen the likelihood of a contest. Examples are the tories' choice of Willson for South Lincolnshire in 1857, and the Liberals' choice of Amcotts for the mid division in 1868. There were certainly times when the old concept of the 'peace of the county' appeared to triumph over more modern notions of party warfare: such was the case in both divisions of the county between 1859 and 1868. In the latter year there were even signs that an understanding had been come to respecting the whole shire, whereby a Liberal and a Conservative were to be returned for all three divisions. W.S. Northcote wrote to his mother of the 'shameful compromises' in Lincolnshire,[5] and Packe's supporters in the southern division claimed to have been the victims of a breach of faith when a second tory candidate came forward.[6] In 1857 the tories were said to have proposed that in return for allowing Cholmeley to resume his seat in North Lincolnshire they should be allowed to occupy the two South Lincolnshire seats unopposed.[7] The county leaders liked to think that they could settle the political affairs of the county as a whole, and it was in this spirit that they discussed boundary proposals, aiming at a nice adjustment of interest between the various divisions.[8]

The reluctance of the gentry to foster contests is perhaps best shown in the North Lincolnshire election of 1841.

[4] Gash, *Politics in the Age of Peel*, pp. 240, 268.
[5] Quoted by Moore, 'Politics of Deference', p. 280. [6] See above, p. 169.
[7] Diary of Weston Cracroft Amcotts, 14 Jan. 1856, *ex. inf.* Sir Francis Hill.
[8] See above, p. 162.

Christopher, the sitting Conservative Member, was made to join battle with the Yarborough interest very much against his will, and succumbed only to a combination of pressures from different sources—the yeomanry of the Louth neighbourhood, the offer of a second Conservative candidate from Brownlow, and the encouragement of the party management in London.[9] Without the militancy of the farmers the other two pressures would have been easier to resist. But at least the Louth movement absolved the gentry from the accusation that they had made 'a set against Lord Yarborough'.[10] For one tory gentleman, T.G. Corbett, that excuse was inadequate. He wrote to Christopher that, living close to Brocklesby as he did, he had no intention of going down to his estate and canvassing personally against the Yarborough interest.[11] And this was the man who had fought the division only six years before.

When there was a contest such as that for North Lincolnshire in 1841, it was the candidates and their aristocratic supporters who had to pay the bills. But they preferred that to the alternative, the launching of candidates by means of a public party organization, with all the democratic notions which that implied. As long as registration and election machinery was controlled by a small private group, so long could the choice of candidates be kept exclusively aristocratic. If party associations were founded, their tasks were confined, at least before 1868, to registration, leaving the leadership free to decide election policy. Lord Yarborough, for instance, had no wish to follow the example of the West Riding, a division where a man like Cobden could be returned by the urban politicians in spite of the Fitzwilliam phalanx.[12] Resistance to election pledges was another feature of aristocratic county politics, and this again can be seen as a sign of the determination of the country gentlemen to remain immune to all political influences beyond those of their own small circle.

[9] He recalled in 1868 that 'the late Mr. Bonham' had pressed him to contest the division against his judgement. (Hughenden MSS., B/XX/T/102, Nisbet-Hamilton to Col. Taylor, 20 Oct. 1868.)

[10] See above, p. 110, and compare the attitude of the South Lincolnshire tories in 1837, p. 112.

[11] Ogilvy of Inverquharity MSS., Portfolio 15, Corbett to Christopher, 29 June 1841.

[12] See F.M.L. Thompson, 'Whigs and Liberals in the West Riding, 1830-60', *Eng. Hist. Rev.* lxxiv (1959), p. 229.

It would be wrong to exaggerate, however, the extent to which non-political considerations affected the political behaviour of the country gentlemen.[13] After 1832 it is possible to describe the politics of most if not all the Lincolnshire gentry in terms of national party labels, even though (especially before 1841) they did not always give straight party votes. Most of them, moreover, exercised political influence on their estates in a consistent fashion. There were some changes of allegiance, and one or two instances where a son differed from his father in politics. But more often it was family tradition which perpetuated, rather than diluted, party attachments.

Despite all the talk of compromises, there is no proof that a hard and fast agreement, regarded as binding by both parties, was ever entered into during the period of Lincolnshire politics under discussion. Even in South Lincolnshire in 1868 all that really took place was a communication from one party to the other, not a negotiation between them. Nor was there ever a concrete understanding about more than one of the Lincolnshire divisions. Whatever might be schemed or hinted at, in practice each party in each division made its independent decision whether or not to fight an election.[14]

A one-and-one return without a contest might suggest collusion. But it was generally the result of a lack of confidence on one or both sides that they could carry the second seat. At times—as with the Conservatives in 1868—excessive

[13] Professor Gash, for instance, contrasts the aims of national party politics with the triumph of 'local and personal interests' in some county constituencies, with reference particularly to 'compromised' elections, and states that 'personal and family influence withdrew some constituencies entirely from the currents of national feeling' (*Politics in the Age of Peel*, pp. 240, 268). Professor Moore goes farther, and argues that 'in most counties, party, even in the limited sense to which it is applicable in Parliament, existed hardly at all.' Even the county contests, which Gash sees as evidence of genuine popular feeling, Moore describes in terms of personal feuds between opposing magnates (Politics of Deference pp. 191, 293).

[14] Professor Gash gives the examples of East Norfolk in 1835, where one party made a definite overture to the other, and Staffordshire in 1841, where there was an agreement in writing concerning both divisions of the county. In the former case, however, a contest did eventually take place, the truce having been abandoned; and in the latter case (as Gash's own account makes clear) the uncontested returns were as much the result of a balance between the parties, and of the money that both sides had spent in 1837, as the product of the negotiations that preceded the election. (See *Politics in the Age of Peel*, pp. 246-57.)

timidity might argue a want of party spirit.[15] But in other cases it argued a want of funds, the lack of a good candidate, or an unfavourable register. In South Lincolnshire the return of Packe in 1859 and 1865 did not perhaps reflect a true balance of power between the parties. But in North Lincolnshire in 1837 the absence of a contest reflected the outcome of the previous election, when it was shown that neither side could hold both seats. The speeches of Worsley and Christopher at the 1837 nomination certainly did not breathe a spirit of compromise.

The gentry, then, did think in terms of parties, but it was in terms of local rather than national party politics. Wielders of influence themselves, they naturally assessed local party strengths in terms of personalities and interests. At times this habit could lead them seriously astray, as when the North Lincolnshire tories overestimated the power of the decaying Yarborough interest in 1868. At other times they could be proved right. In 1841 the Yarborough interest withstood the Conservative assault, whilst in other counties the whigs suffered defeat after defeat.[16]

Other counties were perhaps more prone to compromises and had a less partisan gentry class. In undivided counties, for instance, the stronger survival of county feeling after 1832 may have led to the adoption of more independent and less partisan candidates. And where counties were given a third Member there was ample scope for avoiding contests and arranging amicably for the representation of minorities. In Berkshire, for example, politicians like Philip Pusey and John Walter,[17] men of local standing but uncertain party affiliation, were able to secure the third seat, the other two being taken by more conventional partisans. In Cambridgeshire it led to a convenient arrangement whereby the whigs held the third seat. (In 1852 it was not a whig but a farmers' candidate who was the third man.) Buckinghamshire was another county where a two-and-one return was usual.[18] The

[15] One of their excuses, however, was that both Packe and Yarborough were thought to be 'coming round' of their own accord.

[16] Only in E. Cumberland, S. Durham, and N. Lincolnshire, among the English county divisions, were Conservative challenges unsuccessful in preventing the return of whigs or Liberals (Moore, Politics of Deference, p. 271). Another five whig or Liberal candidates, however, were unchallenged.

[17] For whom see Gash, *Politics in the Age of Peel*, pp. 270 ff.

[18] Hughenden MSS., B/I/D (Buckinghamshire politics, 1852-76).

development of party organization, whose tendency was to foster contests, was probably slower in these three-Member counties than elsewhere. In Dorset there was still no regular Conservative organization in 1880.[19]

It was probably the spread of party organizations in the county constituencies, especially after 1868, that finally eliminated the independent country gentleman. In Lincolnshire the last of this class was Tomline, who stood for North Lincolnshire in 1881. But he was an oddity. The tory county Members became noticeably less independent in 1868, with the arrival of Henry Chaplin, Rowland Winn, and Edward Stanhope. Chaplin inherited his uncle's popularity, but none of his old-fashioned independent ideas. Rowland Winn was that least independent of Members, a party whip, and Edward Stanhope might as well have been a borough Member, for all that he seemed to care about agricultural politics. All three were strong believers in local and national party organization. After 1868 it is difficult to detect those demarcations between more and less independent elements which had played an important part in Lincolnshire politics in the early nineteenth century. With the retirement of Banks Stanhope and Nisbet-Hamilton the difference between independent and ministerialist Conservatives in North Lincolnshire faded away. With the passing of Trollope the moderate party in South Lincolnshire, with its leanings towards independence and the grazing interest, merged into the wider Conservative tradition. Among the Liberals the old antipathy between whigs and radicals appeared to have been lost by 1880. And Sharpe proved but a feeble revivalist of the Handley tradition in the southern division. Split voting among the gentry, so widespread before 1832, had declined sharply by as early as 1841. The inclination of some Liberal gentry to favour compromises in the 1850s, as evinced by Hutton and Dymoke, was not a sign of revived independent principles, but a sign that already the lesser whigs were moving towards their natural home in the Conservative party. By 1880 there were still Liberal peers in Lincolnshire, but very few Liberal gentry.

[19] Salisbury MSS., E. Stanhope to Salisbury, 12 May 1881. Since 1832 Dorset had nine times returned two Conservatives and a Liberal, eight times without a contest.

'It is true that provincial politics were not immune from central influence; it is equally true that national politics were given their peculiar colour and flavour largely by provincial representatives and provincial interests and opinions.'[20]

The inter-communication between national and local politics is often claimed as one of the distinguishing features, almost one of the glories, of the British parliamentary system. And never, perhaps, was it more glorious than between the first and third Reform Acts. Parliament was more responsive to popular movements than ever before. And yet those movements were reflections of local interests and opinions that had not yet been submerged in the colourless national amalgam known as 'public opinion'. Between 1832 and 1885 Members of parliament really were representatives and not delegates, and it was principally through them that Westminster and the constituencies maintained their dialogue. The county Member in particular was conscious of his dual role. When he visited his constituents during the recess he came as the national legislator, willing to explain the various measures that he had assisted in passing for the public good during the preceding session. When he returned to Westminster, however, he might then appear as the representative of local interests, more concerned with, and often more faithful to, the good of his constituents than the good of his party.

The Lincolnshire evidence, however, does not always confirm this interpretation. For what emerge time and time again are the contradictions between local and national politics. Members were constantly facing one way in Lincolnshire and another at Westminster, finding that what they said in one place was brought up against them in the other, offending both their party whips and their divisional supporters in the vain attempt to please both, and generally exposing themselves to charges of inconsistency, if not dishonesty. Of course, not all was discord. Members, though of opposite parties, often co-operated in parliament for the benefit of local and sectional interests. Worsley and Christopher, for instance, were used to working together on such matters as the promotion of the General Inclosure Act. Lincolnshire Members, as befitted representatives of

[20] Gash, *Politics in the Age of Peel*, p. 240.

a great agricultural county, were prominent advocates of the farming interest, from Handley's efforts on behalf of the graziers in the 1830s to Henry Chaplin's attempts to procure cattle plague legislation in the 1880s. It was when party became entangled in political questions of local importance that difficulties began.

The difficulties were perhaps more acute for the whigs and Liberals than for the Conservatives. It was part of whig philosophy to put the national welfare above class or sectional interests, and part of whig strategy to keep moderately up-to-date with current views of what the national interest was. Protectionist whig county Members were thus in an uncomfortable position in the 1830s: after 1846 they were an anomaly. Worsley and Cholmeley maintained the whig representation in Lindsey between 1841 and 1852 only because, when addressing their constituents, they neither said what they meant nor meant what they said. In later years, with Protection a lost(or mislaid) cause, the Liberals might have expected to find things easier in rural constituencies. But those constituencies only became more rather than less out of touch with national political trends. The farmers did not want Reform in 1867 or 1884, though some of them may have done so in 1832. Lincolnshire may have swung to the Conservatives in 1841, in conformity with the prevailing fashion: it certainly did not swing to the Liberals (as far as the county divisions were concerned) in 1868 and 1880.

The Conservatives were more the party of landowners and farmers. But even they had their embarrassments. Christopher is a good example. On the one hand he was, or fancied himself to be, an independent country gentleman. He opposed Peel over Catholic emancipation, and opposed him again over Repeal. He had a country seat and a large estate in the division he represented, and relied upon his local interest to secure his claim to a seat in parliament. He did not like election contests, and withheld his approval, as long as he could, from oppositions to his whig colleague. His period of influence and importance in national politics was 1846-52, when he was among the leaders of the Conservatives who were independent enough to break with Peel and form their own party. Yet he was an ambitious man, and his ambition was to be a minister of the Crown. He was chagrined that

Peel never offered him more than very minor office. He was anxious to see the protectionists achieve a working Commons majority in the late 1840s and early 1850s, and to that end was prepared to see the issue of Protection itself pushed into the background.[21] He was eventually rewarded with the chancellorship of the duchy of Lancaster in 1852, an office which, however, he regarded as 'quite independent'.[22] He had shown what his independence really amounted to when he acted as Peel's pilot balloon in 1841, and he showed it again when he voted for Palmerston's motion in November 1852. On both occasions he very naturally aroused the indignation of his constituents. These were times, of course, when his party was in power, and had therefore a particularly strong hold over his allegiance. When the Conservatives were in opposition Christopher got along much better, both in Lincolnshire and in the House.

Like Christopher, Trollope was generally in favour of compromise locally and partisanship nationally. Trollope managed better because his local interest was stronger. But he had the same difficulty in reconciling independent principles with the acceptance of office. It was not simply a personal dilemma. The principal factor was the refusal of the rural elector to understand the rules of the party games played at Westminster. As long as this made for quietness in county politics Christopher and Trollope were safe. But when the farmers were roused to demand a contest, the local leaders could find themselves caught between the very different forces of national and local militancy.

Difficulties of this kind were acute in Lincolnshire, partly because of its strong protectionism, but partly because it was a long way from the political centres of the country. Even the protectionist movement tended to draw its leaders from the home counties.[23] But it was also in the home

[21] In October 1849 he wrote to Disraeli advocating the creation of 'a diversion between John Russell and the Manchester school. If that were once achieved the better class of whigs would join us and we should get rid of the Peelites.' To this end the Conservatives should, he thought, concentrate on a fiscal policy that included revenue rather than protective duties. (Hughenden MSS., B/XXI/H/77.)

[22] Ogilvy of Inverquharity MSS., Portfolio 15, Christopher to Lady Mary Christopher, 26 Feb. 1852.

[23] Among peers, the 10th duke of Richmond (Sussex) and the 4th earl Stanhope (Kent); among farmers, Robert Baker of Essex and C.H. Lattimore of Hertfordshire.

counties that non-protectionist contenders for the farmers' favour were most active. The movements for the repeal of the malt tax appear to have been well supported in counties bordering on London, although the important barley-growing counties of Sussex and East Anglia were also prominent in anti-malt tax agitations. The Cobdenite remedies of 'financial reform' were thought to be spreading among the farmers of Surrey and Buckinghamshire in 1849; and it was with the purpose of providing a Conservative fiscal policy to counter the Cobdenites that Disraeli adumbrated his curious programme in the autumn of that year.[24] Around Birmingham the reform of the currency system appears to have been the more favoured programme amongst the farmers.[25] County Members whose divisions lay near the great cities could perhaps count on a better-informed, as well as a less exclusively rural, electorate, than the Lincolnshire M.P.s. But they could still be misled by local grievances into a misjudgement of national issues, as when Disraeli pleased his own county, only to annoy many others, when he advocated the equalization of the land tax.[26]

(ii) THE FARMERS

It may be doubted whether, despite the fears of some Conservatives, Cobden had a large following among the agriculturists during the period 1848-52. Certainly when he dwelt on the wrongs that tenants suffered at the hands of their landlords he did not appear to strike a very sympathetic chord. He may have had the blood of a Sussex yeoman in his veins, but his politics were essentially those of a Manchester industrialist; and as such he was more concerned to flay the landlords than aid the tenants. Lincolnshire had plenty of yearly tenancies, and plenty of game. But throughout the period 1832-85 there was little interest shown by local farmers in the tenant-right question, and very little bitterness demonstrated over the matter of ground game. At times of

[24] Disraeli wrote to Christopher on 15 Oct. 1849: 'if the farmers, at this "crisis", are not made to understand the financial question, as I am trying to make them understand it, it will all go to Cobden' (Ogilvy of Inverquharity MSS., Portfolio 16).

[25] See G.S.R. Kitson Clark, 'The Electorate and the Repeal of the Corn Laws', *Trans. Roy. Hist. Soc.* 5th Ser. 1, p.122.

[26] Hughenden MSS., B/III/61, Christopher to Disraeli, 22 Nov. 1849.

distress farmers might complain that landlords were not meeting them with sufficient generosity. In the early 1880s there was some public support for compulsory tenant-right legislation of an effective kind; and a leading Brocklesby tenant like William Frankish could even flirt with the Farmers' Alliance. Yet Frankish remained a Conservative: and he also remained a staunch protectionist. Farmers, at least in Lincolnshire, put Protection first. The radicals could not tell them how to raise the price of grain.

The ballot was another issue which fell flat in the rural English constituencies. For Scotland and Wales the radicals no doubt had a case: in both those countries landlord-tenant relations were sometimes characterized by political as well as economic oppression. But in Lincolnshire the ballot was seldom mentioned on platforms after the 1830s, and its eventual passage into law in 1872 had very little effect on the politics of the county.

This was not because the farmers were too thoroughly under the domination of their landlords, or too 'deferential' to speak their minds. When they were thoroughly roused they could pursue their objective with a determination that showed little deference to the aristocracy or to the idea of the 'peace of the county'. The gentry were not directly challenged in the matter of choosing candidates, as we have seen. But they were compelled to enter into controversies, and to conduct sometimes bitter campaigns against each other. It was the farmers who instigated the Lindsey contest of 1852, and it was their leaders who followed them. Only when the farmers were contented and prosperous, as for instance in 1859, could the gentry arrange the county representation to suit themselves. When the agriculturists had a direct economic grievance, they showed that, whatever their attitude to normal party politics, they felt parliament should do something for them.

Lincolnshire politics between 1832 and 1885 were *farmers'* politics. The real themes of those five decades were ones of direct relevance to the farming community—Protection, local taxation, the malt tax, and so on. It was seldom that landowners addressed the county on the subject of their own political interests, as distinct from those of agriculture. Even if they sometimes felt directly threatened by movements to restrict their sport or their estate management, they seldom attempted to mobilize rural opinion on their behalf.

Of the political demands made by the Lincolnshire farmers in the nineteenth century, there can be no doubt that the most frequent and the most insistent was that first for the retention, and then for the restoration, of Protection. Local taxation, though often mentioned, took second place at times of crisis in the farming economy. In the 1860s, though abandoned as a practical programme, protectionist thinking informed the farmers' demand for the repeal of the malt tax. And when the great depression deepened in the 1880s, Protection, even if in thin disguise, once more emerged as a living political question. There is little to suggest that the farmers of Lincolnshire became converts to Free Trade in the 1850s and were then reconverted in the 1880s. Most of them remained protectionists all along.

Protection was particularly attractive to arable farmers, and it is not surprising that it was popular in the predominantly arable county of Lincolnshire. Even those large farmers who made a good part of their livelihood from stock were dependent on wheat as an integral part of their agricultural system, whilst the small farmers of the Fens and the Isle of Axholme had little to fall back on when the wheat harvest failed them. Just as important as the crop systems of the county was the structure of the farming class. There was a large admixture of freeholders among the smallest farmers, and it was the small freeholders who were most economically sensitive to fluctuations in the price of corn. They had no landlords to give them assistance, and their mortgagees were seldom willing to grant relief on account of bad times.

But men such as these, though able, from their weight in the electorate, to influence the fate of political movements, were not likely to initiate them. The class of men who took the lead in the Lincolnshire protectionist movements were the large landowning farmers. Such men were to be found not only managing their own agricultural estates but also providing, as tenants, the capital and skill necessary for the cultivation of such highly farmed estates as those of the Chaplins and the Anderson Pelhams. These were the men, the Healeys, the Skipworths, the Lofts, the Brailsfords, and the Heanleys, who cried 'forward' when the Chaplins and Christophers cried 'back'.

Perhaps economic factors contributed also to the weakness of the latter-day protectionist movement of the 1880s. Encouraged by steadier prices for meat and wool, and assisted by improvements in communications and marketing, Lincolnshire farmers were able to go a little way towards emancipating themselves from their dependence on wheat prices. Between 1876 and 1886 the breadth of permanent pasture in the county (including pasture for hay) increased from 419,730 acres to 474,449, and the breadth of wheat sown decreased from 274,284 acres to 218,756.[27]

Another phenomenon of the later years of the century was the decline of the yeoman class. Some of the old yeomen may have been bought out by the larger landowners, and many who remained found themselves too poor to maintain their former activities in the hunting field and on the public platform. Still others may have retired from active farming in the middle years of the century, joining the already large number of absentee landlords. On the death of Thomas Kirkby, formerly of Cuxwold, in 1883, the *Stamford Mercury* commented that he had been 'almost the latest survivor of the old school of "gentlemen farmers" peculiar to North Lincolnshire'.[28] In 1906 G.E. Collins could record that 'a few of the old yeomen are still to be found up and down the country',[29] although in the Brocklesby country, which he knew best, many of the old hereditary tenant families had disappeared.[30] Perhaps the principal factor was that so few new yeomen rose in the second half of the century to fill the places of those older farmers who had pioneered the great improvements of the first half. The high farmers of the 1880s were not so high, and not so remarkable for being high, as their predecessors of the 1830s.

But Protection as a political demand was not the mere reflection of the economics of contemporary farming. It was a symbol of the cultural gulf between town and country, that gulf whose political consequences were of such significance

27 *Parl. Papers,* 1876, lxxviii, 37; 1886, lxx, 56. For the less severe and protracted depression in stock prices, compared with wheat prices, see T.W. Fletcher, 'The Great Depression of English Agriculture, 1873-96', *Econ. Hist. Rev.* 2nd Ser. xiii (1960-1), pp. 417-32.

28 *Stamf. Merc.*, 27 July 1883.

29 *V.C.H. Lincoln*, 1906, ii. 406.

30 See G.E. Collins, *Farming and Fox-Hunting,* with a Foreword by the Earl of Yarborough, 1935.

in the early and mid nineteenth century. A hatred of the towns and of the bourgeoisie was a phenomenon not confined to Lincolnshire among the rural counties of England. But the fact that Lincolnshire was so extremely rural in its economy makes it a particularly useful object of study. For the Lincolnshire farmers the programme of Protection offered a remedy for low prices. But it was also a means of asserting the rights of the producers as against the consumers. It exalted the principle of indirect taxation over that of direct taxation. And it provided an opportunity for countrymen to show their antipathy towards the towns. It was their enemies, the cotton spinners of Manchester, who encouraged the import of foreign goods and preached the odious doctrine of cheapness, just as it was they who led the campaign against the Corn Laws. When the farmers later fell back on the local-taxation question, it was partly because that, too, had overtones of the same division between urban and rural interests.

The division showed itself in political strategy as well as political philosophy. The towns of Lincolnshire, particularly in the period 1840-76, contributed very little to county politics, and this was not only because of the fact that their electoral weight in the county was small. It was also because they could find little interest in a way of conducting politics so different from their own. Perhaps South Lincolnshire provides the most obvious examples. Boston and Grantham, despite the fact that they were connected by strong economic ties with the countryside around them, were more a liability than an asset to the party organizations in the county.

This was particularly the case within the Liberal party, for the obvious reason that the Liberals were much more of an urban party than the Conservatives. The rural difficulties of the Liberals were sometimes concealed by the success, or apparent success, of whig candidates and whig interests in the county constituencies. But a close look at a rural whig interest such as that of the Anderson Pelhams reveals how difficult a thing it was to create and sustain. In North Lincolnshire the Yarborough interest rested on two supports, both of them rickety. One was the estate tradition and the personal influence of the head of the family. The other was the existence of nonconformity amongst the farmers. But the maintenance of the family tradition involved the continual and personal work of its head. If he spent most of his time out of the county, leaving the estate management to an agent, and the political management to an incompetent squire such as Cholmely, the local patroitism gradually began to cool and the grumbling began. Rural nonconformity, moreover, or at least rural Wesleyanism, was a somewhat ambivalent feature of the political scene. In times of economic depression it was not strong enough to keep farmers loyal to the Liberal party.

What might appear to have been the whig revival in North Lincolnshire in 1880 was in fact the penetration of a rural constituency by urban Liberalism. Little evidence has been found for a swing to the Liberals among the depressed farmers either in the northern or the southern division of the county. In North Northamptonshire, to venture once more over the county boundary, the case seems to have been similar. The successful candidate in 1880 was the Hon. C.R. Spencer, the scion of a whig house. But he was standing in a division in which his family owned no property to speak of; and his programme emphasized the game, tenant-right, and county franchise issues, none of which endeared him to the whigs. His return was made possible at least partly because of the progress the Liberals had made in organizing the division since 1867, a movement that was initiated by the urban politicians of Wellingborough and Kettering, and supported by the nonconformist shoemakers of the division. Whig interests were not strong in North Northamptonshire, and had long ceased to provide a leadership for the Liberal movement.[31]

What, after all, had the Liberal party to offer the farmers in 1880? In Lincolnshire at any rate the agricultural vote was not to be wooed with promises of land law reform or county financial boards. And the farmers were as little moved by tenant-right and game law questions in 1880 as they had been

[31] *Stamf. Merc.*, 23 July 1852, 22 Feb. 1867, 31 May 1867, 27 Dec. 1867 26 Mar. 1880; Salisbury MSS., 3rd marquis of Exeter to Salisbury, 21 Mar. 1880; Janet Howarth, 'The Liberal Revival in Northamptonshire, 1880-95 ...' *Hist. Journ.* xii (1969), p. 78.

in 1850.[32] They could not forget, moreover, that 'agricultural' Liberals such as Sharpe or Tomline were nevertheless members of a free-trading party. And when it came to practical measures, a moderate Conservative like Lawrance could offer as much as any tenant farmer candidate.

If any class of candidate could bridge the cultural and political gap between town and country it was perhaps the rural entrepreneurs, the market-town business men with wide rural clienteles—bankers, corn merchants, and the like. Sleaford did produce one county Member and one candidate from this class, Handley and Sharpe. But both found that they had a difficult game to play. Handley kept in with the farmers for some years, despite his lukewarm protectionism. But then, perhaps, he had more of the rural radical in him than of the urban Liberal. Neither he nor Ingilby was in love with the whigs, and both had tory backgrounds. If there was, indeed, such a thing as rural radicalism, then it was radicalism with a reactionary flavour.[33] Sharpe, on the other hand, kept in with the townsmen up to a point—certainly up to the point where he met with distrust from the farmers.

The enmity between town and country subsided after the middle years of the century, a development in which the cessation of the protectionist agitations certainly played some part. But perhaps equally important was the widening of rural horizons, the decline of intense local feeling and prejudice, and the improvement in communications between the county and the outside world. This development may form yet another part of the explanation of the weakness of the protectionist revival in the last quarter of the century. And it may also have contributed to the decline of the great aristocratic interests of Lincolnshire. No doubt it also assisted the spread of those urban ideas and methods which characterized the politics of the county in the period 1875 to 1885. And here it may be remarked that the two principal influences on the agricultural labourers, the union movement and the

[32] The Farmers' Alliance programme dwelt on these questions, and it was adopted by 59 Liberal and 3 Conservative candidates (T.O. Lloyd, 'The General Election of 1880, in England, Scotland and Wales', Oxford D. Phil. thesis, 1959, p. 381). But what evidence is there that the Alliance gained for the Liberal party a single genuinely rural seat in 1880?

[33] Of this kind of radicalism Cobbett (whom Ingilby admired) is the classic example.

Primitive Methodist connexion, were both urban in sympathy, if not also in origin.

But the appeal of Protection, and the rural resentment of urban ideologies, are still inadequate to explain the abiding and ever-strengthening attachment of the Lincolnshire farmers to the Conservative party. After all, the party of Peel did little for the farmers, and the parties of Derby and Disraeli did less. Nor might the party of the Church—for such it always was in Lincolnshire politics, from the 1830s to the 1880s—be expected to have much attraction for rural nonconformists. Nor again might it be supposed that any party at all could secure the constant allegiance of such a non-partisan body as the Lincolnshire farmers. The broad but intangible truth is that the 'heavy' agriculturists of Lincolnshire,[34] and particularly the arable farmers, suffered from Conservatism almost as an occupational disease. They seemed to inhale it from the very furrows that they ploughed.

34 The adjective was that of a Conservative, Sir James Graham (*Parl. Deb.* 3rd Ser. lviii, 954, 28 May 1841).

Map III. Lincolnshire c. 1885, showing towns, communications, country seats, and other places mentioned in the text

Map IV. Lincolnshire—parliamentary boundaries, 1832, 1867, and 1885

APPENDICES

A: THE COUNTY ELECTION RETURNS, 1832-1885

(W = whig, T = tory, C = Conservative, L = Liberal, R = radical, P = protectionist)

I *North Lincolnshire, 1832-68*

Dec. 1832	PELHAM, Hon. C.A. (W)	6,554
	INGILBY, Sir W.A. (W)	4,748
	Sheffield, Sir R. (T)	3,858
Jan. 1835	PELHAM (W)	4,479
	CORBETT, T.G. (T)	4,450
	Ingilby (R)	3,984
July 1837	WORSLEY, Lord (W)	
	CHRISTOPHER, R.A. (T)	
July 1841	WORSLEY (W)	5,401
	CHRISTOPHER (T)	4,522
	Cust, Hon. C.H. (T)	3,819
Jan. 1847	CHOLMELEY, Sir M.J. (L), *vice* Worsley	
Aug. 1847	CHRISTOPHER (P)	
	CHOLMELEY (L)	
Mar. 1852	CHRISTOPHER re-elected	
July 1852	CHRISTOPHER (C)	5,585
	STANHOPE, J. Banks (C)	5,577
	Cholmeley (L)	4,777
Mar. 1857 / May 1859 / July 1865	STANHOPE (C)	
	CHOLMELEY (L)	

II *South Lincolnshire, 1832-68*

Dec. 1832 / Jan. 1835 / July 1837	HANDLEY, H. (L)	
	HEATHCOTE, G.J. (W)	
July 1841	TURNOR, C. (T)	4,581
	TROLLOPE, Sir J. (T)	4,563
	Handley (L)	2,948
Aug. 1847	BURGHLEY, Lord (P)	
	TROLLOPE (P)	
Mar. 1852	TROLLOPE re-elected	
July 1852	BURGHLEY (C)	
	TROLLOPE (C)	

Apr. 1857	TROLLOPE (C)	4,020
	WILLSON, A. (C)	3,636
	Packe, G.H. (L)	3,188
May 1859 }	TROLLOPE (C)	
July 1865 }	PACKE (L)	
Apr. 1868	WELBY, W.E. (C), *vice* Trollope	

III *North Lincolnshire, 1868-85*

Nov. 1868	CHOLMELEY (L)	
	WINN, R. (C)	
Jan. 1874	WINN (C)	
	ASTLEY, Sir J. (C)	
Apr. 1880	LAYCOCK, R. (L)	4,159
	WINN (C)	3,949
	Astley (C)	3,865
Sept. 1881	LOWTHER, Rt. Hon. J. (C)	4,200
	Tomline, Col. G. (L)	3,729
July 1885	ATKINSON, H.J. Farmer- (C)	4,052
	Thompson, Sir, H. Meysey- (L)	2,872

IV *Mid Lincolnshire, 1868-85*

Nov. 1868	AMCOTTS, Col. W. Cracroft- (L)	
	CHAPLIN, H. (C)	
Feb. 1874 }	CHAPLIN (C)	
Apr. 1880 }	STANHOPE, Hon. E. (C)	
June 1885	CHAPLIN re-elected	
June 1885	STANHOPE re-elected	

V *South Lincolnshire, 1868-85*

Nov. 1868	WELBY, W.E. (C)	4,514
	TURNOR, E. (C)	4,078
	Packe (L)	2,714
	Taylor, J. (indep.)	3
Feb. 1874	GREGORY, Sir. W.E. Welby- (C)	
	TURNOR (C)	
Apr. 1880	LAWRANCE, J.C. (C)	4,518
	GREGORY (C)	4,290
	Sharpe, C. (L)	3,583
Feb. 1884	HATTON, Hon. M.E.G. Finch- (C), *vice* Welby-Gregory	

VI *The Lincolnshire Boroughs, 1832-85: Summary of Members*

BOSTON:
1832 – J. Wilks (R), B. Handley (L)
1835 – J.S. Brownrigg (C), Wilks (R)
1837 – Brownrigg (C), Sir J. Duke (L)

1841 – Brownrigg (C), Duke (L)
1847 – Duke (L), B.B. Cabell (C)
1849 – Hon. D.A. Pelham (L), *vice* Duke
1851 – J.W. Freshfield (C), *vice* Pelham
1852 – G.H. Heathcote (L), Cabell (C)
1856 – H. Ingram (L), *vice* Heathcote
1857 – Ingram (L), W.H. Adams (C)
1859 – Ingram (L); M. Staniland (L)
1860 – J.W. Malcolm (C), *vice* Ingram
1865 – Malcolm (C), T. Parry (L)
1866 – Staniland (L), vice Parry
1867 – Parry (L), *vice* Staniland
1868 – Malcolm (C), T. Collins (C)
1874 – W.J. Ingram (L), Parry (L)
Malcolm (C), *vice* Parry
1878 – T. Garfit (C), *vice* Malcolm
1880 – Garfit (C), Ingram (L)

GRANTHAM: 1832 – Hon. A.G. Tollemache (C), G.E. Welby (C)
1835 – Tollemache (C), Welby (C)
1837 – Welby (C), Hon. F.J. Tollemache (C)
1841 – Welby (C), Tollemache (C)
1847 – Welby (P), Tollemache (C)
1852 – Sir G.E. Welby (C), Lord M.W. Graham (C)
1857 – W.E. Welby (C), Tollemache (LC)
1859 – Welby (C), Tollemache (L)
1865 – J.H. Thorold (C), Welby (C)
Apr. 1868 – E. Turnor (C), *vice* Welby
Nov. 1868 – Tollemache (L), H.A.H. Cholmeley (L)
1874 – Sir H.A.H. Cholmeley (L), H.F.C. Cust (C)
1880 – J.W. Mellor (L), C.S. Roundell (L)

GREAT GRIMSBY: 1832 – W. Maxfield (L)
1835 – E. Heneage (W)
1837 – Heneage (W)
1841 – Heneage (W)
1847 – Heneage (W)
1852 – Earl of Annesley (C)
1857 – Lord Worsley (L)
1859 – Worsley (L)
1862 – J. Chapman (C)
1865 – J. Fildes (L)
1868 – G. Tomline (L)
1874 – J. Chapman (C)
1877 – A.M. Watkin (L)
1880 – E. Heneage (L)

LINCOLN: 1832 – G.F. Heneage (W), E.G.E. Lytton Bulwer (L)
1835 – C. de L.W. Sibthorp (T), Bulwer (L)
1837 – Sibthorp (T), Bulwer (L)

1841 – Sibthorp (T), W.R. Collett (C)
1847 – Sibthorp (TP), C. Seely (R)
1848 – T.B. Hobhouse (L), *vice* Seely
1852 – Sibthorp (T), Heneage (W)
1856 – G.T.W. Sibthorp (C), *vice* Sibthorp
1857 – Sibthorp (C), Heneage (L)
1859 – Sibthorp (C), Heneage (L)
1861 – Seely (L), *vice* Sibthorp
1862 – J.B. Moore (C), *vice* Heneage
1865 – Seely (L), E. Heneage (L)
1868 – Seely (L), J.H. Palmer (L)
1874 – E. Chaplin (C), Seely (L)
1880 – Seely (L), Palmer (L)
1884 – J. Ruston (L), *vice* Palmer

STAMFORD: 1832 – T. Chaplin (T), G. Finch (T)
1835 – Chaplin (T), Finch (T)
1837 – Chaplin (T), Marquis of Granby (T)
1838 – Sir G. Clerk (C), *vice* Chaplin
1841 – Granby (P), J.C. Herries (P)
1852 – Herries (C), Sir F. Thesiger (C)
1853 – Lord R.T.G. Cecil (C), *vice* Herries
1857 – Thesiger (C), Cecil (C)
Mar. 1858 – J. Inglis (C), *vice* Thesiger
July 1858 – Sir S.H. Northcote (C), *vice* Inglis
1859 – Cecil (C), Northcote (C)
1865 – Viscount Cranbourne (C), Northcote (C)
1866 – Sir J.C.D. Hay (C), *vice* Northcote
May 1868 – Viscount Ingestre (C), *vice* Cranbourne
Nov. 1868 – Hay (C)
1874 – Hay (C)
1880 – M.C. Buszard (L)

[Sources: *Parl. Papers*, 1880, lvii, p. 6; 1882, lii, p. 374; Lincolnshire poll books; McCalmont's *Parliamentary Poll Book.*]

B. THE REGISTER OF ELECTORS, 1832-1884

I *North and South Lincolnshire, 1832-68*

Year	N. Lincs.	Kesteven	Holland	S. Lincs.	Lincs.
1832-3	9,134	3,953	4,003	7,956	17,090
1834-5	8,872	3,835	3,859	7,694	16,566
1835-6	10,165	4,125	4,090	8,215	18,380
1836-7	10,063	4,125	4,090	8,215	18,278
1837-8	10,141	4,090	4,010	9,100	19,241
1839-40	10,147	4,379	4,350	8,729	18,876
1842-3	11,363	4,713	5,027[a]	9,740	21,103
1845-6	11,398	4,476	4,687	9,163	20,561

North and South Lincolnshire, 1832-68 continued

Year	N. Lincs.	Kesteven	Holland	S. Lincs.	Lincs.
1846-7	11,424	4,519	4,707	9,226	20,650
1848-9	11,298	4,357	4,427	8,784	20,082
1849-50	11,166	4,272	4,368	8,640	19,806
1850-1	11,288	4,247	4,341	8,588	19,876
1851-2	11,677	4,202	4,279	8,481	20,158
1852-3	12,348	4,196	4,221	8,417	20,765
1853-4	12,382	4,133	4,112	8,245	20,627
1854-5	12,262	4,081	4,010	8,091	20,353
1855-6	12,373	3,986	—	—	—
1856-7	12,435	4,085	4,202	8,287	20,722
1857-8	12,401	4,536	4,899	9,435	21,836
1858-9	12,481	4,536	4,907	9,443	21,923
1860-1	11,490(b)	4,333	4,849	9,182	20,672
1862-3	12,296	4,480	4,737	9,217	21,513
1863-4	12,251	4,484	4,664	9,148	21,399
1864-5	12,372	4,504	4,756	9,260	21,632
1867-8	12,732	—	—	8,943	21,675

(a) Probably an error.

(b) The original register, among the Lindsey quarter sessions records, gives 12,323.

[Sources: *Parl. Papers,* 1833, xxvii, p. 74; 1836, xliii, pp. 366-76; 1837-8, xliv, pp. 553 ff.; 1844, xxxviii, p. 427; 1846, xxxiii, p. 145; 1847, xlvi, p. 336; 1850, xlvi, p. 199; 1852, xlii, p. 309; 1857 (2), xxxiv, p.83; 1858-9, lv, p. 45; 1860, lv, p. 49; 1862, xliv, p. 708; 1864, xlviii, p. 227; 1865, xliv, p. 549; 1867-8, xx, p. 461.]

II *North, South, and Mid Lincolnshire, 1868-84*

Year	North	South	Mid	Total
1868-9	9,436	10,476	8,694	28,606
1873-4	10,117	11,020	8,549	29,686
1879-80	10,639	10,710	8,822	30,171
1883-4	10,435	11,232	9,699	31,366

[Sources: *Parl. Papers,* 1868-9, l, p. 113; 1874, liii, p. 99; 1880, lvii, p. 53; 1884, lxii, p. 213.]

III *Qualifications, North and South Lincolnshire, 1832-68*

	Freehold	Copyhold	Leasehold	Rental	Others	Total
N. Lincs.:						
1839-40	6,572	439	35	2,992	109	10,147
1864-5	8,807	591	0	2,801	173	12,372
S. Lincs.:						
1839-40	5,303	526	37	2,541	322	8,729
1864-5	6,062	574	0	2,565	48	9,260

IV *Qualifications, North, South, and Mid Lincolnshire, 1882-3*

	Free-, Lease-, & Copyhold	Rental (£50)	Occupation (£12)	Total
North Lincs.	6,521	1,184	2,706	10,411
South Lincs.	6,340	1,396	3,537	11,273
Mid Lincs.	5,691	1,206	2,808	9,705

[Source: *Parl. Papers,* 1883, liv, p. 369.]

V *Lincolnshire Divisions, 1885 (total electorates)*

Brigg	10,323	Louth	10,252
Gainsborough	11,107	Sleaford	9,863
Horncastle	9,941	Spalding	11,597
	Stamford 9,741		

[Source: *Parl. Papers,* 1886, lii, pp. 641 ff.]

C. AVERA(C. AVERAGE PRICES OF WHEATQUARTER), (PER IMPERIAL QUARTER), UNITED KINGDOM, 1828-1886

Year	*s. d.*	Year	*s. d.*	Year	*s. d.*
1828	60. 5	1848	50. 6	1868	63. 9
1829	66. 3	1849	44. 3	1869	48. 2
1830	64. 3	1850	40. 3	1870	46.11
1831	66. 4	1851	38. 6	1871	56. 8
1832	58. 8	1852	40. 9	1872	57. 0
1833	52.11	1853	53. 3	1873	58. 8
1834	46. 2	1854	72. 5	1874	55. 9
1835	39. 4	1855	74. 8	1875	45. 2
1836	48. 6	1856	69. 2	1876	46. 2
1837	55.10	1857	56. 4	1877	56. 9
1838	64. 7	1858	44. 2	1878	46. 5
1839	70. 8	1859	43. 9	1879	43.10
1840	66. 4	1860	53. 3	1880	44. 4
1841	64. 4	1861	55. 4	1881	45. 4
1842	57. 3	1862	55. 5	1882	45. 1
1843	50. 1	1863	44. 9	1883	41. 7
1844	51. 3	1864	40. 2	1884	35. 8
1845	50.10	1865	41.10	1885	32.10
1846	54. 8	1866	49.11	1886	31. 0
1847	69. 9	1867	64. 5		

[Source: B.R.Mitchell, *Abstract of British Historical Statistics,* Cambridge, 1962, pp. 488 f.]

Note: The average price of wheat in Lincolnshire was slightly lower than in the United Kingdom as a whole.

BIBLIOGRAPHY

A. MANUSCRIPT SOURCES

(i) Major national collections
(ii) Collections deposited at the Lincolnshire Archives Office
(iii) Collections in other custody

B. PRINTED SOURCES

(i) London newspapers and periodicals
(ii) Local newspapers
(iii) Parliamentary Papers
(iv) Primary Sources – General
(v) Primary Sources – Local
(vi) Secondary Sources – General
(vii) Secondary Sources – Local
(viii) Maps

Among the great national MS. collections only the Hughenden (Disraeli) MSS. proved of substantial value. The absence of material on local county politics is particularly noticeable in the papers of Liberal statesmen. In some cases, such as that of the Ripon MSS., this may be due partly to the sorting out and destruction of 'unimportant' material before deposit. In the case of an extremely full collection such as the Gladstone MSS. the reason would seem to lie in the lack of intimate contact between the small group of agricultural backbenchers, peers as well as commoners, and the party leadership.

As for the papers of Lincolnshire Members and leading politicians, extensive searches and a thorough circularization of descendants have uncovered little that was not already deposited in or listed by the Lincolnshire Archives Office. There may still be one or two relevant collections remaining undisclosed in private hands, but none, it may safely be assumed, that are likely to come to light in the near future. The local MS. collections used in this work are of a very patchy and random nature, with the outstanding exceptions of the Monson MSS. and the Stubbs Deposit. They fall into two main categories: the papers of leading resident landowners, such as the Monsons, Heathcotes and Heneages; and the papers of professional party agents, surviving in solicitors' deposits, such as those of Stubbs; Burton; and Taylor, Glover, and Hill.

Two distressing gaps in the MS. material should be noticed. The Yarborough collection includes only a few items of family correspondence, perhaps in part the result of a destructive fire at the end of the nineteenth century.[1] Endeavours to trace the whereabouts of the Chaplin MSS., in England and Northern Ireland, have been fruitless. It

[1] *Ex inf.* the late earl of Yarborough.

is probable that Henry Chaplin's daughter destroyed much valuable material after using it for her biography of him.

It has proved almost impossible to locate and discover MS. collections of farming families. Farmers are notoriously bad at writing letters and keeping records, and the chances of valuable survivals have been further diminished by the exodus of old farming families in the depressions of the 1890s and 1930s.[2] Inquiries revealed only one farmer, Mr. Ellwood of Mareham-le-Fen, who is directly descended from a farmer prominent in county politics around 1850, and who still holds the same tenancy on the same estate. The great Brocklesby tenant families of the nineteenth century have vanished from the estate, and the 'inheritance' of Lincolnshire farms through several generations seems to be a thing of the past.

Fortunately the work does not depend wholly or even principally upon MS. material. The major contemporary sources used have been the county newspapers, and in particular the *Lincoln, Rutland, and Stamford Mercury*. The files of this paper, at the Colindale library of the British Museum, have provided a perspective and a degree of continuity otherwise unobtainable.

Of the most use among reference works have been the poll books of Lincolnshire contests, and the county directories of White and Kelly. The local collections (Gough Additions) of the Bodleian Library, Oxford, are rich in both.

A brief survey of secondary sources must begin with the work of Sir Lewis Namier and his pupils on county politics in the eighteenth century. His study of Shropshire in *The Structure of Politics*[3] has been followed by a number of detailed studies, such as those of Eric G. Forrester on Northamptonshire[4] and Brian Bonsall on Cumberland and Westmorland.[5] It may be, however, that the rich MS. collections to which they gained the entry led them to overestimate the importance of the great landed magnates in eighteenth-century politics, and the extent to which the county electorates were mere pawns in the game of interest and influence.[6] It would be presumptuous to carp at the subtle and understanding work of Namier himself, who was generally circumspect in his treatment of the claims of landowners respecting their own power and prestige. But the crudities of his pupils and popularizers may have had regrettable effects on the historians of nineteenth-century politics.

The foundations of work on English local politics in the nineteenth century have been laid by Dr. Kitson Clark and Professor Gash.[7] But

2 Lincolnshire Archives Committee, *Archivists' Reports*, 18 (1966-7), p. 27.

3 Sir Lewis Namier, *The Structure of Politics at the Accession of George III*, 2nd edn., 1957, pp. 235 ff.

4 Eric G. Forrester, *Northamptonshire County Elections and Electioneering, 1695-1832*, Oxford, 1941.

5 Brian Bonsall, *Sir James Lowther and Cumberland and Westmorland Elections, 1754-75*, Manchester, 1960.

6 Forrester, op. cit., p. 114; Bonsall, op cit., p. 6.

7 G.S.R. Kitson Clark, *The Making of Victorian England*, 1962; Norman Gash, *Politics in the Age of Peel*, 1953.

as yet no extended study has been made of a single rural county between 1832 and 1885. D.C. Moore, in his Columbia thesis, takes Cambridgeshire as an example of a rural country,[8] but references to it are scattered through the work. Studies of party organization have concentrated on the central machinery rather than the 'grass roots',[9] and recent work on the landed interest, extremely valuable in itself, has tended to perpetuate the legend of the farmer as a shadowy cypher in rural politics.[10] Recent studies have remained content to dismiss landlord-tenant relations with a few glib references to 'coercion', 'deference', and 'feudalism'.[11]

For the agricultural interest and party politics between 1832 and 1885 the historian is still dependent to a great extent on hoary authorities such as Donald Grove Barnes and C.R. Fay.[12] There have been short studies of early pressure groups such as the Old Board of Agriculture,[13] the Agricultural Association,[14] and the Anti-League.[15] Attention has also been given to the political background and implications of the repeal of the corn laws.[16] But surveys of the role of Protection, local taxation, and the malt tax throughout the period are still awaited, and organizations such as the Central Chamber of Agriculture have not yet found their modern historian.[17]

[8] David Cresap Moore, 'Politics of Deference . . .', Columbia Univ. Ph.D. thesis, 1959. [Bodl. Diss. Films 159.]

[9] See, for instance, E.J. Feuchtwanger, *Disraeli, Democracy, and the Tory Party*, Oxford, 1968.

[10] F.M.L. Thompson, *English Landed Society in the Nineteenth Century*, 1963, esp. at p. 204; David Spring, *The English Landed Estate in the Nineteenth Century: its Administration*, Baltimore, 1963, esp. at p. 178.

[11] See, for instance, H.J. Hanham, *Elections and Party Management in the time of Gladstone and Disraeli*, 1959, p. 11; O.R. McGregor, in Lord Ernle, *English Farming Past and Present*, 6th edn., with Introductions by G.E. Fussell and O.R. McGregor, 1961, pp. cxxviii-cxxx.

[12] C.R. Fay, *The Corn Laws and Social England*, Cambridge, 1932; Donald Grove Barnes, *A History of the English Corn Laws from 1660 to 1846*, 1930.

[13] Rosalind Mitchison, 'The Old Board of Agriculture', *Eng. Hist. Rev.*, lxxiv (1959) p. 41.

[14] David Spring and Travis L. Crosby, 'George Webb Hall and the Agricultural Association', *Journ. Brit. Stud.* ii (Nov. 1962), p. 115.

[15] G.L. Mosse, 'The Anti-League', *Econ. Hist. Rev.* xvii (2) (1947), p. 134; Mary Lawson-Tancred, 'The Anti-League and the Corn Law Crisis of 1846', *Hist. Journ.* iii (2) (1960), p. 162.

[16] G.S.R. Kitson Clark, 'The Electorate and the Repeal of the Corn Laws', *Trans. Roy. Hist. Soc.* 5th Ser. i (1951), p. 109; G.S.R. Kitson Clark, 'The Repeal of the Corn Laws and the Politics of the Forties', *Econ. Hist. Rev.* 2nd Ser. iv (1) (1951), p. 1; Betty Kemp, 'Reflections on the Repeal of the Corn Laws', *Vict. Stud.* v (1961-2), p. 189; D.C. Moore, 'The Corn Laws and High Farming', *Econ. Hist. Rev.* 2nd Ser. xviii (1965), p. 544; David Spring, 'Earl Fitzwilliam and the Corn Laws', *Amer. Hist. Rev.* lix (1959), p. 287; J.T. Ward, 'West Riding Landowners and the Repeal of the Corn Laws', *Eng. Hist. Rev.* lxxxi (1966), p. 256; William O. Aydelotte, 'The Country Gentlemen and the Repeal of the Corn Laws', *Eng. Hist. Rev.* lxxxii (1967), p. 47.

[17] There is an official history of the Central Chamber (A.H.H. Matthews, *Fifty Years of Agricultural Politics: The History of the Central Chamber of Agriculture, 1865-1915*, 1915), but it conceals more than it reveals.

A. MANUSCRIPT SOURCES

(i) *Major national collections*

British Museum:
Gladstone MSS., Addit. MSS. 44,086 ff.
Iddesleigh MSS., Addit. MSS. 50,037 ff.
Peel MSS., Addit. MSS. 40,302 ff.
Ripon MSS., Addit. MSS. 43,621 ff.

Christ Church, Oxford:
Salisbury MSS.

The National Trust, Hughenden, Bucks.:
Disraeli MSS.

Public Record Office:
Russell MSS., P.R.O. 30/22.

(ii) *Collections deposited at the Lincolnshire Archives Office, The Castle, Lincoln*

Ancaster MSS. [Of particular value are the Grimsthorpe estate correspondence and the political correspondence of G.J. Heathcote, 1st baron Aveland.]

Anderson Deposit. [Journal of Sir C.H.J. Anderson, 1807-42.]

Brownlow MSS.

Burton Deposit. [Conservative agency, 1868-81.]

Daubney Deposit. [Political agency, Grimsby.]

Heneage MSS. [Estate and political correspondence of Edward, 1st baron Heneage, 1867-1905.]

Methodist Records. [Horncastle circuit, baptismal registers.]

Monson MSS. [Estate and political correspondence of the 6th and 7th barons Monson.]

Revesby MSS. [Political papers of the Hon. E. Stanhope.]

Stubbs Deposit. [Liberal agency, 1841-81.]

Taylor, Glover and Hill Deposit. [Conservative agency, 1841-85.]

Tennyson d'Eyncourt MSS. [Political correspondence of the Rt. Hon. Charles Tennyson d'Eyncourt, 1831-59.]

Yarborough MSS. [Estate papers; letter books of the 2nd earl, 1846-57.]

(iii) *Collections in other custody*

Minutes of the Congregational Church, Brigg, in the custody of the Revd. R.F. Taylor, 49 Albert St, Brigg.

Casewick (Trollope) MSS., in the possession of the Hon. Mrs. N. Trollope-Bellew. [Political papers of Sir John Trollope, 1st baron Kesteven.]

Helmsley (Anderson) MSS., in the possession of Mrs. G.G.V. Duncombe. [Correspondence and diaries of Sir. C.H.J. Anderson.]

Minute Book of the Central Conservative Association, Horncastle Division of Lincolnshire, in the custody of Edward Warner, Esq., Secretary to the Association, the Old Town Hall, Spilsby. [Minutes from 1893.]

Ipswich and East Suffolk Record Office:
Barne Family Archives. [Boucherett papers.]
Pretyman-Tomline Deposit. [Tomline papers.]

Messrs. Burton and Dyson, solicitors, of Kirton-in-Lindsey. [Liberal agency, 1841-58.]

Leicestershire County Record Office:
Prestwold Hall (Packe) MSS. [Accounts and notebooks of Col. G.H. Packe.]

Lincoln City Library:
'A List of the Freeholders of the County of Lincoln . . ., 1825.'

Mareham-le-Fen (Ellwood) MSS., in the possession of C.J.S. Ellwood, Esq. [Family papers.]

National Union of Conservative and Unionist Associations, 32 Smith Square, London, S.W.1. [Conference minutes from 1867.]

Nostell Priory (Winn) MSS., in the possession of the Rt. Hon. the Lord St. Oswald. [Correspondence of Rowland Winn, 1st. baron St. Oswald.]

Northumberland County Record Office:
Middleton of Belsay MSS. [Political papers of Sir Charles Monck, 1852.]

Bodleian Library, Oxford:
Wilberforce MSS. [Letters from Sir C.H.J. Anderson.]

Scottish Record Office:
Ogilvy of Inverquharity MSS., GD/205 [Political and other correspondence of R.A. Christopher (later Nisbet-Hamilton).]

Borough Museum, Scunthorpe:
Sheffield of Normanby MSS.

Spalding Gentlemen's Society:
Banks Stanhope MSS. [A few Stanhope papers.]

Diaries of H.J. Torr (1864-1935), in the possession of Mrs. H.N. Nevile, Aubourn Hall, Lincoln.

B. PRINTED SOURCES

(i) *London newspapers and periodicals:*

The Times.
Morning Herald [protectionist].
Bell's Weekly Messenger.
Farmers' Journal.
Mark Lane Express.

(ii) *Local newspapers*

(Listed under places of publication, with date of foundation and political character; see also above, Part One, cap. 8.)

Boston:
Boston, Stamford, and Lincolnshire Herald, 1832; later (1854) *Lincolnshire Herald* [Conservative].
Boston Gazette, 1860 [Conservative].
Boston Guardian, 1854; later *Boston and Louth Guardian;* later *Lincolnshire Guardian*; later *Boston Guardian, Skegness Advertiser*, and *Lincolnshire Independent* [Liberal].

Gainsborough:

Retford, Worksop, Isle of Axholme and Gainsborough News, 1855 [neutral].

Grantham:

Grantham Journal, 1854 [neutral].

Grimsby:

Grimsby Advertiser, 1853-71 [neutral].

Grimsby News, 1874 [Liberal from 1876].

Hull:

Hull and Eastern Counties Herald, 1838 [Liberal from 1856].

Lincoln:

Lincoln Standard, 1836-48; 1862-9 [Conservative].

Lincoln Gazette, 1835-41 [Liberal].

Lincolnshire Times, 1847-61 [Liberal].

Louth:

Louth Advertiser, 1859 [independent Conservative].

Louth Times, 1872 [Liberal from 1878].

Market Rasen:

Market Rasen Weekly Mail, 1856 [neutral].

Sleaford:

Sleaford Gazette, 1854 [independent Conservative].

Spalding:

Lincolnshire, Boston, and Spalding Free Press, 1847 [Liberal (independent from 1859)].

Stamford:

Lincoln, Rutland, and Stamford Mercury, 1695 [Liberal].

Lincolnshire Chronicle, 1833 (published at Lincoln from 1862) [Conservative].

Stamford News, 1809-34 [radical].

(iii) *Parliamentary Papers*

Select Committee, Wool Trade, *Parl. Papers,* 1828 viii.

S.C., Election Expenses, 1834 ix.

Royal Commission, Municipal Corporations, 1835 xxvi.

S.C., Agricultural Distress, 1836 viii.

S.C., Commons' Inclosure, 1844 v.

S.C., Votes of Electors, 1846 viii.

S.C., Game Laws, 1846 ix.

S.C., Agricultural Customs, 1847-8 vii.

S.C., Parochial Assessments, 1861 xiv.

S.C., Poor Law Administration, 1862 x; 1864 ix.

S.C., Registration of County Voters, 1864 x.

Statistical Returns, agricultural, 1866 lx; 1876 lxxviii; 1886 lxx.

R.C., Childrens' Employment, 1867 xvi.

R.C., Agricultural Employment, 1867-8 xvii.

S.C., County Financial Arrangements, 1867-8 ix.

Departmental Report, Cattle Plague, 1867-8 xviii.

Reports, Boundary Commissioners, 1867-8 xx, lvi; 1884-5 xix, lxii.
S.C., Malt Tax, 1867-8 ix.
S.C., Local Taxation, 1870 viii.
Return of Owners of Land (1873), 1874 lxxii.
Return of Election Expenses, 1880 lvii; 1882 lii.
R.C., Agricultural Distress, 1881 xv-xvii; 1882 xiv-xv.
S.C., Tenants' Compensation, 1882 vii.
S.C., Charitable Trusts, 1884 ix.
S.C., Smallholdings, 1889 xii; 1890 xvii.

(iv) *Primary Printed Sources – General*

(The place of publication is London unless otherwise stated.)

The Baptist Hand-Book for 1870, 1870.
Banks. *A Directory of the Joint-Stock and Private Banks in England and Wales, 1851-2*, 1852.
Bateman, John, *The Great Landowners of Great Britain and Ireland*, 4th edn., 1883.
Baxter, R. Dudley, *Local Government and Taxation, and Mr. Goschen's Report*, 1874.
Bischoff, James, *A Comprehensive History of the Woollen and Worsted Manufactures*, 2 vols., 1842.
Burke's . . . Landed Gentry.
Burke's . . . Peerage, Baronetage, and Knightage.
Caird, J.A., *English Agriculture in 1850-51*, 1852.
Catholics. *The Complete Catholic Directory*, by W.J. Battersby, Dublin, 1846.
Clayden, A., *The Revolt of the Field: a Sketch of the Rise and Progress of the Movement among the Agricultural Labourers*, 1874.
The Clergy List.
Cobbett, William, *Rural Rides*, new edn., 1853.
The Congregational Year Book for 1846, 1847.
Crockford's Clerical Directory.
Disraeli, Benjamin, *Lord George Bentinck, a Political Biography*, 1852.
Dod, C.R., *Electoral Facts, 1832-52*, 2nd edn., 1853.
Dod's Parliamentary Companion.
Ernle, Lord, *The Land and its People: Chapters in Rural Life and History*, [1925].
Gorst, J.E., *An Election Manual*, 1883.
Goschen, J.G., *Reports and Speeches on Local Taxation*, 1872.
Grant, James, *History of the Newspaper Press*, 3 vols., 1871-2.
Green, J.L., *The Rural Industries of England*, 1894.
Hope, George. *George Hope of Fenton Barns: a Sketch of his Life, compiled by his Daughter*, Edinburgh, 1881.
Kelly's Directory of the Titled, Landed, and Official Classes.
The Law List.
Long, Walter, *Memories*, 1923.
Lowther, Rt. Hon. J.W., *A Speaker's Commentaries*, 1925.

Morley, J., *The Life of Richard Cobden,* 2 vols., 1896.
The Newspaper Press Directory, 1846 –.
Oldfield, T.H.B., *The Representative History of Great Britain and Ireland,* 6 vols., 1816.
Parliamentary Debates, 3rd Series.
Pell, Albert. *The Reminiscences of Albert Pell, sometime M.P. for South Leicestershire,* ed. T. Mackay, 1908.
Rogers, Francis Newman, *The Law and Practice of Elections, Election Committees, and Registration,* 7th edn., 1847, etc.
Royal Blue Book, Fashionable Directory for 1832 [etc.], 'containing the town and country residences of the nobility and gentry . . .'.
Sanderson, James, *Tenant Right,* 1875.
Saunders, William, *The New Parliament,* 1880.
Tindall, Revd. Edwin H., *The Wesleyan Methodist Atlas of England and Wales,* [1878].
Walford, E., *The County Families of the United Kingdom,* 1860, etc.
Wolf, L., *Life of the First Marquess of Ripon,* 2 vols., 1921.

(v) *Primary Printed Sources – Local*

Anderson, Sir C.H.J., *The Lincoln Pocket Guide,* 3rd edn. ed. A.R. Maddison, 1892.
Astley, Sir J.D., Bart., *Fifty Years of my Life,* 2 vols., 1894.
Barker, Revd. J.T., *Congregationalism in Lincolnshire,* 1860.
Chaplin, Henry. *Henry Chaplin, a Memoir,* ed. the Marchioness of Londonderry, 1926.
Chaplin, Henry. *Fox-hounds, and their Handling in the Field,* by Lord Henry Bentinck, with an Introduction by Viscount Chaplin, 1922.
Church Rates, Horncastle. *An account of persons assessed to the Poor Rate, in the parish of Horncastle, and of the manner in which they voted at the poll for a Church Rate of Sixpence in the Pound, commencing on Friday, 2 September, 1836 . . .*, Horncastle, pr. James Babington, 1836. [Local collection, Lincoln City Library.]
Church Rates, Louth. *The Law, Practice and Principles of Church Rates, being a report of the proceedings of a numerous vestry meeting in Louth, 2 October, 1834, when a Church Rate was refused, published under the superintendence of the Committee for opposing the Rate,* London, 1834.
Clarke, J.A., 'On the Farming of Lincolnshire', *Journ. Roy. Ag. Soc.* xii (1851), p. 259.
Cocking, Thomas, *The History of Wesleyan Methodism in Grantham and its Vicinity,* 1836.
Collins, G.E., *History of the Brocklesby Hounds, 1700-1901,* 1902.
Collins, G.E., *Farming and Fox-hunting,* with a Forward by the Earl of Yarborough, 1935.
Collins, G.E. 'Agriculture', *Victoria County History of Lincoln,* ed. W. Pope, 1906, ii. 397.
Dale, F.T., *The History of the Belvoir Hunt,* 1899.

Dixon, Revd. Joseph, *The Earnest Methodist: a Memoir of the late Mr. Thomas Dixon of Grantham,* 1871.

Everard, Robert, *The Effect of Free Trade on the Various Classes of Society, in a Letter Addressed to the Members of the Spalding Protection Society,* 1850.

Handley, Henry, *A Letter to Earl Spencer (President of the Smithfield Club) on the Formation of a National Agricultural Institution,* 1838.

Handley, Henry. *The Speech on the motion of Sir Robert Peel, of 'want of confidence in the ministry', House of Commons, 2 June, 1841, by Mr. Handley, M.P. for South Lincolnshire.*

Heron, Sir Robert, *Notes,* pr. at Grantham, 1850.

Kelly, E.R., ed., *The Post Office Directory of Lincolnshire,* 1849, 1855, 1861, 1868, 1876, and 1885.

Larken, Revd. Edmund R., *A Few Words on the Ten Hours Factory Question,* 1846.

The Lincoln Date Book, [1867].

Lincolnshire Agricultural Society. *Rules ... and Reports of the ... Society,* 1869-72. [Brit. Mus.]

Louth Free Methodist Church. *The Regulations of the Louth Free Methodist Church, with Introductory Observations,* Louth, 1854.

Maddison, Revd. Canon A.R., ed., 'Lincolnshire Pedigrees', *Harl. Soc.* l-lii (1902-4).

Nevile, Revd. Christopher, *A Letter to Lord Worsley, M.P., upon his vote of Confidence in Ministers,* 1841.

North Lincolnshire Agricultural Society. *Rules and Annual Reports,* 1863-7. [Brit. Mus.]

Perks, Sir Robert W. *The Life-story of Sir Robert W. Perks, Bart., M.P.*, by Denis Crane, 1909.

The Poll for the County of Lincoln, 1807, Lincoln (William Brooke), 1807.

The Poll for the . . . County of Lincoln, 25-27 June 1818, Lincoln, 1818.

The Poll for the County of Lincoln, 26 Nov.-6 Dec. 1823, Lincoln, 1824.

The Poll for the Northern Division of Lincolnshire, 21-22 Dec. 1832, Lincoln, n.d.

The Poll for the . . . Lindsey Division of Lincolnshire, Jan. 1835, Stamford, n.d.

The Poll Book for the Parts of Lindsey, Aug. 1841, Lincoln, n.d.

The Poll Book for the Southern or Kesteven and Holland Division of the County of Lincoln, Sleaford, 1841.

Poll Book of the North Lincolnshire Election Taken in July, 1852 . . ., Boston (Thomas Fricker), 1852.

The Poll Book for the Election of two Members to Represent in Parliament the Southern Division of the County of Lincoln . . ., Apr. 1857, pr. W. Fawcett, Sleaford, n.d.

The Poll Book . . . for the Southern Division of the County of Lincoln, Nov. 1868, Sleaford, n.d.

Pusey, Philip, 'On the Agricultural Improvements of Lincolnshire', *Journ. Roy. Ag. Soc.* iv (1843-4), p. 287.

Richardson, Charles. *The Peasant Preacher: Memorials of Mr. Charles Richardson,* 2nd edn., 1866.

Richardson, Mary E., *The Life of a Great Sportsman, John Maunsell Richardson,* with an Introduction by Victoria, Countess of Yarborough, 1919.

Sidney, Samuel, *Railways and Agriculture in North Lincolnshire,* 1848.

Simpson, Justin, *Obituary and Records for the Counties of Lincoln, Rutland and Northampton, 1800-59,* Stamford, 1861.

Sowerby, F. *A Memorial Sketch of Mr. Francis Sowerby, of Aylesby, Grimsby,* pr. at Grimsby, n.d.

Trollope, Ven. E., *The Family of Trollope,* Lincoln, 1875.

White, William, *History and Gazetteer of Lincolnshire,* Sheffield, 1842, 1856, 1872, 1882.

Wordsworth, Christopher, *A Pastoral to the Wesleyan Methodists, with a Friendly Appeal on the Owston Epitaph,* Lincoln, 1875. *Christopher Wordsworth, Bishop of Lincoln,* by J.H. Overton and E. Wordsworth, 1888.

Thompson, Pishey, *The History and Antiquities of Boston,* 1856.

Young, Arthur, *A General View of the Agriculture of the County of Lincoln . . .,* 1799.

(vi) *Secondary Sources – General*

(A select list of works of historical analysis published after 1900, excluding titles already referred to on pp. 258-60 above.)

Andrews, Julia H., 'Political Issues in the County of Kent, 1820-46', London M.Phil. thesis, 1967.

Best, R.H., and Coppock, J.T., *The Changing Use of Land in Great Britain,* 1962.

Beynon, V.H., and Harrison, J.E., *The Political Significance of the British Agricultural Vote,* University of Exeter, Department of Economics, Report No. 134, July 1962.

Brown, Benjamin H., *The Tariff Reform Movement in Great Britain, 1881-95,* New York, 1943.

Davies, E., 'The Small Landowner, 1780-1832, in the Light of the Land Tax Assessments', *Econ. Hist. Rev.* i (1927-8), p. 87.

Dictionary of National Biography.

Dow, George, *Great Central,* Vol. 1: *The Progenitors, 1813-63,* 1959.

Gash, Norman, *Reaction and Reconstruction in English Politics, 1832-52,* Oxford, 1965.

Grinling, Charles H., *The History of the Great Northern Railway, 1845-1902,* new issue, 1903.

Hayes, B.D., 'Politics in Norfolk, 1750-1832', Cambridge Ph.D. thesis, 1959.

Howarth, Janet, 'The Liberal Revival in Northamptonshire, 1880-95', *Hist. Journ.* xii (1969), p. 78.

McCalmont, F.H., *The Parliamentary Poll Book of all Elections from 1832 . . .,* 7th edn., 1910.

Mitchell, B.R., *Abstract of British Historical Statistics,* Cambridge, 1962.

Moore, D.C., 'The Other Face of Reform', *Vict. Stud.* v (1961) p. 7.

Namier, Sir L., and Brooke, J., *The House of Commons, 1754-90,* 3 vols., 1964.

Peerage, The Complete, by G.E.C.

Pelling, Henry, *Social Geography of British Elections, 1885-1910,* 1967.

Pennock, J. Rowland, 'The Political Power of British Agriculture', *Pol. Stud.* (1959), p. 291.

Pressnell, L.S., *Country Banking in the Industrial Revolution,* Oxford, 1956.

Robb, J.H., *The Primrose League, 1883-1906,* New York, 1942.

Sedgwick, Romney, *The House of Commons, 1715-54,* 2 vols., 1970.

Smith, Derek Walker-, *The Protectionist Case in the 1840s,* Oxford, 1933.

Smith, F.B., *The Making of the Second Reform Bill*, Cambridge, 1966.

Shannon, R.T., *Gladstone and the Bulgarian Agitation, 1876*, 1963.

Self, Peter, and Storing, Herbert J., *The State and the Farmer,* 1962.

Stewart, Robert, *The Politics of Protection: Lord Derby and the Protectionist Party, 1841-52,* Cambridge, 1971.

Thompson, F.M.L., 'Whigs and Liberals in the West Riding, 1830-60', *Eng. Hist. Rev.* lxxiv (1959), p. 214.

Vincent, J.R., *Pollbooks, How Victorians Voted,* Cambridge, 1967.

Watson, Professor J.A. Scott, *The History of the Royal Agricultural Society, 1839 to 1939,* 1940.

(vii) *Secondary Sources – Local*

Baker, Frank, *The Story of Cleethorpes and the Contribution of Wesleyanism through Two Hundred Years,* Cleethorpes, 1953.

Chambers, J.D., 'Enclosure and the Small Landowner in Lindsey', *Lincs. Hist.* i (1947), p. 15.

Corns, A.R., *Bibliotheca Lincolniensis,* 1904.

Grigg, David, *The Agricultural Revolution in South Lincolnshire,* Cambridge, 1966.

Hill, Sir Francis, *Georgian Lincoln,* Cambridge, 1966.

Lee, J.M., 'Stamford and the Cecils, 1700-1885, a Study in Political Control', Oxford B.Litt. thesis, 1957.

Lester, George, *Grimsby Methodism, 1743-1889, and the Wesleys in Lincolnshire,* 1890.

Mumby, Eileen H., *Methodism in Caistor,* Caistor, 1961.

Obelkevich, James, 'Religion and Rural Society in South Lindsey, 1825-75', Columbia Ph.D. thesis, 1971.

Olney, R.J., 'The Battle of Epworth, 3 June 1852', *Lincolnshire History and Archaeology,* no. 5 (1970), p. 39.

Russell, Rex C., *The 'Revolt of the Field' in Lincolnshire,* Lincolnshire Committee of the National Union of Agricultural Workers, 1956.

Smith, Alan, 'Politics and Power in Nineteenth-Century Lincolnshire', unpublished article.

Stamford. *The Making of Stamford,* ed. Alan Rogers, Leicester, 1965.

Thirsk, Joan, *English Peasant Farming: The Agrarian History of Lincolnshire from Tudor to recent Times,* 1957.

(viii) *Maps*

Bryant, A., *Map of the County of Lincoln, made from actual survey in the years 1825-26, 27 . . .,* 1828.

Ordnance Survey, One-Inch Survey, 2nd edn., 1891. [Lincolnshire surveyed 1883-91.]

Philips' Atlas of the British Isles, [1904].

INDEX

(Places are in Lincolnshire unless otherwise indicated)

BOADICEA

BOADICEA

J. M. Scott

Constable London

Published in Great Britain 1975 by
Constable and Company Ltd
10 Orange Street London WC2H 7EG

ISBN 0 09 459580 1

Set in Monotype Garamond
Printed in Great Britain by
Ebenezer Baylis & Son Limited
The Trinity Press, Worcester, and London

Contents

Illustrations

Preface

Boadicea is remembered, more than nineteen centuries after her death, as one of the most romantic figures in our island story. This is remarkable for several reasons, apart from the great span of time.

The only historians who can have any claim to contemporary knowledge of the events concerned are Roman writers—who must be considered as the enemy. However objective they tried to be one cannot expect them to describe her and her actions sympathetically; and they do not. Many hundreds of years were to pass before a British account appeared, and by that time this island must have been thoroughly indoctrinated with the Roman point of view.

Then, we know so little about her personally. There is only one quite short description of her appearance. That is certainly impressive. But we know almost nothing about her early life. At the time of her rebellion, when there is first mention of her, she was a widow with two young daughters. She was beaten by the Romans, her daughters were raped and her people dispossessed. She rose against the oppressors, gathering other tribes to her standard. Thereafter, for a few months at most, her followers behaved with a savagery which is shocking even by the standards of the time. Her followers sacked three Roman-dominated towns and Boadicea came near to driving across the sea the army of the greatest empire in the world. Then, when the odds were numerically very much in her favour, she was routed—and disappears from history by an unknown end, while what remained of her people suffered the consequences.

There are points both good and bad in this, to attract and to repel. But is there enough of the former to create a national heroine? The fact remains that Boadicea is in that category. And the sceptic is entitled to wonder whether she had been 'built up' by fact or fiction, history or legend.

Let us enumerate the points which have made her name remembered, without at this stage separating the legendary from the authenticated. The first is childish, literally so. It is in our schooldays that almost all of us learn our ancient history. This is uninspiring to the schoolboy. Then he comes upon a person—a woman!—who rose against the Romans and dashed about in a chariot with scythes on the axles cutting off the legs of the people whose dead language he has to endure in other uninspiring lessons. That is something he remembers for the rest of his life! He may have acquired no more information about the lady, but that is enough.

The writer cannot speak with the same authority about schoolgirls. It is possible that Boadicea has for them a less bloodthirsty and more feminist appeal. And certainly a woman warrior can be a romantic image for any adult—unless he happens actually to have met a female revolutionary. In the more exalted plane, Joan of Arc was our enemy, but she is admired in this country scarcely less than in France.

Then, Boadicea rose against oppression, against an omnipotent conqueror. That has a very strong appeal, bolstering national pride. Such defiance has inspired our finest emotions, our best prose. As Lewis Spence wrote in 1937: 'If the fire of her rebellion glows like a torch at the gateway of our history, it continues to burn because of the deathless and intrepid patriotism which lit and inspired it.'

Winston Churchill in his *History of the English-Speaking Peoples* described the burdens and abuses which led up to the revolt, and wrote: 'There followed an uprush of hatred from the abyss, which is a measure of the cruelty of the conquest. It was a scream of rage against invincible oppression and the superior culture which seemed to lend it power. . . . Her monument on the Embankment opposite Big Ben reminds us of the harsh cry "Liberty or Death" which has echoed down the ages.'

As for the horrors, they happened long enough ago for us to accept them with far less revulsion than we would feel at some minor cruelty read of in today's newspaper. But, paradoxically, a heroic or dramatic act keeps its value irrespective of time and distance—and *almost* irrespective of accuracy. If a story has sufficient heroism and drama it will go on moving people from generation to generation, whether it be true, not quite true, or downright fiction.

The story of Boadicea's rebellion has dramatic quality. No doubt about that. But is this sufficient in itself to explain its survival? And in what proportions does it depend on facts and on legend? The historical sources are limited. The most trustworthy and illuminating is Tacitus. His father-in-law, Agricola, was in Britain at the time of the rebellion, and Tacitus heard the story from his lips. Tacitus is a careful historian, unconvicted by scholars of any deliberate false statement in his records. He gives a short account in his *Agricola* and a longer one in his *Annals*. The other main classical source is Cassius Dio, or Dion, who was born in about A.D. 155—some ninety-five years after the rebellion. For his account, which is at greater length, he evidently drew on Tacitus, but he may have had other contemporary sources which have been lost. If there is no corroboration for much that he says, in addition to what Tacitus has told us, at least it all fits in with our background knowledge. This background knowledge is uneven but in some fields adequate. We have from Roman sources plenty of information about the Roman civil and military organization, and a certain amount about the British tribes. Added to this are very considerable archaeological discoveries, many directly concerned with the Iceni, Boadicea's tribe. Thus it is possible to sift out a fairly detailed story which may be taken as historically true.

The plan of this book is to start with a chapter on the legend, giving the unauthenticated and frankly fictional versions. The remaining chapters tell the actual story—history borne out and expanded by archaeology. We begin with the scene in Britain at the beginning of the first century. In this we are to a certain extent helped by Julius Caesar's account of his two deep raids of 55 and 54 B.C. Then comes the invasion by Claudius of A.D. 43, the partial conquest, the beginnings of colonization. Then the build-up and outburst of rebellion; and finally its course and aftermath. The object is to give Boadicea's story a proper setting in history—a beginning, a middle and an end. Whether this contains the necessary dramatic ingredients, the reader must decide for himself.

One final point. Recorded history has given us facts to go on. Archaeology in the widest sense—digging up the past—has provided a wealth of data. But these facts and data are of comparatively little help in *seeing* a story without imagination—or deduction, which is imagination disciplined by facts. For instance, we know that a historical character did a certain thing. But to discover his or her motive, imagination must be used. The same is true for the interpretation of a find which science tells us is of appropriate date. So imagination has been used here and there—frankly and admitted as such—by the writer. And it is still more necessary in the reader.

Scholars are now agreed that the person with whom this book is concerned should be named Boudicca, or perhaps Boudica, the derivation being from the Welsh *buddug*, or more ancient word *buddig*—both meaning 'victory'.

Surely the main purpose in using a name is to let people know to whom you are referring. If our title were *Boudicca* some people would recognize the subject and be satisfied that the right word had been used. With *Boadicea* as the title some may be critical. But at least everyone will know whom the book is about.

For a similar reason I have generally referred to Colchester, St. Albans, London, etc. instead of Camulodunum, Verulamium, Londinium. (For list see below.) But since the narrative is inevitably peppered with the names of people and tribes which have no modern equivalents it has seemed best to simplify wherever possible.

For his background reading the writer is chiefly indebted to the following books: *Boadicea*, by Lewis Spence; *Roman Britain*, by I. A. Richmond; *Roman Britain and the English Settlement*, by R. G. Collingwood and J. H. L. Myers; *The Rebellion of Boadicea*, by Donald R. Dudley and Graham Webster; and *The Roman Conquest of Britain*, by Donald R. Dudley and Graham Webster.

J. M. Scott

Roman names of places mentioned

Anglesey—Mona

Caernarvon—Sagontium

Canterbury—Durovernum

Chester—Deva

Colchester—Camulodunum

Exeter—Isca

Gloucester—Glevum

Isle of Man—Monavia

Lincoln—Lindum

London—Londinium

Richborough—Rutupiai

St. Albans—Verulamium

Silchester—Calleva

Staines—Pontes

Towcester—Lactodorum

Wall—Letocetum

Wroxeter—Viroconium

I

The building of the legend

In the days when families played round games there was one which consisted of the telling of a story by the first player to the second, who repeated it to a third, who repeated it to a fourth—and so on until perhaps a dozen people had heard a version and then told their own. At the end the final result was compared with the original.

The story of Boadicea has been treated somewhat like that during the last nineteen hundred years.

Tacitus told it first, briefly as follows. Sixteen or seventeen years after the conquest of southern Britain in A.D. 43, Prasutagus, king of the Iceni, died. He left half of his considerable riches to his two daughters and the other half to the Emperor Nero, hoping thereby to win continued freedom for his kingdom. But the Roman chief Treasury official confiscated everything in the name of the Emperor, dispossessed the Icenian nobles and took many as slaves. His followers flogged the widow of Prasutagus, Boadicea, and raped her two daughters. This was the culmination of a long series of oppressions. The whole of south-east Britain rose in revolt under the leadership of Boadicea.

The Roman Governor, Suetonius Paulinus, was at that time engaged in the conquest of Anglesey and the north-western mainland of Wales. He at once rode to London with his cavalry, but before he felt strong enough to engage the British host, Boadicea had destroyed Colchester, London and St. Albans, and cut to pieces a strong legionary rescue force from Lincoln. In the final battle, however, the British were routed and Boadicea killed herself.

Dio Cassius repeated this story, adding further details. The only other classical historian concerned is Suetonius—the second-century writer, not the Governor of Britain mentioned above. In the Dark Ages the voices of those writers were lost, not to be heard again until the Renaissance. During that period some strange tales passed as history. Even when the original sources could once more be consulted, a story which engaged the emotions as much as did that of Boadicea was handled in different ways, with variations of fact or emphasis. The Queen of the Iceni has by no means always been treated as a heroine. It may be useful, and it is certainly diverting, to trace her ups and downs in popularity and the various versions of her story. The final result is in this case the original, borne out and amplified—considerably amplified—by the detective science of archaeology.

Gildas the Wise, born about 516, is our first British historian. A monk and a saint, he was chiefly concerned in pointing out the wickedness of mankind in general and his own countrymen in particular. For him the Romans, who had been gone from this island for rather more than a century, were the best of a bad lot. As for his sources, he refers without naming them to 'foreign writers', but the chief value of his *Liber querulus de excidio Britanniae* is as a record of contemporary legend. From such a writer we could hardly expect a complimentary reference to Boadicea, and we do not get it. But at least she is no worse castigated than many other leaders:

This island, stiff-necked and stubborn-minded, from the time of its being first inhabited, ungratefully rebels, sometimes against God, sometimes against her own citizens, and frequently, also, against foreign kings and their subjects . . . .

For when the rulers of Rome had obtained the empire of the world, subdued all the neighbouring nations and islands towards the east, and strengthened their renown by the first peace which they made with the Parthians, who border on India, there was a general cessation from war throughout the whole world; the fierce flame which they kindled could not be extinguished or checked by the Western Ocean, but passing beyond the sea, imposed submission upon our island without resistance, and entirely reduced to obedience its unwarlike but faithless people, not so much by fire and sword and warlike engines, like other nations, but threats alone, and menaces of judgement frowning on their countenance, whilst terror penetrated to their hearts.

When afterwards they returned to Rome, for want of pay, as is said, and had no suspicion of an approaching rebellion, that deceitful lioness [Boadicea], put to death the rulers who had been left among them, to unfold more fully, and to confirm the enterprises of the Romans. When the report of these things reached the Senate, and they with a speedy army made haste to take vengeance on the crafty foxes, as they called them, there was no bold navy on the sea to fight bravely for the country; by land there was no marshalled army, no right wing of battle, nor other preparation for resistance; but their backs were their shields against their vanquishers, and they presented their necks to their swords, whilst chill terror ran through every limb, and they stretched out their hands to be bound like women: so that it has become a proverb, far and wide, that the Britons are neither brave in war nor faithful in time of peace.

The Romans, therefore, having slain many of the rebels, and reserved others for slaves, that the land might not be entirely reduced to desolation, left the island, destitute as it was of wine and oil, and returned to Italy, leaving behind them taskmasters, to scourge the shoulders of the natives, to reduce their necks to the yoke, and their soil to the vassalage of a Roman province.

A thousand years went by before Boadicea was again mentioned, for although Bede referred briefly to the rebellion in his *Ecclesiastical History* he did not name its leader. It remained for an Italian, Polydore Vergil, to write of 'Voadicia' in his history of England. Apart from a few geographical errors (he confused the Isle of Anglesey, Mona, with the Isle of Man) his account is reasonably accurate from the moment when the rebels 'didde sodaynelie slide from the Romaines, in headlong rage with weapon rising against them', until their final defeat by Suetonius. Then, 'Voadicia, cheefe governess of the battale, lest shee shoulde fall into the hands of her enimies, ended her life bie empoysoninge her selfe. The estate of the Ile from that time forth was more quiet.'

Polydore Vergil spent most of his life in England, and it was at the wish of Henry VII that he undertook his history of Britain. He is adjudged by far the most scholarly and painstaking historian who wrote of England at that date. An interesting incident is that he asked

James IV of Scotland for information on the Scottish kings. This request was refused on the grounds that only a Scotsman was suitable to write Scottish history. So this task was given to Hector Böece.

Böece (1465–1536) called Boadicea 'Voada' and moved the scene of her rebellion a few hundred miles to the north. As with Polydore Vergil, the Isle of Anglesey is the Isle of Man. But most of the action is in Scotland. Berwick and Carlisle are destroyed by the rebels, and almost all the characters are Scottish.

> Voada send ane secrete servand to hir bruther Corbrede, king of Scottis, schawing the incredibill iniuries done to hir bi Romanis, hir dochteris brocht to sik calamite that pacience is bot place to mair displesour.

King Corbrede plays an important part. This is not the only occasion in the development of the legend when a man helps Boadicea. It is as if it could not be accepted that a woman had done so much on her own! But the ladies as a whole are often to the fore, for good and ill. When the Roman fortress of Carlisle was taken, 'the Scottis were so kendillit in hatrent to revenge the iniuries done bi Romanis, that the wemen cessit fra na maner of cruelty that mycht be devisit aganis thame'. And for the final battle, 'Voada gadderit an ehuge noumer of Britonis, with mony ladyis with manis corage in bricht harnes'.

Böece describes the battle with fair accuracy. In fact there is a salting of truth throughout the whole account, enough to show that he had read Tacitus. But the magnet of nationalism pulled it all to the north.

Böece does, however, add a pleasant final touch. Though Voada kills herself, her two daughters are captured with weapons in their hands. And one of them marries a valiant Roman named Marius, 'quhilk bereft hir virginite afoir'. They became king and queen of Britain. One hopes that they lived happily ever after.

A few years after the death of Böece, Pietro Ubaldini came from his native Italy to England. He illustrated manuscripts, taught Italian, and fought in Scotland under Sir James Crofts in 1549. He was the author of *Vite delle Donne Illustre di Regno dell' Inghilterre e della Scotia*. A *Life* of one illustrious lady of the kingdom of England is that of Voadicia, and there is another of Bonduica—for Ubaldini has been confused by the various forms of Boadicea's name and the different versions of her story. He seems to have been listening to Tacitus, Dio and Böece talking all together. But this matters little, for he is less concerned with the details of a life story than with the moral that can be drawn from it. This, in translation, is what a critical Italian commented—of Voadicia: '. . . and thirty thousand men were cut to pieces, and thus was she constrained to yield up the country to her conquerors, and though adverse fortune had so cruelly reduced her from her former greatness to a state of extreme wretchedness, she none the less recalled her former nobility, and, in order that she might die free, not wishing to be paraded in triumph before her proud captors, she killed herself with poison, leaving for posterity the memory of a rare strength of character and a respected and generous wisdom.'

And of Bonduica: 'She was indeed worthy to be numbered among the great women of this kingdom because of her wondrous nobility, nor should the cruelty used by her towards her enemies be allowed to exclude her from that band of praiseworthy women when it was done on impulse and in the heat of revenge rather than as a manifestation of her natural inclination—either that or that the vices of the Roman soldiers, learnt from the wicked Nero, their Emperor, were such that they called for a punishment in keeping with their gravity.'

Ubaldini was writing for Italians, who no doubt were as interested then as they are now in the eccentricities of British ladies. But he is of importance to the theme of this chapter because, like Böece with his happy ending, he provides something for the imagination to catch hold of. He widened the audience.

Edmund Spenser widened it still more in England. In *The Ruines of Time* Boadicea is:

> Bunduca, that victorious Conqueresse
> That lifting up her brave heroick thought
> 'Bove womens weakness, with the Romans fought:
> Fought, and in field against them thrice prevailed.

In *The Faerie Queene* she fights the Romans on the Severn:

> But being all defeated, save a few,
> Rather than fly, or be captiv'd, her-selfe she slew.

Thus, during the reign of Queen Elizabeth, the queen of the Iceni is for the first time given the status of a heroine. But the audience was still small and comparatively sophisticated, limited to those who could read.

The next phase was the telling of the story visually and vocally. This brought it within the range of everyone—

but at the price of drifting even further from the original, for historical drama is history as it *ought* to have been.

Ben Jonson included Boadicea in his *Masque of Queenes*. She appears eighth in an illustrious company of female rulers who range back into antiquity and legend. She is thus presented: 'The eygt, our owne honor, Voadicea, by some Boadicia, by some Bunduica, and Bunduca: Queene of the Iceni, a people that inhabited that part of the Iland which was call'd East-Anglia . . . since she was borne here at home, we will first honor her with a home-borne testimony from the grave and diligent Spenser.'

He quotes the verse given above, then gives specimens of what Tacitus and Dio had to say of her; and sums up: 'All which does waygh the more to her true prayse, in coming from the mouthes of Romanes and enemies.'

Jonson appreciated that the original versions derived from hostile propagandists. Although a minor point, this deserves notice.

After the masque, Boadicea appeared in straight theatre. Unfortunately Shakespeare did not write about her. His plays come within a generation and a neighbouring tribe of hers in *Cymbeline* who was, historically, the early first-century monarch of south-east Britain, his capital at Colchester—Camulodunum, the first city which Boadicea sacked.

In Shakespeare's lifetime John Fletcher wrote *Bonduca*, which was performed in 1610 by the Shakespearian Kings Men with Richard Burbage in the lead. Either because Burbage had to have the chief part or because after the long reign of Elizabeth the public had had enough of female rule, Boadicea is not the most important character in this play. Burbage's Catarach dominates. He is the quintessence of self-righteous masculine virtue. He commands the army of his cousin, the queen, and reacts in the most superior manner to all her noble utterances, telling her to 'go spin'. When the younger daughter lures the Roman who is in love with her into a trap which she has baited with herself, Catarach appears, tells her that sort of thing isn't done, and sets the trusting Roman free.

Boadicea is allowed to die nobly, proclaiming:

> If you would keep your laws and Empire whole
> Place in your Roman flesh a British soul.

But Catarach gets the final curtain, Suetonius ordering:

> March on, and through the camp, on every tongue
> The virtues of great Catarach be sung.

The plot has only a very vague similarity with the Tacitean narrative.

There were two other plays about Boadicea, by Richard Hopkins in 1697 and by Richard Glover in 1753. In the second of these Garrick took the part of Dumatrix, who is the commander of her army in this version; for once again she is not allowed to lead herself. She dies off stage, 'blind with despair and disappointed fury'. It seems that her brief phase of popularity is over.

But Milton poured the coldest water on her. In his *History of Britain* he wrote: 'The truth is that in this battle and whole business the Britons never more plainly manifested themselves to be right barbarians: no rules, no foresight, no forecast, experience, or estimation, either of themselves or of their enemies: such confusion, such impotence, as seemed likest not to a war, but to the wild hurry of a distracted woman, with as mad a crew at her heels.'

adicea, her reputation had never sunk so low! he suffered from one poet writing prose was by another writing verse. In 1782 Cowper published his Ode. In this he introduces a Druid prophesying future greatness. A shrewd stroke, that! The queen might lose the war but her race would inherit the earth—as the British were busily doing at that time. And ten thousand read it for every one who read Milton's *History*. The legend received the kiss of life.

When the British warrior queen,
 Bleeding from the Roman rods,
Sought, with an indignant mien,
 Counsel of her country's gods.

Sage beneath a spreading oak
 Sat the Druid, hoary chief;
Ev'ry burning word he spoke
 Full of rage, and full of grief.

* * *

Rome shall perish—write that word
 In the blood that she has spilt;
Perish, hopeless and abhorr'd,
 Deep in ruin as in guilt.

* * *

Then the progeny that springs
 From the forests of our land,
Arm'd with thunder, clad with wings,
 Shall a wider world command.

Regions Caesar never knew
  Thy posterity shall sway,
Where his eagles never flew,
  None invincible as thee.

Such the bard's prophetic words,
  Pregnant with celestial fire,
Bending, as he swept the chords
  Of his sweet but awful lyre.

She, with all a monarch's pride,
  Felt them in her bosom glow;
Rush'd to battle, fought, and died;
  Dying, hurl'd them at the foe.

Ruffians, pitiless as proud,
  Heav'n awards the vengeance due;
Empire is on us bestow'd,
  Shame and ruin wait for you.

Tennyson also wrote of Boadicea. But his poem was aimed at a more cultured audience—and is one of the least known of his works. It imitates the difficult metre of Catullus's *Atys*. It begins:

While about the shore of Mona those Neronian legionaries
Burnt and broke the grove and altar of the Druid and Druidess,
Far in the East Boadicea, standing loftily charioted,
Mad and maddening all that heard her in her fierce volubility,
Girt by half the tribes of Britain, near the colony Camulodune,

Yell'd and shriek'd between her daughters o'er a wild confederacy.

Its middle is prophecy:

Fear not, isle of blowing woodland, isle of silvery parapets,
Tho' the Roman eagle shadow thee, tho' the gathering enemy narrow thee,
Thou shalt wax and he shall dwindle, thou shalt be the mighty one yet!

And it ends with a moral:

Out of evil evil flourishes, out of tyranny tyranny buds
Ran the land with Roman slaughter, multitudinous agonies.
Perish'd many a maid and matron, many a valorous legionary,
Fell the colony, city, citadel, London, Verulam, Camulodune.

We have covered various ways in which the story was carried on through eighteen hundred years, and the legend built up—history, more or less honest or manipulated, drama, poetry. The most effective of all was sculpture. In 1856 Thomas Thornycroft began work on his statue group, *Boadicea and her Daughters*. It was a brilliant conception, well suited to the current mood. The late Victorians sympathized with Boadicea as the first British woman to stand up for what was right, and as symbolic of the beginnings of our far-flung battle line. They also approved of the Romans as empire builders.

They managed to reconcile the two, comparing Boadicea's revolt with the Indian Mutiny—after which the Empire went on stronger than ever.

Thornycroft worked at his statue group for fifteen years. The Prince Consort took warm interest in its progress—lending horses from the royal mews as models. In passing, one may note that these splendid beasts cannot have been much like the Icenian ponies, which were used in pairs to pull chariots because they were not strong enough to carry an armed man; it is also interesting that the German Prince Albert should have been attracted to so essentially a British figure. But our chief interest is in the public reaction. This was where the legend as we know it was born.

In July 1871 the art critic of *The Times* saw the plaster cast in Thornycroft's studio in Wilton Place, and wrote of it with enthusiasm:

> Mr. Thornycroft has given us fine statuary before now, but he has done nothing, as he has attempted nothing, so great as this. It is not perfect; it has, indeed, faults which at once strike us, but it is not only without doubt the most successful attempt in historical sculpture of this barren time; but it is an achievement which would do credit to any time and any country. The group is nearly twice the size of life, for the figure of Boadicea measures 10 ft. A car, the body of which is wicker-work and the wheels thick circles of solid wood, is drawn at speed by two unbridled horses rudely belted to the heavy pole. They plunge asunder as they sniff battle in the wind; one would dart forward and the other attempts to hold back. In the car, naked to the waist, crouch the Queen's two daughters, and

> strain their gaze towards the Roman host. The face of one is full of a proud and eager hope, that of the other freezes with horror. Between them stands Boadicea. She lifts her arms high above her head; her right hand is closed round the shaft of a spear, the left is extended, and the whole gesture is of supreme grandeur. Her face and her entire manner finely convey the impression that she is addressing the multitude of the warriors of her tribe. It is the pause before battle, and borne rapidly along the whole array of her people, she calls upon them to take vengeance once and for all and to destroy these Roman soldiers from off the face of British earth. The speed of the car is shown by the incline forward of the figures, the blowing manes and tails of the horses, and the drapery pressed against the outline of the Queen's body. Her face and attitude are instinct with commanding grandeur; she orders the extinction of her foes; she appeals to her people not in frenzy and tears; in tones heart-stirring and eloquent no doubt, but with more pride than rage in them, and her haughty spirit does not dream of defeat.

Thornycroft died in 1885, before the work was cast in bronze. But his son saw to that, with the help of a public subscription. *Boadicea* was presented to the nation.

Then arose the question of where it should be placed. The first suggestion was the tumulus in Parliament Hill Fields, another Hyde Park Corner, another Kensington Gardens, 'on a rocky eminence of moderate height, surrounded by water to keep the spectators at the distance from which it should be viewed'. In 1902 it was unveiled on its present site by the River Thames at Westminster. Probably more than anything else the statue established

Boadicea as a national figure. And it certainly established the scythed chariot.

Parliament Hill had seemed appropriate because it was a traditional site of Boadicea's tomb. But when this was opened it was found by the Society of Antiquaries to be nothing of the sort. A number of other places have been put forward as the Queen's grave. An eighteenth-century suggestion was Stonehenge. But though romantically appropriate, it was difficult to explain the gap of a good many centuries between the construction of the memorial and Boadicea's death. In Essex one traditional grave is the tumulus known as the Barlow Hills, and the claim is made for the Bubberies that the name derives from Boadicea. Harrow Weald also claims her grave.

It will be remembered that Dio said she was given a costly funeral. Very likely whatever remained of the fortune of Prasutagus was buried with her. Until it is found, the legend will remain. If it is found, her personal legend will be all the stronger.

2

The scene

Before starting on the historical account, we need in our mind's eye a picture of this island in the first half of the first century A.D. The topography of the country—its ups and downs—and of course its geology were the same then as now. And the native flora was the same, for the habits of nature do not change in a period equivalent to the life span of three or four great oaks. But a drastic change has taken place in what grew where—because man has increasingly interfered, cutting down and planting, and improving what he planted. What we have to picture is the natural distribution of the vegetation. This varies with different soils, exposures and altitudes. The rough and ready way to arrive at our first impression is to see what finally survives on a patch of land left to itself. Botanists call this the vegetational climax.

In this now crowded island only high land which cannot economically be cultivated or land with a deep top layer of unfertile soil is left more or less to itself. But during the last war and the years directly following it we saw bombed areas where vegetation sprang up and battled for survival according to its own laws; and we have all seen patches which for some reason have been left to themselves for a number of years. The strongest plants, best adapted to the particular soil, take over, ousting any delicate strangers which may have been put there and beating off all comers in the form of naturally scattered seeds. Thus, on a small scale, we have seen the Britain of old when most of the land was not cleared or cultivated because the labourers were unskilled, ill-equipped and very few—so few that one of the hardest imaginative tasks is to appreciate the smallness of the population. Probably in the whole island there were not more than half a million people. Naturally they tilled only the most amenable soils and lived in the areas which suited them best, leaving the remainder—90 per cent or more of the whole—at its vegetational climax.

That only the most suitable areas were cultivated does not rule out the high lands, meaning in this context land of over 1,000 feet above sea level. The high lands were natural fortresses and suitable for habitation for that specific reason. They were of very great importance in our history. But in this story the only mountainous area we are concerned with is Wales, and with it only incidentally. Our scene is the southern half of England, with most of our interest concentrated on the south-east—East Anglia and to a lesser extent Kent and Sussex. Since there are no mountains here it is soil, drainage and cultivation rather than altitude which tint our picture with varying shades of green.

A major factor which has not significantly changed throughout the whole era of history is that Britain gets too much rain. Without drainage, only absorbent or permeable soils carry away the excess. Chalk, sand and gravel are in that class. So is limestone, but this lies outside our particular area. Untilled clay is almost as watertight as putty, and there is a lot of clay in the south-east. In primitive human terms one can cultivate and live in comparative comfort on permeable soils. On clay one cannot. (A pit dwelling in clay inspires nightmares of rheumatism!) Therefore there must be a few paragraphs here on the geology of the south-east.

Chalk and clay are the chief ingredients. The Geological Map of Great Britain shows a striking pattern of different colours. The chalk sprouts like a three-fronded plant from Salisbury Plain. The most northerly frond extends north-eastwards, to end on the north coast of Norfolk, though it reappears beyond the Wash in Lincolnshire. To use names one knows well, the highest and most significant part of this frond consists of the Wiltshire Downs and the Chilterns. As it passes through Cambridgeshire, Suffolk and Norfolk it is scarcely elevated.

The middle frond of chalk is narrow, high and distinct: effectively it is the North Downs which end on the Kentish coast between Sandwich and Dover, with an island of chalk to the northwards between Margate and Ramsgate.

The southern frond is the South Downs which end in the lofty cliff of Beachy Head.

North of the most northerly frond are the clays of Buckinghamshire, Bedfordshire, Cambridgeshire and Lincolnshire. Between the two upper fronds, covering Greater London and Essex, is another big area of clay. Between the bottom two fronds, east of Hampshire, which is almost all chalk, is yet more clay—in the area of the Weald of Sussex.

So the geological map shows us (ignoring lesser formations) three fronds of permeable chalk interspersed by heavy, moisture-holding soils. But unfortunately for early man—and perhaps for modern man as well!—that is not quite the surface picture. The geological map shows the basic geology, not the superficial deposits. And the glaciers of the Ice Age deposited a lot of heavy clay on the low ground of East Anglia. The surface chalk was there reduced to a thin band lying up against the marshes of the Fens, which before drainage were uninhabitable except on the islands. Most of the rest is covered with boulder clay. Only in the north-east corner, and in a fringe round the rest of the coast, are there lighter soils, gravel and sand subsoils.

Considering this geological picture, one is not surprised to learn that Salisbury Plain was the cradle of corporate life in this country. Migrants arrived from Brittany and Iberia, and settled on Salisbury Plain. From there they radiated along the fronds of chalk. Thus some reached East Anglia, though Norfolk, Suffolk and Essex received most of their immigrants by sea from northern Europe. But it was on the chalk that the first roads were trodden out. As every walker knows, the Ridgeway, Icknield Way, Pilgrim's Way follow these fronds on dry and springy turf above the sticky clays. On the chalk are the White Horses and the 'Roman' camps—many of them much older than the Romans.

The clay land was dangerous if not impenetrable. Anyone who lives on clay, or heavy loam which is clay well charged with decayed vegetable matter, notes that the natural vegetation is forest. The elm with its extensive and flat root system throws out a jungle of suckers which help to anchor it to the ground—and grow into trees themselves. In summer its seeds fall thick as snowflakes in a storm, and its seedlings are wonderfully persistent. The oak is scarcely less prolific. Elders, thorns and briars sprout between. All these grow up and shut off the light from lesser vegetation. The gardener or farmer can easily picture what he would wake to if he fell asleep for twenty years, let alone two thousand. So the lower levels of this island were almost entirely covered by forest.

About three quarters of East Anglia was bordered by sea or by the Fens. To the south-west lay the marshy Thames valley. (All slow-flowing rivers had wide fringes of marsh.) The only easy land approach was by the narrow frond of chalk which had remained upon the surface after the Ice Age. East Anglia might be considered a peninsula within an island. As such we will try to picture it in more detail.

Much of it was clay or heavy loam and had therefore remained in its natural state, although men had for centuries possessed iron instruments capable of cutting down trees. Only farmers were going to alter the vegetational pattern, and farmers have been inclined to do work that is not rewarding. It was no good felling and burning the forest until they had some means of cultivating the clay or heavy loam surface. The primitive plough could not do that.

The primitive plough was derived from a hooked stick used as a hoe. Someone had the excellent idea that instead of pulling this scraper through the earth himself he should arrange for an ox or horse to pull a larger instrument while he steered it from behind. But this did not turn the soil over. It merely left a furrow, as a pig's snout does when it rootles. ('Furrow' and 'farrow' both derive from the Old English word for a pig.) This primitive plough—called by the Romans *aratrum* and by the Scandinavians *ard*—is still used in certain parts of the world where the soil is light and dry. In such conditions it leaves a fine tilth suitable for seed, particularly if the ploughing is done twice—first down and then across. That is why the early Celtic fields were roughly square, as we know from air photographs that they were. The pattern is still in some areas discernible.

The scratch method of ploughing is impracticable on clay. There the point merely sticks in, and the harder the pull and push the deeper it sticks. Until there was a more efficient plough the only way of preparing such soil for crops was by the primitive hand method, still employed by gardeners. But digging can only have been practised on a small scale.

Until quite recently it was believed that a more efficient plough only appeared in Britain with the Anglo-Saxons, well after our period. But now there is strong evidence that the Belgae possessed a heavy metal-shod plough so designed that, with more animals pulling, it could not only cut through clay but turn it over.

The Belgae, probably of German origin, had come to England over the North Sea, first as raiders and then as settlers. One tribe, the Atrebates, settled in the Silchester area of Hampshire, and another, the Catuvellauni, around the present St. Albans in Hertfordshire. A third tribe, the Trinovantes, occupied Essex. The two latter tribes were thus neighbours of the Iceni of Norfolk and Suffolk. They began to cultivate the clay and heavy loam. This not only provided a bigger farming area but also better crops, for chalk soil is not particularly fertile. Their ploughing method was naturally copied by their neighbours.

Thus the south-east of Britain, ahead of the rest of the island, ahead of most of Europe including the country of the Romans, had achieved a break-through in a double sense. Its people were on the way to proving that agriculture could do more than supply the basic needs of man, that it could make him rich if intelligently practised. It was making East Anglia—although lacking minerals—

richer than neighbouring districts. Its corn and hides were in demand on the Continent. Its balance of payments, already on the right side in spite of an increasing demand for luxuries, was constantly improving.

The botanist-archaeologists have even identified the seeds which were sown. Lord Ernle listed them as follows in *English Farming Past and Present*. The wheats were Emmer (*Triticum diococcum*), Spelt (*T. spelta*) and Broadwheat (*T. vulgare*). The barley was Bere (*Hordeum vulgare*). The oats were *Avena strigosa* and *A. brevis*. The bean was the pea-sized *Vicia fabia*.

The detective-like techniques employed to discover secrets of the past are fascinating. The close study of pollen is an excellent example. Pollen, the minute male element of plants which nature throws abroad with her usual profligacy—and few grains of which find a chance of fulfilling their function of fertilizing the ovule—possesses a skin which is practically indestructible—except when in close contact with its female counterpart. In its bachelor state the skin, the exine, remains intact for tens or hundreds of years, for thousands in bogland. And the exine of every species is characteristically marked. Thus it is possible to determine under the microscope what plants formerly grew in the place where the pollen grains are found. More than that, one can know (calling in another science) when they grew. Still more than that, by taking out a cubic unit of soil from a fixed depth one can identify and proportion the various species. A paper entitled *Pollen-Analytic Evidence for the Cultivation of Cannabis in England*, kindly provided by its author, Dr. H. Godwin of Cambridge, begins: 'A detailed pollen diagram from an East Anglian Lake, Old Buckenham Mere, registers vegetational changes from late Glacial times to the present. When a chronology is projected upon it this allows the reconstruction of the effects of historic and prehistoric man upon local vegetation through the last 5,000 years.'

This is not quoted to suggest that Boadicea's people took drugs! In fact cannabis was not grown in any quantity before Anglo-Saxon times. But it helps the layman to accept that even the most detailed statements about the first century may have adequate scientific backing.

By no means all the open ground was tilled. Most of it was pasture. The margins of the Fens provided excellent grazing. Our ancestors bred cattle, similar to the present Highland Cattle of Scotland, also pigs, goats, sheep, horses, fowls—a variety of domestic animals almost as wide as now, though the goose was treated as a semi-sacred pet and not eaten before the Romans came. The edible snail was a Roman importation, which never became a popular form of diet. This island was, apparently, already conservative in its tastes.

A pleasant incident about a Roman snail may perhaps be interpolated. In *Thirteen Rivers to the Thames* Brian Waters tells of the finding of one (they are large, round, white and unmistakeable) within an hour's walk of the Roman villa at Chedworth. It and its ancestors had taken at least fifteen hundred years to cover three miles.

On food of their own choosing and production the inhabitants of first-century East Anglia lived well. Their skeletons show them to have been a sturdy people, nearly as tall as the present average. They ground their grain by hand and baked bread. Having pottery they could cook by other means besides roasting and grilling. Since the scythe had come with the iron age they could cut hay to keep their beasts alive in the winter. And of course they could make weapons. They needed weapons, not only against human enemies. With forest surrounding the farmsteads and settlements, prowling wolves, bears and foxes would take toll of the farm animals—though the British lion is only heraldic, and of later date at that. But the forest also supplied game to supplement the food supply.

The people used a currency on the Roman pattern. Some of the developments and comforts of Roman civilization came by the hands of traders from the Continent before the Roman conquest. Clothing was of wool and perhaps linen too, coloured with vegetable dyes. (We are still to describe Boadicea's striking costume.) Gold ornaments were worn. Continental wine was drunk as well as the native barley beer.

The settlements were small and scattered. The idea of a large centre of population, containing law courts, market and theatre, was a Roman importation. The houses were huts of the simplest design and of perishable materials, wood and thatch. Stone could only be used when suitable stone was easily available, and there is none in East Anglia. Bricks were scarcely if at all used before the Roman invasion. But living conditions, at least for the better-off members of the community, were probably almost as comfortable as in the early Middle Ages. Wattle and daub was already being used—these words are written in an East Anglian thatched cottage, partly built of wattle and daub—so there is a link even with a still existing type of building!

Finds of highly decorated weapons, shields and armour, and also of gold ornaments, have helped to build up a picture of an aristocracy as well as a peasant class. The chiefs were gorgeously arrayed. They wore armour in battle, and helmets richly embossed and decorated with the effigies of animal heads, which it has been suggested anticipated the medieval crest. In fact the tribal warfare was already tending towards that of the days of chivalry. One champion would call out another from the enemy ranks to settle the issue by single combat while their hosts stood watching. This form of spectator warfare suited the peasant who went into battle half naked, perhaps painted with woad as Caesar said, but armed and protected by nothing better than blunt-pointed slashing sword and wicker shield.

Chariot fighting was a speciality. This preceded the use of cavalry, because the lively little horses were not strong enough to carry an armoured man. The tactics of chariot warfare will be described later. But a negative discovery about the chariots themselves must be admitted at once. Not one with scythes on the axles has been found in England.

They may have been tried (Tacitus does mention them as once used in Caledonia), but a moment of thought untinged by romance will show that they would soon be discarded as impracticable. They would cause havoc in the enemy lines. But at some stage of the battle the charioteers would have to return to their own ranks—where they would cause similar havoc. A Celtic chariot has been reconstructed from fragments found in Anglesey. Lightness is the guiding principle of its design, for the vehicle had to bump and bounce over the most uneven ground. The Anglesey chariot consists of two strong wheels, a long axle with a yoke for the harnessing of two horses, and an open wooden framework for the driver to stand on, partly protected by wicker sides. It is about as different as it could be from the chariot in the statue group at Westminster in memory of Boadicea. This may be sad but it is true.

Of things which are not material, and which therefore cannot literally be dug up—social behaviour and organization, for instance—we know much less. There were no native records whatever until after the Romans had left. All that we have are Latin inscriptions and Roman memorial sculptures. Certainly the Romans, with Julius Caesar well to the fore, described some of the native customs. But one cannot help suspecting propaganda or inadequate knowledge. For instance, Caesar speaks of the Britons of his day having their wives in common—an arrangement which strikes one as still more impractical than having scythes on chariot wheels.

It is almost certainly impossible to get at the whole truth as regards social structure and habits. An ignominious attempt is made by M. E. Seebohm in *The Evolution of the English Farm*. She summarises the Celtic tribal laws and customs as set down by Howell Da in the tenth century in Wales. Admittedly this is some nine hundred years after our period. But the conservatism of mountain people, particularly those of Wales, has been proved whenever a point is provable, and it is at least probable that these laws and customs were based on a much more ancient Celtic structure.

The law regarding the status and independence of a wife certainly deserves mention for its direct bearing on this story. She was entitled to leave her husband before the end of the seventh year of her marriage, taking her share of the household goods, children and stock with her. This remarkably long probationary period might well account for Caesar's remark about wives being held in common. And the evident high standing of women among the Celts helps to explain why Boadicea was accepted as the leader of the rebellion.

Let us stand back from the easel to look appraisingly at the picture we have been painting of first-century East Anglia. The convex eastern side of this bow-shaped projection of the British island thrusts forward towards the north coast of Europe. It is in effect a peninsula, largely surrounded by sea or marshland, and further protected by forest except along a thin causeway of chalk. Within itself it was largely forested, and by this forest divided into north and south—except along the thin line of surface chalk. In the southern half lived the Belgic tribes, the Catuvellauni and Trinovantes. In the north, principally in Norfolk, lived the Iceni. They were of mixed ancestry but had no Belgic blood.

The two halves quarrelled, threw up fortifications between each other across the only practicable line of advance. Most of the earthworks which remain are of later date, but at least one—at Wandlebury near Cambridge—belongs to this period.

The Belgic tribes had felt the weight of Julius Caesar's hand in the middle of the preceding century. The Iceni were beyond its reach. When nearly a hundred years had passed without a return of the Romans they may well have felt that they would never come back. We can be sure at least that the Iceni were more concerned about the ambitions of their Belgic neighbours, whose swords were as good as their ploughshares, than they were of distant Rome. And meanwhile they profited by the ever increasing trade with the Continent.

The poorer class lived a hard but not undernourished life. The farmers had the power to increase their holdings.

The artisans and craftsmen—tool-makers, armourers, blacksmiths, carpenters, cloth-makers, jewellers—found an ample market for their goods. The aristocracy lived a life of barbaric splendour, eating and drinking well, uncultured and uninhibited, stimulated by such fighting as there was, much as they were stimulated by hunting. One cannot suggest that there was a national spirit, but the people enjoyed their way of life and had no fear that it would ever be upset.

3

The Roman invasion

We must now look at Britain through Roman eyes, first those of Julius Caesar, then of his successors; for the climax of this story is an explosion, and we must know all the ingredients.

Caesar said he crossed the Channel in 55 B.C. because the Belgae in Britain were aiding, morally or materially, their kinsmen in northern Gaul, with whom he was directly engaged. No doubt this was a main reason (he had crossed the Rhine with a similar purpose) but it was not the only one. Caesar was ambitious, and even a partial conquest of the British island would add enormously to his prestige. Therefore he took the greatest risk of his adventurous career.

We now think of ourselves as an island race, different from the rest of the world. The geographers of the early civilizations, Greek and Roman, considered Britain as monstrously different. Their world was bounded by seas of which the ocean which lapped the European continent was part. Britain was outside the mass of land; therefore it was another world, an excrescence which ought not to be there. It was *alter orbis*. Ancients of the mental level of those who now read science fiction peopled Britain with creatures quite as strange as our modern Martians.

It was a magic island, favoured by the Gods—probably because it was the homeland of the Druids. But also it was a rich island. Merchant adventurers had been there and brought back gold and other metals, including silver which was always needed by Rome for her coinage; also hides, clever hunting dogs, and handsome slaves, the produce of tribal wars.

Caesar gathered together all the Gallic merchants who had traded with Britain, and questioned them. They would tell him nothing. But he knew the Belgae, close relatives of the British Belgae; and he had probably seen Britons in Gaul. They were fairer and taller than the Romans, but they were men like other men. They might be conquered. He sent a ship to examine the coast, for he rightly anticipated that the greatest danger lay in crossing the Channel—the Ocean, as he called it.

He crossed with two legions in seventy ships, which included warships as well as transports. He faced an opposed landing, and the water was too shallow for his ships to reach the shore. The legionaries, brave as they were under conditions which they knew, hesitated to disembark until the standard bearer of the X Legion jumped into the water, calling out, 'Leap down, men, unless you want to abandon the Eagle to the enemy. . . .' This is another incident remembered from school days, though not by so many as those who learned the name of Boadicea: national pride plays its part. Once the well-drilled legions had drawn up in tight formation on the shore—a solid line of shields from which there darted out the short, sharp stabbing swords—they soon had the ascendancy. The British attacked bravely, wildly, swinging their longer swords, which failed in effect against the Roman armour. Their own magic protection of woad was not effective. They withdrew.

Caesar could not follow because the ships which carried

his cavalry had been driven back by contrary winds. Another storm wrecked or damaged a number of his transports at anchor. In spite of his initial success he was in a weak position. In these circumstances he could hope for little, and he achieved nothing of military significance —unless one considers the operation only as a reconnaissance. He was fortunate to get his forces back to Gaul before the October storms.

He was much more successful in the following year with a force of no less than five legions and auxiliaries—28,000 infantry and 2,000 cavalry. Faced by Cassivellaunus, who led the mixed army of British tribes, he forced his way first across the River Stour and then across the Thames.

The British, having been beaten in pitched battle, continued to oppose the Romans by guerilla tactics. But Caesar, helped by the Trinovantes, managed to find, capture and destroy the stronghold of Cassivellaunus. This was, it appears certain, the earthworks still to be seen at Wheathampstead, near St. Albans (the Roman Verulamium). Cassivellaunus escaped, to continue his guerilla tactics while Romans remained on British soil. But Caesar had achieved enough to justify his second expedition. He had won the allegiance of the Trinovantes, enemies of the Catuvellauni. He had been in a position to demand hostages and tribute—though whether he ever received either is far from certain. He withdrew to Gaul after a brilliant campaign.

It is tempting to wonder what would have happened if he had returned again, or if any Roman commander had launched an invasion while the ruthless efficiency of the legions was still within living memory. But almost a century was to pass before a Roman soldier again stood on British soil. Memories of discomfiture are short, particularly when there are no written records, so the British tribes remembered only that Caesar had twice been forced to withdraw. As for Rome, she was occupied elsewhere.

Caesar's attention was fully engaged during his last ten years, first by revolt in Gaul and then by all that followed his crossing of the Rubicon. Augustus, the first Emperor, who inherited from the man who was assassinated from fear that he might declare himself Emperor, spent his long reign in consolidation. He made no attempts at invasion. Tiberius also left Britain alone. The mad Caligula assembled an invading force in the Channel ports about Boulogne. It never sailed. What exactly happened is obscure, but the legions refused to embark and were withdrawn.

So the invasion was delayed until A.D. 43, when Claudius saw his opportunity. The most thorough preparations were made, not only military but political, for it had always been the Roman way to divide their adversaries, seeking allies by bribes and promises. Thus at least the Trinovantes, who had submitted to Caesar, had been kept friendly. Certain princes, ousted by their rivals, had fled to Rome—where they were put to good use.

The invasion coincided, no doubt intentionally, with a critical phase in the leadership of the powerful Belgic tribes whose hatred of the Romans had not faded in three generations. Their rule and influence stretched from their capital of Colchester up to Newmarket, where they bordered the Iceni, through Northamptonshire and the Cotswolds and down to the south coast. In A.D. 40 their king, Cunobelinus, died; and the Belgic realm was divided between his sons. Togodumnus inherited the eastern part, and Caractacus the south and west. The

Romans evidently hoped to drive a diplomatic wedge between these two. But they failed. Whatever the individual ambitions of the brothers may have been, they were united in their hostility to Rome.

The feelings of the other tribes were different. They tended to prefer the devil they did not know. The people of Kent, afraid of complete absorption by the aggressive, imperialistic Belgae, welcomed Roman intervention. The Iceni did not go as far as that, and did not in any case expect to be occupied by Roman soldiers, as Kent was bound to be. But they were under continual pressure from the Belgae to their south, and had recently lost to them their outpost fortifications on the Gog and Magog hills near Cambridge. They needed help.

Their king played his hand with care. We cannot be certain that Prasutagus, husband of Boadicea, was already king; but the Icenian ruler of the day behaved with a caution which fits the character of Prasutagus. He was ready to acknowledge a greater invader, to pay lip service and even tribute, if his kingdom was guaranteed against further incursions by the native enemy. Prasutagus was a rich man, primarily concerned with the conservation of his wealth and the peaceful development of Icenia.

It must have been clear enough that invasion was intended. One does not have to go far out into the Straits of Dover to see the coast of France, and from very early in the year 43 there had been a great deal of activity there. Ships were built or modified, and concentrated at Boulogne. Stores poured in by the wagon load and were piled up ready for loading. Some 40,000 troops and a large number of horses were collected in camps. Preparations on such a scale must have been evident to fishermen. And the Gallic merchants, who since Caesar's day had been coming to Britain in increasing numbers, would carry detailed accounts. It was abundantly clear that the Romans meant to cross the Straits.

But week after week went by, and still they did not come. Something had evidently gone wrong. It began to look as if once again the invasion had been called off.

The soldiers were unwilling to cross the 'Ocean'. They were part of the proudest, best-trained and disciplined army in the world; but they were superstitious, and they had heard stories about this island outside the world. Some years before, a part of the army of Germanicus had been embarked from the mouth of the River Ems for winter quarters further south. It should have been a short and easy passage, but a storm blew up.

'The Atlantic is the stormiest of all the seas . . .' wrote Tacitus, who was not generally given to exaggeration. 'Here, then, was disaster on a new and unprecedented scale. On the one side were the shores of enemy country, on the other seas so wide and deep that this is thought to be the last, landless ocean. Some of the ships were sunk: more were cast away in far, uninhabited islands, where the troops either starved to death or ate the bodies of the horses washed up with them . . . . Some had even been driven ashore in Britain, and were sent back by the petty kings of the island. As they came in from their far adventures they had marvels to tell: fearful hurricanes, strange birds, strange monsters, half human, half animal. All these they had seen or imagined in their fears.'

It is interesting that the 'petty kings' of eastern Britain were careful to avoid any cause of quarrel with the Romans. They sent back the castaways. But the stories of the soldiers who were returned would lose nothing with each re-telling, and they must have been told a hundred times. The troops of Caligula had set a precedent by refusing to sail. This was repeated.

The military commander, Aulus Plautius, was at a double disadvantage. Sound general though he was, he lacked the spark of personality which inspires men beyond reason, out of reason. And he was unknown to three of the four legions which had been placed under his command. He shrank from disciplining the mutineers, and sent to Rome for help and guidance.

Narcissus, a freed man, a Greek ex-slave who by quickness of mind had achieved high office, was sent from Rome. At first he offered himself as a butt to the soldiers, allowing them to let off steam. Then he talked them round. They embarked without further protest. All this must have occupied about two months, and the campaigning season was short.

Aulus Plautius may not have been an inspiring general, but he was a lucky one. He carried his army over to Richborough, between Ramsgate and Deal, where he made an unopposed landing. The British force which had been waiting for him—not a regular army in any sense but a force made up of chiefs and their retainers, farmers and the like—had broken up and gone home. It must have seemed to them that this was another false alarm.

That was Plautius's first piece of good fortune. The potentially dangerous landing on a hostile coast was achieved without loss in the landlocked roadstead of Wantsun Channel, which was then navigable. This success paid a dividend, for the soldiers who had successfully overcome their fears were enormously pleased with themselves. Morale could not have been higher. The Roman plan included diversions and decoy landings. But this did not prove necessary.

In our knowledge of the invasion we are much poorer than we might be because the relevant books of Tacitus have been lost. But the details at this stage matter little to this story. The Roman advance, wonderfully efficient, brave, and ingenious in overcoming obstacles, had to proceed a long way before the Iceni were pricked by it. It may be described briefly. It almost appears a game of chess with the pieces of one side moving systematically, logically, almost safely across the board until they had reached the half-way line.

The British forces quickly regathered under Caractacus and Togodumnus. The defenders were superior in numbers to the invaders, but that was their only advantage. While the Romans were perfectly co-ordinated and trained as a whole, the British were a collection of units under individual leaders—wild, brave men, trying to outdo each other. But as the Romans never forgave a defeat, they never forgot a lesson; and in one part or another of their vast Empire they had always been fighting. Therefore they had moved with the times in warfare. The British tribes had not. For almost a century they had only experienced squabbles with their neighbours, and had not progressed at all in the Continental sense. They still practised the same chariot tactics which Caesar had noted with professional interest:

> Chariots are used in action in the following way. First of all the charioteers drive all over the field, the warriors hurling javelins; and generally they throw the enemy's ranks into confusion by the terror inspired by their horses and the clatter of their wheels. Then, having driven between the ranks of their own cavalry, the warriors jump off their chariots and fight on foot. The

drivers meanwhile gradually withdraw from the action and range the chariots in such a position that, if the warriors are hard-pressed by the enemy, they may easily get back to their vehicles. Thus they combine the mobility of cavalry and the steadiness of infantry. And they become so efficient from constant practice and training that they will drive their horses at full gallop, keeping them well in hand, down a steep slope, check and turn them in an instant, run along the shaft (between the horses) and skip back again into the chariot with the greatest nimbleness.

Such circus-skilful tactics must have been hypnotising, terrifying to an enemy—at first. But once the novelty had gone they could not succeed against a Roman unit moving as an armoured mass. They could not win a pitched battle.

A pitched battle was fought on the Medway. Plautius had under his command troops highly trained and experienced in river crossings. These swam over fully armed and succeeded in holding the bridgehead thus formed. They reduced the charioteers to lightly-equipped infantry by killing their horses. While this fighting was going on Vespasian, the future emperor, got another force across unopposed in a different place. Presumably with boats or a pontoon bridge he quickly built up his strength on the further bank. So the first day of the battle ended. Next morning the Britons renewed their assaults on the bridgehead, but the Romans, who had no doubt used the dark hours to reinforce their position, were strong enough to hold their ground, and by evening they had consolidated. They drove the British tribal units into the woods.

This was the crucial battle. The Thames at low tide proved a lesser obstacle. The Romans even managed to capture a bridge intact, which suggests that the British forces were thoroughly disorganized. Togodumnus had been killed. Caractacus withdrew to the west. No other serious resistance could be expected on the way to the Belgic capital at Colchester.

The campaign so far had been swift and ruthlessly efficient. But on the borders of Essex it was checked for many weeks. For the Emperor had to come all the way from Rome to lead the final advance, and although a messenger using relays of horses could cover the thousand miles in a fortnight, an imperial suite was much slower. Dio tells us that Claudius brought elephants. If so it dates the first appearance of these animals in Britain. One cannot help wondering how they were got across the Channel.

This halt by Plautius was tactful, not tactical. It allowed Caractacus to get clear away. The Roman commander and Governor-designate of the Province of Britain may not at the time have realized that this mattered. For what could Caractacus do in the wild and mountainous lands of the west after his own Belgic forces had been so thoroughly routed?

He could have achieved nothing—except for the Druids. The Druids were implacably opposed to Rome as were the Jews. They may be likened to the Jews in that their cult knew no frontier. They were the only unifying power among the Celts, in both Gaul and Britain. They provided, too, the tutors for the youth of all the aristocratic families. Thus their influence was both subtle and profound.

The Druids saw in Caractacus a leader who could be

counted upon to oppose the Roman domination. With their backing he was accepted as war leader by the Silures and Ordovices of southern and central Wales. Here where Druid influence was strongest, where the country was difficult to penetrate and the people most stubborn in their opposition, a centre of resistance built up which endured until the time of Boadicea's rebellion, and in fact was then of crucial importance.

But to return to the late summer of A.D. 43, Claudius came from Rome, fought a battle with the people of Essex, and led the victorious entry into Colchester. There he made treaties with the various tribes, and returned to Rome for his triumph. What remains of the dedicatory inscription on the Arch of Claudius states that 'eleven kings of the Britons' submitted to him. Professor Donald Dudley says wittily that no British XI is harder to pick, but it is at least possible that Prasutagus was one. It would have fitted with his cautious and conciliatory policy. In any case the Iceni were for the moment left alone.

Aulus Plautius, following this first stage of the invasion, appears to have been instructed to establish a viable Roman province as quickly as possible. The first necessity was to make it secure. Vespasian was ordered to sweep westwards along the south coast of the island. This he did, finding it necessary to reduce a whole series of hill forts, Maiden Castle among them. Plautius himself established Colchester as his base, then cautiously explored in a north-westerly direction. He recognized the line of the Fosse Way as the best natural frontier he could hope to find. Though far from impregnable, it ran northeastwards, parallel to the Bristol Channel and the River Avon. It continued along the limestone escarpment which limits the Cotswolds, looking down into the thickly forested country to the northward. It continued through Leicester to Lincoln—though thereabouts in less defensible terrain. The River Trent helped to seal off the eastern end. He did not aim to make this a fixed defensive line, like that which Hadrian later built between the Solway and the Tyne. Instead, the Fosse Way was the axis of a belt of fortified encampments some thirty miles in depth.

When Plautius relinquished his appointment in A.D. 47 he considered that the south-eastern corner of Britain was effectively under Roman control.

Ostorius Scapula took over the governorship in the autumn, as the legions were going into winter quarters. Caractacus chose that moment to strike. He had spent the last four years establishing his military leadership in Wales, and in indoctrinating his followers with hatred of the Romans. He had first-hand experience of their cruelties, but the surest threat to rouse the independent Welsh was that of slavery. The Romans needed slaves to work the mines. They fought to gather prisoners for this purpose.

The Silures crossed the Severn and drove deep into the province between the Fosse Way forts, shattering the *pax Romana* and waking among the subject people memories of ancient freedom. The new governor had to take the legions out of winter quarters and drive Caractacus back into Wales.

That was only a beginning, to tide over the winter months. Caractacus could not be left to attack again at will and at any point of his own choosing along the Fosse Way frontier. Therefore Scapula decided to hunt him down by launching a many-pronged advance into Wales, along the coast and up the valleys.

There was a major objection to this typically thorough Roman plan. Scapula lacked sufficient reserves to maintain his garrisons in East Anglia and at the same time to invade Wales. He got round this by establishing a colony for old soldiers in the Colchester area. These men were retired from active service but by no means too old to fight in an emergency. There was the disadvantage that the *colonia* could only be created by expropriating land, which naturally alienated the native owners. But the old soldiers released garrison troops for the Welsh campaign.

Scapula took another gamble also. He ordered that the eastern tribes should be disarmed. The weapons and armour of the Celts were, as we have said, heirlooms passed down from father to son. They were not things that a man of spirit was prepared to part with. Added to this, disarmament involved search, aggressive intrusion into the home. The Iceni rose in revolt. This was evidently a burst of anger, an unplanned uprising. It was quickly suppressed. So sure was Scapula of the effectiveness of this suppression that he left Prasutagus on the throne.

With his full force in the field, Scapula encircled Caractacus. The Celtic chief moved northwards through the high country of the Ordovici, but was headed off. At last in a steep and narrow place he turned at bay. After a day of hard fighting the Romans were the victors, but when they counted the dead Caractacus was not among them.

He had escaped to the north across the line between the Mersey and the Humber where the extensive territory of Brigantes began. But he had chosen badly. The Queen's party of the Brigantes was pro-Roman, and Queen Cartimandua handed over Caractacus to Scapula in chains.

If the Governor believed that the Welsh question was thereby settled he was quickly undeceived. The Silures were made only more obstinate and troublesome by this defeat and treachery. Avoiding pitched battles, they kept up a continuous series of raids, skirmishes and ambushes. Harassed by this elusive enemy, Scapula's health broke down, and he died.

During the long governorship of Didius Gallus, which followed, the situation in Britain did not materially change. But it changed in Rome. Nero became emperor at the age of seventeen. At first, while still swayed by his tutor, Seneca, and by Burrhus, prefect of the Praetorian Guards, his policy was moderate and cautious. He saw Britain as an investment which had paid no dividends. Trouble in the west had prevented the exploitation of tin and silver mines, while the expense of patrolling the frontier remained as high as ever in lives and money. The province came near to being written off as uneconomic.

But by the year 57 Nero felt strong enough to ignore his advisers, and began to decide policy in his own wilful way. Britain must be *made* to pay. The reasons why it had not yet done so could be summed up by the single word, Wales. Therefore, Nero decided, the Welsh question must be settled once and for all.

The man chosen by the Emperor to implement this decision was Quintus Veranius. He was a man in the prime of life, with a reputation for initiative and drive. He stated confidently that he would conquer the whole of Britain within two years.

The British climate killed him in one.

4

The conquest of Wales

Nero could not abide being thwarted by God or man. But it took a long time for the new Governor of an outpost of the Empire to take up his appointment, particularly if his predecessor had not been relieved of his post in the ordinary course of routine but had died unexpectedly. First, news of the death had to be carried to Rome. The letter sent by messenger relay from Britain might take two weeks to cross the Channel with its often unfavourable winds, be carried to Marseilles and thence on by ship to the capital. The land route round the head of the Ligurian Sea and down half the length of the Peninsula could scarcely be quicker, and in the early stages would be dangerous.

In Rome, when the successor had been agreed upon, it would be necessary to recall him from wherever he was serving. With an empire which virtually surrounded the Mediterranean and covered Europe as far east as Germany, the man selected might have to be brought from a thousand miles away. Having been given his appointment, he required thorough briefing by the various departments of state before he was ready to leave. The Governor was primarily a military man. He was responsible for the frontiers of his province and for the maintenance of law and order within them, the army being directly under his command. Many matters—customs dues, the collection of taxes and so on—were the concern of the Procurator, the senior Treasury official. But the Governor was finally responsible if anything went wrong. He needed to master a great deal of information on his province. And then he had to travel there with his staff, both military and clerical. He could not hope to take up his appointment in less than three or four months.

The new Governor, Suetonius Paulinus, reached Britain in the autumn of 58. He was essentially a man of action, which was why he had been chosen.

Some fifteen years earlier he had been Governor of Mauritania, roughly corresponding with Morocco and Algeria. The Mauritanians were wild hillmen who attacked from their fortresses in the Atlas Mountains and could never be pinned down. Suetonius had led his legions over the range and down to the oases from beyond which the tribesmen drew their provisions and reinforcements. There he systematically destroyed the enemy's power to resist. It was a daring and masterly campaign, involving a passage through very difficult country, ideal for ambuscades. By his success he finished in the shortest possible time a war which might well have been indefinitely protracted. In recognition of this he was awarded a triumph and made consul. Thus he had a background of governmental experience. But there can be little doubt that his new appointment was due to his reputation as a dashing general of proved ability in mountain warfare.

There must have been a vast number of administrative questions awaiting decision in a province which had been without a governor for so long. Suetonius did not spend much time on them. He left most to the Procurator, Catus Decianus, whom he had found in office on his arrival. There are many instances in Roman history of trouble between Governor and Procurator. Apart from their different yet interdependent responsibilities, they were almost always of quite different origin. The Governor was a soldier, a traditionalist, a patrician. The Procurator was a businessman or civil servant. They were most unlikely to get on socially together. They tended to see as little of each other as they possibly could. Suetonius and Catus were not exceptions to this rule.

Suetonius considered the position in military terms. The capital of the province was Colchester, tucked away in the south-east with good sea connections with northern Gaul. It lay in the country of the Trinovantes, a conquered tribe which meekly accepted subjugation. In fact they had co-operated in the process of Romanization. Colchester was being built up—by Trinovantine labour—into a showpiece Roman town. There was a senate house, a theatre, and a temple to Claudius. This last, which was of great significance later, needs explanation. Every Roman emperor automatically became a god when he died. But Claudius decided that, as far as Britain was concerned, he would be considered as divine while still alive. So he commanded the building of a temple to himself when he entered Colchester in triumph in A.D. 43. No doubt he was in euphoric mood, and the Senate in Rome had given their approval in advance to any arrangements that he saw fit to make.

The temple was large and expensively constructed—as one can still see from the excavations—elevated above the surrounding ground and with an altar in front. Apart from the fact that Claudius was still in this world when it was inaugurated, the temple at Colchester was part of the established process of Roman colonization and integration. We have seen modern dictators insisting on everything short of divine worship. The Romans carried the cult of personality to its logical extreme. They found that this served to unify a province, to give it a focus and a means of expressing proper gratitude for the *pax Romana*.

But maintenance of such a cult cost money, which the Romans themselves had no intention of expending. The Roman idea of worship—of whatever god—demanded the observation of a series of festivals throughout the year. These included not only religious sacrifices but games and musical and literary competitions. These were the responsibility in both time and money of the priests. The priests were members of the local aristocratic families, elected in rotation. Only a few tribes could be involved in the Colchester cult. Therefore the burden of maintenance fell heavily on the few. As Tacitus put it, 'in the guise of religion the chosen priests poured out their whole fortunes'. And for those who were not priests, the temple to Claudius remained a symbol of Roman conquest.

The patient Trinovantes had another burden put upon them—the provision of agricultural land for veteran legionaries living in Colchester. These tough old soldiers soon had the former owners working for them as slaves. And they constantly increased their holdings by grabbing more land. This was outside the law, but the Governor turned a blind eye to it because they could be relied upon to keep the local people quiet.

Besides Colchester, there was the newly-born and rapidly growing business town of London. This was inhabited by merchants and their families and did brisk trade with the Continent. Twenty miles to the northwest, in the country of the conquered Catuvellauni, was

St. Albans—Verulamium. This had earthworks dating from before the invasion. But the other two towns were entirely unfortified, in Colchester all the effort being directed towards amenities, and in Londinium to trade.

The triangle formed by these three towns was the heart of the new province. It was screened from the rest of Britain by client kingdoms. The establishment of such vassal states was a stage in colonization which had been proved successful in other parts of the Empire. The principle was as follows: the rulers were left in power. It was in their interest to see that their people behaved themselves, their own positions depending upon this. For further encouragement they might be assisted by financial loans or grants. This form of control suited the Romans, who were bound to be over-extended in a new country, and did not want to have too much on their hands at once. It relieved them, for instance, from the cares of local government. It was only a temporary arrangement. The states could be completely taken over and digested into the province one by one on suitable occasions in the future, such as at the death of the reigning monarch. They were not told this, of course.

The states of the eleven kings who submitted to Claudius were among those which formed a buffer for the prosperous south-east. Icenia was one. Safe at last from the ambitions of neighbouring tribes, Prasutagus could be counted upon to follow the Roman line. Brigantia was another, or at least that part of it over which Queen Cartimandua had authority. Her violently anti-Roman husband was a cause for anxiety, but the Queen, who had proved her loyalty by handing over Caractacus, provided a certain amount of security to the north. So the buffer of passivity swung down through the lands of Dobuni and

Atrebates to Sussex by the sea where the Regni observed the obligations which King Cogidubnus had accepted. And Kent was firmly under the Roman heel. All in all, the south-east was well protected by the British themselves. But the Welsh, of course, were outside the pale.

Suetonius Paulinus would have learned this much before he left Rome. He would also have been informed of the disposition of the army, while the details of its deployment, and above all the efficiency of the legions and auxiliaries, was his over-riding interest when he reached Britain. Exactly where the units were then located we do not know. Lincoln was the headquarters of the IX Legion, Leicester of the VIII. The II Legion may have been near Gloucester. The XIV was, or had been in the time of Scapula, near Shrewsbury. The XX was somewhere in the frontier area. There were, besides, cavalry units and auxiliaries making up a total of about 50,000 armed men.

The five legions which Suetonius had under his command, and most of the auxiliary troops besides, were all facing outward from the secure south-east. They could be switched at a marching rate of twenty miles a day, or even faster in an emergency, for a good road system had already been constructed.

The Fosse Way stretched from Exeter to Lincoln. Thus the Fosse Way was the long side of the (roughly) right-angled triangle which formed the province, the other two sides being the east and south coasts. From London a number of roads radiated to points on the Fosse Way, and in some cases beyond it. Only three are of importance here, and all were improvements or extensions of existing ancient tracks. One was Ermine Street, which ran north to Lincoln and beyond. The north-western artery was

Watling Street, which crossed the Fosse Way at High Cross (Venonae) and led towards Chester, though it had not yet reached that town at the time of Suetonius's arrival. The south-western highway from London led through Silchester and Ilchester to Exeter, the southern extremity of the Fosse Way.

The past tense has been used, but the present would be applicable, for this is part of the skeleton of our present road system. Watling Street, with which we will be mainly concerned, is the A5, which leads to Holyhead. The later Roman road did the same, but at the time when Suetonius became Governor it stopped short of Wales.

One more road of the period must be mentioned. Chester was connected with Gloucester. This route ran roughly parallel with the eastern extremity of the Welsh mountains.

Suetonius was fortunate to inherit a province which had adequate communications. Such roads took time to build. In nothing does Roman thoroughness stand out more clearly than in their road-making. The causeway, about sixteen feet across and drained by lateral ditches when necessary, was dug down to a firm foundation. On this was laid a nine-inch thickness of flat stones, then an equal thickness of brick and stone bound with lime concrete. The roads were aligned by instrument and by smoke signals, and if they had to change direction it was done on the crest of a rise. The labour both for construction and maintenance was provided by the local communities, only the surveyors, engineers and supervisors being Romans. These solidly built avenues, fit for any traffic in any weather, cut straight and purposefully through the thickly-forested countryside and over the downland.

The result of this road system was that news from Gloucester could be carried to the central London–St. Albans–Colchester area in two or three days by relays of messengers riding day and night. A legion could cover the distance in a week, its heavy baggage following by wagon. And even Chester was less than twice as far away in time. This may at first reaction appear slow to our motor-conditioned minds. But East and West had never been so close before. The legions marched with full equipment. Their uniform was armoured, and they wore it whether fighting or not—when digging their protective camps, for instance. The legionary had a metal helmet and a cuirass of thick leather furnished with metal strips. His main protection was his shield, a long semi-cylinder of heavy leather with a central boss projecting in front. Held close to the body it covered him from chin to knees, while the boss could be used as a punch against close opposition. His weapons were a short sword, a dagger and two seven-foot javelins. He carried, besides, two sharpened stakes and an entrenching tool which were used for the construction of the ditch and palisade which encircled the marching camps. And he carried a mess tin and a fortnight's ration of corn. For the Roman legionary was a vegetarian and only ate meat, grumblingly, when there was nothing else. His total load was about sixty pounds. That he was able to march twenty miles a day and then fortify a camp before he cooked, ate and slept is a measure of the fitness demanded. Any failure for a reason other than sickness or wounds was severely dealt with.

This is a convenient place to say something about the method of fighting. The legions were the heart and spear-point of the battle line. For command, each legion of five or six thousand men was divided into cohorts of about five hundred. Each cohort comprised six centuries—actually of eighty men. The legions advanced, or awaited the enemy, in open order so that the throwing arm was free. When the two forces were within forty yards of each other the first javelin was cast. The second was delivered as soon as possible after that. If the enemy was charging, the range would by then be twenty yards or less. A well-thrown javelin either transfixed an enemy or pierced his shield. In the latter case the effect was almost as deadly as the first. The point was of hard metal, but the shank was of soft iron and bent under the weight of the long wooden shaft. It was as a result impossible in the time available to pull it out of the shield, which therefore had to be discarded.

As soon as the second javelin had been thrown the order was given to close ranks. The legionaries came together almost shield to shield. They lowered their helmeted heads and shuffled forward in a jog-trot charge. The bosses of the shields butted into the enemy ranks. Between the shields the short sharp swords flicked and stabbed. An unarmoured enemy was then at a terrible disadvantage, whereas the legionaries were covered in every vital part.

By trumpet call the formation or direction of attack could be changed. The legions were meticulously drilled. The wedge formation was commonly used. One may imagine how it could split up a barbaric horde. The British tribesmen's swords were long and made for slashing only. The points were not sharpened. They were of little use against these close-packed armoured wedges. Nor had the tribes the organization, training or discipline to change their form of attack or defence in the middle of a battle. There was no single combat here, nothing to which they were accustomed—half-naked man against half-naked man. They were opposed by a multi-pronged killing machine directed by trumpet blast.

As soon as the enemy wavered, or if they held firm in places, the wings of Roman cavalry, the *alae*, were brought in, charging with lances. And the auxiliaries, men of conquered Continental tribes, let loose their sling bolts and arrows.

It is not surprising that the Romans never lost a pitched battle in Britain. But although they were left in possession of the field they by no means always followed up successfully. Only the cavalry could catch a lightly-accoutred fleeing enemy, and the cavalry were comparatively few in numbers.

In skirmishes the legionaries often had the worst of it. If they could be caught off guard in an ambush or by a rush from cover, before they had time to form up, a swift enemy could do serious damage and get away again. This was the sort of fighting that Caractacus had led after being beaten in the pitched battle of the Medway. These raids continued. And when the Romans penetrated into the Welsh mountains they were up against other difficulties as well. They did not know the country, and their heavy baggage trains could not follow the mountain trails. Besides, they were at a disadvantage to these tough little Celts in their own climate.

Wonderful as was the strength and fitness of the legionaries they lacked the sheer stamina and ferocious determination of the Welshman. It was said the Celts could live on roots, could crouch all day up to their necks in water and take no harm from it. Probably the stories were exaggerated, but they show the respect that the well-armed Romans had developed for their mountain enemies.

There were three Welsh tribes which the Romans at that period encountered. The Silures were in the south-east, above the Bristol Channel and the Severn estuary. The Ordovices, a large tribe, covered the mountainous area between Snowdonia and Wroxeter on the upper Severn. The Degeangli lived in Flintshire.

It was as war leader of the Silures that Caractacus had made such damaging raids through the Roman lines before he moved north-westward into the country of the Ordovices for his final and disastrous battle. Both tribes had ever since been implacably hostile to the invaders. The Ordovici, living further removed among their mountains, had had less direct contact with the Romans. But the Silures had never ceased from bothering, and although each military governor after Plautius had tried to impress them with the might of Rome, the Silures had managed to cause quite as much damage as they suffered.

That was the background on which Suetonius could make his military appreciation. Like Veranius, he had a free hand regarding further conquest—so long as he made the province pay. This was all the more urgent after so much time had been wasted. The problem of the Celts in Wales took priority over any other that might exist in the rest of the country.

Suetonius was not a young man when he came to Britain. He was a hardened veteran. We have authoritative information on his governorship, since Agricola, the father-in-law of Tacitus, was on his staff. We are not told very many details, but enough to piece together the General's plan. Briefly this was to converge upon the heart of Welsh resistance. The final fortress was

Snowdonia in the far north-west. And behind Snowdonia lay Anglesey, a fertile island which provided food and respite for the warriors.

The similarity with the conditions which had existed in Mauritania was striking—fields of corn out of harm's way behind the range. But Anglesey was more than that. It had become the refuge of all who would not endure the Roman yoke, and it was the stronghold of the Druids.

How to get at it? The old soldier did not underestimate the difficulties. Snowdonia was not as high as the Atlas range, but it was rugged, its climate was much worse, and tracks were rudimentary. The Roman lines of communication would be very long and difficult to defend in the mountain section. Anglesey, the goal and the only place where food could be obtained if hostilities were prolonged, was separated from the mainland by a sea channel. The presence of the sea introduced a factor which had not been present in the Mauritanian campaign. On the one hand it complicated the final assault; on the other it provided a further opportunity for outflanking the mountains. Rome had a small fleet in southern British waters. Suetonius ordered it up via Bristol and the Outer Ocean and made a base at Chester which was then —before the River Dee silted up—an excellent natural harbour.

It is important to make plain how extended was the Roman line of communications and how deeply committed were the fighting forces. Suetonius had with him two legions, the XIV and the XX. With a large number of auxiliaries and additional forces his army may have numbered 25,000 men—half of Rome's total strength in Britain. The other half had to police the indefinite northern frontier, South Wales, the still uncertain tribes south of the Bristol Channel, and the whole of the south-east. Nor was this only for a short period. It took Suetonius two campaigning seasons to complete his pincer movement round Snowdonia and mass his forces for the final assault across the Menai Straits.

Part of his army, starting from Chester, followed the north coast of Wales through Flintshire. By what route the other part advanced south of Snowdonia we do not know. The walker and the motorist may make their guesses how his troops and baggage train found a way from Wroxeter or elsewhere on the upper Severn to Portmadoc on the west coast. But in the spring of A.D. 60 all that remained of Suetonius's army in Wales was drawn up on the shore facing Anglesey. They had with them flat-bottomed boats built in the new yards at Chester and towed into position by the fleet. Facing them across the strip of water was the hard core of British resistance, military and religious. It was literally a last ditch stand—except that the Menai Straits are more considerable than any ditch.

The infantry were carried across on the flat-bottomed boats. The cavalry swam with their horses. . . . From water level, as every swimmer knows, the shore seems further than it is, and in any case 300 yards is a long swim. The young Agricola vividly remembered the scene, and the impression it made upon him is conveyed in the written description of Tacitus.

The shores of Anglesey swarmed with armed men. The Roman soldiers were used to barbarian hordes. But this was different. Among the warriors were Druid priests who raised their arms to heaven, shouting prayers and curses. There were fanatical women dressed in black, their hair dishevelled and with torches in their hands, who ran about screaming and shouting in an ecstasy of fury.

The Romans were superstitious. For all their conviction of superiority they never went into battle until the auguries had been considered. Presumably the signs had been favourable. But, up to their necks in water or borne on this strange element in little boats, they were faced by something utterly unknown and terrifying. 'This weird spectacle,' wrote Tacitus, 'awed the Roman soldiers into a kind of paralysis.'

If the Britons had then possessed a leader of the quality of Caractacus he would undoubtedly have led an attack, in the water or on it in coracles. But there was no attack, and the Roman trumpets blared. That harsh material noise had given the orders in battle drill since every veteran was a recruit. The legionaries vaulted overboard and splashed ashore, javelins poised. The cavalry mounted their staggering horses and formed up. They charged.

There was little effective resistance. Fanaticism is no counter once the fear of it is overcome. The multitude of men and women, soldiers and priests, was stabbed down and trampled under foot. The Roman army swept on to loot and pillage and burn and massacre and cut down the sacred groves of the Druids.

One cannot avoid trying to imagine the feelings of Suetonius at this moment. It is given to few to be the victor of two exceptionally difficult campaigns. As a young man he had conquered Mauritania. Now, well past middle age, he had reduced the furthest corner of Britain.

Whatever were his feelings, they quickly changed. An exhausted messenger delivered a rolled parchment. Rebellion had broken out in Icenia, two hundred miles behind him.

5

Fire in the East

Much had happened in East Anglia while Suetonius had been in the west. Seeds of trouble planted long before had sprouted and grown harvest ripe, while other damaging weeds had sprung up more quickly.

One such sowing had been the disarming of the tribes by Ostorius Scapula ten years before. Although the resistance to this by the Iceni had quickly been suppressed, it cannot be supposed they had forgotten. Besides, they and their neighbours would be most unlikely to hand over all their weapons—any more than the Scottish Highlanders did after the Jacobite rising of 1745—and in any case ample replacements could have been made and concealed during the following decade.

The indifference of the Romans to this danger, and to that caused by other provocations which will be mentioned, was due to their conviction of superiority. They were the best organizers in the world, with the best army. They were a civilization, and scorned the barbarians. They took scant notice of human feelings. Icenia, for instance, was due to be absorbed into the province on the death of its king. The Roman-type towns would be built with temple, senate house, theatre—as was done at Colchester. Then youth of good families would be educated in Roman schools, trained in the Roman army. Latin would become the official language, gradually replacing the

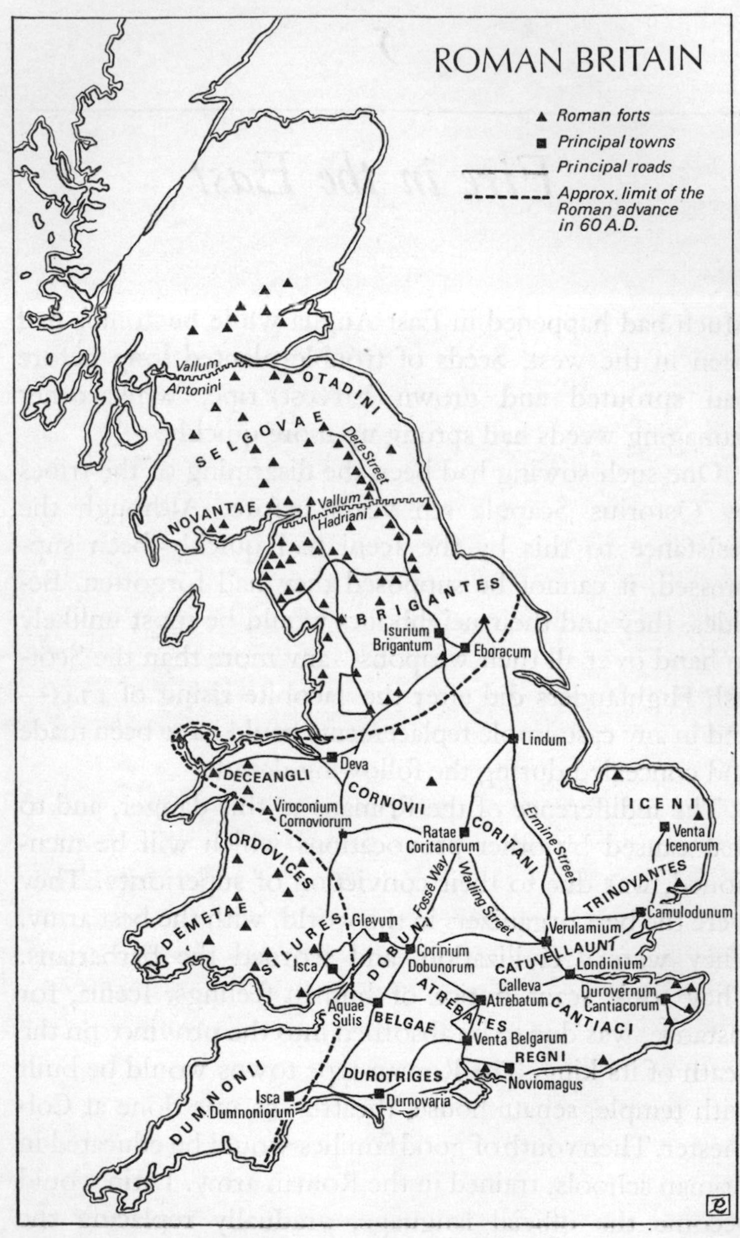
ROMAN BRITAIN
Roman forts
Principal towns
Principal roads
Approx. limit of the Roman advance in 60 A.D.
Vallum Antonini
OTADINI
SELGOVAE
Dere Street
NOVANTAE
Vallum Hadriani
BRIGANTES
Isurium Brigantum
Eboracum
Lindum
Deva
DECEANGLI
CORNOVII
Viroconium Cornoviorum
ICENI
Venta Icenorum
Ratae Coritanorum
CORITANI
Ermine Street
ORDOVICES
Fosse Way
Watling Street
TRINOVANTES
Camulodunum
DEMETAE
SILURES
Glevum
DOBUNI
Verulamium
CATUVELLAUNI
Corinium Dobunorum
Isca
Londinium
Calleva Atrebatum
Durovernum Cantiacorum
ATREBATES
CANTIACI
Aquae Sulis
BELGAE
Venta Belgarum
REGNI
Noviomagus
DUROTRIGES
Durnovaria
Isca Dumnoniorum
DUMNONII

indigenous tongue. Slowly, perhaps, but surely the Iceni would be Romanized.

If they were foolish enough to revolt at any time they would quickly be crushed. A legion was stationed at Lincoln, not far from their borders, and there were small garrisons in forts at strategic points. Rome had no fear of a single tribe and believed the British incapable of uniting. Had they not been squabbling like cats and dogs before the invasion? And had they not proved that they were helpless since then? The Romanization could proceed unhurriedly, as planned, and meanwhile the tribes would pay for the amenities of civilization which were being brought to them.

These payments were another source of trouble. For both the people of the province and the client kingdoms they were by no means light. Their labour or their lives as soldiers might be required of them. They were taxed on their lands, their property, their trade, and were forced to provide corn at fixed rates to feed their conquerors. It seems likely also that during the brief governorship of Veranius, or at the start of his successor's, a census was made and a revision of taxes ordered. Not only were the official taxes high, but the Roman bureaucrats did not scruple to squeeze out something extra for themselves. There were also Roman businessmen, private moneylenders, prepared to make loans, at high interest, to those who found difficulty in paying what was demanded of them. Dio tells us that Seneca, Nero's counsellor and former tutor, had forty million sesterces—about £40,000—out on private loan in Britain. This may not be true, but certainly the new province was being increasingly exploited in a variety of ways, and the client kingdoms scarcely less.

But if the eyes of the Procurator and the Roman businessmen were on Icenia, this was because they considered it worth exploiting. In the 50s the tribe must have been as prosperous as at any time in its history. Prasutagus is spoken of by Tacitus as rich, and there is no reason to doubt it. Ever since the revolt of 48 there had been peace with Rome and security from the once-threatening Belgae. The agricultural revolution brought about by the iron-shod plough had borne fruit. The Icenian landowners were growing more corn than ever before. But their greatest riches were probably their flocks and herds, and their hardy little horses.

The large landowners were the aristocracy, many of whom were connected with the royal house. Boadicea is quoted by Dio as speaking with scorn about the softness and luxury of the Roman way of life. But the Icenian nobles did themselves well enough. We have no way of knowing where the royal palace was. Caister near Norwich is of later date, though there might have been an earlier settlement there. Professor Dudley has suggested the Thetford area, though archaeology has so far failed to settle this question. This negative evidence suggests that the Icenian capital was neither large nor built of durable materials.

Of more interest is the Icenian royal family. All that we know from the records about Prasutagus has already been mentioned—that he had a long and prosperous reign. Being of great possessions he would be inclined to be cautious: the *status quo* suited him best. Such would be the ideal monarch from the point of view of the Governor. Prasutagus could be relied on to keep his people in order, leaving Suetonius free for his adventures in the west. The point of view of the Procurator might well be different—but of him later.

It is a little difficult to picture Boadicea as the wife of Prasutagus. She is a vivid personality after all these centuries, he no more than a vague shadow of a type. A woman with the qualities of generalship, with the passion and the courage of the rebel, would not naturally ally herself, one would have thought, with the sort of person we have pictured as the king. 'She was huge of frame,' says Dio, 'terrifying of aspect, and with a harsh voice.' He was describing her later on, when there was reason for her aspect to have changed and her voice hardened. But the big frame was there already. However, if Prasutagus married a large and dominating woman he would not be the only mild man to have done so. And it may well be that the qualities which Boadicea was later to reveal were at that time hidden, for there had not yet been cause to bring them out. At the time we are dealing with she must have been in her thirties. So she would only have been a teen-aged girl during the tribal squabbles before the invasion.

She and Prasutagus had two daughters. We do not know their names, and we can only guess at their ages. Judging by the probable date of their parents' marriage, the elder was perhaps fifteen or sixteen in 59—not more; the younger a year or two less. We know from our own experience of monarchy that the family life of the royal house is of great sentimental interest to the people. The Iceni were to demonstrate a very lively sympathy for their Queen and princesses, so it is not extravagant to suppose that it was a happy family. Although we are deducing on scant evidence, Boadicea can be imagined in character as well as appearance. The features and garments which Dio describes—bright red hair which fell to her knees, a big gold chain, a brooch to hold her outer mantle and a dress of many colours—would fit a robust person who enjoyed life as well as a fiery warrior. One cannot know which character fitted her more naturally, but one must admit that either is possible.

The lightly-built chariot with its two lively horses was the state coach of the day, as much as it was an instrument of war. There was scarcely room for more than two in a chariot; so one may suppose that when the Queen and the princesses rode abroad, one of them must have been the driver. Driving fast, without roads, without springs, was a fiercely athletic, even acrobatic skill. If the Queen drove in a tribe of charioteers she must have driven well. One can picture this big, strong woman standing balanced on the bumping car, leaning forward with the reins in both hands, shouting to her horses, her face alight, her hair flying. . . . As for the colour of her hair, all which was not black or blond was, to dark-complexioned conquerors, red. (Much later, the Chinese called the British 'the red-headed Barbarians'.) So the bright hair was possibly no more brilliant than chestnut. But of whatever colour, hair a yard long and streaming in the wind—it is a picture! And the two young girls, freckled perhaps and happy, clinging tightly and laughing as the chariot swerved and jumped—one does not need to be sentimental to see with the mind's eye a picture of barbaric domesticity which catches the imagination.

The census would cause a loss of privacy, an invasion of inquisitive agents, for the main purpose was to make an all-round evaluation. Tacitus is surely referring to increases of taxes and perhaps conscription too when he summarizes the complaints of the British in these words: 'That the only effect of their patience was more grievous impositions upon a people who submitted with such facility. Formerly they had one king over them; now there were two, the Governor and the Procurator, the former venting his rage upon their life's blood, the latter on their property. The union or discord of these two was equally fatal to those whom they ruled, while the officers of the one and the centurions [the old soldiers of the *colonia*] of the other joined in oppressing them by all kinds of violence and contumely, so that nothing was safe from their avarice, nothing from their lust.'

Extortion rather than legal tax collection is strongly suggested. It is also pertinent that the union or discord of the Governor and Procurator are referred to. There is ample evidence that Suetonius and Catus did not like each other. Suetonius was a ruthless general, capable of great cruelty, but one does not fail to detect nobleness in his behaviour. In Catus there was none. In every reference to him he comes out as gracelessly cruel and avaricious. The Governor, while in East Anglia, would have imposed a certain restraint and caution on the Procurator, but he was in Wales.

It must have been common gossip among the men of business who were Roman citizens or cognizant of imperial custom that Icenia would be absorbed on the death of her king. Rome had always shown that she was entirely cynical about the peoples whom she ruled or meant to rule. They were, so to speak, fattened up in a state of semi-freedom, and then when the time was ripe, engulfed and digested. The death of the monarch was a generally suitable occasion. Therefore if Prasutagus became ill, or if there were any doubt about his health, those who had private funds invested in that kingdom would want to retrieve them before they were absorbed by

Rome. Certain it is that there was a descent of usurers on Icenia intent on getting their money back.

Troubles rarely come singly. The Procurator saw what was happening, and was in a position to know the imperial intention. Whether or not he had funds of his own to call in, he was responsible for seeing that Rome got her full share. At the time of the submission of the eleven kings, the Emperor Claudius had made certain grants—economic aid to buy co-operation. Catus decided to treat these as loans and to call them in, plus the unpaid interest of more than fifteen years. This alone would have been crippling, but it was not the only exaction. Tacitus quotes the Iceni as complaining that their houses were seized and their children forced away from them, presumably as conscripts or slaves. As for the Trinovantes, they had trouble enough. The veterans of the *colonia* 'were ejecting the inhabitants from their houses, and driving them from their lands, calling them slaves and captives; in which high-handed proceedings they were encouraged by the soldiers, whose lives were like their own, and who looked forward to a similar licence for themselves'.

The soldiers referred to were those still with the colours who had been detailed as guard for the Procurator. There were not many of them. The Governor had taken to the west every man he could. But it appears that those whom Catus had under his command were of a similar type to himself, more interested in spoils than war.

When things turn from good to bad, and from bad to worse the sufferer may reach a stage at which he feels that there is nothing more unpleasant left to happen. But what the Iceni had endured was only a prelude to what lay in store for them. The unhappy year 59 was not yet over when Prasutagus died.

Caractacus brought before Claudius

Overleaf—*Boadicea haranguing the Iceni*, by H. C. Selous

Reconstruction of a British chariot from remains found in Anglesey

Bronze shield from the Thames at Battersea

Cautious to the end, he had left a will by which half of his great fortune went to the Emperor Nero. The half remaining was to be divided between his daughters. His widow inherited nothing. We have some record in Tacitus and Dio of Boadicea's sayings in the months which followed. There is no evidence whatever that she was in any way aggrieved. It is at least possible that she knew the terms of her husband's will while he was still alive, and that she approved of his intention. This, clearly, was voluntarily to pay so great a death duty that imperial Rome would be satisfied and leave the Iceni in peace. Tacitus says as much: Prasutagus acted in this way 'in the belief that this mark of attention would result in the kingdom and his household being left alone'.

Nothing happened immediately. Both the Procurator and the men of business had their agents already in the country. The extortions in the name of rightful recovery continued, with sequestration of property from those who could not pay. News of the king's death, and the terms of his will, had to be carried to Romc, and an answer received. Thus there was no change during the winter months, which in any case were unsuitable for travel. The Governor would have been informed within a week or two of what had happened, even if he was in Chester or the furthest corner of Wales. Settlement of the Icenian question was a matter of government. It was much more than fiscal, and therefore out of the province of the Procurator. Furthermore Suetonius must have known that Catus was a crook. But his eyes were set on Anglesey and the completion of his campaign. He never looked over his shoulder.

Catus went into Icenia with the strongest force he could collect. This consisted of some regular troops and a number of the old soldiers—Tacitus calls them centurions—from the *colonia* at Colchester. In Icenia they joined forces with those already in that kingdom. So far Catus was technically within his rights: he was on his way to collect the legacy due to Nero. But his interpretation of Prasutagus's will put his action beyond all reason. He considered that not only half of the dead king's estate belonged to the Emperor, but all of it; and he ruled that the estate was not only the personal possessions of the deceased but the whole kingdom. He took the lands and property of the nobles and carried off the able bodied as slaves.

The climax was the behaviour of his men at the royal palace. Tacitus does not mention fighting, but even if Boadicea was in some way deprived of her guard she would not take such an intrusion quietly. We already know something of these centurions. 'Nothing was exempted from their avarice, nothing from their lust.' Resistance by someone they considered of an inferior race, and particularly by a woman, would only incite them further. What Boadicea did one would dearly like to know. One feels sure that she at least slapped their faces. This big woman must have been very angry. But she was overpowered and bound. She was flogged. And her young daughters were raped. Then these not-so-noble Romans departed with all the loot they could carry.

It was remarked briefly in the Preface that the rebellion of Boadicea was marked by atrocious cruelties. This is the moment to weigh that up. If a mother of today saw her daughters raped by hooligans, would her feelings be less violent than those of a mother of two thousand years ago? Would she not want to kill? If she could not do that, she would have the law to aid her. For Boadicea there was no man-made law, but she had the power of her tribe behind her passion. Their homes had also been looted and one supposes there had been sexual outrage in other households. The wild men of Catus were out on the spree. Their behaviour with the Queen and her daughters would be for the Celts like a torch thrown into dry straw.

The wonder is that there was not an immediate outburst. Had that resulted it would no doubt have been quickly suppressed. The mother's fury would have flared and died, leaving no trace in history. But Boadicea possessed qualities which even she may have been unaware of at the time. As a first step she controlled herself, and found that she could also control her naturally undisciplined supporters. Then her power must have dawned on her, and she set to work with the skill of an experienced general.

One would give a great deal for an Icenian description of the months that followed. We have only the Roman historian, Tacitus, laconic and biased; and Dio, sometimes verbose but quite as biased. But the achievements of this remarkable woman are set down and we have only to assess them.

Spring had come. Tacitus says, later, that the Britons did not sow corn that season because they expected to have taken over the Roman supplies by autumn. This does not ring true. Farmers would always sow their fields if they could. Besides, the Roman supplies were of British corn. Probably the sowing was hindered or prevented by the troops and pillage gangs of Catus.

It is true, however, that the Icenians were busy with other matters besides farming. 'Relieved from present dread by the absence of the Governor,' says Tacitus, 'the Britons began to hold conferences in which they painted the miseries of servitude, compared their several injuries, and inflamed each other . . .'. The participants are spoken of as Britons, not exclusively Icenians. The representatives of other tribes must have been involved from an early stage. But these conferences were held on Icenian soil. Their country was surrounded by the sea, by the Fen marshland and by forest except for the narrow chalk strip; and this strip had been left barren in the Newmarket area as protection against the once hostile Trinovantes. These obstacles had been the natural defences of the Iceni against attack by their neighbours. Now they made the country an ideal rallying ground for counter-attack against the common invader. One must imagine agents and representatives slipping through the forest or crossing the Fens by tracks known only to local guides. Later, when the representatives had been won over, forces of fighting strength would begin to converge by the same routes.

All this was organized with extraordinary skill. The Romans had a well-developed intelligence service which included a widespread network of spies. But they discovered nothing about the preliminary moves.

Before saying more about these preparations we must decide who was in charge and by what right. Boadicea was the inspiration, and it was she who led the army when it formed. But it is open to question whether she had, by virtue of her position, the right to lead even the Icenian section. She was the widow of the king, the queen mother. It is just possible that she was the queen regnant and that Prasutagus had become king by marrying her, or as a nominee of the Romans; but there is nothing to support this. No coinage has been found bearing Boadicea's name or image, or that of her husband. There is no numismatic clue. Nor have we a precedent for Icenian royal inheritance. In neighbouring tribes the kingdom went to the eldest son, or was divided between the sons. But Boadicea was certainly treated as their ruling queen by the Iceni. And she was accepted as war-leader by all the tribes. She was elected to this position as Caractacus had been in Wales and Vercingetorix in Gaul. Since she had no previous experience in war this must have been from force of her personality and ability in conference.

The Celtic tribes were notoriously individualistic, yet she welded a confederacy. Meanwhile there were weapons, stores and men to be collected and a plan of campaign to be worked out—all in complete secrecy. The first objective was Colchester. Camulodunum was the capital of Roman Britain, the centre of its culture. The temple of Claudius was symbolic of imperial rule, god-like in its omnipotence. Most compelling of all, in Colchester were the centurions who had done the outrage.

While the army was mustering, a form of psychological warfare was launched against Colchester. 'At this time,' wrote Tacitus, 'for no understandable reason the statue of Victory at Camulodunum fell down, with its back turned as if flying from the enemy. Frenzied women sang of coming destruction. Weird cries were heard in the senate house and inhuman howlings in the theatre. An image of the colony in ruins was seen in the estuary. A blood-red ocean and the impressions of human bodies left by the receding tide were interpreted as hopeful signs for the Britons and omens of disaster for the veterans.'

However these things were contrived, they had a powerful effect. The roughest men are often the most superstitious. They began worrying about the town's lack of defences. But when they made plans for the building of moat and rampart they were persuaded that these were unnecessary. The local Britons were if possible more passive and subservient than ever. It was impossible to imagine trouble in the heart of the province after seventeen years of peace.

The Celt is quickly roused to passion, and no doubt was all the more inflammable then. How he was made to hide his feelings so that the Roman intelligence was deceived is a mystery. Meanwhile, Boadicea was swelling her forces by fiery speeches and cogent arguments. We do not know all the tribes which joined the Iceni. The Trinovantes certainly did, some of the Catuvellauni of the St. Albans district probably, and perhaps detachments from the Durotriges of Dorset, from the Dobuni to the north of them, from the Coritani, and from the Brigantes and the Parisii from as far afield as Yorkshire. Certainly the Governor was in Wales with half the army. But there remained a legion in Gloucester, another on the upper Severn, another in Lincoln. Also there were occupied forts on all the roads, and detachments in Colchester, London, St. Albans. There were spies everywhere. Yet Boadicea managed without detection to concentrate an army which Dio says numbered 120,000 men.

This is probably an exaggeration, but the host must have been enormous, for the Celt went to war with his wife, children and domestic animals. War was a family affair. Certainly the country was thickly forested, but it almost passes belief that such an undisciplined multitude could have been gathered together, and kept secret, under the Roman noses of the authorities. Yet it is a Roman historian who states it.

One cannot say that Boadicea had chosen her time well, for events had forced her to action. But the timing was favourable to her. Suetonius was poised for his final attack in Wales, all his resources, all his supporting troops looking towards Anglesey. And because this was his objective—Mona, the sacred island of the Druids—the cult of Druidism supported the Queen. Although officially suppressed, there were Druid priests throughout the land. Their influence and oratory must have helped considerably in the enlistment.

It was probably April or May when Suetonius was in position to attack Anglesey and Boadicea felt ready to lead her army southwards. It is at this stage that Dio gives the description of her which has already been quoted in part. She stood on a rostrum in the middle of the host, her face terrifying in its fury, her voice harsh, her bright hair hanging to her knees. 'She wore a great twisted golden necklace, and a tunic of many colours, over which was a thick mantle fastened by a brooch. Now she grasped a spear to strike fear into all who watched her . . .'.

The speech which Dio puts into her mouth is very long and not very impressive—a recapitulation of all the grievances, all the hopes. It is almost certainly invented by the historian and therefore best left unquoted. But imagination needs no stimulus to picture the scene as this big woman with long hair and blazing eyes made the final call to battle.

6

The fire gets out of control

When Boadicea's followers poured down from the forests of Norfolk and Suffolk into Essex the well-kept secret of the rebellion was out. Its strength and direction of thrust were known. The host swept past military posts, ignoring them as an incoming tide flows around rocks later to be submerged. From these strong points, when left alone again, must have gone the gallopers who brought the news to Suetonius in Wales and Cerialis at Lincoln.

Suetonius Paulinus is a particularly interesting character in contrast to Boadicea. We know more about him than we do of the queen, for Agricola's admiration for his general flows through the stylus of his son-in-law. Tacitus in any case had great respect for the characteristics of ancient Rome, many of which were possessed by Suetonius. He was on the one hand a careful and thorough organizer, exacting in discipline and the precision of battle drill. On the other he was a man who took risks. He was personally fearless to the point of foolhardiness. He had the reputation of always taking a personal part in the battles where he commanded. And he could stake his reputation and the thousands of lives for which he was responsible as unemotionally as a gambler putting chips on a number. Human lives meant nothing in themselves. If he was not actively cruel, he was without sympathy for suffering. He was hard, efficient. Also he was ambitious, a rival of Corbulo who had won a great name in Armenia. He was a soldier first and last, a governor only by appointment. Law and civil administration were of far less interest to him than military concerns. Finally, Suetonius was not a young man. To do what he did in late middle age he must have been exceptionally hard in body as well as mind. Britain would be his last command. His reputation would stand or fall by what he achieved.

He had done what his predecessors had failed to do, captured the granary of Wales and the stronghold of the Druids. But the news which he then received nullified this victory. It looked as if he had won the Island of Anglesey at the cost of the Island of Britain. That would happen unless he moved very quickly and Boadicea slowly. She was within a few miles of Colchester, within easy reach of London and St. Albans. He was two hundred and seventy miles away. She was reported to have over 100,000 followers, fresh men at the start of a campaign. The army he had led into Wales had been reduced by casualtics and was tired. In any case all this force could not be turned against the queen, for although the enemy in Anglesey had been wiped out there were still plenty of Welshmen in the mountains. The same restriction applied to possible reinforcements from the legionary bases at Gloucester, Wroxeter, Lincoln. Even if these forces could be concentrated, few men could be spared from police duties in these areas. The spirit of revolt might spread like an epidemic, particularly if the garrisons were moved.

Suetonius weighed the chances and took his decision. It was too late to help Colchester, but London might be saved if he could get there before Boadicea. Speed was more important than numbers. He had with him in Wales the XIV and XX Legions. The infantry could not reach

London in much less than a fortnight, by which time the British host would almost certainly be there. So he rode off with the cavalry, ordering the infantry to follow him.

This was bold, quite apart from the fact that he would have to ride through potentially hostile country all the way. His striking force was small. Each legion had on its establishment little more than a hundred horsemen. He had with him, too, some of the auxiliary cavalry, units of 500 enlisted from conquered territories on the Continent. But the total is unlikely to have exceeded fifteen hundred. In any case cavalry alone would be of limited value, particularly for defending a town. That he might as soon as possible achieve a more balanced force he sent gallopers to the II Legion at Gloucester ordering it to meet him on the road. As for food stores and baggage, they would travel even more slowly than the infantry, at the pace of mules or oxen. For two or three weeks each soldier would have to depend upon what he carried.

We do not know what route Suetonius followed. But the most direct available to him was Watling Street. If he took it, one may suppose that he ordered II Legion to meet him at High Cross, where the Fosse Way coming up from Gloucestershire crosses Watling Street. There is doubt on the detail of all Suetonius's movements, as there is of Boadicea's, for neither Tacitus nor Dio give itineraries. This matters comparatively little to the general reader, and the position of the rendezvous ordered for II Legion matters least of all, for it was not kept.

When the gallopers from North Wales reached Gloucester the Legate of II Legion was not in command, being ill or absent on some operation. In his place was the Camp Prefect, Poenius Postumus. He refused to move the legion. So he has come down in history as a coward.

Possibly he was, but it seems unlikely. He had risen from legionary—private soldier—to acting command. During the last seventeen years the legion had seen much hard fighting in Britain, first under Vespasian against the tribes of the south-west and then against the Silures, whom it still opposed. A soldier in the field does not climb the slippery pole of promotion from the ranks if he lacks physical courage, while to give a flat refusal to one's general requires moral fibre. Why Poenius Postumus disobeyed the order to march seventy units or so to the nearest point on Watling Street we shall never know. Perhaps no one knew even at the time, for he killed himself by falling on his sword after hearing of the battle he had avoided. He may have anticipated a serious threat to his sector of the frontier. He may well in his own opinion have acted for the best. But the absence of II Legion destroyed the general's logistic plan which would have enabled him to reach London with a balanced force.

To the great credit of Suetonius he did not hesitate a moment. He rode straight on with the cavalry at a rate of about fifty miles a day. He was in the thickly-forested Midlands which might have concealed in ambush an enemy of twenty times his strength. Travelling with such urgency he could not have allowed himself to be slowed down to the pace of lateral patrols working through the thickets on either side of the road. At night it was Roman standing orders for the legionaries to build a marching camp protected by a seven-foot ditch and a palisade. The cavalry, busy with their horses, were excused this chore. It is not to be supposed that they undertook it now, when there were no infantry. By day they clattered on at their best pace, and by night they slept under the rain or stars, still more vulnerable to attack. The only precaution which Suetonius took—which he could take in the circumstances—was to move fast, to arrive before Boadicea could expect him.

The cavalry were the élite of the Roman army. They wore brilliantly-coloured cloaks, their armour and accoutrements were highly polished. Our nearest modern equivalent is the Household Cavalry in a state procession. As they cantered down the long, straight road through the forests of the Midlands one can imagine the awe with which the half-naked woodsmen saw them pass.

One cannot help wondering what were the general's thoughts as he rode, saddle-sore, aching and tired. He could not usefully plan ahead without knowing more of the situation. In conditions of weariness and discomfort the mind is resentful. He must have been furious with Poenius Postumus. To one whose whole working life was attuned to the mechanical reactions of discipline the behaviour of this ranker officer must have been inexplicable and inexcusable. Roman law provided for a slow and painful death for one who, as Tacitus puts it bluntly in this instance, 'disobeyed the commands of his general, contrary to his military oath'.

But the anger of Suetonius must have been directed far more fiercely against Boadicea. This is more than a guess. His subsequent behaviour displayed a vindictive cruelty which went far beyond military and governmental needs. Even the materialistic Roman Senate saw this. Suetonius hated Boadicea, and through her all the Iceni. One does not know if he and she had met. It is quite possible that he saw her with Prasutagus at some governmental gathering in Colchester soon after his arrival in Britain, before he set out for the west. If so he no doubt remembered her appearance, a big, striking woman. The Romans were not large. She was very likely taller than he. And she was a barbarian, queen of a tribe he despised. He would not be favourably impressed. Now she had turned the brilliant success of his Welsh campaign upside down, made a fool of him in the eyes of Rome and the barbaric world. He must have boiled with personal indignation against her.

He reached London before her, covering five times the distance which had separated her from it at Colchester. But he did not know that in the meantime she had doubled back to fight another and harder battle.

It requires an effort of the imagination to picture London as it then was. It was scarcely older than the Roman conquest, but in recent years it had grown like a mushroom patch, too fast for the usual Roman town planning. This sheltered natural harbour within easy reach of the Continent had attracted merchants from Rome, north and south Italy, Gaul, Spain, Greece, all parts of the Empire. Many had built themselves houses and settled down. The place had sprung up anyhow, a cluster of wooden houses with some superior villas. The river was full of shipping, the banks lined by wharves and sheds. The untidy little town was prosperous and busy. The imports were stores for the army and luxuries for the rich, its exports metals, hides, mastiffs, and slaves. No doubt many Britons were among the twenty or twenty-five thousand inhabitants. They had accepted the new way of life. Londinium was an international market, polyglot in speech, but to the rebellious Celts an example of Rome's handiwork and therefore to be destroyed.

When Suetonius arrived with his tired cavalry he found the *municipium* a very anxious place. The threat of death hung over the inhabitants. The Procurator, Catus, who had sparked off the rebellion, had left the Londoners to their fate and fled to Gaul. It would not have been possible for many civilians to escape to the Continent on the little merchant ships, while to scatter into the country would have been as dangerous as remaining. They were branded as Roman sympathizers, and who could tell how widely the rebellion had spread? They greeted Suetonius as their saviour. He, on his side, was brought up to date with the situation—and took a different view.

It is convenient to describe what had happened during the last fortnight or so from the point of view of Boadicea.

She marched straight on Colchester. For her it stood for the men who had outraged her family, for all the Iceni the same. For the Trinovantes it stood for their slave masters. For the other tribal contingents its Temple of Claudius was the symbol of Roman conquest. But although the objective was clear and approved of by all, the host would travel slowly. If its numbers were anything approaching the 120,000 recorded, the column would stretch on a road for well over thirty miles. Apart from other considerations, this gives reason to doubt Dio's estimate. But, divided by three or four, the column remains unwieldy. As anyone who has travelled in a big convoy knows, the speed is slower than the individual speed of the slowest—whatever mathematics may say! If one imagines the wagons carrying food and families, the picture is an organizational nightmare. How long, for instance, would it take to camp and break camp, to halt for rest and food and start again? In a military command orders pass quickly down a chain of subordinates to every man. With a collection of tribal units held together only by enthusiasm there would be less of a chain than a tangle.

Boadicea had been elected war-leader, but she would have to depend on tact and inspiration in place of discipline. When considered realistically, what she achieved appears supernatural.

As she started southwards in her chariot after the long and anxious period of secret preparations, she must have felt the intoxication of having swayed a multitude with her words. Then the problems of leadership would begin. What these were will be best conveyed by looking more closely at the composition of the host. Not only was it made up of tribal detachments, but each detachment was subdivided under its nobles or strong men. Rivalries would be inevitable, and the tribes themselves had been at war within the memory of many. Quarrels or arguments about precedence would be inevitable. There was no uniformity in equipment. The nobles were well armed and armoured—if they had managed to save their weapons from confiscation. The simple men had hunting spears, bows and arrows, home-made swords, clubs. Some were on horseback and most on foot. The wagons had different loads and draught animals. They carried women and children and food—food for the multitude must have been an endless problem. It is interesting to conjecture whether there were women in the fighting force. It is put forward with diffidence that some of the refinements of killing and mutilation recorded by the Roman historians suggest the feminine touch. In later history, both among the North American Indians and in the East, it was the women whom the captives chiefly feared. And in this case the Iceni had reason—among other things—to hate the enemy as masculine creatures. This must not be stressed.

Certainly there were many women with the host.

Would they, especially with a woman commander, remain as camp followers and spectators? But the last argument is strongest of all. Suetonius is reported by Tacitus as telling his legionaries before the final battle, 'There are more women than soldiers in their ranks.' This is a direct statement, though not necessarily a true one. Whether there were Amazons in Boadicea's fighting ranks must remain in doubt. But certainly her host was as mixed as it could be, and the administrative problems must have been enormous.

We are not told by what route the host advanced on Colchester, and since we do not know from where it started there is little profit in trying to deduce this. But the tumult of its coming must have given at least a few days' warning to the doomed town. It is difficult to believe that the veterans would not try to throw up some sort of defence in that time. But Tacitus says, 'Thwarted by men in the secret of the conspiracy, they dug no trenches and erected no palisades. They omitted to send the old men and women away so as to leave none but young men inside. And having taken no more precautions than in a time of profound peace, they were surrounded by a multitude of barbarians.'

With a fifth column among them and an overwhelming force surrounding them the veterans had no chance. The outlying buildings were immediately overrun and burned to the ground. The garrison made their last stand in the Temple of Claudius. There they held out for two days. Then they were overwhelmed and all the inmates slaughtered. It was a ruthless, barbaric massacre.

With the destruction of Colchester and its garrison the emotional objective was achieved. But even if Boadicea wanted to stop there she could not. The IX Legion was stationed at Lincoln, 120 miles away. Its commander had been deceived throughout the weeks of preparation. But he must have known of the march south almost as soon as it began, and he would move fast. At any moment he might attack the host in the disorganization of victory.

Boadicea detached a powerful force to deal with this threat. It cannot have been easy. Facing a legion was a very different task from overrunning an unprotected town. One doubts if she could have got the force moving without leading it herself. In any case she must be given full credit for this tactical move. The Roman historians clearly show resentment that their reverses were suffered at the hands of a woman. Had they been able to point to some man, some mastermind, behind her they would certainly have named him. But no other individual is mentioned at all. The angry mother had become a general.

The direct route for the legion would be Ermine Street as far as Godmanchester and then by the Via Devana through Cambridge. The forces may have met near Godmanchester. Tacitus is laconic. 'The victorious Britons went out to meet Petilius Cerialis, Legate of the Legion, who was advancing to the rescue. They routed the legion and slaughtered all his infantry. Cerialis himself escaped with the cavalry, and found shelter behind the defences of his camp.' From this one supposes that he was chased all the way back to the Lincoln fortress. The legion later required 2,000 infantry to bring it up to strength. The well-armed and disciplined Romans almost invariably inflicted far more damage than they received, so Boadicea may have lost two or three times as many.

The capture and sacking of Colchester had been of psychological value, but in their second battle her army had won a harder and more militarily important victory. Apart from Suetonius, wherever he might be, there remained no Roman force capable of opposing her in the whole eastern half of Britain.

Now there could be no stopping or going back. Rome never forgot an affront, least of all a military defeat. Neither she nor her people could be safe until every Roman soldier had been killed or driven from Britain.

This consummation suddenly appeared possible. The only serious threat remaining was Suetonius. If he could be eliminated the garrisons of Gloucester, Wroxeter, Chester and the lesser forts could be snuffed out one by one.

It was at this stage of Boadicea's campaign that Suetonius and his cavalry arrived in London. If her thinking had become as military as her behaviour suggests she would be glad of this. He had travelled much faster than expected, therefore his force would be tired. Instead of having to march west and look for him she had him in an indefensible town harassed by thousands of frightened non-combatants. She gathered up her scattered forces and descended on London.

But Suetonius, with all the facts before him, had made his own appreciation. London could not be held with the cavalry alone. His infantry marching from Wales could not arrive in less than a week. Before that Boadicea would probably attack. Therefore he must withdraw. That he would thereby be condemning many thousands of civilians to death made no difference to this military evaluation.

The despair of the townspeople when they saw those whom they had looked upon as their saviours preparing to desert them can easily be imagined. Tacitus puts

Suetonius's action in the best light he can. 'He decided to save the whole province by the sacrifice of this single town. No tears, no lamentations from those who begged his help could prevent him from giving the signal for departure. Those who could keep up with him were given a place in the column: but all who, because of their sex or age, or love for the place, chose to stay, were butchered by the enemy.'

The British horde burst into London on the heels of Suetonius and there was an orgy of slaughter and destruction. Dio goes into details about the outrages perpetrated by the Britons, the skewering of Roman women on long stakes, and more besides. Tacitus is vivid enough. 'The Britons were not interested in taking prisoners or selling them as slaves, nor in any of the usual commerce of war,' he says, 'but only in killing by the sword, the gibbet, by fire and the cross.'

It is as if Boadicea was losing control of her enormous and ill-integrated host. Perhaps this entered into the calculations of Suetonius. Once his infantry and baggage train caught up with him he would have a force of about two legions' strength, plus auxiliaries. This would still be far inferior in numbers to the British host, but the morale of his men would not deteriorate. Hers, on the other hand, had no training, no discipline. Still more important, they had no pay. No one who had received the attention of the Procurator had any money left; and they were not, we are told, interested in 'the usual commerce of war'. A period of inactivity or of fruitless hunting for their chief enemy might tempt many to drift off to their homes.

What the host did was to double back to St. Albans, where the same story of slaughter and destruction was repeated. Recent excavations at Verulamium have disclosed a thick layer of burnt débris which undoubtedly dates from this time. The third Roman town was utterly destroyed. But the military situation had not improved for Boadicea since her defeat of IX Legion. If the revolt was to succeed, Suetonius had to be beaten in battle.

This would have been easier if she had followed him closely as he retreated from London. But if she intended this she did not succeed as she had at Colchester. He had got away, and she did not even know where he was. So the capture of London was in effect a tactical defeat.

7

The final battle

The climax of the rebellion was the final battle. One is in a hurry to hear about it and its result. The classical historians were no less impatient to tell of it. Tacitus, having described the sack of London, and given the fearful figure of 70,000 Roman citizens and allies slaughtered there and at Colchester and St. Albans, begins the next paragraph:

> By now Suetonius Paulinus had with him the XIV Legion and a detachment of the XX, together with auxiliary troops from the nearest fort, a total of 10,000 men, and he decided to make an end of delay and seek engagement in battle.

What delay? Tacitus has certainly not delayed. Dio says:

> Paulinus . . . was not willing to risk a conflict with the barbarians immediately, as he feared their numbers and their desperation, but was inclined to delay battle to a more convenient season. But as he grew short of food and the barbarians pressed relentlessly upon him, he was compelled, contrary to his judgement, to engage them.

Here is another mention of delay. There is no hint of how long it lasted. We have to arrive at the duration of the revolt by other means. The tribes had not sown their corn before they went to war. When organized fighting ended they had no crops to harvest. From this one may deduce that thc hosting was in March or April and the final battle in July or August—four months at least. Since the first moves were certainly swift it appears that the later manœuvring was protracted. During the final weeks or months the moves of the two sides—the reinforcing, the concentration or dispersal—must have had their effect upon the final result. But nothing has been found to fill this gap in time. The only evidence is of a negative nature. So we must do the best we can by putting ourselves in the place of the two leaders.

Suetonius withdrew from London because he was too weak to face the British host. Where could he go? The north and north-east were swarming with enemies. There was not enough shipping for him to have evacuated from the Thames estuary. But he certainly would not have done this even if it had been possible. Catus had run away by ship—and broken his career thereby. That he was a crook was less venal in Roman eyes than that he was a coward.

Suetonius was certainly not a coward. But he might have withdrawn to the south with the intention of concentrating his forces in Kent and Sussex. There he could have awaited reinforcements from the Continent. The Cantiaci were completely under the Roman heel—ever since forty-three baggage trains and columns of reinforcements had been travelling the road from Richborough through Canterbury and Rochester to London. This almost daily exhibition of Roman riches and strength had kept them quiet. And the Regni of Sussex were ruled by Cogidubnus, the most Romanized of all the client kings. He had been rewarded with Roman citizenship and the title *Rex et legatus Augusti in Britannia*. (One may mention in passing that after forty years of faithful service his kingdom was absorbed into the province like all the rest.) In Kent Suetonius would have been safe enough. But it would have been both dangerous and time-consuming for his legions to concentrate there. The IX at Lincoln would have had to pass right through the enemy-occupied territory, but was in no state for fighting its way anywhere. The legions in the west could have joined him with less difficulty. But this would have amounted to throwing away all the conquests of seventeen years without a fight, just because the rebels had overrun three scarcely defended cities. Evacuation, we may be sure, was never in the aggressive mind of Suetonius, unless directly ordered by Rome.

The possibilities remaining open to him were to withdraw to the west or north-west. A hundred miles to the west lay Gloucester and II Legion which was intact as far as we know. Intact, but at the very best untrustworthy since its acting commander had disobeyed a direct order. Every argument favoured the north-west. If he withdrew by the way he had come, within a few days he would fall back on his well-tried infantry, following him from Wales.

We may take it that that is what he did. Possibly he did not leave London by Watling Street, which passed through St. Albans. Even if the British host was still in Essex he would have been too close to it for comfort. He may have put the Thames between himself and Boadicea and made a detour by Staines or even Silchester, thirty miles further on, which was a growing Roman town. If so he must then have doubled back along the line of the Chilterns to meet the legions, which would in that case have been halted by galloping messengers. For meet them he did. Tacitus says he had with him the XIV and detachments of the XX legion when he decided to give battle, and these formations had been with him in Wales.

Some authorities have doubted whether he could have made such a manœuvre swiftly enough to avoid Boadicea with his column hampered by refugees. But there is no reason to suppose that he was thus encumbered. The sentence where Tacitus refers to the people of London reads, 'Those who could keep up with him were given a place in his column.' Since his column was of cavalry, only fit men with horses could have kept up with him. These might be useful. All the rest were left behind. A general who could abandon a town of some 25,000 inhabitants to destruction did so for a good reason, and we may take it that he was consistent.

Thus we suppose that he met XIV Legion and a detachment of XX somewhere on Watling Street. But he needed further reinforcements and he needed food. At or near High Cross, at the junction with the Fosse Way, he would be well placed to gather additional forces from the west or centre of the frontier region. But he could only do this by weakening the forts from which they came. If their strength was too much reduced, the uncommitted tribes would be encouraged to throw in their lot with Boadicea. Thus he would gain reinforcements at the cost of adding considerably to the ranks of the enemy. There were the Brigantes to be considered, the Welsh tribes, and perhaps the Cornovii. According to Tacitus he summoned only 'auxiliary troops from the nearest fort'.

There remained the question of food for his 10,000 men. The baggage train was following from Wales, but at the end of a campaign it is unlikely that there would be much corn available from that source. It was by this time summer, ten months or so from the last harvest. The supplies of the local Britons would be running low, and they would hide their grain rather than have it commandeered, particularly if they had not sown that spring. But Suetonius could order in a certain amount from the nearest forts. He could do this best if he remained in one place, with good communications in all directions. When he had gathered enough food, and as many reinforcements as he dared, there would be no advantage in delaying the final battle any longer. So: 'He decided to make an end of delay and to seek an engagement.'

The suggestion that the final battle was fought on or near Watling Street in the area of High Cross is only acceptable if it fits with the probable, or at least possible, movements of Boadicea. Several authorities, Lewis Spence among them, have suggested that she remained on the northern side of London, somewhere in Epping Forest. As a result they place the final battle thereabouts—in Essex, or, in the opinion of Spence, the site of Kings Cross Station. But the arguments for this depend primarily on the assumption that Suetonius withdrew southwards into Kent or Sussex, which we have discounted. The battle has also been sited as far afield as Chester, by the German scholars Mommsen and Domaszewski. This would be a very long way for Boadicea's ill-organized army to march through a country of unknown and possibly hostile tribes. And it would mean that Suetonius returned almost to his starting point, which hardly fits in with his shortage of food and anxiety to settle the issue.

Boadicea reached London shortly after Suetonius left it. That she failed to follow him closely and bring him to battle before he was reinforced and could choose his own

D*

battleground was her first bad military error. The scope and secrecy of the mobilization, the descent on Colchester and quick turn-about to deal with IX Legion were brilliant. So why this failure? As suggested earlier, she might already have begun to lose control of her heterogeneous host. But so early in the campaign, and after nothing but successes, her prestige must have been high, and it is hard to believe that on so important an issue she was thwarted by disobedience alone.

A possible explanation lies in the extent of the early successes, and in Celtic religion. London offered less resistance than Colchester. There was no strongly built temple to hold out against fire and battering ram. But there was more destruction to be done, more killing, and perhaps more sacrifice to the deity held responsible for success. Dio says that the worst atrocities, including the skewering of women on long sharp stakes, were committed in the sacred groves of Andastra. Nowhere else is there mention of this goddess. But it has been pointed out by Dr. Anne Ross that the names of Celtic deities varied from place to place, from Ireland through England to Gaul, although what they stood for was generally the same. Their commonest function was in war and fertility—in other words killing and sex. It is a particularly unpleasant thought that at the dawn of Christianity, when some Christians may already have been in the country, the Britons were practising such revolting religious rites. But it may have been so, and it may well have been this that robbed them of their best chance of winning freedom. The name Andastra has been interpreted as Victory. The Irish Morrigan, Queen of Nightmares, seems more appropriate.

A more acceptable reason for the delay in London

might have been the collection of corn from Roman store houses. But it is hard to believe that an old soldier like Suetonius would not have destroyed the remainder after supplying his own men and the inhabitants. Nor does that explanation fit with the subsequent descent on St. Albans where similar enormities—or religious rites—were done.

The sacking of St. Albans is in any case difficult to understand. Colchester and London were Roman towns. Verulamium was certainly Romanized. It was a *municipium*. But it was the capital of the Catuvellauni, many of whom had flocked to the hosting in Icenia and taken their part in the fighting, which should have created an *esprit de corps*. But Verulamium was burnt to the black layer of ashes still to be seen. Was it another sacrifice to Andastra or an act of mere destruction by men and women intoxicated by it and seeking for more? Certain it is that Boadicea went from London not on the trail of Suetonius but to St. Albans.

But after that there was no more to destroy, or not without hard fighting, for apart from tribal centres against which there could be no animosity there remained only the Roman garrisons, all many miles distant. The destruction of Suetonius was the next step. If Boadicea had the clarity of mind which her organizational ability suggests she surely saw this was essential. To her host, which had put IX Legion out of action and frightened Suetonius out of London, this must have appeared quite easy. It was an article of British faith that Caesar had been driven out; Dio puts this thought into Boadicea's rallying speech:

To speak the plain truth, it is we who have made

> ourselves responsible for all these evils, in that we allowed them to set foot on the island in the first place instead of expelling them at once as we did their famous Julius Caesar.

The Romans could be beaten and driven out. But where was Suetonius and his army? Boadicea had no intelligence service. Her tribal units knew no more of England than their own districts. They could not have drawn a map even of the southern third of the country. Rumours there would be in plenty, but it would be difficult to evaluate them—as it would have been comparatively easy for Suetonius to arrange for false information to be carried.

Things must have been extraordinarily difficult for Boadicea at this time. An army of tribal units was notoriously brittle. In defeat it splintered and disappeared. In success it was almost as likely to break up and go home with its booty. Inaction was the most dangerous state of all. The Romans had been allowed to land unopposed at Richborough because they did not appear until two months after they were expected, and the temporary British soldiers had gone back to their farms. After the sack of St. Albans there were tasks to be done, reorganization and the collection of food by forage and hunting. But it was no doubt difficult to organize this for the good of the whole host as opposed to that of the foragers and hunters. And there would always be the temptation for a man to slip back to his own land where his presence was so necessary.

Boadicea must have been relieved when at last she had news of Suetonius. It is by no means impossible that he actively enabled her to have this information; for if she did not go and look for him he would have had to hunt for her, which would have prevented him from preparing a position. With numbers so heavily in favour of the British it was essential for him to choose his own ground. However obtained, the information was that the Romans were on Watling Street. The British host trundled off north-westward with their chariots, foot soldiers and family wagons—a column many miles in length.

There would be signs of the Romans all the way along. The scent was hot. The similarity with a hunt and its followers is inescapable. Noisy, cheerful, certain of victory, the Britons swung down the ancient British track which the Romans had paved and straightened out. One pictures the warriors swaggering along, the creaking wagons, the gossiping women, the children, the dogs, the farm animals, the chariots overtaking on the verges.

There was forest then on both sides, but the slopes were of course the same as they are now. Anyone who travels Watling Street must be impressed by its endless undulations. . . . From the next crest the Roman army might come into view. . . . But a hundred miles of marching disclosed only their overnight camps, and litter thrown aside during the marching and counter-marching of the XIV and XX and of the cavalry. These would be welcomed by the British commander for their effect of maintaining the excitement of the chase. There was no need to urge on the tribal units. Rather it was a race between them to be first at the kill.

One wonders if Boadicea ever suspected that she might be being led into a trap. In country so thickly forested, with scant communications, Suetonius could surely have concealed his whereabouts for much longer. Instead there was this straight road which with every milestone told of the Roman troops.

If she thought she was being invited to attack the Governor's force she accepted the challenge. If a trap was intended it was baited by Roman soldiers whom her own force outnumbered. She could not, of course, know the odds with any certainty, but she would be aware of the size Suetonius's force had been in London and feel confident that it had not been increased to any great extent. Confidence was the key to the British mood.

After a hundred miles they reached High Cross. An examination of Watling Street on the London side of that point reveals no place which fits Tacitus's description of the battlefield. That in itself is not proof. But as we have seen, Suetonius probably withdrew to the area of High Cross the better to build up his forces and supplies. Professor Donald Dudley and Dr. Graham Webster have put forward a site some twenty miles further to the north-west, which seems in every way more likely than the various claims of other authorities. Unless something is discovered to discount it, we can accept their suggestion.

High Cross is a lonely place today, windswept and open, with only three or four houses at the junction of Watling Street and the Fosse Way. Then it was forested, with the two straight roads stretching like a great cross as far as the eye could reach between the trees. There was a small Roman post which would certainly have been evacuated and destroyed by its garrison. Possibly the ashes were still warm.

From there Watling Street led on in long and gentle undulations, but never overlooked by higher ground on either side for a distance of twenty miles. Then there is a slight rise which stretches obliquely across the line of the road, and is indented by defiles. It is composed of older, igneous rocks on which a different vegetation would grow. It rises only some two hundred feet. But it provides a vantage ground above Watling Street.

The brief description of the battlefield given by Tacitus is as follows: 'He [Suetonius] chose a position in a narrow defile, protected from behind by forest. Here he could be sure that there would be no enemy except in front, where an open plain gave no cover for ambushes.'

It is not easy to picture the scene as it was nineteen hundred years ago, even if the choice of site is correct. The suggested place is near to the present village of Mancetter (the Roman Manduessedum) which lies between Caldecote, north of Nuneaton, and Atherstone. The imaginative eye must first sweep away hundreds of modern houses and an industrial estate and then clothe the ground with its original vegetation.

The Roman commander had chosen the place with care so that his 10,000 could not be outflanked or surrounded by the 50,000 or more British warriors. The defile sloped up into the ridge and was weathered out into the shape of the bow of an open boat beached on a sand bank. The ridge was forested, not with big, widely-set trees but with the thicker-growing and more stunted sorts, which survive in an exposed position—elder, thorn, holly, and briars. This also clad the forward side of the ridge, but we can deduce that the defile itself was open. Also in front there was a wide clear space on a soil of sand and gravel which ran down to the road and over it until big trees rose again in the heavy marl beyond.

The first contact which the Britons made would be with outposts on the road some miles in front of the position. Their duty was to gallop back and give warning.

One can well imagine the excited shout of tens of thousands of voices at this unmistakable sign that the clash was near.

Then the Roman army itself came in view a mile or two in front. We have from Tacitus an exact description of how the force was disposed, and a skeletal account of the battle itself. Tacitus was a specialist in battle descriptions, writing for a connoisseur public. The Roman army fought to exact patterns, with well-defined drill and manœuvres. For Tacitus it was only necessary to announce the type of battle (like a gambit in chess), and describe anything unusual or dramatic which resulted; the rest would be understood by Romans brought up on their history of war. So we may be justified, on the basis of other battles, in describing this one in more detail than he did. It was, as it turned out, a textbook encounter between a small, well-drilled force on ground of their own choosing and a huge barbarian horde.

When the advancing British column first saw the Roman army it was drawn up in line across the defile. The Roman legionaries were in the centre, probably six ranks deep. On either side of them were the auxiliaries, men not Italian-born but trained in the same thorough way; and the cavalry were on the wings. The whole line was scarcely a thousand yards across.

The British host poured off the road and spread out on the open flat. They could have made a line far more extensive than that of the Romans, but the defile restricted them to the same frontage for attack. There was procedure of honour in forming centre, right or left. This would take time to work out even though the orders were already agreed.

The interval while the two armies were facing up to

Roman soldiers fighting barbarians, from a bas-relief on Trajan's Column, C. A.D. 110

Overleaf—*Statue of Boadicea and her daughters in Whitehall, by Thornycroft*

Boadicea haranguing her troops

each other, still far out of range, was the time when the commanders gave their orders and exhortations. The history of antiquity is spiced by these harangues, and the reader may have wondered how an army spread over half a square mile could hear. The answer is that they could not, and in fact the recorded speeches probably derive more from the imagination of the historians than the mouths of the generals. But orders at least had to be heard. The Roman custom was to call the unit commanders together to hear the General's plan and exhortation, then dismiss them to their units to pass on the essence. This scarcely differs from present-day custom—except that modern generals reserve their eloquence until they write their memoirs.

Suetonius is credited by Tacitus with a short speech—which Agricola, as a staff officer, would have heard.

> Pay no attention to the noise these savages make. Ignore their empty threats. There are more women than soldiers in their ranks. They are not warlike and they are badly armed. When they experience the weapons and courage of troops who have often beaten them before, they will turn and run. In an army of many legions, few win battle honours. What glory will be yours, a small band which fights for the honour of the whole army! Keep your ranks. Throw your javelins. Strike with your shield bosses. Then drive on. Do not pause for booty. Win the battle and you win it all.

Boadicea is also said to have addressed her followers, though how her words could have been recorded it is hard to know. In any case few of the host could have heard her, for the Britons were notoriously noisy when the intoxication of battle gripped them—blowing their horns, clashing sword on shield, shouting war cries. She visited each tribal unit, proclaiming that although their people were accustomed to the leadership of women in battle, she was among them not as a royal person but as a woman fighting for freedom, to avenge the bruising of her body and the rape of her daughters. The gods would grant this vengeance. The Romans would never face the roar and din of the British thousands, still less their charge and hand-to-hand attack. Numbers were on their side, justice was on their side. It was victory or death. As a woman she was resolved not to live as a slave. The men could do as they liked.

It was exhortation, not orders. The men cheered wildly. Those who could not hear her saw her driving round in her chariot in her striking clothes, her long hair flying. Her two daughters were with her, by their presence conveying her message even without words.

Such battles opened with the swift manœuvres of skirmishes between the hosts. The auxiliaries on the Roman side, recruited from Spain, the Pyrenees, Gaul, Thrace and Germany, were allowed to keep their traditional weapons. So there were archers, both mounted and on foot, slingers, cavalry, spearmen. They harassed the enemy units while they were forming up, sling bolts and arrows flying. With the British this task of disorganization belonged chiefly to the charioteers. They had bowmen too, but the British archers had not yet won renown.

This was only the curtain raiser. When the last arrow and sling bolt had flown, the auxiliaries fell back precipitately before the main encounter. For the Celts the encounter was the charge. It was almost the whole gamble of the battle, a rush of such wild impetuosity that it often settled the issue within minutes.

No doubt on this occasion it would have been wiser to use their advantage in numbers more circumspectly. Only a force equal to that of the Romans could actually oppose them in a charge because there was room for no more on that narrow front. But others, before the charge, could have infiltrated on either side of the defile, worked their way through the thick woodland and caused a lot of trouble on the flanks and at the rear.

The Britons were too impatient for such tactics, too certain of success. They charged in a solid mass, the tribal leaders in front and their men behind them. By all accounts the noble Celt was a splendid figure, tall, athletic, bearded and with long hair, fair or auburn. They towered over the stubby little legionaries, and they came on with all the clamour of war cry and trumpet. They were handicapped by charging up hill, but they came on recklessly. When running at full speed it is more natural for a man to hold his arms wide rather than cover his body with shield and weapon.

The legionaries were in line, five or six ranks deep. When the enemy were forty yards distant the front rank threw the first light javelin. Each man then immediately reached behind him and to the right, took the second javelin from his companion in the second rank and threw that close behind the first. That done, the drill was for the front rank to side-step and fall back while the second rank repeated the throw, either with light javelin or heavy, according to the range. This was repeated with the quickness born of long and careful practice until the enemy were within ten yards or so.

It does not take charging men many seconds to cover

thirty yards—not if they have a clear run and do not check. The Britons were charging up a slope. Many of their leaders must have been transfixed by the first javelin volley, more by the second, more by the third and fourth. Those who had opposed their shields in time would be struggling with seven-foot shafts. The men behind could only continue their advance by pushing past them or jumping over the dead. It is a shock to see a man skewered right through, writhing like a worm on a hook. It would be only natural if the bravest checked for a moment.

In this moment, at trumpet blast order, the legionaries closed ranks, raised their long shields, drew their short broad swords and shuffled forward down the slope in wedge formation. To achieve this wedge one century went in front, two others following in echelon, a fourth in reserve to plug any gap or reinforce success. The units might be larger than the century—a cohort in a large army. But that was the principle. The effect was a series of wedges which hammered into the enemy mass. Hammer is the apt word, for the shield boss was used with the force of a trotting man behind it. His left arm punched with the shield while the sword in his right hand stabbed like a serpent's tongue.

The enemy, out of breath and shocked by the javelin volleys, were generally divided by the wedges into triangular shaped groups of men who suddenly found it necessary to fight on two fronts. This was demoralizing.

The Celts were by this time fighting hand to hand in a general mêlée which left little room for manœuvre. No man however strong can fight with the energy of a boxer for more than a minute or two without gravely deteriorating in skill through weariness. In single combat the opponents tire and deteriorate together. But another item of Roman battle drill, similar to that of javelin throwing, was for the front rank swordsman to side-step and fall back to the rear, leaving the man behind him to take his place. Therefore the Briton was faced by a fresh opponent.

Each Roman had to kill five or more Britons to win. But they worked in shifts, cutting through the leaders to the men behind. In a tightly fought battle it only needs a break in one place to cause the beginning of a rout. When hard-pressed men know that something has gone wrong and cannot see what it is, fear quickly turns to panic.

The *alae* of cavalry, the élite of the enemy, were on the wings waiting for this break. A good general was quick to see the chance when it came, and to order a charge with lances. There was a scream of trumpets and a thunder of hooves from both sides. The British mass, wedged into in front, pierced from the best men to the worst, and now charged upon with all the impetuosity of a downhill gallop from the flanks, broke and fled.

But they could not retreat far. This battle had as macabre an ending as it is possible to imagine. The wagons full of women and children, the families of the warriors, had been drawn up as closely together as they could be parked near the foot of the defile to watch their menfolk win their final victory. They blocked the line of retreat. The running men were crowded in a helpless, seething throng against the wagons. The terror of mass hysteria is well known to us from crowd accidents when no enemy is about. With attacking Romans stabbing their way on one side, women and children shrieking on the other, the horror is fortunately beyond the scope of our experience.

Steadily, inexorably, the legionaries and auxiliaries

butchered their way through to the wagons. They climbed over these on the piles of dead, killing the women and children and the draught animals. The cavalry raced after those who had managed to escape from the shambles of the wagon park, cutting them down.

Tacitus wrote: 'It was a glorious victory, like those of the good old days. Some estimate as many as 80,000 British dead. There were only 400 Romans killed, and scarcely more wounded.'

8

The pax Romana

Boadicea's last battle resulted in the greatest slaughter this island has ever known. Tacitus suggests that it was all over in a matter of hours. The casualty figure he gives is the same as that for Hiroshima in 1945 when the first atomic bomb was dropped. In both cases, of course, women and children were included as well as combatants. The difference is in the duration of the killing, hours as opposed to seconds, and to the fact that Hiroshima, with Nagasaki following, brought the end of that war. In Britain in the year 60 the battle marked the beginning of a much wider destruction by sword, hunger, exposure and disease which obliterated many more people. Exact figures are impossible to arrive at. But if one is right in estimating that the whole British population amounted to half a million—as opposed to fifty million now—the resultant shock of casualties would, mathematically, be a hundred times as great. Without stressing an unsatisfactory type of argument one may make the point that Boadicea's revolt and its aftermath caused an upheaval and destruction of maximum significance.

It was remarked earlier that Suetonius must have hated Boadicea for turning upside down his victory in Wales. Through her he hated all her people. The policy he adopted during the remainder of his governorship went far beyond punitive repression. He seemed vindictively determined upon the annihilation of whole sections of the British community—the Iceni and Trinovantes, at least—and on the most harsh suppression of other tribes.

Tacitus says in the *Annals*: 'The whole army was concentrated and kept in tents to finish the war. . . . The territory of all tribes that had been hostile or neutral was laid waste with fire and sword.'

It was not enough to have refrained from joining the rising. To have fallen short of active support of the Roman side was a crime. Order had been re-established before winter came, but the killing went on. There is a significant passage in the *Agricola*. 'The issue of a single battle restored it [Britain] to its old obedience. Even so, many of the rebels remained under arms, very conscious of their disloyalty, and naturally apprehensive about the Governor, fearing that—however admirable in other respects—he might act harshly to those who surrendered and pursue a cruel policy, for he was a man who avenged every wrong done to him.'

The Trinovantes, placed as they were within the road system of the three towns, had no more chance than rabbits in a hayfield with reapers scything towards them from all sides. The Iceni, scattered throughout their forested and marshy country, and with no villages or towns of any size, were harder to hunt down. Many no doubt were killed that autumn or rounded up and sent as slaves to the mines of Britain, or by chain gang to Rome. But the operation was not completed that winter. The elusiveness of the Iceni is remarkable, for Tacitus's phrase, 'the whole army was concentrated', must mean that very large forces were used in the hunt.

The wooden houses were quickly found and burned,

the farm animals slaughtered or driven off. The people too old or too young to move were treated according to the mood of the hunters or the orders they had received. The rest took to the forest. There they were hunted like vermin. For soldiers from warmer, drier lands to live under canvas instead of in the comparative comfort of winter quarters was already a hardship. One pictures the sullen, sodden men searching through wet woods.

If it was hard on the hunters, how was it for the hunted? They had no roof, no warmth, no safety, no future. And they had no food except for the little they could hunt while being hunted. That spring 'they had omitted to sow the crops and brought every man into the army'.

If they had sown they would have been granted no chance to reap. So perhaps it made no diffcrence. But the result was famine. Few people in our civilization have experienced real hunger. The present writer happens to have done so at sub-zero temperatures and feels justified in obtruding himself to mention one result. It subordinates all the better feelings, leaving only the most primitive and selfish. Here they would feel hate for their well-fed hunters. What else was there to feel except their hunger pangs?

The hunters, cold and resentful at their winter task, felt equal hatred. Some of them had seen the skewered Roman women at Londinium, and the atrocities at the other two towns. The rest had heard of them. The men they were actually hunting might not have been responsible, but they were of the same race. It was hatred to the death of one race for another.

As for the personal hate of Suetonius for Boadicea, that was thwarted because she was dead. She and her daughters disappeared from the eyes of the Romans, and from history, after the chariot drive through her ranks before the battle. We do not even know her daughters' names. Apparently the Queen got back to her own country, and there died—Dio says from a disease and Tacitus by taking poison. Perhaps the latter is the more acceptable end. She had nothing more to live for, only to be marched in chains in a Roman triumph before execution. Certainly she could do nothing for her people. But if she thought that by eliminating herself she might reduce the retribution she was wrong. The killing continued into the spring. When the hunters could not find the men and women they destroyed the means by which they lived, which came to the same thing in the end. There can have been little more sowing in the spring of 61 than there had been in 60. Dr. Godwin's paper on *Pollen-Analytic Evidence*, quoted in the second chapter, states, 'The Romanization of Norfolk was tardy and less intense than in other areas of Britain, possibly because the Early Roman period was marked by the abortive revolt of the Iceni under Boudicca and its subsequent cruel repression.'

Let us look at the situation for a moment from the Roman viewpoint. The prime intention of making the province pay was further than ever from being realized. There was no lack of slave labour for the mines, of course. But this was only one source of revenue, and a comparatively small one, for the north Midlands had not yet been reached, while the extreme west of Cornwall with its tin, and Wales with copper and gold, were still unpacified. For the rest, you cannot extract taxes from people whom you kill or drive into the woods.

The state of Britain was the more chaotic because Procurator Catus, when he ran away, had taken with him all his staff and most of the records. The rest had been destroyed in the flames of the revolt. When a new procurator was sent to fill the vacancy, before the end of the year 60, he had to start from the beginning—in a province seventeen years old.

It will be as well to remind ourselves of a procurator's function and powers. He was the head of the civil service and treasury in the country. Being of slightly lower status than the governor he could not act against his orders, but he had the right to report directly to the emperor, and to put forward his own recommendations. Catus had acted during the absence of Suetonius in Wales, and therefore not directly against orders, but rather as a deputy on his own authority. The interest of Suetonius was now mainly concentrated on East Anglia, and we may suppose that he never left it for long. A great deal would therefore depend upon the character of the new procurator and how he and the governor got on together, for they would be working together, seeing each other almost every day.

The new Procurator, Julius Alpinus Classicianus, was not a Roman. He came from Trier—Trèves on the Moselle—a place which, incidentally, contains the most remarkable Roman remains of any town in northern Europe. Professor Birley has proved that he must have obtained Roman citizenship at least twenty years earlier. But since by birth and upbringing he belonged to a province he was not blinded by imperial prejudice against the British. He was middle aged, perhaps in later middle age, married, with one daughter. He has come down to us as a man of absolute integrity and great moral courage.

He and Suetonius did not work well together. Suetonius was honest. It had become all too common for a governor to make money out of his province, but it is certain that Suetonius did not make a denarius out of Britain. Class difference, if it had existed as it did with Catus, would have been less apparent, since he and the Procurator were of different nations; but in any casc Classicianus was of a noble family. He and the governor were both educated and intelligent men. But their points of view were diametrically opposed.

Suetonius had proved himself an Ancient Roman in the way he had refused to accept defeat, had faced up to odds of five or more to one, and conquered. The Ancient Roman had faults as well as virtues. With courage and determination went lack of imagination. Kindly feelings were to be subordinated in oneself and ignored in others. Pride was admirable. So was revenge—which should be far more severe than the damage received. Suetonius continued his policy of ruthless destruction. The approach of summer made the task less uncomfortable and more rapid.

Classicianus was totally opposed to this. Whether he had sympathy for the Iceni and the other rebel tribes we do not know, but he pointed out the difference between destruction and construction as it affected revenue. Suetonius would not listen. The harrying continued. Classicianus had no power to stop it, but he wrote direct to the Emperor saying that matters could never be bettered until the governor was replaced.

Tacitus strongly disapproved of this behaviour. Classicianus, he says, 'allowed his private quarrels to obstruct the public interest, stating that it would be wise to wait for a new governor who, lacking the hate of an enemy or the arrogance of a conqueror, would be inclined to show mercy to those who surrendered'.

One may be sure that the new Procurator was unpopular in all Roman circles in Britain. He had not seen the horror of the rebellion, and here he was advocating mildness. But Classicianus was as obstinate as Suetonius. He continued to speak his mind and to write on the same theme to the Emperor.

Nero did not at once commit himself. He was twenty-three years old and less interested in government than in his pleasures. The Terror of his later years had not yet begun and he still retained his old counsellors, Burrhus and Seneca. This was a difficult matter for them to advise on. The argument of Classicianus could not be ignored, for it was borne out by the finances of Britain. Everything pointed to the advisability of a change of policy. But not, for other reasons, to a change of governor. Militarily, Suetonius had done brilliantly. Both with the legions in Britain and the public in Rome his prestige was very high indeed. To recall him before the end of his governorship would cause an outcry if nothing worse. Also there was the possibility that Classicianus was wrong. Another and totally unbiased opinion was needed. Therefore it was decided to send out a commission of enquiry.

Meanwhile the campaign—for it was no less than that—against the remnants of the rebels continued. There may still have been bands at large in the Midland forest. There was certainly a hard core in Norfolk. It would be fascinating to know how and where they held out. Professor Dudley and Dr. Graham Webster speak of excavations at Thornham, on the Norfolk corner of the Wash, which suggests that the Iceni made a last stand there. Another possibility is the Fens, where Hereward the Wake retained his freedom as an outlaw almost exactly a thousand years later. In this stubborn resistance of the Iceni there lies more courage than in the whole rebellion. It has been suggested that it was inspired by the hope of a more lenient governor being appointed. In the quotation from Tacitus given above, Classicianus is in fact held responsible. But it is hard to see how these lonely men and women who lived among reeds or thorny undergrowth could have known what was being discussed in the high places of the enemy. A simpler explanation is more plausible—that they were the sort who do not give in.

While they continued their extraordinarily uncomfortable existence the commission of enquiry was getting under way. It was headed by Polyclitus, secretary to the Emperor. A confidant of Nero was naturally a person of the highest dignity and importance. We may safely presume that he was also a voluptuary. Polyclitus travelled through Italy and Gaul very slowly and with an enormous staff, clerical and household.

He was a freedman. It will be remembered that when Claudius's invasion force refused to embark at Boulogne the freedman Narcissus had been sent for and had talked the legionaries round. Since then freed slaves had been increasingly employed. That a man had risen from less than nothing to the highest rank proved his intelligence and personality. But a freedman had another, and special, value for an emperor. He was unpopular with every class of Roman society—aristocrat, soldier, civil servant, business man—and therefore could be presumed to be impartial. His only loyalty was to the Emperor who had given him his freedom. It was a curious situation. After the terrible convulsion of Boadicea's revolt, and the hundred thousand deaths that had resulted, the fate of Britain was to be adjudged by a man who had been a slave.

The reader must have felt the gaps in this story. The writer has longed for the freedom of fiction to fill them by imagination. What sort of man was this ex-slave sent to give judgement on the treatment of Britain? We shall never know, for character is not a thing dug up by archaeologists; nor was Polyclitus important enough in the Roman Empire to have left a memorial. George Shipway, who recently wrote a very good novel, *Imperial Governor*, about Britain in the years 58–61, gives a convincing sketch of him. He describes Polyclitus at the end of his tour of inspection as going to the slave market and choosing twelve beautiful Trinovantine boys and twelve girls—as one might buy souvenirs to take home.

It is history that Polyclitus made a thorough tour of inspection. The deference shown to him by both the military and civil side of the Roman administration puzzled and possibly amused the British, who knew that he had been a slave. They surely deserved that small diversion.

The report submitted to Nero by Polyclitus recommended that the policy of attrition be changed to one of conciliation and reconstruction. Suetonius, proud and certain of his own rightness, refused to be deflected from his course of vengeance. Fifty thousand soldiers were behind the victorious general. He was a force to be reckoned with.

He was finally recalled in the summer of 61 in connection with the loss of a number of ships and their crews. We are told no more than this. But we know that he was impatiently concerned with wiping out the last pockets of Icenian resistance, and one cannot help supposing that he had used the fleet as he had used it in the Welsh campaign for a combined operation. He went quietly back to Rome, neither as a triumphant general nor in disgrace. He was once more made consul. The awkward old soldier was allowed to fade away.

Thus, undramatically, the two main figures in this historical episode have disappeared. Life in Britain went on without them. Our final interest is in the revised policy which was adopted as a result of the rebellion. To put it another way, did Boadicea's revolt bring about anything that was good?

Great care was taken in the choice of men to govern Britain, and by them of subordinates for positions of authority over the native people. Rome digested the lesson that human feelings matter, and that rule by force alone is a barren policy.

The successor of Suetonius was Petronius Turpilianus, who was governor for three years; and although we know little of him apart from the grudging praise of Tacitus that he was 'more kindly disposed towards repentance' and 'settled the former disorders' without attempting anything further, it is clear that he put an end to the killing—which resulted in the cessation of armed resistance. The stout-hearted remnants of the Iceni could come out of hiding and rebuild their farms. So peaceful in fact did Britain become in this short period that Rome felt able to appoint as the next governor a man with no military experience at all. Trebellius Maximus was popular with the Britons but had considerable trouble with the legions which were always most difficult to handle when they had nothing to do.

Under these two governors the foundations of peace and prosperity were laid in Roman-occupied Britain. But credit for the initiation of this better way of life must be given to Classicianus. If he had not made a bold stand against Suetonius—who cannot have been a pleasant man to oppose—things would have gone on as before for some time longer at least. As things worked out, once the change of policy had been made it was the Procurator's duty to implement and oversee the details of the new administration. Classicianus inherited from Catus a tradition of corruption, peculation and downright vice. He built up a civil service of probity and justice. It was his seemingly impossible task to get tribute out of people and also to win their good will. If dead men cannot pay taxes, neither can those who are bankrupt. Classicianus must have possessed humanity, patience and imagination. He should be the patron saint of the Inland Revenue.

It is curious and satisfactory that although we know so little about him personally, except by implication, we have his memorial. His tombstone is in the British Museum. One broken part of it was found on Tower Hill in 1852. This massive piece of stone had been used in strengthening the Roman city wall. It was not generally accepted for what it was until another find which fitted to it put its identification beyond doubt by adding enough to the inscription to make it understandable. This second large fragment was unearthed in 1935. It includes the name of the daughter of Classicianus, Placata, which means Peace.

While still concerned with personalities, we may mention two minor characters of the main story who had a continuing influence in Britain. Both Petilius Cerialis, Legate of IX Legion which was so roughly handled by Boadicea's forces, and Gaius Julius Agricola, the staff officer, became governors of the province.

Cerialis carried the border at least as far as York, setting up a camp there which became the base for all subsequent operations in the north.

The ambition of Agricola was no less than the conquest of all Britain. He went a long way towards achieving it, defeating the Caledonians at Mons Graupius—

whatever that name may be in Gaelic. He was recalled before he put to the test his final plans for conquering Scotland. Tacitus paints his military achievements in glowing colours. He is equally laudatory about the advances Agricola made in the more peaceful fields of life.

Authorities are generally agreed that Tacitus overpraised his father-in-law, giving him credit which belongs more rightly to his predecessors. We may, however, cover the developments of the quarter century following the rebellion without ascribing credit to any individual, for this was Romanization, the process applied to every province once it became militarily secure.

Peace was the first essential. That achieved, attention could be given to encouraging the form of life characteristic of Roman civilization. It might be supposed that the first change was towards centralization in towns as opposed to the numerous small tribal settlements. This was Roman policy, as contributing to a better control of the country than existed under a multiplicity of local leaders; and perhaps the growth of towns was the first visible sign. But before that the people had to be educated to accept the change. Colchester, the showpiece town of Camulodunum, failed—apart from the abuses which led to violence—because the whole idea of such a place was inimical to the Celtic point of view. So the nobles were encouraged to send their sons to Roman schools. When they learned to appreciate the Roman conception of civic responsibility, government, recreation, domestic comfort, then they were helped by Roman planners and architects, and possibly by grants of money, to build a town with comfortable houses, forum, theatre, temple and so on. In a town so established the rich citizens vied with each other in providing amenities and in the various forms of public service. But in Caistor-by-Norwich, the Icenian post-rebellion capital, building and development were particularly slow because there were no rich families left.

London on the other hand grew rapidly from its own ashes. It became the capital city, displacing Colchester. The Governor and Procurator had their headquarters there. Nothing could keep London down for long. It had to grow and spread. But the new London was not a ramshackle collection of buildings as the first had been. It was a planned city, well laid out and walled.

In the country Roman forms of building were soon established because they provided a house more convenient and comfortable than the native type. It is a mistake to think of Roman villas as the houses of rich Romans. Most developed from British farms as the native farmers became more prosperous and were imbued, almost imperceptibly, with Roman ideas. The face of the country changed little and slowly, but the straight roads stretched further, connecting the towns which grew up from trading marts about the camps or in places geographically suitable for trade.

According to Strabo, the main British exports at the beginning of the century had been corn, cattle, hides, hunting dogs and slaves. To these were added an increasing quantity of metals as the mines were developed. There were lead ores in many parts of the country, and from these silver was extracted by the smelting process known as cupellation. Iron, tin and copper were also mined, and gold in Carmarthenshire. Coal was also mined, but the only actual record of its use was on the altar of Minerva at Bath.

Ornaments were made from the shale of the Isle of

Purbeck and from the jet of the Whitby Lias. British pearls were also popular, though perhaps less so than the oysters themselves. Their shells are dug up in large quantities on the site of almost every military camp. Professor I. A. Richmond suggests that the oyster tavern was the Roman soldier's equivalent of the fish-and-chips shop.

Three breeds of dog are known to have been exported, the Irish wolf hound, the bulldog and the spaniel, while the greyhound is depicted in pottery. Both sealskins and bearskins were used in trade, live bears also being sent to the arenas. Professor Richmond mentions their use for lacerating criminals. The *pax Romana* was not in every sense benign. Cloth from British wool was a valuable product, the most popular abroad being the *birrus Britannicus*, which was waterproof.

Perhaps the most lasting change was in speech. At first Latin was only the official language, spoken when Roman and Briton were concerned together in government, justice, military and civil questions. But it was the only written language, and therefore all who would write must learn it. It spread downwards from the upper levels of society. It spread upwards too—the vulgar Latin of the legionaries and the traders—from their contact with the local people. Since the native tongue was also spoken there was a period of bilingualism.

Latin unquestionably gave a great deal to the language. Take away from modern English every word of Latin derivation and see what is left! Latin was the most concise and precise of the ancient languages. There were many other linguistic influences in this country later—Norman, Saxon, and so on—but the result is that English is as precise as any living tongue and is at the same time the ideal language of poetry. It is interesting, if not paradoxical, that the Scottish, who for geographical reasons were slow to be affected by any foreign influence, speak the best English. The Welsh, still more resistant, kept the Celtic tongue with the addition of a few hundred Latin loan words.

It would be beyond the scope of this book to deal in more detail with the effects of Romanization, or carry the story further. In conclusion we need an assessment of Boadicea for good or ill and of where she stands as a character in our history.

If she had beaten Suetonius in the last battle the Romans would almost certainly have been compelled to evacuate the island. Very likely they would have come back. Britain was not only a potentially valuable province but also a strategic base of great importance. But supposing they had gone for good, would Britain have been the gainer or the loser?

Rome had in the year 60 given only from her worse side—aggressive, cruel, subjugating. What she had to offer in culture, administration, standard of living, came later; and so it would have been missed or at least postponed, as it was for the countries she never visited—such as Scandinavia. Put another way, Rome was a civilization, Britain a collection of barbaric tribes. The influence of Rome must have been progressive.

If so it would seem that Boadicea was a retrogressive influence. She slowed down Romanization—at enormous cost; as in effect though not by intention she made it more humane and considerate. But even if one grants her this, she did not alter the course of history.

She struck the spark which lit the fire. She struck when it was both courageous and right to strike. But she could not, or at any rate did not, control the fire it caused.

She is remembered chiefly through tradition, which takes little account of facts. She is a national figure, more substantial than Britannia because she was a real woman. Tradition has snatched out of the fire she lit one brand which gives only an inspiring light—resistance against oppression and wrong. For that she is rightly remembered. But her voice is the last fierce cry of something old and savage rather than the first expression of noble feeling; and as such, without straining after romanticism, it should be heard.

9

What remains to be seen

The evil that men do lives after them,
The good is oft interred with their bones.

The funeral speech of Mark Antony in Shakespeare's *Julius Caesar* was intended to rouse sympathy for the dead; the speaker is not presented as essentially sincere. But the lines are appropriate for the Queen of the Iceni. She reacted in a way which was originally right. Perhaps the good was later blotted out by evil—interred in an unknown grave.

Certainly she does not appear well in archaeology. All she has left is a layer of ashes. Visually recorded are the good works of the Romans in stone, brick, statuary, inscription, ornament; their cruelties and callousness are gone without trace. That being understood, let us see what remains to be seen of the time of Boadicea.

One can get a strong feeling of the past by visiting the scenes of her destruction. This is less so in London than elsewhere. London is so large. So much else has happened there, so much has been built. In fact the archaeologist has to act quickly if he is to read anything from a foundation site before it is covered by another building. And what has been found can be seen only in the museum. But the relics there leave a vivid impression. There are, for instance, seventeen coins of the reign of Claudius which were in the stratum of ash seventeen feet below

Lombard Street. They are partly fused together. The heat was so intense that the natural clay below them was reduced to powder.

London, of course, has known many fires. But those which can be dated by coins, pottery or glass give an indication of the lay-out of the municipium in A.D. 60. It was within the present city limits, north of London Bridge, but straggled out along the high roads to north and west.

In Colchester you see the past around you in the street—the Roman walls with present-day houses and shops built against them and on them. The town walls, of course, were constructed after the disaster, to make sure that the same thing could not happen again. They were built so strongly that, some fourteen hundred years later, they withstood a long siege and cannon fire during Cromwell's rebellion.

The durability of everything the Romans did makes one feel that such people would have come back even if Boadicea had driven them out of Britain. Whatever they set up was meant to last for ever. One feels this in the 'vaults' which pass through the foundations both of the Temple of Claudius and of the Castle which the Normans built upon the site. The original temple, though for worship and not defence, was strong enough to hold out for two days until the tens of thousands of besiegers burnt it over the heads of the people inside. One can imagine it being almost covered with firewood to make an immense bonfire.

The temple was certainly built again. The Normans pulled it down and used the stones to build their castle—which is what remains above ground level today. But in the late seventeenth century an attempt was made to pull *it* down as a source of building material. In the course of this semi-demolition a tunnel was driven under the castle, the walls of which are about twenty-five feet thick. Passing through the tunnel, known as the vaults, one sees a section of both the Norman and Roman temple foundations. Both are of concrete. If scratched with a piece of blunt metal, a key or a coin, the Norman concrete comes off in powder. The Roman is hard as stone.

What remains of the castle contains the museum. Here one sees objects of everyday life which were being used in A.D. 60. Most moving are a child's toys made of terra-cotta —a pig, a monkey, a rabbit. And there is a glass feeding bottle for a baby. Such fragile objects have survived even better than metal, which has been corroded.

Excavations have disclosed a similar layer of ash to that found in London. There is besides a tombstone which conveys the destructive rage of the attackers. The stone is carved to depict an auxiliary cavalryman riding his horse over the body of a naked Briton. The figure of the Briton is untouched. So is the inscription, which would have meant nothing to Boadicea's warriors. But the face of the cavalryman has been smashed off.

There is also the cast of a head of the Emperor Claudius which was fished out of the River Alde in 1907. It is deduced that the original, now in the British Museum, had been hacked from a statue, and later thrown away— probably at the time of the persecution, to get rid of the evidence. The man who found it, when he was a boy, is still about. He received five shillings for it. It was recently sold for over £50,000.

The Catuvellauni of Hertfordshire had experience of the Romans more than a century before the time of the rebellion. The fortress of Cassivellaunus which Julius

Caesar captured was at Wheathampstead, six miles north of St. Albans. The Belgic tribe then moved to the slopes above the River Ver where the first town of Verulamium was built. From the first there was Roman influence in lay-out, drainage, type of building, and very likely also in dress and food. It was this collaboration which made the place an object of hatred to Boadicea's people. They burnt it to ashes although, as has recently been shown, it possessed defensive earth works.

The second town plan was completed during the governorship of Agricola. Thereafter Verulamium continued to develop throughout the centuries of Roman occupation. Then the first English saint, Alban, who was executed by the Romans, gave it its present name.

The excavations have been brilliantly carried out. The ruins of this comfortable and important Roman town are there to see—theatre, hypocaust, beautiful mosaics. But once again the only relic of Boadicea is a layer of ashes.

There is still a great deal to be learned. Boadicea's grave will probably never be found, but the site of the final battle may be exactly fixed. Work continues along Watling Street, and also in the land of the Iceni. 'Archaeological excavation,' Dr. Graham Webster wrote in 1962, 'has over the last few decades become a very precise operation, carried out with the delicate skill of a surgeon and interpreted with the stiff logic of a scientist.' During the lifetime of some of us the main gaps in the story of Boadicea are likely to be filled.

HISTORICAL APPENDIX

Chronology

	Events in Britain	*Events in Rome and the Empire*
B.C. 55	Caesar makes a reconnaissance and returns to Gaul.	Reforms of Crassus and Pompey. Caesar bridges the Rhine.
54	Caesar invades Kent: defeats Cassivellaunus, retires to Gaul. Celtic chieftains regain power.	Break-up of First Triumvirate begins with death of Julia.
51		Publication of Caesar's *Commentarii de Bello Gallico.*
B.C. 30 to A.D. 14	Transference of power from Trinovantes to Catuvellauni.	Reign of Augustus.
A.D. 43	Roman expeditionary force under Aulus Plautius lands at Richborough; Caractacus defeated at Medway, Emperor Claudius occupies Colchester.	Claudius (accession A.D. 41) decides on invasion of Britain.
47	Ostorius Scapula moves against Caractacus, leader of the Silures.	Claudius revives censorship and the famous secular games.
51	Caractacus seeks refuge with Cartimandua, Queen of the Brigantes; he is betrayed to the Romans.	

	Events in Britain	Events in Rome and the Empire
53	Silures fight on. Ostorius succeeded by unenterprising Didius Gallus.	Marriage of Nero and Octavia, daughter of Claudius.
58	Suetonius Paulinus made Governor; marches into Wales.	St. Paul imprisoned in Rome.
60	Paulinus reaches Menai Straits, invades Anglesey and attacks Druids. Revolt of Boadicea; Colchester sacked; IX Legion cut to pieces; St. Albans and London destroyed. Victory of Suetonius Paulinus; massacre of Britons. Suicide of Boadicea. Reprisals taken: Britons hunted down.	Nero establishing his personal brand of Oriental-type despotism in Rome. Neglects to cultivate the army, notably the Praetorian Guard. St. Paul brought to trial in Rome; appeals and is released.
61	Suetonius Paulinus recalled to Rome; replaced by Turpilianus.	
63–69	Trebellius Maximus Governor. Comparative peace in Britain; Romanization of Britons.	Rome burns in a nine-days' fire; Christians blamed and persecuted. Death of Nero; succeeded by Otho then by Vespasian.
71	Brigantes restless. Cerialis sent to subdue them.	New buildings begun in Rome under Vespasian; Nero's buildings destroyed.
74	Julius Frontinus Governor; suppresses Welsh tribes.	Censorship of Vespasian and Titus.
78	Julius Agricola Governor. Extinguishes Welsh and Brigantine resistance.	Tacitus: *Dialogue on Orators.*
79	Agricola advances north along eastern coast from	Death of Vespasian. Accession of Titus. Eruption of

	Events in Britain	*Events in Rome and the Empire*
	York to the Tweed.	Vesuvius buries Pompeii.
81	Agricola master of Scotland as far as the Forth and Clyde.	Death of Titus. Accession of Domitian.
83	Agricola thrusts into Highlands. Victory over Caledonians at Mons Graupius.	Domitian crosses Rhine against Chatti; begins building series of defensive forts and ramparts.
84–97	Agricola recalled at climax of Governorship to bring aid to Domitian's campaign on continent. Scanty records exist for this period.	Death of Agricola in Rome, A.D. 93. Assassination of Domitian, A.D. 96. Publication of Tacitus' *Life of Agricola* and *Germania*, *c.* A.D. 97.
98	Avidius Quietus Governor (until A.D. 103).	Trajan becomes first provincial Emperor (born near Seville).
117		Hadrian becomes Emperor.
120	Revolt of Brigantes; defeat IX Legion at York.	Death of Tacitus.
122–7	Emperor Hadrian visits Britain. Platorius Nepos constructs Hadrian's Wall from Tyne to Solway Firth.	Hadrian travels extensively in provinces. Has many new buildings erected, particularly in Greece.
140–3	Lollius Urbicus builds the Antonine Wall across Forth-Clyde isthmus.	
180	Caledonian eruption through Antonine Wall. Military initiative passes from Romans to their enemies.	Commodus succeeds Marcus Aurelius as Emperor. Unrest on Rhine and Danube frontiers.
184	Ulpius Marcellus pacifies Britain.	Commodus assumes title 'Britannicus' to commemorate victory in Britain.
185	Helvius Pertinax succeeds	

	Events in Britain	*Events in Rome and the Empire*
	Ulpius Marcellus. Suppresses mutiny of Roman army in Britain.	
193	Clodius Albinus, successor of Pertinax in Britain, proclaimed Emperor by British legions; crosses with troops to Gaul.	Assassination of Commodus. Pertinax elected Emperor by Praetorian Guard ; then murdered by them. Civil war in Rome. Septimius Severus seizes power.
196	All north England overrun by barbarians after removal of garrison by Albinus. Fall of Hadrian's Wall, York, Chester.	Severus marches on Albinus at Lyons. Albinus defeated and killed.
208	Recurrence of trouble in Britain ; Severus himself leads campaign. Attacks Caledonians; withdraws to Hadrian's Wall, which he rebuilds.	Severus leaves Rome for Britain.
211	Death of Severus at York. Pacification so effective that Britain enjoys peace, unlike continent, for many years.	Caracalla murders a colleague and a brother on death of Severus to become sole Emperor. Frequent attacks on all frontiers; revolts in some areas.
286	Aurelius Carausius, Roman commander of British fleet, proclaims himself Emperor of an independent Britain.	Diocletian and Maximian acknowledge Carausius as one of the Augusti.
293	Constantius Chlorus instructed to seize Carausius' French possessions. Allectus murders Carausius, replaces him.	Constantius and Galerius appointed Caesars in West and East respectively.

	Events in Britain	Events in Rome and the Empire
297	Constantius crosses Channel. Defeats Allectus, reorganizes Britain.	Galerius defeats Narses and recovers Mesopotamia.
306	Death of Constantius at York after protracted encounter with Picts.	Constantine the Great, son of Constantius, assumes title of Caesar Imperator.
368	Spanish Count Theodosius clears out barbarians established in Britain.	Reign of Valentinian. Picts, Scots, Saxons, Franks and Attacotti make concerted attacks on the Empire; Roman troops routed.
383	Britain left defenceless; last stand made at Hadrian's Wall. Wholesale barbarian invasions.	Magnus Maximus denudes Britain of its garrison to seize Empire from Gratian, son of Valentinian.
393	Stilicho, regent of Theodosius, liberates Britain.	
396 to 402	Stilicho enlists help of Cunedda (British chieftain) to help pacify Britain.	Stilicho forced to use British troops to drive Visigoths out of Greece. Alaric the Goth defeated at Verona in Italy.
403–6	British troops set up successive usurpers called Marcus, Gratian and Constantine to defend country from invasions.	Fresh Gothic invasion into Italy led by Radagaisus; defeated.
410	Roman legions withdrawn from Britain to protect Rome; effective end of Roman occupation of Britain; Britons left to defend themselves from invasions of Caledonians and German tribes.	Rome captured and sacked by Alaric.

Prehistoric Britain up to the Romans

Our story begins with the age of Neolithic man—from 3000 B.C. onwards. By that time earthquakes, volcanic action and glaciers had finished their work and England's rivers had found something like their modern level. Inviting routes lay open for invasions which seem to have run much the same course many times over. The invaders, steering in dug-out canoes far into the country by easy inlets, would then take the upland drier tracks, conquering the previous occupants or driving them inland. They would halt at the Midland forests, or skirt them with dislike. Finally, they would be arrested by the rocky hills where the successively displaced cultures could find refuge, and the new world painfully and very slowly fuse with the old. From such fusion—in Wales, Scotland and elsewhere—would emerge something very different from the pattern triumphant in the coastal plain.

Until the first century B.C. all invaders pursued much the same objectives—they wanted room, dry grazing and good water. Therefore, though some would stay to fish and fowl by rivers and estuaries, most would seek at all costs to get away from the forests they dreaded, from oak and ash which their weapons could not cut, and from clays and water-logged soils where their animals would fare badly. The higher hills they found useful for refuge camps and summer pasture, but in general they made for the upper fringes of the lowland plain. Thus relics of their dwelling places, their tombs and ornaments have been found thickest on the Thames gravel terraces, the chalk downs of northern Wessex, the porous water-bearing ridges which stretch from the Severn to east Yorkshire, or the East Anglian heaths. In such regions, connected by trackways of unknown antiquity, and above all in the Salisbury Plain centre, lay the heart of the first historic England.

These early civilizations overlapped, so that clear divisions of time are difficult to determine. Thus flint arrow heads persisted for ages after the introduction of bronze, and barrow burials continued up to the time of the Romans. Moreover any particular migration or culture might affect only one small part of the island: in the hill regions, especially Dartmoor or the Yorkshire moors, life went on with little visible change, or changed in different ways than the oft-conquered south.

The first written account of Britain comes from the Greek Pytheas of Marseilles, who explored its coasts about 325 B.C.; before that we must depend upon what archaeology can make of camps and hut-circles, metal weapons, ornaments and pottery, or on anthropology's deduction from discovered skeletons and later human types, or the verdict of philology regarding speech development. It is often practically impossible to separate evidence of invasion from evidence of trade, or to build conclusions on the grave ornaments of many centuries during which some settlers inhumed their dead and others cremated them.

The little we can detect of Neolithic man is all-important. In the third millennium before Christ, there were three invasions of Britain—a northern one from the Baltic area, one from southern France; and a third dominant stock arrived by way of the Atlantic and the Irish Sea. The majority of these were people of a dark, slight, long-headed Mediterranean type, flintminers, who had domesticated animals and sowed a little wheat.

From about 1900 to 1000 B.C., there followed what are styled the Early and Middle Bronze Ages, though where and by what divided is less easy to say. The so-called 'Beaker Folk' who began this new set of invasions, if originally of Mediterranean stock, absorbed in their wanderings some Nordic strain since broader heads and a sturdier build marked them out from their predecessors. Most appear to have come last from the Rhineland and settled in great numbers over the whole east, from the Yorkshire wold to the Thames estuary. They inhumed their dead in many sorts of round barrows and may have practised human sacrifice. Bronze, mixed perhaps from Irish copper and Cornish tin, was the material used by their chieftains and fighting men, and was a medium of their trade, which also embraced a flourishing commerce in Irish gold and jet from Yorkshire. They were a more organized people than any yet existent in Britain, since the first works at Stonehenge and the circles of Avebury date from this era. Theirs was the power that brought giant blue stones from Pembrokeshire to Salisbury Plain, cut ditches fifty feet deep and morticed lintels into vast shaped uprights.

From about 1000 B.C. we enter the Late Bronze Age which shades, by degrees unproven, into the Early Iron Age around 500 B.C. It is an age primarily of amalgamation of conquerors and conquered, of population expansion by a people who wove cloth and smelted charcoal, introduced a rude plough to carve out the small rectangular terraced fields, still visible on the downs and, most marked of all, greatly increased the quantity and quality of metal-working. New types of metal work were introduced—socketed and hollow-cast axes, swords with a cutting edge, and sickles, wheeled vehicles and cauldrons. Arts and crafts appearing at this time seem to denote new immigrations—of an Alpine element and of a western link with Spain—but although both of these were to recur, it is true to say that from this time on the trend of immigration came predominantly from the North, notably from the Rhineland and the Ardennes. We have, in fact, reached the epoch of the Celts and the beginning of those folk-wanderings which for a thousand years convulsed Europe.

Caesar called the inhabitants of Britain, 'Britanni' and the island, 'Britannia', evidently confusing the more correct form 'Pretanni' which the Greek explorer Pytheas found in Gaul. But by Caesar's time the majority of the inhabitants of Britain were Celtic, like the Gauls. They were part of a powerful nation called variously Keltoi, Celtae, Galatae and Galli by the inhabitants of the Mediterranean basin. Not a unified nation in the modern sense, the Celts were a people composed of tribes of varying size, usually politically independent of one another but with certain common characteristics, which first became apparent in the area north of the Alps at the beginning of the sixth century B.C. It was at this time that the iron-using warrior chieftains, centred on Hallstatt in Austria, first gained power, and from this base they expanded west, east and south—as far east as Asia Minor, where they gave their name to Galatia, and in the west to

Spain and Britain. They plundered Greece and Italy, and in 390 B.C. a group of them, returning from a raid in central Italy, captured Rome and held it to ransom.

The Mediterranean peoples recognized in them at once a people different from themselves, taller and more powerfully built, fairer in skin and hair (their blondness accentuated by their custom of washing their hair in lime), blue-eyed and differently dressed, wearing trousers and tunic. They were certainly taller than the average Roman, and more warlike also. The lure of the rich civilizations in Italy was a powerful magnet for a people fond of personal adornment, such as gold torcs. After 390 B.C. nearly two centuries were to pass before the Romans were able to master the Celts settled in northern Italy; and the remainder of the Continental Celts, in Gaul, were not defeated until the campaigns of Julius Caesar.

How precisely, and when, the Celtic invaders affected the British Isles is disputed in every detail. Two different families of Celtic tongues were later developed, respectively called Goidel ('Q' Celtic, retaining the original Indo-European 'Q' sound) represented by Irish and Gaelic, and Brythonic or Gallo-Brittonic ('P' Celtic, modifying the 'Q' sound to 'P') represented by Gaulish, with insular versions in Welsh, Cornish and Breton. But it is still not known when that distinction was made, whether before or after reaching these islands. In one way or another archaeology seems to establish a continuous arrival of many groups of Celts from about 800 to 450 B.C., coming from Swiss lake-villages, from Champagne and Brittany, and even more so from the northern French and lower Rhine regions, where Celt and Teuton had met and mixed. They made their way to Scarborough headland, into the Fens and the Thames and the Hampshire harbours; another wave, sailing from the Atlantic ports, reached the tin workings that exported through St. Michael's Mount, and by way of the Severn passed into the Midlands.

These tall, fair-haired people called the natives whom they defeated 'Pretanni' or painted folk. They were experienced warriors and brought with them the power of iron—later on they would mine the ores of the Sussex Weald and the Forest of Dean—making six-foot ash-hafted spears, chariots with iron-rimmed wheels, and horse harness. They were the builders of the fortified camps which stud many cape promontories and all the southern downs, often with vast ditches and guarded gates—Maiden Castle in Dorset is a famous example. Their pottery and carefully-wrought brooches and artistic bronze work suggest a wide trade and a powerful aristocracy. Between 250 B.C. and about A.D. 100 we have evidence of two further, widely separated settlements, well advanced in culture. One, identified in Yorkshire, which spread through the Fens to East Anglia, is of a people who buried their chieftains with horse and chariot and daggers; while far away at Glastonbury other invaders raised log-platform dwellings over the marshes and worked in iron, bronze, stone and bone, also smelting lead and killing man or game with pellets from slings.

About 75 B.C. began a final sequence of Celtic invasions which were to bind Britain in a permanent relation with Europe. Some twenty-one years before Caesar the third and most advanced group of all, the Belgae, who would prove his most powerful enemies, began to arrive in Britain. Centred on the Marne and Aisne, and part-German in culture, they had already won some footing in these areas when they appeared in force in Kent, headed by the tribe of the Catuvellauni, and spread from thence over the Thames basin into Essex and Hertfordshire, where at Wheathampstead they began building a fortified capital, while lesser branches continued on to the Midland streams lying between Oxford and Cambridge. The enormous earthwork at Wheathampstead was the headquarters of Cassivellaunus, leader of the Catuvellauni, who was responsible for the chief opposition to Caesar—it was successfully stormed during Caesar's second campaign. Formal tribute was then exacted and further expansion forbidden, but before long the Catuvellauni had transferred their mint and presumably their tribal centre from Hertfordshire to Camulodunum (Colchester), conquering the Trinovantes of Essex.

Some thirty years after the first Belgic invasion, when Caesar had come and gone, another Belgic tribe, the Atrebates, refugees from Roman power, crossed from Normandy, fixed a capital at Silchester in Berkshire, and ruthlessly attacked the peoples of West Sussex and Somerset. The Belgae brought with them a rude vigour, and some positive improvements such as the introduction of a heavier form of plough which could really turn the sod, and they undertook a certain amount of land clearance. From the horse of their chariots perhaps descends the white horse cut on the Berkshire downs.

Although their power was considerable enough to make sizeable states, at the opening of the Christian era we find many British kingdoms, and no united Britain or a uniform culture. Outside the two substantial Belgic states mentioned, there survived strong Celtic communities; the Dobuni, extending from the Cotswolds to the Welsh foothills, with one wing stretched into Dorset; the Trinovantes in Essex, the Iceni in East Anglia, and the Brigantes in the north. Both in the north and in the Cornish west and Wales, a bronze age civilization, or an even ruder life, was perpetuated, ranging from chiefs in hill-forts down to villages of pit-dwellings or stone huts. The Belgic areas were wealthy, with much wheat-growing and iron-making, but a finer sense of art lived on in the Celtic middle west, where pottery retained the bold curves and spirals of an earlier age, and from which some magnificent bronze ornament was derived. Everywhere we seem to stumble on separate communities, sometimes wholly disconnected, sometimes at war with one another. Whether Breton immigrants defending Maiden Castle with slings, subterranean dwellers in Wales, pile-dwellers in Yorkshire or merely isolated farmers, all alike were barely touched by the series of conquests.

The coinage of the different British chiefs or kings reflected their different policies, and illustrated also the growth of trade and social complexity in pre-Roman Britain. By 100 B.C. a gold coinage had emerged in many areas, replaced later by silver and bronze, which in turn had gradually replaced the currency of iron bars or ingots attested by Caesar and apparently of the form of sword blanks of standard weight. The coinage of the Atrebates closely copies Roman originals and bears the Latin word 'rex', a sign that the Atrebates knew some Latin, for the word was anathema to the Romans but was granted to allies of the Roman people. One coin issued by the Catuvellauni, by contrast, bears the Celtic word 'ricon', meaning king like 'rex', but by its choice of language probably indicating independence of Rome. Likewise the Catuvellaunian coinage was designed in spirited artistic independence of the Roman coinage. One difference between the two British coinages is particularly striking:

that of Cunobelinus, leader of the Catuvellauni (Shakespeare's Cymbeline), carries an ear of barley while that of Commius of the Atrebates shows a vine leaf, extolling the merits of wine imported from the Roman world rather than British beer!

In art these tribes possessed a native late-Celtic style, descended from far-off Mediterranean antecedents and more directly connected with the La Tène culture of the Continental Celts. Its characteristics were a flamboyant and fantastic treatment of plant, animal and, more rarely human forms, a brilliant use of curved, geometrical forms and much skill in enamelling. Its finest products were achieved in bronze, but the same patterns spread to woodwork and pottery.

For a generation before A.D. 43 the Belgae had thrown open their territories to Roman commercial enterprise. Some decades before the establishment of Roman rule, Roman or Romanized craftsmen were working in the service of Belgic kings such as Tasciovanus and Cunobelinus. Roman bronzes, Roman pottery, Roman silver vessels were trafficked in Britain in return for (as Strabo tells us) corn, cattle, gold, silver, iron, skins, slaves and hunting dogs. An astonishing result of the excavation of Cymbeline's capital at Colchester was the discovery of some of the finest products of Italian factories on the floors of the primitive hutments of the Belgic population. The Roman invader, following the Roman trafficker, was confronted with this curious and paradoxical mixture of commercial prosperity and native squalor.

It can be seen that the political system of the Celts was essentially tribal and in fact non-political. Their traditions and temperament were those of an incurably nomadic people, as volatile and lightfooted as the half-wild herds driven and corralled by their forefathers. In both Britons and Gauls Tacitus notes the same audacity in provoking danger, and irresolution in facing up to it. The frequent absence of a permanent water supply in their hill towns is characteristic of them in their proto-historical environment; on the cut-and-run principle of warfare, provision for a momentary siege was adequate. Wars were waged between meals.

Similarly their essays in political development appear to have been lacking in certainty and direction. Occasionally a tribal king would acquire by force or diplomacy a suzerainty over neighbouring tribes, normally a transient union. On the other hand, there was a tendency in Caesar's time for the tribal councils to increase their authority at the expense of the kinglet, and sometimes an oligarchical system of government succeeded, at least momentarily, the monarchical. The Celtic world was ill at ease in its new environment, riddled with faction and irresolution; its conquest by Rome was not premature. Celtic Europe was thereby enabled to pass through the discipline of Roman paganism, and thereafter to reassert itself for a while in the gentler precincts of the Romano-Celtic church.

Britain as a Roman province

Had Caesar never lived, the destiny of Rome must have taken her to the Atlantic. She had destroyed Carthage, absorbed Greece, crushed Asia Minor and carried her frontier to the Euphrates. Only on the north and north-west was she exposed to the barbarians who, since the first Celtic drive three centuries before, had never rested. To meet the emergency they had created in Gaul, Caesar accepted a five-years' command in 58 B.C. In three successful campaigns he removed the threat and at midsummer in 55 B.C. decided on an exploratory expedition to Britain as a preliminary to conquest.

After the departure of Julius Caesar from Britain the Island was not troubled by Rome for nearly ninety years. In that interval Caesar destroyed Pompey and was himself slain, Mark Antony and Octavian fought over the succession, Tiberius reigned, and Christ was crucified, while the British scene saw the important transfer of power from the Trinovantes to the Catuvellauni, whose chief began to style himself 'King of the Britons'. All this while Roman sentiment expected, and even demanded, the annexation of Britain.

The Empire established by Augustus gave the Mediterranean world for the first time a single political form. There was one Emperor over all, one army, one civil service and in the end one religion, although it was never possible to speak of one nationality or one culture. During his forty-five years of unchallenged power, ending with his death in A.D. 14, Augustus consolidated the far-flung provinces, established a large degree of local self-government in them, revitalized the economy, stabilized the Treasury, created a widespread and heretofore unmatched prosperity, reduced, disciplined and tamed the Army, arranged for his successor (while signally failing to establish an acceptable system for later selections) and, in the process of all this achievement, introduced to history the comparative felicity of the *pax Romana*—order, peace and obedience to law within the long-battered world of Mediterranean civilization. His success, so monumental in character, so lasting in history, rested on his understanding and practical use of two Roman creations long antecedent to his reign, both of which he developed and moulded to serve his farsighted purpose: the Law and the Army.

When Augustus planned the stabilization of the Empire he seems originally to have intended to make its northern boundary in Europe the River Elbe. Through the lands between that river and the Rhine, his generals, Drusus and later Tiberius, brought about the sullen submission of the surly forest tribes. With this pacification apparently complete, Tiberius turned over his command to Quintilius Varus, who in A.D. 9 allowed his army of three legions to be ambushed and totally destroyed in the trackless wastes of the Teutoburg Forest. Augustus, appalled, summarily gave up hopes of further expansion and set the Rhine and the Danube on the north and the Channel on the west as the Imperial frontiers, earnestly recommending to his successors that they go no farther afield.

Nevertheless his awareness of popular opinion in Rome made Augustus careful to convey, through his court poets, the impression that the conquest of Britain was always imminent. Tiberius followed this example, for it seems that although the island of Britain lay on the fringes of Roman influence and came late within the sphere of Rome, the imaginations of all classes of the Roman people were stirred by the idea of annexing Britain.

Thus Tiberius, like Augustus, may have contemplated invasion but never initiated it. The reasons are not hard to find; his policy was one of consolidation rather than of expansion; moreover the Augustan settlement, the 'Principate', held within itself a contradiction which made it difficult for the machinery of Imperial government to embark upon a policy of foreign conquest. The system inaugurated by Augustus demanded that the Emperor preside over a delicately balanced administration in which one party (the Princeps) held the reality of power and another party (the Senate) held the semblance of it. This system was not of Tiberius's making and probably not to his liking, yet he had to direct its further development. To this fault in the constitution created by Augustus can in fact be traced the fundamental weakness which brought increasing instability into Roman political life and made it a prey to the corrupt intrigues of various factions surrounding the Imperator—a weakness which spread through the hierarchy of soldiers and civil servants serving the far-flung empire and in time brought it to its knees.

During the reign of these first two emperors, the internal condition of the Empire steadily improved. The Gallic provinces in particular, reaching to the Rhine, speedily embraced the standards of Roman civilization, and participated fully in its economic life. Tranquillity and order, peaceful trade and commerce, replaced the quarrelling anarchy the Gallic peoples had known before Caesar. In three generations, with only occasional flare-ups, the concept of being part of a civilized world community had taken root and flourished. The resulting prosperity was not without effect across the Channel in Britain, where raiding one's neighbour was a traditional and honoured means of livelihood. This had indeed been so in Gaul before Caesar; but in Britain it remained a way of life, subject to possible retribution, but never to moral condemnation.

The irritations and the compensating satisfactions of a growing commerce with Britain were another factor in the increasing interest with which Roman officials looked across the Channel, and an added incentive was provided by the fury of the Druid priesthood. Refugees from Gaul, opposing the imposition of Roman customs and law, fled to Britain and there harangued their faithful followers on the crimes of Roman tyranny. As Gaul became Roman in thought, language and custom, Britain, in the eyes of many peaceful provincials, as well as in those of the responsible officials, was slowly becoming a nuisance. Whereas Augustus considered the Channel a frontier that required no defence, the Britons, in their greed for other people's property and their capacity for intrigue, proved it otherwise.

Gaius Caesar, 'Caligula', succeeded his great-uncle without incident on March 18th, A.D. 37. More truly a Julian than his father Germanicus, he conceived that a revival of the scheme to conquer Britain would enable him to get to know the army, and would fire the popular imagination. The pretext was at hand—that a renegate British prince, Adminius (Amminius) son of Cunobelinus, had submitted to him personally and requested his aid. According to the historian, Suetonius, who loved gossip more than history, Caligula interpreted the personal submission and request for aid of Adminius as carrying with it the submission of the entire island. Be this as it may, he abruptly ceased his 'pseudo-military clowning' on the Rhine in the spring of 40 and marched what troops were on hand to the Channel, in the meantime ordering ships to be made ready.

It is virtually impossible to assess whether Caligula intended this conquest or merely imagined it. It seems probable that his troops behaved at this stage as those of Claudius two years later and refused to embark, and that Caligula could not wait for them to recover their nerve for fear of what might be happening back in Italy. The most he could do was to issue a public manifesto formally announcing the annexation of Britain. The actual military occupation he could not attempt and perhaps was incapable of. He returned to Italy in August with his mind a prey to the suspicions and fears which the conspiracy of his nearest relatives had engendered. In 41 he died in Rome, killed by a tribune of the Praetorian Guard. His short reign brought into startling relief the despotism inherent in the Principate and the hopeless dependence of the Senate on the Emperor.

Contemplating their deed, the murderers must have realized that their sole hope of safety lay in selecting the next incumbent. Chancing on a grandson of Augustus, Tiberius Claudius Drusus Germanicus, they convinced him that his duty to Rome required not only his ascent to the Principate but the payment to them of a liberal donation for supporting his candidacy. Claudius agreed—it is difficult to see how he could have refused, and have lived.

He further agreed to the suggestion of a new conquest, to be followed by a glittering triumph and the honorific title 'Britannicus', bestowed by vote of the Senate. In fact, given the spirit of the times, the arguments for the conquest of Britain had by now become nearly unanswerable.

Claudius had a keen sense of Rome's historical mission, believing that Rome should assimilate, as well as expand by setting up client kingdoms: he coveted the title of 'Extender of Empire'. In invading Britain he could plead that he was fulfilling a civilizing mission to stamp out barbaric rites, was ensuring the integrity of Gaul, and was safeguarding Roman traders and exploiting British wealth in the form of metal, timber, cattle and slaves. However his chief motive was undoubtedly the conviction that Roman public opinion strongly favoured the adventure.

From the time of Caesar onwards the opportunity Britain afforded for the winning of prestige and military honour, and the satisfying of personal ambition, provided the principal motive for Roman interference. Caesar himself probably hoped to refill his war chest from the much-rumoured British wealth, as well as from the sale of prisoners; the Claudian invaders, too, came expecting to find considerable mineral wealth. They were disappointed in this, but they did find in Britain a lowland area which could be easily controlled, but with too much woodland for intensive cultivation, and a highland area which they were to hold loosely and never properly exploit. The best tribute that Britain would bring to Rome was her man-power for the Imperial armies; the invaders soon realized that the economic and financial liabilities would outweigh any gains that might be won. Strabo stated his opinion quite clearly: Britain should *not* be conquered, because the profits to be derived therefrom would not even cover the cost of the garrisons which would have to be maintained there.

Thus after the Claudian conquest Britain lost the El Dorado character it had previously held for imaginative Romans and even became, as the remotest of all the provinces, something of a Roman Siberia for troublemakers, both political and religious—it is recorded of Marcus Aurelius that in the 170s, when he had to deal with Tiridates, a dissident native ruler in the East, 'Marcus did not put him to death, but merely sent him to Britain'. But for its first 150 years as a province Britain was one of the senior appointments for a Senator with military ambitions; a theatre in which renown could be won to justify the celebration of a triumph at home. Moreover the addition of the legions stationed on the island of Britain and the fleet at the disposal of the Governor altered the delicate balance of military power among the various frontier commanders.

This was a danger that Augustus had been well aware of—he had found from personal experience that loyalty to a general rather than to Rome was the major motivation of the legions—and had laid down a policy that the forces entrusted to the several provincial governors, while necessarily varying in size according to their military responsibilities, should in no single case be large enough to make a particular governor, on the death of an emperor, a nearly unchallengeable candidate for the succession. But nothing was ever set up to ensure the maintenance of this policy—nor could it have been, as every succeeding emperor became increasingly dependent on military power. Any successful general became a source of anxiety to the Emperor. Thus Suetonius, for his success in suppressing Boadicea's rebellion, suffered the fate reserved for Nero's abler commander: he was recalled to Rome, unhonoured, in A.D. 61. Britain became the ideal province in which a governor might consolidate his power and build up his forces undisturbed, prior to making a bid for the Empire itself, as the careers of Clodius Albinus (193–196) and of Magnus Maximus (*c.* 383) clearly illustrate.

The vitality of Roman Britain and the grasp which Roman administration had over the province of Britain is well symbolized by the fortunes of Hadrian's Wall. Built between the years A.D. 121 and 127 by the Emperor Hadrian's friend and governor of Britain, Nepos, its construction reflected Agricola's pacification of the country and the conviction, which always followed the first flush of conquest, that Rome would last for ever. Falling in 196 to the Caledonians, it was almost immediately rebuilt by Governor Senecio; not until 383 was it breached by the northern hordes for the last time, as a result of the removal of British garrisons by Magnus Maximus in his bid for the imperial throne. Then wholesale barbarian invasions of Roman Britain followed, but these did not or could not entirely destroy the wall—it stands today as perhaps the most tangible memorial to Roman power in Britain.

The Roman occupation of Britain lasted for as long as 360 years, and to divide this time into a period of offensive conquest and one of defensive peace seems to blur the main truth. For if within forty years of the Claudian conquest Roman armies reached the extremities of Wales and Scotland, several times a military disaster or rebellion threatened a premature end to the entire Roman occupation. The story seems rather one of a border province, always weakly held, and often with inferior troops, responding instantly to a spell of good government in Rome, but in its own character never self-sufficient, and drawing all its energy from the heart of the Empire. When Rome sagged under Nero, or rose in new glory under the Antonines in the second century, was restored in the fourth by Constantine, and broke at last before the Goths and Huns, so, correspondingly, Roman power in Britain faltered, flowed again and then ran dry. There were years of a forward policy and years of economy, but the disease of Empire was incurable. A date can be found after which the loss of Britain was certain, although the end is best visualized not as one of sudden, fierce destruction, but rather as a fading away into a slow, long-drawn-out dusk.

Britain as seen by the Roman historians

The most rewarding classical descriptions of the Celts are those by Diodorus Siculus and Strabo, who wrote at or shortly after the time of the Roman conquest of Gaul and were therefore in a position to describe the Gauls of France in their pre-Roman state. The Celts of Britain must have been very similar.

> In stature [declared Diodorus] they are tall, with rippling muscles and white skins; red-haired, not only naturally but they do all they can to make it redder by art. They often wash their hair in water boiled with lime, and turn it backward from the forehead to the crown of the head, and thence to their very necks, that their faces may be more fully seen, so that they look like satyrs and hobgoblins.... The persons of quality shave their chins close, but their moustaches they let fall so low that they even cover their mouths: when they eat their meat hangs dangling by their hair, and when they drink the liquor runs through their moustaches as through a sieve.... In the very midst of feasting, upon any small occasion it is ordinary for them to rise, and, without any regard for their lives, to fall to with their swords. ... In their journeys and fights they use chariots

> drawn with two horses, which carry a charioteer and a soldier, and when they meet horsemen in the battle they fall upon their enemies with their throwing-spears then, quitting their chariots, they set to with their swords. . . . When at any time they cut off their enemies' heads they hang them about their horses' necks.

Their clothing seemed strange to Graeco-Roman eyes. Unlike the more barbaric Germans, whom Tacitus describes as 'either naked or lightly covered with a small mantle', they wore parti-coloured coats with sleeves 'interwoven here and there with divers coloured flowers', and wide and flowing trousers (*bracae* or *anaxyrides*)—a costume of oriental origin derived possibly through the Scythians of southern Russia. It may have been introduced thence into the West first by Germans rather than by Celts. The trousered costume was essentially that of a horse-riding people, and it is suggestive that in Caesar's time, when the Germans were thrusting strongly westwards, the old Celtic usage of chariots was, in Gaul, being superseded by cavalry, although in remoter Britain, where breeds of horse large enough for riding were seemingly not yet available, Caesar found the Celtic pony-drawn chariots still in full vogue.

The defensive arms of the Gauls, according to Strabo, were:

> . . . a shield proportioned to the height of the man, garnished with their own ensigns. . . . Upon their heads they wore helmets of brass, with large pieces of work raised upon them for ostentation's sake . . . horns of the same metal or shapes of birds and beasts carved on

them. They have trumpets after the barbarian manner, which in sounding make a horrid noise, to strike terror fit and proper for the occasion.

These people are of a most terrible aspect, and have a most dreadful and loud voice. In their converse, they are sparing of words, and speak many things darkly and figuratively. . . . Among them they have poets, who sing melodious songs, whom they call bards, who to their musical instruments, like unto harps, chant forth the praises of some and the dispraises of others. . . There are likewise among them philosophers or divines whom they call Druids, who are held in veneration and esteem.

In his account of his first invasion of Britain Caesar, writing as usual in the third person, describes how the Roman troops were thrown into confusion 'by the novel character of the fighting', so that only his own arrival saved the day: 'Caesar brought assistance in the very nick of time, for his coming caused the enemy to halt, and enabled our men to recover from their fear.'

After his second invasion he wrote the following account of the inhabitants of Kent:

Of all the Britons the inhabitants of Kent, an entirely maritime district, are by far the most civilized, differing but little from the Gallic manner of life. Of the inlanders most do not sow corn, but live on milk and flesh and clothe themselves in skins. All the Britons, indeed, dye themselves with woad, which produces a blue colour, and makes their appearance in battle more terrible. They wear long hair, and shave every part of the body save the head and the upper lip. Groups of

> ten or twelve men have wives together in common, and particularly brothers along with brothers, and fathers with sons; but the children born of the unions are reckoned to belong to the particular house to which the maiden was first conducted.

When evaluating Caesar's accounts it must be understood that, whereas Strabo and Diodorus were concerned with the writing of history and geography, Caesar was an astute politician and military commander writing self-justificatory despatches after the event. Tierney has gone so far as to say that 'Caesar had no interest in Gallic ethnography as such', and that the ethnographical passages in the *Gallic Wars* are there because literary convention ruled that historical works should contain such material. Caesar's general, Hirtius, who wrote the concluding Book VIII of the work, seems to have been well aware of this. 'Caesar not only wrote with supreme fluency and elegance,' he said, 'he also knew superlatively well how to describe his plans and policies.' Dr. Grant writes moreover that 'Caesar's apparent simplicity and lack of rhetoric were deliberate artifices based on mastery of the most elaborate rhetorical theory'.

Nevertheless the popular appeal of the *Gallic Wars* is undeniable and it seems that criticism of the work is based on the bias with which the facts are presented to the reader rather than on inaccurate reporting of them. Here, for instance, is Caesar's account of his first landing in Britain:

> These arrangements made, he caught a spell of fair weather for sailing, and weighed anchor about the third watch: he ordered the cavalry to proceed to the

further harbour, embark, and follow him. . . . He himself reached Britain about the fourth hour of the day, and there beheld the armed forces of the enemy displayed on all the cliffs [near Dover]. Such was the nature of the ground, so steep the heights which banked the sea, that a missile could be hurled from the higher levels on to the shore. Thinking this place to be by no means suitable for disembarkation, he waited at anchor till the ninth hour for the rest of the flotilla to assemble there . . . and catching at one and the same moment a favourable wind and tide, he gave the signal, and weighed anchor, and moving on about seven miles from that spot, he grounded his ships where the shore was even and open [probably between Walmer and Deal]. . . . Disembarkation was a matter of extreme difficulty for the following reasons. The ships, on account of their size, could not be run ashore, except in deep water; the troops—though they did not know the ground, had not their hands free, and were loaded with the grievous weight of their arms—had nevertheless at one and the same time to leap down from the vessels, to stand firm in the waves, and to fight the enemy. The enemy, on the other hand, had all their limbs free, and knew the ground exceeding well; and either standing on dry land or advancing a little way into the water, they boldly hurled their missiles, or spurred on their horses, which were trained to it. . . .

While our troops hung back, chiefly on account of the depth of the sea, the eaglebearer of the Tenth Legion after a prayer to heaven to bless the legion by his act, cried: 'Leap down, soldiers, unless you wish to betray your eagle to the enemy; it shall be told that I at least did my duty to my country and my general.' When

F*

he had shouted this aloud, he cast himself forth from the ship, and began to bear the eagle towards the enemy. Then our troops exhorted one another not to allow so dire a disgrace, and leapt down from the ship with one accord. And when the troops on the nearest ships saw them, they likewise followed on and drew near to the enemy.

Further difficulties lay in store for navigators accustomed to the tideless Mediterranean:

That same night, as it chanced, the moon was full, the day of the month which usually makes the highest tides in the Ocean, a fact unknown to our men. Therefore the tide was found to have filled the warships, in which Caesar had caused his army to be conveyed across, and which he had drawn up on dry land; and at the same time the storm was buffeting the transports, which were made fast to anchors. Nor had our troops any chance of handling them or helping. Several ships went to pieces; and the others, by loss of cordage, anchors and the rest of their tackle, were rendered useless for sailing. This inevitably caused dismay throughout the army. For there were no other ships to carry them back; everything needful for the repair of the ships was lacking; and as it was generally understood that the army was to winter in Gaul, no corn had been provided in these parts against the winter.

When they became aware of this, the British chiefs who had assembled at Caesar's headquarters after the fight took counsel together. As they knew that the Romans lacked cavalry, ships, and corn and perceived the scantiness of the army from the smallness of the camp (further emphasized by the fact that Caesar had brought the legions over without baggage), they thought it best to renew the war . . . for they were confident that when the present force was overcome or cut off from return no one thereafter would cross over to Britain to make war upon them. . . .

If the Britons did count on this, the following year proved how wrong they were: when the Roman fleet hove in sight of land not an enemy was to be seen, 'for,' says Caesar, 'alarmed at the number of ships, 800 of which had been seen at once, they had concealed themselves on high ground away from the shore.'

In Book V we are given an account of the campaign against Cassivellaunus—

. . . whose territories are divided from the maritime states by the river called Thames, about eighty miles from the sea. Hitherto there had been continuous wars between this chief and the other states; but our arrival moved the Britons to appoint him commander-in-chief for the conduct of the whole campaign. . . .

Having obtained knowledge of their plans, Caesar led his army into the borders of Cassivellaunus as far as the River Thames, which can be crossed at one place only on foot, and that with difficulty. When he had arrived there he noticed that on the other bank of the river a large force of the enemy was drawn up. The bank was fortified with a fringe of sharp projecting stakes, and stakes of the same kind fixed under water were concealed by the stream. When he had learnt these details from prisoners and deserters, Caesar sent the cavalry in advance and ordered the legions to follow up instantly. But the troops moved with such speed and such spirit, although they had only their heads above water, that the enemy could not withstand the assault of legions and cavalry, but abandoned the banks and betook themselves to flight.

When Cassivellaunus had thus relinquished all hope of a struggle, and disbanded the greater part of his force, he kept our marches under observation with the remainder—about 4,000 chariots. Withdrawing a little from the route, he concealed himself in entangled positions among the woods. In whatever districts he had learnt that we intended to march he drove all cattle and human beings from the fields into the woods; then, whenever our cavalry dashed out over the fields to plunder and devastate more freely, he sent out charioteers from the woods by every road and path, engaging our cavalry to their great danger, and preventing them from ranging further afield by the fear thus caused. The only course left to Caesar was to allow no party to remove very far from the main column of the legions, and to do as much harm to the enemy in laying waste the fields and setting fire to the country as the marching powers of the legionaries could accomplish. . . .

The *Life of Agricola* by Tacitus was published with his *Germania* in A.D. 97–98. In the *Agricola* we have a portrait of Britain at the time of Boadicea's revolt written in a style that never loiters, often sparkles, is never dull. The book has exercised a steady attraction on generation after generation for in it can be traced an ideal that commands admiration—belief in Rome, in Roman destiny, and in Roman ways and standards of life. Of the private life of

Tacitus we know very little indeed—he married the daughter of Agricola in A.D. 77 but he never mentions her. We know that he was planning to write a general history of the years A.D. 68–96, and the account of Britain might be regarded as a preparative study; but in it the biographical interest is always to the fore—details of both geography and history are cut down to a minimum. Tacitus had the obvious advantage of a close relationship with Agricola, who as a Governor of Britain knew it as no Roman had ever known it before.

Nevertheless it is hard to accept his claim that he put research on a new basis, with solid fact to replace guess-work. He might possibly have done so had he taken more trouble. But he is often amazingly careless about military and geographical detail, and throws the achievements of Agricola on so uncertain a background that they begin to become blurred themselves. He writes as though any province, any provincials, any army, any enemy might serve equally well to illustrate his hero's virtues, as in the following account of events following one of Agricola's victories:

> Night brought our men the satisfactions of victory and booty. The Britons wandered all over the countryside, men and women together wailing, carrying off their wounded and calling out to the survivors. They would leave their homes and in fury set fire to them, and choose lairs, only to abandon them at once. Sometimes they would try to concert plans, then break off conference. Sometimes the sight of their dear ones broke their hearts, more often it goaded them to fury. Some, it was afterwards found, laid violent hands on their wives and children in a kind of pity. The next day revealed the

> quality of the victory more distinctly. A grim silence reigned on every hand, the hills were deserted, only here and there was smoke seen rising from chimneys in the distance, and our scouts found no one to encounter them. When they had been sent out in all directions and had made sure that everything pointed to indiscriminate flight and that the enemy were not massing at any point, Agricola led his army into the territory of the Boresti. Summer was almost over, and it was impossible for operations to be extended over a wider area. There Agricola took hostages and ordered his admiral to coast round Britain. The forces allotted were sufficient, and the terror of Rome had gone before him. Agricola himself, marching slowly in order to inspire terror in fresh nations by his very lack of hurry, placed his infantry and cavalry in winter-quarters.

One of the highlights of Tacitus's account of the career of Agricola in Britain is his description of Boadicea's revolt and the events leading up to it:

> The Britons submit to the levy, the tribute and the other charges of Empire with cheerful readiness, provided that there is no abuse. *That* they bitterly resent, for they are broken in to obedience, not to slavery. . . .
>
> After the governor Didius Gallus, Suetonius Paulinus enjoyed two years of success, conquering tribes and establishing strong forts. Emboldened thereby to attack the island of Anglesey, which was feeding the native resistance, he exposed himself to a stab in the back.
>
> For the Britons, freed from their repressions by the absences of the dreaded legate, began to discuss the

woes of slavery, to compare their wrongs and sharpen their sting in the telling. 'We gain nothing by submission except heavier burdens for willing shoulders. Once each tribe had one king, now two are clamped on us—the legate to wreak his fury on our lives, the procurator on our property. We subjects are damned in either case, whether our masters quarrel or agree. Their gangs of centurions or slaves, as the case may be, mingle violence and insult. Nothing is any longer safe from their greed and lust. In war it is the brave who take the spoils; as things stand with us, it is mostly cowards and shirkers that rob our homes, kidnap our children and conscript our men. Any cause is good enough for us to die for—any but our country's. But what a mere handful our invaders are, if we reckon up our own numbers. The Germans, reckoning so, threw off the yoke, and they had only a river, not the Ocean, to shield them. We have country, wives and parents to fight for; the Romans have nothing but greed and self-indulgence. Back they will go, as the deified Julius went back, if only we can rival the valour of our fathers. We must not be scared by the loss of one battle or even two; success may foster the spirit of offence, but it is suffering that gives the power to endure. The gods themselves are at last showing mercy to us Britons in keeping the Roman general away, with his army exiled in another island. For ourselves we have already taken the most difficult step—we have begun to plot. And in an enterprise like this there is more danger in being caught plotting than in taking the plunge.'

Goaded by such mutual encouragement, the whole island rose under the leadership of Boadicea, a lady of royal descent—for Britons make no distinction of sex in their leaders. They hunted down the Roman troops in their scattered posts, stormed the forts and assaulted the colony itself, in which they saw their slavery focused; nor did the angry victors deny themselves any form of savage cruelty. In fact, had not Paulinus, on hearing of the revolt, made speed to help, Britain would have been lost. As it was, he restored it to its old obedience by a single successful action. But many guilty rebels refused to lay down their arms out of a peculiar dread of the legate. Fine officer though he was, he seemed likely to abuse their unconditional surrender and punish with undue severity wrongs which he insisted on making personal. The government therefore replaced him by Petronius Turpilianus. They hoped that he would be more merciful and readier to forgive offences to which he was a stranger. He composed the existing troubles, but risked no further move before handing over his province to Trebellius Maximus. Trebellius was deficient in energy and without military experience, but he governed his province like a gentleman. The barbarians now learned, like any Romans, to condone seductive vices, while the intervention of our Civil Wars gave a reasonable excuse for inactivity. There was, however, a serious outbreak of mutiny, for the troops, accustomed to campaigns, ran riot in peace. Trebellius fled and hid to escape his angry army. His self-respect and dignity compromised, he now commanded merely on sufferance. By a kind of tacit bargain the troops kept their licence, the general his life, and the mutiny stopped short of bloodshed. Vettius Bolanus, likewise, as the Civil War still ran its course, declined to disturb Britain by enforcing discipline. There was still the same paralysis in face of the foe, the same indiscipline in the camp—only Bolanus was a decent man, with no sins to make him hated, and had won affection where he lacked authority.

But when Vespasian, in the course of his general triumph, recovered Britain, there came a succession of great generals and splendid armies, and the hopes of our enemies dwindled.

The Druids

The gods of the Britons were many and of all sorts—gods of war and thunder, or local deities of some holy well or haunted wood. The Scottish forests were especially feared as the dwelling place of demons. But the chief feature of their religion was the priesthood of the Druids which, as in Gaul, practised magical arts and horrific rites of human sacrifice, taught a secret lore, and wielded great influence in society. The Britons like the Gauls deferred to the Druid caste, with whom lay the secrets of their sacred songs, the taking of auspices, the award of punishment and the dread power of 'taboo', which created a class of untouchables. Unfortunately there exists no written or archaeological evidence to tell us of the spiritual life in Britain. The centre at Glastonbury and the forts outside Winchester and Chichester fell to the Belgae before new towns were built on the ancient sites, first by the Belgic tribes themselves, later by the Romans, but confusing and obscuring the archaeological evidence.

Moreover the Celtic world, like the rest of barbarian Europe, held to the non-literate oral tradition, which was of course the time-honoured and socially approved method for the conservation and transmission of law, genealogy, story, song and myth in the vernacular. The Druids were in fact specifically charged with the preservation and continuance of this ancient tradition, which deliberately avoided the use of writing. No authentic pre-Christian inscription includes any word for 'Druid' in Greek, Latin or Celtic forms, and all the written evidence for Celtic religion belongs to the latest phase, when Gaul and Britain had been incorporated in the Roman Empire. Our earliest tolerably reliable evidence about Druids comes from Julius Caesar and his sources—especially the Stoic philosopher Posidonius, whose work is no longer extant; but three later Greek authors, the historian Diodorus Siculus, the geographer Strabo, and the writer of miscellanies, Athenaeus, have reproduced parts of his writings. The material on the Druids in Caesar's *Gallic Wars* is taken from Posidonius, without acknowledgement and with significant additions, and exaggerations.

For the following two generations little is heard of the Druids—tradition merely states that they were banned by Tiberius and Claudius on account of superstitions and human sacrifices, while Pliny in his *Natural History* enlarges on the magical cures possessed by 'this race of prophets and physicians'. No classical writer ever fully described or even uncovered the philosophy of the Druids, which was elusive and exerted no influence on classical thought. The understanding of the barbarian world around them by the classical *literati* was inevitably coloured by contemporary modes of thought and current philosophical schemes. Thus Posidonius wrote from the Stoic viewpoint, stylizing the Druids as representative of the *logos* or higher power of the soul.

When we come to the Renaissance rediscovery of the past, and the incidental rediscovery of the Druids, we find them recreated by men who were themselves steeped in the philosophy and scholarship of the Greek and Roman thinkers who had first commented upon this obscure barbarian priesthood. The climate of thought was congenial to an acceptance and a development of the classical philosophers' view, and when fashion shifted from classical to romantic, the Druids were quietly waiting to take on a new life in the contemporary modes of Western thought and emotion. And so, as curiously satisfactory symbols, they have kept their place for a couple of thousand years or more: barbarian sages, primeval Christians, champions of liberty, repositories of mysterious wisdom. Certainly the tradition about them stands in need of reappraisal in the light of modern scholarship and archaeology.

The word DRUI (neuter plural DRUID) is found in Old Irish and may be analysed as DRU-UID or DRU-VID, the second element of which means 'he who knows' or 'the far-seeing', and the first element of which may be either an intensive prefix or the word meaning 'oak'.

How far in fact the Druids were originally a Celtic or even Aryan institution is itself a moot point. It is sometimes argued that when the Celts appeared in history Druidism was already in decline and the military caste of Aryan Celts were in revolt against this foreign priesthood, which had previously conquered them. Caesar observes that 'their sacred lore is believed to have originated in Britain and to have been carried thence to Gaul; and today those who wish to study it deeply, as a rule cross to Britain to learn it'. The relative antiquity which this prestige implies for the Druidic organization in Britain, on the fringe of the Celtic world, does indeed suggest a non-Celtic origin for the system. About 500 B.C., according to Caesar, Druidism spread from Britain to Gaul. Megalithic monuments have been taken as evidence that Druidism flourished in neolithic Ireland and spread thence to Britain well before 500 B.C., finding its refuge in Ireland again after the Roman conquest. But if this is so, and Druidism is of pre-Celtic origin, it is at least evident that the cult and priesthood had become thoroughly naturalized in the Celtic world by the first century B.C. After that time the Druids were members of an Indo-European social order, practising a religion which probably contained many elements by then already ancient.

Druids were encountered in person, probably by Posidonius, certainly by Caesar; Suetonius Paulinus and his army were publicly cursed by Druids on the shores of the Menai Straits, as Tacitus describes. Moreover copying from one text to another brought the Druids by report into the writings of those who had not travelled in Celtic lands. Provided it is remembered that Posidonius was looking at the Druids hopefully for confirmation of his ideas of a golden age of innocence, and that Caesar was thinking primarily about his political prestige in Rome, the writings of the Posidonian group give us a remarkably objective picture of the Druids, and of the Celtic culture of which they were an expression.

This culture was multiple and diverse, rural and uncentralized. There were no formal buildings for religious purposes. The teaching of novices for the priesthood took place in lonely forest clearings which were the usual Celtic sanctuaries. Oral teaching and learning by heart of sacred verses was given by Druids to the sons of the warrior nobility entering for instruction into the priesthood, whose status must always have been high. Strabo and Posidonius distinguish between three classes: the bards, the seers, and the Druids proper; Caesar merely between two: the knights and the Druids. The diviners or seers seem to have drawn auguries from the sacrifices performed by the Druids, while the bards were poets or composers of eulogy or satire, as well as the singers of these poems for ceremonial or entertainment purposes. Druids may in some circumstances have acted as diviners, but their function was distinct from that of the bards. All matters of knowledge, sacred and profane, were the province of the Druids, who also wielded considerable juridicial power as 'the most just of men'. Settlement of property disputes, of boundaries and the judging of all crimes and controversies was carried out by them. They could bar from attendance at sacrifices any individual or tribe who did not accept their rulings, thus making them outcasts without religious or legal status.

It is hardly realistic to exculpate the Druids from participation, probably active, in both the beliefs and practices involved in human sacrifice (which after all had only been brought to an end in the civilized Roman world in the early first century B.C.). Caesar writes of the use of 'huge figures woven out of twigs whose limbs they fill with living men and set on fire'; Strabo confirms this strange rite, which remains unexplained and unparalleled and has caught the imaginations of all who have subsequently written on Druids. Other forms of human sacrifice included impaling or shooting to death by arrows, and Diodorus and Strabo describe how victims were stabbed in the back and omens deduced from their death throes.

Our information on Druid ceremonies mainly centres on sacrifice. Pliny gives us the only detailed account of a Druid ceremony, which was concerned with the growth of mistletoe on an oak tree, a circumstance of rare occurrence. The time chosen for the rite was the sixth day of the moon and preparations were made for a feast and a sacrifice of two white bulls. A Druid in a white robe climbed the tree and cut the branch of mistletoe with a golden sickle. The branch was caught on a white cloak as it fell. The bulls were sacrificed. The golden sickle is inexplicable: if it really existed it would have been unable to cut the tough stem of mistletoe: gilded bronze is more likely. Pliny's account of the ritual necessity of gathering the plant *samolus* left-handed and fasting, and of plucking *selago* without using an iron knife, barefoot, and with the right hand through the left sleeve of a white tunic, are performances of private magic rather than public ceremonies.

Druidic philosophy or doctrine is harder to reconstruct than their ritual observances; they are unlikely to have held the coherent body of dogma attributed to them by Posidonius, to whom the Druids are leaders of humanity particularly endowed with the *Logos* principle, and holding as chief tenets the immortality of the soul and the indestructibility of the universe—although from time to time it is temporarily consumed by fire or water. Yet Posidonius was one of the most acute observers of antiquity, and Strabo and Mela confirm that the Druids had knowledge 'of the magnitude and form of the earth and the world'; also their belief in successive transformations of an eternal matter and in the alternate triumph of the two elements, fire and water. Caesar and Mela state that, 'They profess to know the motions of the heavens and the stars and their movement, the size of the universe and of the earth.' The Druids in Diodorus are 'skilled in the divine nature', and are able to communicate with the gods.

The item of Druidic belief that struck the classical writers most forcibly was that of literal, personal immortality. In Posidonius, as quoted by Diodorus, the Celts held that 'the souls of men are immortal and that after a definite number of years they live a second life when the soul passes to another body'. From this, Diodorus continues, followed the idea of the redemption of one life by another, while Caesar makes the chief point of doctrine that 'men's souls do not suffer death, but after death pass from the one to the other'. Ammianus, Valerius Maximus and Diodorus associate the belief in immortality with the Pythagorean theory of metempsychosis—equating the Celtic doctrine with the beliefs of Pythagoras—or making the Druids 'members of the intimate fellowship of the Pythagorean faith'. This is hardly conceivable, although it is reasonably likely that similar beliefs were held by the Pythagoreans and the Druids.

The references in the classical authors on which our knowledge of the very existence of the Druids is based range in date from around the end of the third century B.C. to the fourth century A.D., and relate to Western Europe and to Britain. The earliest vernacular texts in Old Irish represent written recensions of an oral tradition dating from somewhere shortly before the fifth century A.D., and relate only to Ireland. There is therefore a virtual continuity over five hundred years, so far as actual chronology is concerned, but an abrupt shift of scene between the comments of the Greek and Roman writers and the indigenous Celtic record. But all the literary sources are set within a consistent framework which can be historically, linguistically and ethnographically defined as that of the ancient Celts.

To place the Druids in their proper setting therefore we must form a picture of the Celtic world to which they belonged—a self-sufficient and remarkably homogeneous, iron-using, barbarian economy, based on its flocks and herds and its ploughlands, with a warrior-aristocracy supporting skilled artists and craftsmen, the whole economic and social structure dependent for its strength and inspiration on the ritual, magic and religious beliefs controlled and directed by the Druids.

Index